In Search of
Deeper Learning

In Search of Deeper Learning

THE QUEST TO REMAKE THE AMERICAN HIGH SCHOOL

Jal Mehta AND Sarah Fine

 Harvard University Press

Cambridge, Massachusetts
London, England   2019

Second printing

Library of Congress Cataloging-in-Publication Data
is available from loc.gov.
ISBN 978-0-674-98839-2 (alk. paper)

Contents

In Search of
Deeper Learning

Introduction

IT WASN'T UNTIL we stepped outside for a mid-afternoon break that the doubts became too serious to ignore.

On the surface, all was well. Our flights were on time. The West Coast weather was sunny and warm—a welcome respite from the New England winter. Adults and adolescents at Inspire Academy (a pseudonym) were gracious.[1] Leaders took the time to talk with us; teachers welcomed us; students didn't balk when we joined them at lunch. When we said that we had come to Inspire as part of our research on how American high schools could create powerful learning experiences for more students more of the time, people nodded knowingly. Their school, they told us, was leading the charge on that front—using project-based learning to support students in developing both deep academic knowledge and "twenty-first century skills" such as collaboration and creative problem-solving.

By the middle of the second day, however, it was clear to both of us that something wasn't right. Despite the time and effort that had gone into choosing Inspire as a site for our research, it was becoming hard to shake the thought that we had picked the wrong place. In a tenth-grade English class, students slumped their way through a scene from *Othello*, reading out loud only when threatened with detention and spending much of the period filling out a worksheet that told them to summarize what they had read. In an eleventh-grade biology course, students spent thirty minutes passively listening as their teacher read out the directions for a highly structured experiment, the outcome of which everybody already knew. In a ninth-grade social studies class, a young teacher shouted over her students' side conversations, her voice increasingly shrill. When we asked students why they were doing what they were doing, their most common answers were "I don't know," "because the teacher told us to," or, in one memorable instance, "ask that girl over there—she's the one who knows what's going on in this class."

There was one bright spot. In Ms. Ortiz's eleventh-grade English classroom, tucked away in an upstairs corner of Inspire's sprawling building, students had spent a month reading and analyzing Kate Chopin's *The Awakening*. Now, drawing on the themes from the novel, they were working on a project that asked them to use original art to challenge narratives they found oppressive. The room hummed with purposeful activity. Some students clustered around tables, immersed in their creations, while others worked on the accompanying written analyses. When we asked them to discuss their work, they did so thoughtfully and articulately, explaining how, unlike Chopin's protagonist, who saw suicide as the only escape from society's expectations, they were using art to challenge the narratives they saw as constraining. Next week, they would exhibit and explain these creations to an audience of peers and teachers.

As we sat on a patch of grass near the school's front entrance, we compared notes and tried to work through the questions that were bubbling up. Why were there such gaps between Inspire's espoused values and its enacted practices? How could a school that had been recommended as a leader in the field—in foundation-commissioned case studies and by many educators and reformers—so dimly resemble its reputation? How did Ms. Ortiz learn to do what she did, and why was Inspire unable to spread such effective practices to more of its teachers? Was Inspire really among the best the United States had to offer when it came to engaging underserved high school students in powerful learning experiences? If it was, what did that say about our project—and about our field?

These were not the questions that had brought us to Inspire. We began 2010 in an optimistic frame of mind, having secured a small grant to study a range of successful American public high schools—particularly, but not exclusively, those serving disadvantaged students—and try to understand what made them tick. In an era when standardized testing reigned supreme, we wished to question the logic that labeled "good" schools as those whose students did well on tests, and instead study places that were not merely achieving academic minimums but helping students to *flourish*—to think critically, to become engaged in their learning, and, in a variety of ways, to prepare for the demands of twenty-first-century life.

Since we suspected that the answers to these questions might be multiple rather than single, we wanted to capture a variety of different approaches to achieving these goals. We would visit schools that varied widely in pedagogical approaches, governance, and design, including traditional comprehensive high schools, charter schools, magnet schools, pedagogically traditional and pedagogically progressive schools, urban schools, and suburban schools. Our plan called for us to immerse ourselves in these places using ethnographic methods—observing classes, talking with teachers and students, examining artifacts—to try to understand the varied approaches to bringing public high schools into the modern age.

The timing for such a study was ripe. While there had been a spate of studies on high schools in the 1980s—captured in classic works such as Sizer's *Horace's Compromise*, Lawrence-Lightfoot's *The Good High School*, Powell et al.'s *The Shopping Mall High School*, and Goodlad's *A Place Called School*—shifting trends in scholarship had moved away from the kind of holistic and humanistic perspectives that characterized this well-known work.[2] In addition, the creation of charter schools in the early 1990s, along with the small school movement in the late 1990s and early 2000s, meant that there was now a much greater range of institutions to study.

We also wanted to tap into the increasing public desire to improve high schools, which many had come to see as the final, and most challenging, frontier of K–12 school reform. While there has been some progress in student achievement in math and reading in fourth and eighth grades over the past several decades, high school achievement in math and reading in the United States has been flat.[3] The International PISA test, which asks high school students not only to recall information but also to apply knowledge and problem-solve, consistently places the United States at the midpoint, or lower, of international rankings.[4] Data also consistently demonstrate that the longer students are in school, the less engaged they feel: 75 percent of fifth graders feel engaged by school, but only 32 percent of eleventh graders feel similarly.[5] Since this range of indicators suggested that high school continues to be the hardest place to make progress, we were hoping to study "break-the-mold" high schools to understand what it would take to create engaging, equitable, and intellectually vibrant learning environments for all adolescents.

The problem was finding such schools. Inspire was not an exception. At school after school, as we shadowed students through their days, we found gaps between aspirations and realities. Most classrooms were spaces to sit passively and listen. Most academic work instructed students to recall, or minimally apply, what they had been told. When we asked students the purpose of what they were doing, the most common responses were "I dunno—it's in the textbook," and "maybe it'll help me in college." We had seen such lackluster classrooms before, of course, but these were in highly recommended schools where we had hoped to find a model that would transcend the norm. All too often, things looked the way they had at Inspire: big ambitions and significant struggles.

So, what to do? One option was to abandon the project. There would be some funding wasted and some time squandered, but, perhaps, better to accept the sunk costs and move on. A second option was to turn our project into an indictment of the American education system. In the tradition of Jonathan Kozol, John Holt, Charles Silberman, and many others, we could write a scathing critique of American schooling, drawing on our observations to show the ways in which even schools that were meant to be innovative were falling far short of their aspirations. But this ground had been covered many times over—and part of why we wanted to write about good schools was that we sought an antidote to the pessimism that governs so many school reform discussions.

As we looked more closely at our data, we realized that there might be a third option. While the dominant patterns we had observed reflected a school system that was trapped by a "grammar of schooling" that was cast a century ago, there were exceptions—many different kinds of exceptions—which, cumulatively, perhaps could help to light a path forward. Often these exceptions were in classrooms, like Ms. Ortiz's, where teachers had found interesting ways to engage students in intellectually complex subjects. If the bad news was that our recommended schools, as a whole, were struggling to achieve their ambitions, the good news was that at every site we found individual teachers who had found ways to transcend the norm. In fact, it became a predictable part of our research: if we spent a day shadowing a student, we would find one and sometimes two classes that were intellectually lively and demanding. Over time, these classrooms became their own data set. What were these teachers doing, how were they doing it, and how had they come to do it? There seemed to be much to learn from them.

Another bright spot came from widening our view. In many of the high schools we visited, much of the most powerful learning seemed to occur not in core classes, but rather at the school's "periphery"—in electives, clubs, and extracurriculars. Hidden in plain sight, these peripheral spaces often had a very different "grammar" than the one that usually dominated core classes. In these spaces, students had real choices, learning by doing was the norm, there was time to explore matters in depth, and students were welcomed as producers rather than receivers of knowledge. What made these spaces tick? How could they exist, almost entirely unnoticed, within the same schools in which core learning was so often passive and disengaged? Might there be lessons that the "core" could learn from the "periphery"?

Finally, as we continued our search, we did find a small number of high schools that consistently were able to translate their espoused values into enacted practices. In particular, we identified three very different schools—a project-based school, a "no excuses" school, and an International Baccalaureate-for-all school—that were able to actualize their visions in powerful ways. What enabled these schools to make such headway? How had they countered the classroom-to-classroom variation in quality that was so prevalent elsewhere? Why were administrators and teachers in these places able to achieve their aspirations when many with similar ambitions could not? Viewed this way, our experiences at Inspire and other struggling schools became useful data: contrasting cases that could be lined up against our positive cases to help us identify exactly what enabled some schools to transcend the norm.

The profound differences across these three schools also allowed us to explore a range of approaches to the remaking of the American high school. During the course of our study, educators and scholars began to refer more and more often to "deeper learning," an umbrella term evoking a range of ambitions that extends beyond rote learning.[6] These goals were not exactly pathbreaking—many schools, particularly private schools, had embraced such ambitions for years—but the idea of bringing them to *all* students would be new. We saw close relationships between our study and the notion of deeper learning. In fact, as we considered it further, we realized that these three schools were each working on different parts of the deeper learning equation. The no-excuses school, which we call No Excuses High, was particularly focused on the challenge of equity; its leaders were trying to take the type of traditional learning that is often found in the upper tracks of affluent schools and make it available to high-poverty students of color. The project-based school, which we call Dewey High, was focused on reimagining the grammar of schooling—on breaking down barriers between disciplines, on connecting the school to the broader world, and on having students create and contribute knowledge rather than just passively receive it. The IB school, which we call IB High, lay somewhere in the middle: drawing on an examination system created for highly privileged students, the schools' administrators and teachers were striving to help students do authentic work within the traditional academic disciplines, while simultaneously seeking to extend such learning to a wide array of learners. These schools, then, provided three distinct visions of what the reinvented high school might look like, each with corresponding advantages and tradeoffs.

If these high schools offered starkly divergent possibilities for the future of schooling, we were also coming to recognize that our most successful teachers, electives, and extracurricular spaces, wildly varied as they were in methods, goals, and populations, all held one trait in common: they *integrated* different virtues of learning. In particular, we came to think that our own distinct vision of deep learning—not simply in school, but in life—emerges at the intersection of three virtues: *mastery, identity,* and *creativity.* In the spaces that teachers, students, and our own observations identified as the most compelling, students had opportunities to develop knowledge and skill (mastery), they came to see their core selves as vitally connected to what they were learning and doing (identity), and they had opportunities to enact their learning by producing something rather than simply receiving knowledge (creativity). Often these spaces or classrooms were governed by a logic of apprenticeship; students had opportunities to make things (newspapers, collections of poetry, documentary films, theater productions, debate performances) under the supervision of faculty and/or older students who would model the creative steps involved, provide examples of high-quality work, and offer precise feedback. Not coincidentally, the most successful teachers and extracurricular leaders whom we encountered had themselves been apprenticed into their fields in a similar way—and these experiences had helped them develop a *stance* about what they were doing that differed from the "teaching as transmission" view that was so prevalent.

We widened our lens in other ways, too. While we initially planned to write about schools, it became impossible to make sense of what we were seeing without considering the interplay of external forces that had shaped these schools. For example, Inspire and schools like it were working against the grain in so many respects: most teachers were teaching as they had been taught, short class periods inhibited in-depth explorations, district-mandated curricula and teacher evaluation systems were not aligned with efforts to emphasize critical thinking, and parental and college pressures mitigated against change. In fact, we came to think that many of the most successful classrooms, extracurriculars, and schools that we encountered were successful because they had found ways to *buffer* the expectations of the external ecosystem in order to create space to do something different. Thus, when we began to write about particular schools and learning spaces, we tried to move back and forth between describing practices on the ground and considering the broader forces that shape or constrain those practices. As we drafted our conclusion, we considered how these forces might be transformed to support, rather than inhibit, powerful efforts on the ground.

The good news is that there seems to be a growing interest in making these shifts. When we began in 2010, this project felt far outside of the mainstream; the attention of both the public and the K–12 world was still focused on the test-score emphasis of No Child Left Behind. During the intervening years, however, there has been a distinct shift. The Common Core State Standards initiative signaled a focus on more ambitious learning goals; policymakers and practitioners increasingly started talking about "twenty-first-century skills"; the Obama White House held a summit on high school reinvention; Apple funded XQ: The Super School Project to run a nationwide competition to reinvent schools; High Tech High, a network of project-based schools in San Diego, now attracts more than a thousand practitioners to its annual Deeper Learning conference; and deeper learning is now part of many state and district policy strategies. At the beginning, we struggled to find funding for the project; now, we find ourselves increasingly invited to address gatherings of educators seeking to undo old systems and create powerful learning environments for the future. And while part of what motivated our research was the middling performance of U.S. schools on international yardsticks, many of those who attend our sessions come from other countries—they too, are trying to figure out how to integrate mastery, identity, and creativity into a twenty-first-century school system.

In the end, we visited thirty schools, spent more than 750 hours observing classrooms and other learning spaces, and interviewed more than three hundred students, teachers, administrators, parents, and other stakeholders. The picture that emerged is of an institution that is betwixt and between when it comes to deeper learning. Schools are actively trying to shed the long hand of the past, but have not yet arrived at the future. This effort is truly a quest: a journey that, as yet, has no clear path—but whose stakes make it well worth undertaking.

This is not the book we set out to write. We were seeking inspiration; we found complexity. Our friend and colleague Marshall Ganz, who teaches organizing, says that significant change is about urgency combined with hope. The story we tell here has elements of both. On the one hand, our research underscores the difficulty of deepening the work of most American high schools, given that their core designs are often unspecified and / or incoherent, and that their core programs of academic study are often fundamentally disconnected from who students are and what they can do. In documenting these realities, we try to show, in unvarnished terms, the size of the problem; we argue that the change needed at scale is more one of kind than of degree. On the other hand, we show that there are already many classrooms, electives, and extracurriculars, as well as a few individual schools, that can light the path, showing what powerful and purposeful learning would look like. With humility, we suggest that if we wish to be neither paralyzed by the scale of the problem nor seduced by the promise of easy solutions, we need to look carefully at exactly what makes this work so hard—and also at why, and under what conditions, it is possible to achieve success. Our hope is that by sharing what we've learned we can spark an informed conversation about what it would entail to build a system in which deep learning is no longer the exception, but the rule.

1 ∽

The State of Deeper Learning in American High Schools

WHAT IS "DEEPER LEARNING" and why should it be a central goal for schools? This question is more complicated than it might seem. Deeper learning is an umbrella term that has emerged over the past decade to encompass a range of desirable attributes of schooling, attributes rooted in the premise that schooling needs to move beyond rote learning and shallow testing. The Hewlett Foundation, which helped to popularize the term, defines it as those combined characteristics of schooling that enable learners to "develop significant understanding of core academic content, exhibit critical thinking and problem-solving skills, collaborate, communicate, direct their own learning, and possess an "academic mindset."[1] The National Research Council's 2012 report on the term describes it as fostering "cognitive, intrapersonal, and interpersonal" competencies.[2]

Later in this chapter, we will explain what we see as distinct about our own view of what deeper learning entails. But for now, we will simply note that for the purposes of organizing our journey, we like the phrase "deeper learning" because the connotations of "deeper" are consistent with much of what we would hope for in a significant learning experience. When one goes deeper into a discussion, or explores a topic more deeply, or becomes more deeply versed in an area, one is moving toward the kind of learning that a serious education should enable.

While the term "deeper learning" is new, many of the aspirations it represents are longstanding. For instance, Paulo Freire, in 1970, decried the tendency of "banking" models of pedagogy, where children are treated as empty vessels in which teachers "deposit" knowledge, and argued for "problem-posing" as an alternative.[3] Alfred North White-head, in 1929, discussed the difference between "active" forms of learning and "inert" knowledge.[4] Joseph Mayer Rice, in 1893, contrasted "old education," which emphasized drilling and recitation, with "new education," which aimed "to lead the child to observe, to reason, and to acquire manual dexterity as well as to memorize facts—in a word, to develop the child naturally in all his faculties."[5] Modern scholars describe this contrast as between "ambitious instruction," which asks students to reason and understand underlying conceptual structures, and "conventional instruction," which does not.[6] While there are some differences among these formulations, in a fundamental way they share an emphasis on "deep" versus "shallow" education, that is, on education that asks students to think versus education that asks them to follow directions, and education that has purpose and meaning for students versus education that does not.[7]

If the goals are not new, what is new are the external expectations of what the school system needs to produce. These expectations have changed for three fundamental reasons. The first is economic. Economic changes have hollowed out a large cadre of middle-class jobs that formerly could be claimed by high school graduates; these students increasingly need post-secondary credentials to be competitive in the job market. The types of skills that employers value have also shifted. In 1970, the top three skills employers asked for were reading, writing, and arithmetic; in 2015, they are complex problem solving, critical thinking, and creativity.[8] Thus the education that would have sufficed in 1970 will not prepare students for the workforce today. A second reason relates to equity. To the degree that the goals of deeper learning have already been met, they have mostly been realized in affluent private schools and in the highest-track classes at the most advantaged public schools; what is new is the idea that these opportunities need to be extended to all students, regardless of color, economic status, or initial skill level. A third reason comes from the civic arena. Students now live in a world plagued by complex global problems, including climate change, massive economic inequality, ideological warfare, and a technological revolution marked by a chaotic proliferation of sources of opinion, fact, myth, paranoia, and disinformation. The generation of students coming of age today will be asked to navigate, survive, and, if they can, help to heal the world they have inherited. Schools will need to do their part to develop skilled, creative, educated, informed, and empathetic citizens and leaders—the kind of people that our economy, society, and democracy demand.

Perspectives on Deeper Learning

Our vision of deeper learning builds on antecedents from various disciplines, fields, and traditions. We think that more conversation and integration across these strands will be helpful, because deeper learning generally emerges when a number of the associated elements come together. In particular, we think that three kinds of integrations—*the cognitive and the affective, the short-term and the long-term, and the individual and the social*—are important foundations for thinking about how to create deeper learning experiences.

To begin at the beginning: what does it mean to understand something deeply? Cognitive scientists think of deep learning—or what they might call "learning for understanding"—as the ability to organize discrete pieces of knowledge into a larger schema of understanding. Research suggests that deep learners have schemas that enable them to see how discrete pieces of knowledge in a domain are connected; rather than seeing isolated facts, they see patterns and connections because they understand the underlying structures of the domain they are exploring.[9] For example, a shallow understanding of the biological cell might enable one to label its parts; a deep understanding would enable one to understand how a cell's components function together as a system and, thus, to anticipate what might happen if a particular component was damaged. A related idea is that deep understanding allows you to transfer knowledge—not only to use it in the context in which it was taught, but also to understand or explain something in a related context.[10]

This example brings to the fore another aspect of deep understanding: it requires both a significant repository of factual knowledge and the ability to use that factual knowledge to develop interpretations, arguments, and conclusions. While "deeper learning" is sometimes critiqued in the popular press as the latest round of favoring "skills" over "content" or "concepts" over "facts," research clearly demonstrates that people who possess deep understanding of a domain move with ease across this false divide.[11] The ability to offer a historical interpretation of the causes or consequences of the French revolution, for example, is rooted both in a detailed knowledge of the key players, structures, and events and in the ability to draw inferences, construct historical arguments, and use evidence to support one's point.

Much of the work in this cognitive tradition draws its inspiration from research on expertise, which explores how people who are experts in a field construct their understandings. Studies of such experts reveal that they notice aspects of a situation that are not apparent to non-experts because they have cognitive schemas for understanding the domain; for example, expert teachers are more able to assess and respond to students' thinking and adapt lessons midstream than are novice teachers, who tend to proceed more mechanically through more subject-centered lessons.[12] This idea relates to Jerome Bruner's notion that to truly understand a domain requires understanding the structure of how that field organizes its knowledge.[13] This kind of epistemological understanding, he argues, is critical to building the conceptual schemas that enable transfer within a domain.

This understanding of deep learning has also spurred a different vision of teaching. Scholarship in the late 1980s and early 1990s that advanced this perspective under the banner of "teaching for understanding" suggested the ways in which both learning and teaching would need to change if this perspective were embraced. Milbrey McLaughlin and Joan Talbert wrote in a 1993 introduction to the book *Teaching for Understanding*, "These visions depart substantially from conventional practice and frame an active role of students as explorers, conjecturers, and constructors of their own learning. In this new way of thinking, teachers function as guides, coaches, and facilitators of students' learning through posing questions, challenging students' thinking and leading them in examining ideas and relationships."[14] In this new role, they continue, teachers would have to leave behind the longstanding view of themselves as "knowledge transmitters" and embrace the more constructivist notion of teachers co-constructing knowledge with learners.[15] More recent writing by Magdalene Lampert on what she calls "ambitious instruction" or "deeper teaching" has taken a similar perspective, arguing that teachers need to teach in ways that bring to the fore student thinking, help students do work that parallels the work of professionals in the discipline, and create a collaborative culture in which this kind of thinking and learning can thrive.[16]

Lampert's work begins to integrate what we think of as the cognitive and affective aspects of deeper learning. In other words, while deeper learning stems in part from increasing the level of rigor of the cognitive processes, it also relies in part on cultivating the motivation and identity of the students involved. Our experiences observing, teaching, and learning in powerful classrooms suggest that the "cool" descriptions of the cognitive dimensions described earlier must be married to "warmer" qualities such as passion, interest, and "flow"— qualities that give the learning life and create forward momentum. In their work on "intellectually authentic instruction," Fred Newmann and his colleagues stressed the ways in which "engagement"—often dismissed as entertaining students without really teaching them—is, in its more substantial manifestations, actually a critical precondition for significant learning: "The most immediate and persisting issue for students and teachers is not low achievement but student disengagement. The most obviously disengaged students disrupt classes, skip them, or fail to complete assignments. More typically, disengaged students behave well in school. They attend class and complete the work, but with little indication of excitement, commitment, or pride in mastery of the curriculum. In contrast, engaged students make a psychological investment in learning."[17] They continue: "Meaningful learning cannot be delivered to high school students like pizza to be consumed or videos to be observed. Lasting learning develops largely through the labor of the student, who must be enticed to participate in a continuous cycle of studying, producing, correcting mistakes, and starting over again. Students cannot be expected to achieve unless they concentrate, work, and invest themselves in the mastery of school tasks. This is the sense in which student engagement is critical to educational success; to enhance achievement, one must first learn how to engage students."[18]

This perspective is given a boost from retrospective studies of deep learners. This work looks at individuals who have become deeply knowledgeable and skilled in their domains and asks them how they arrived where they did.[19] The general pattern is that people initially become interested in their domains by playing around in those fields (for example, by splashing in a pool or experimenting with a musical instrument); then they begin to engage in deliberate practice under the supervision of a coach or someone with more experience in the domain; next their identities gradually shift to reflect their participation in the domain (from "I'm someone who swims" to "I'm a swimmer"); they continue to practice; and then eventually "play" and "creation" reemerge, this time in a much more complex way. We could think of this process as a kind of spiral, in which one returns again and again to the same activities, but each time in a way that is more sophisticated.[20]

This account of how *individuals* become deep learners is complemented by work that emphasizes the role that *communities* can play in this process. To that end, Jean Lave and Etienne Wenger suggest that much of the most powerful learning takes place in communities of practice; these are fields (like midwifery, sculpting, butchering, and many others) in which one begins as a "legitimate peripheral participant" (for instance, an assistant to a midwife) and through the process of observation, modeling, and emulation, is gradually apprenticed into understanding and skills in the domain.[21] Allan Collins, John Seely Brown, and Susan E. Newman have applied similar insights to more classically academic subjects in their argument for "cognitive apprenticeship," in which skilled readers, writers, and mathematicians gradually induct members with less expertise into their crafts.[22] Such a process brings together many elements that are hypothesized to be important for deep learning: the field sets a standard for what good work looks like; there is a significant role for coaching, modeling, and feedback; the desire to do what leading practitioners do provides direction and motivation; and the task is grounded in a human activity that has intrinsic value. The image of moving from a "peripheral participant" to a more central one is also consistent with the language of increasing "depth." From this perspective, deepening one's learning in a given domain happens in part by becoming more centrally enmeshed in a domain-specific community, which links one's individual growth to one's social position. It also suggests a shift in role from passive observer to active participant.[23]

Taken together, we posit that deeper learning emerges at the intersection of the following three elements: *mastery*, *identity*, and *creativity*. *Mastery* captures the dimensions of deeper learning that are tied to substantive knowledge of content, transfer of this knowledge, pattern recognition and expertise, and understanding the structure of a field or discipline. *Identity* captures the way in which deeper learning is driven by intrinsic motivation, the way it is fueled by learners' perceptions of the relevance of the content, and the way in which learning becomes deeper as it becomes a core part of the self. *Creativity* captures the shift from receiving the accumulated knowledge of a subject or domain to being able to *act* or *make* something within that field; taking this step builds on one's understanding of a domain (for example, an analysis of how a play is written) and incorporates it into a creative act (writing a play). In later chapters, we will track how the schools we saw are faring in creating opportunities for mastery, identity, and creativity.

One terminological note: we refer to "powerful learning experiences" when we are referring to a particular classroom or moment—powerful learning can happen in an hour. We use the term "deeper learning" when we are discussing arcs of learning that develop over time, because we think that deep learning is best understood in terms of lengthy trajectories. Mastery, identity, and creativity intersect, Venn diagram style, in powerful learning experiences; they also act as a reinforcing spiral that accumulates over time to produce deep learning.

From Effective to Ambitious Schools

While there are multiple resources one can draw on to assemble a picture of the nature of deep learning, the literature on how to build public schools that would achieve those qualities is surprisingly sparse. There is a body of work that goes back to Ronald Edmonds and others in the 1970s, under the label of "effective schools," describing the qualities of schools that have outperformed their contemporaries on standardized tests. This literature emphasizes the importance of high expectations; creating an orderly, safe climate; use of data to improve practice; and, in some versions, the right of the leader to make core decisions about the school.[24] Largely missing from these studies, however, is an account of how the described positive traits connect to the instructional core—the triangle connecting the teacher, students, and curriculum.[25]

More recent work by Anthony Bryk and his colleagues on "organizing schools for success" seeks to build on this earlier literature and to connect it to the instructional core. They argue that developing both professional capacity and an "instructional guidance system," which helps teachers to know what and how to teach, are critical to academic success, but so is integrating these components into a comprehensive package of school supports comprising school leadership, parent-community ties, and a student-centered learning climate.[26] This work builds on the now sizable literatures on professional learning communities, relational trust, organizational learning, and instructional leadership.

Missing from these studies, however, is an account of what it would take for schools to move toward *deeper* learning, or what the academic literature calls ambitious instruction. Much of the Bryk research was conducted in Chicago elementary schools in the 1990s, all of which, though they varied some on test scores, were subject to low-level state tests and were not seeking ambitious instruction. More generally, as Paul Cobb and Kara Jackson point out, organizational researchers have largely avoided the discussion of what makes for good pedagogy, a gap that limits the utility of their conclusions:

> Research on large-scale instructional improvement has traditionally been the province of educational policy and educational leadership. While much can be learned from these studies, most of this work does not take a position on what counts as high-quality teaching but instead operationalizes it in terms of increasing student test scores irrespective of the quality of the tests. In the course of our work . . . it has become increasingly evident that views on what counts as high-quality mathematics teaching matter when formulating strategies or policies for instructional improvement.[27]

At the same time, there has been an increasing scholarly interest in "ambitious instruction"—instruction that moves away from low-level tasks, asks students to develop ideas and interpretations, and is otherwise consistent with much of what we have described as deeper learning. But although this literature has focused on describing good classrooms and, more recently, on implications for teacher preparation, there has not been an equivalent interest in schools.[28] In short, researchers have explored ambitious instruction and effective schools, but very little attention has been paid to ambitious schools, which were the focus of our study. (Note that while "ambitious" has been the favored term in the literature, in lay language "ambitious" is not necessarily a positive quality; in fact, we later critique some schools for being too "ambitious" in terms of credentialing and, thus, not focused enough on powerful learning. Hence, we will use "deeper learning schools" in this book.)

An Overview of Our Six-Year Study

How do American high schools stack up against the goals of deeper learning? As we alluded to in the Introduction, the overall picture is not pretty, although we did find some bright spots.

While we describe our sample and methods in more detail in the Appendix, a brief summary here is in order. In total, we visited thirty schools across the United States. All of these schools had been recommended as offering deeper learning, "twenty-first-century skills," or particularly rigorous traditional learning. Recommendations had come from a survey we sent to leading researchers, district and state policy leaders, charter management operators, and other knowledgeable observers. We also scoured lists published by magazines or other venues that honor "top schools." Our goal was to study the variety of approaches to deeper learning that schools were taking and to learn from those that were doing the best at this task.

Table 1.1 provides a summary of the schools that we visited. The group includes a heavy representation of progressive, project-based schools, and/or schools from the Hewlett "deeper learning" network (nine schools). We also visited four "no excuses" schools. While some see their controlling approach as the antithesis of deeper learning, they constitute one of the leading school-reform models in the United States and send large numbers of high-poverty students to college; thus, they seemed worthy of examination. We went to five International Baccalaureate schools, which seek to use IB as an anchor to create "deeper learning." We also went to three comprehensive high schools. Table 1.1 describes the orientation, size, and demographics of each of the schools in our sample. While we tried to capture some of the range of diversity of the American high school, we oversampled on schools that served high-poverty, working-class, and minority students.

This is not a representative sample of American high schools. It is rather a strategically chosen sample designed to maximize the variety of contemporary approaches toward promoting deeper learning in public high schools. As such, it is heavier on charter schools, smaller

Table 1.1 Comparison of Schools in the Deeper Learning Study of the American High School

Name (pseudonym)	School Type	Specialty Programs	Location	Number of Students	Population Served
Deep Dive Sites (20–30 days of observation)					
Dewey High	Charter	Project-based	West Coast city	550	Mixed
No Excuses High	Charter	No excuses/Advanced placement	East Coast city	600	High-poverty students of color
IB High	Charter	International baccalaureate	East Coast small city	800	Middle-income students
Attainment High	District-run public	Advanced placement	East Coast suburb	2,000	Middle- and high-income students
Medium Dive Sites (5–10 days of observation)					
Inspire Academy	Charter	Project-based	West Coast city	500	High-poverty students of color
Midwestern Math and Science Academy	State-run magnet	Accelerated math and science	Midwestern town	400	Mixed
Comprehensive High	District-run public	International baccalaureate	Midwestern city	2,500	Mixed
N/A	Charter	No excuses/Advanced placement	East Coast city	600	High-poverty students of color
N/A	District-run public	Project-based/Montessori	Midwestern city	700	Mixed
N/A	Charter	Project-based	West Coast city	600	High-poverty students of color

(continued)

Table 1.1 (continued)

Name (pseudonym)	School Type	Specialty Programs	Location	Number of Students	Population Served
Shallow Dive Sites (1–4 days of observation)					
N/A	Traditional public	N/A	East Coast city	1,400	High-poverty students
N/A	Traditional public	Small school	East Coast city	400	High-poverty students of color
N/A	Traditional public	Small school	East Coast city	300	High-poverty students of color
N/A	Traditional public	Small school	East Coast city	200	High-poverty students of color
N/A	Traditional public	Small school	East Coast city	400	High-poverty students of color
N/A	Traditional public	EL education	East Coast city	500	High-poverty students of color
N/A	Traditional public	International baccalaureate	East Coast city	350	High-poverty students of color
N/A	Traditional public	Blended learning	East Coast city	500	Mixed
N/A	Traditional public	International baccalaureate	East Coast city	450	High-poverty students of color
N/A	Traditional public	International baccalaureate	East Coast city	600	High-poverty students of color

Type	Model	Location	Size	Student population	
Traditional public	STEM Academy	East Coast city	300	High-poverty students of color	N/A
Traditional public	EL education	East Coast city	850	High-poverty students	N/A
State-run public	STEM focus	East Coast city	250	High-poverty students of color	N/A
Charter	Career and technical education	East Coast city	250	Mixed	N/A
Charter	No excuses/Advanced placement	West Coast city	450	High-poverty students of color	N/A
Charter	N/A	East Coast city	300	High-poverty students of color	N/A
Charter	Project-based	West Coast city	400	High-poverty students of color	N/A
Private	No excuses/Advanced placement	West Coast suburb	600	High-poverty students of color	N/A
Private	Project-based	East Coast city	100	Mixed	N/A
Private	Harkness	East Coast rural area	850	High-income students	N/A

schools, and schools that have a thematic orientation because these were the schools that had been granted the freedom to break the mold and innovate toward deeper learning. Since significant research has already been done on the comprehensive high school, we sought instead to examine in detail the different kinds of schools that have been developed in the past few decades, in part due to the charter movement. That said, we did include some traditional comprehensive schools in our sample, and we discuss one of them in detail in Chapter 5.

In particular, our three deep dive thematic schools—a project-based school (Chapter 2), a no-excuses school (Chapter 3), and an International Baccalaureate school (Chapter 4)—offer ways to examine three of the most prominent approaches to re-envisioning American schooling for the twenty-first century. The project-based school was part of Hewlett's "deeper learning" network, which encompasses ten progressive networks of schools, more than five hundred total, serving more than 227,000 students in forty-one states.[29] There is no similar network of networks of no-excuses schools, but when we totaled the students in ten of the largest no-excuses networks, we similarly found that there were more than five hundred schools, serving more than 223,000 students.[30] If either of these networks were districts, they would be larger than Dallas or Philadelphia, and more than twice as large as Baltimore, Denver, or San Francisco. A 2015 study measuring charter orientations across seventeen cities found that "no excuses" and "progressive" were consistently the two largest categories of charter schools.[31] They represent opposing theories of action about what a good education entails, which makes them interesting poles for our study. It is also worth noting that almost all of these schools were created since 1994 (and most were created since 2000); if the goal is to examine new approaches since the last major studies of high schools in the 1980s, these schools provide that opportunity.

International Baccalaureate is an older approach that dates back to 1968. But it, too, has grown significantly in recent years in the United States: from three hundred schools using the IB program in 1999 to more than 1,800 today.[32] Originally intended for elite students abroad who wanted to apply to American or British universities, it has increasingly become a model for public schools seeking to serve poor students; the latest statistics suggest that 46 percent of IB schools had a student body in which at least 40 percent of the students were receiving free or reduced-price lunch.[33] Substantively, IB stands somewhere between the progressive and no-excuses approaches, emphasizing mastery of traditional academic disciplines but favoring an inquiry-oriented approach.

At each of these schools, we utilized the standard tools of the qualitative researcher. We observed classes; interviewed students, faculty, and administrators; hung out in the hallways; and went to practices, rehearsals, games, and performances. In total, we spent more than 750 hours observing in schools and interviewed more than three hundred people. This was an active process—we started by getting a representative picture of a school by attending a variety of classes and interviewing the principal and some faculty and students; then we honed in on areas that were of particular interest. We also found that some schools had more to teach us than others. We did deep dives at three of our most successful schools and at one large comprehensive school, where we spent between twenty and thirty days at each. These became the subjects of Chapters 2, 3, 4, and 5. We did medium dives in six other schools—spending five to ten days at each—these were generally schools that were trying to do many of the same things as the more successful schools but were struggling; they became "negative cases" for our sample. We spent one to four days at the other twenty schools—short visits intended to marry the depth of our ten deep- and medium-dive cases with some breadth. We also did a deep dive on the theater program featured in Chapter 6—following the creation of a production from inception to performance. Finally, we spent extensive time with a subsample of seven of the most compelling teachers we found; they became the subject of Chapter 7. The Appendix describes our process in more detail, including the way we structured our classroom observations.

The Gap between Aspirations and Reality

The most striking overall pattern in our data was that our aspirations before beginning the study bumped up against a disappointing reality. We had hoped to be inspired; instead we felt profoundly disheartened.

Here is one representative example, which evokes the aphorism from the 1980s' studies of high schools, "I pretend to teach, you pretend to learn":

It is a Thursday morning and Mr. Picket's tenth-graders are doing a round-robin oral reading of a scene from *Romeo and Juliet*. Mr. Picket has prompted the students to annotate their texts as they go; they are supposed to draw swords next to lines about hate and hearts next to those about love. Only three of the eighteen students appear to be marking anything. The rest sit quietly, some appearing to follow along in their photocopied text, others staring down at the floor.

Every few minutes, Mr. Picket pauses the reading and asks questions that require one-word answers: "What are most of these lines talking about—love or hate?" "Which family do these lines talk about—Montague or Capulet?" Although a few students mutter answers, Mr. Picket usually answers the questions himself. Eventually he notices that most students are not marking up their texts. "C'mon, you guys," he says. "Somebody tell me: what's one place you can draw a heart?" After a long silence, he sighs in exasperation. "Okay, I'll give you a freebee," he says, and reads a few lines out loud. "Everyone draw a heart there," he says when he is finished.

After the group has finished the scene, Mr. Picket hands out a worksheet with some follow-up questions: "What happened in the fight scene between Mercutio and Tybalt?" "What did the characters say about hate and love?" Each question has two lines provided for student responses. The students are mostly quiet and about two-thirds of them appear to be working on the task. The rest sit quietly. Mr. Picket sits at his desk, frowning down at what appear to be some ungraded tests. After fifteen minutes, a student loudly falls out of her chair; she and three girls nearby burst into laughter. Mr. Picket frowns and prompts the girls to "get started," after which they quiet down.

Eventually, the bell rings. Mr. Picket collects the worksheets but says nothing to those students who hand in blank pages. While the students pack up their bags, I ask one girl what the purpose of today's class was. She hesitates before answering. "I don't know—I don't really see a point. It's English class so we just read stories and stuff," she says. Then, after a minute, she gestures toward a male student at another table. "You should ask him," she says. "He knows stuff like that."

To be specific, one part of the problem was the level of cognitive rigor. In classroom after classroom, students were not being challenged to think. Roughly speaking, about four out of five classrooms we visited featured tasks that were in the bottom half of Bloom's taxonomy, asking students to recall, comprehend, or apply, rather than to analyze, synthesize, or create. Another way of putting this: if we stapled ourselves to a student for a day, we likely would encounter one class, or occasionally two, that presented genuine opportunities for critical thinking or analysis. Consistent with prior studies, teacher talk far outran student talk; the modal task for students continues to be to take notes on teacher-delivered content about pre-established knowledge. Math tasks continued, on the whole, to be algorithmic, asking students to apply existing formulas to a series of practice problems.

What we observed in our "recommended" schools with respect to cognitive rigor was consistent with national evidence about the nature of tasks in classrooms. The largest ever videotaped study of American classrooms, grades four through eight, in which more than seven thousand videos were scored by multiple observers across four different validated instruments, found that American teachers scored high in "behavior management" but were weakest at "analysis and problem solving, regard for student perspectives, quality of feedback . . . and content understanding." Of these competencies, "analysis and problem solving" was the least frequently observed, seen in only about 20 percent of lessons (similar to our one in five estimate). In math, only 1 percent of lessons scored in the top rating for analytic complexity, while 70 percent received the lowest rating.[34] Similar findings were reported in a large-scale analysis by Education Trust, which focused on the tasks that middle-school students are asked to carry out. In evaluating nearly 1,600 tasks at six middle schools, analysts used Webb's depth-of-knowledge scale to examine the complexity of the tasks that students were asked to complete. They found that "only 4 percent of assignments asked students to think at higher levels." Conversely, "about 85 percent of assignments asked students to either recall information or apply basic skills and concepts as opposed to prompting for inferences or structural analysis."[35]

Another frequent pattern we observed was the tendency of teachers to undermine potential opportunities for higher-order thinking. Teachers sometimes asked questions that could elicit open-ended responses; for example, in an English class a teacher might ask students about themes or symbols they noticed while reading. But once students began to respond, teachers would appropriate the early shoots of what students were trying to say (often only a few words) and incorporate them into their own longer comments. We seldom heard students speak more than a sentence or two at a time. This is consistent with prior research by Martin Nystrand and Adam Gamoran, which found, in a study of 224 lessons across nine high schools, that free-flowing discussion in ninth-grade English classrooms averaged fewer than fifteen seconds a day![36]

A related issue was what we came to call the "Waiting for Godot" pattern. Typically we would visit a classroom as part of what was announced to faculty as our "deeper learning" study. We would see a class like the ones just described, then the teacher would tell us, on our way out, that she or he knew that this class wasn't deeper learning but it was building the foundation for a deeper task that would come later in the unit. We would then go back, day after day, to the same classroom, but find that the "deeper" day never came. While there is no world in which there isn't some time spent in learning new skills or building basic factual knowledge, it was notable that the best teachers we saw often started with a puzzling question or authentic overall task, then integrated the content and skill building into the unit. As one observer quipped, most teachers saw the process as "Bloom as ladder"—basics now, higher-order skills later—whereas the most compelling teachers we saw seemed to have a "Bloom as web" approach, meaning that they were moving back and forth between lower-order and higher-order tasks.

We also saw differences across tracks, consistent with prior research. Students in AP and honors tracks more frequently were given some opportunities to discuss texts, look at primary sources, and engage in discussion. Students in the lower tracks (now often euphemistically relabeled as "college prep" or "advanced college prep") spent more time simply reading texts aloud and copying notes from PowerPoint presentations. Because these tracks were often sorted along class and racial lines, they also reproduced inequalities in what students were being offered. There was one memorable occasion when we, separately, each observed a history class in the morning—one was filled with documents and primary-source analysis, and the other featured one of the dullest lectures you will ever hear on the Industrial Revolution. Later that day, as we were discussing our respective history classes in a small lunch area, a woman walked in to grab her food out of the fridge, and we realized *we had seen the same woman teaching in different tracks.* This suggests that the problem is not so much with the teachers who teach low-track students as with the existing knowledge base about how to do so. We did encounter some teachers who had found more successful ways to teach students in the lower tracks and some schools that had moved away from tracking entirely. We will discuss both later.

Another pattern was mistaking faster for deeper. We saw this in class-rooms across curricular levels, but it was particularly prevalent in honors and AP courses. Teachers felt responsible for meeting external pacing expectations—whether they came from districts, state tests, SAT IIs, or APs—and the result was that they felt obligated to move through material quickly but not necessarily deeply. In science in particular, labs were often rushed efforts to demonstrate what the text-book said rather than opportunities for real investigation. In math or chemistry classes it became about learning more rules or molecules. Students who wanted to do well in school (or whose parents wanted them to) would comply with teachers' requests and do the expected homework and in-class tasks, but the goal was the grade and not the subject. "Is this going to be on the test?" is alive and well in American high schools.

If one dimension of the problem was cognitive rigor, another major dimension was engagement. In many of the schools we observed, students who had been chattering excitedly in the hall only a moment before sat stone-faced in class. Students told us over and over that they couldn't see the point of what they were doing, that there was little connection to any real-world application, and that they came to school mainly to see their friends and participate in extracurriculars, or to get to college. A 2015 Gallup poll of nearly a million U.S. students paints a similar picture. The Gallup poll finds that engagement decreases the longer that students are in school: while 75 percent of fifth graders report being engaged by school, the number drops to 41 percent by ninth grade, and 32 percent by eleventh grade. Since students have to be at school to take the poll, even the 32 percent underestimates the level of disengagement, because the most disengaged students have dropped out of school and are not in the data.[37] The Gallup poll is consistent with earlier studies that similarly suggest declining engagement as students get older.[38]

The 2009 High School Study of Student Engagement (HSSSE) offers the most detailed recent examination of engagement patterns in
American high schools. The survey, which sampled more than 42,000
students from 103 schools in twenty-seven states, found that 66 percent
of students say they are bored daily at school, and one in six say they
are bored in every class.[39] Students gave a range of familiar reasons for
this boredom, including that the "material wasn't that interesting"
(82 percent) and "lack of relevance" (42 percent). Teachers' pedagogical choices were another reason for their disengagement.[40] Pedagogies
that we know to be most common in high schools, like "teacher lecture," were rated as engaging by only 26 percent of the students. Conversely, modes that are less frequently used, like "discussion and debate,"
were seen as engaging by 61 percent of the students.[41] While it is
certainly possible for material to be superficially engaging without
going "deeper" (as we will discuss shortly), it is notable that the most
frequent pedagogical mode has students sitting passively, a mode
they themselves overwhelmingly report leads to disengagement and
boredom. Conversely, research on more positive classrooms—ones
that were described by observers as meeting the criteria for what Newmann called "authentic intellectual work"—suggests that such practices are correlated with higher levels of engagement.[42]

According to the HSSSE study, levels of engagement also varied
along axes of stratification: girls reported more engagement than boys;
white and Asian students were more engaged than black and Latinx
students; students who did not receive free or reduced-price lunch were
more engaged than those who did; students in honors and advanced
classes were more engaged than those in lower academic tracks.[43] These
patterns were consistent across three dimensions of engagement, including cognitive/intellectual, social/behavioral/participatory, and
emotional.

The HSSSE study also found that students felt largely disempowered
by their education. In the free response portion of the study, students
wrote things like:

- "This survey is pointless and stupid. Nothing will be done based
  on anyone's answers."
- "Why would we fill these out and find no change when you get
  others' hopes up by doing this, and it fails?"

- "Most of the questions are self-explanatory just by walking into the school."
- "This is pointless. Nobody is going to look at this."
- "If this school has taught me anything, it is that my opinion matters not here."
- "This school does not allow students to have a voice in decision-making, even though they say they do."[44]

Teachers in our study were well aware that students were disengaged from their subjects, but many were baffled by how to respond. Some tried the "you need to learn this because you will need it for college and beyond" approach, but this strategy made little headway with adolescents who tended to think mostly in terms of the now. We also saw the frequent use of hooks that were intended to promote engagement— "write about your weekend"; multiple references to pop culture; and some sharing by teachers about their own lives—but, in our observation, unless these devices were linked to a way to get deeper into the subject, they rarely went anywhere. Further, at times we thought they undermined the teacher's credibility with respect to the subject, as in the case of a young history teacher who ended a class otherwise devoted to the Crusades by asking students to name their favorite cartoons.

Many of the reasons for this disengagement seemed to lie less with the teachers than with the constraints imposed by the overall grammar of schooling. We were struck that despite the formal freedoms granted to many of the charter schools we visited, forces of inertia, isomorphism, or lack of imagination made them look not that different from other high schools. If students are going to be asked to move across 1,500 years of history in one ninth-grade year, with dynasties and emperors changing weekly, it would be difficult for Socrates himself to make that subject engaging. It was not a coincidence that many of the most compelling classes we found were electives, which had in some way altered this core grammar—focusing on one subject in more depth and examining it from multiple angles; moving away from batch processing to individualized pathways of learning; doing more hands-on work; or connecting student effort and energy to a product or project that would be presented to an outside audience (we discuss this further in Chapter 5).

At the same time, a different kind of problem emerged in progressive or project-based schools or classrooms, where we sometimes thought that teachers were mistaking student-centered learning or active learning for deeper learning:

It is a Wednesday afternoon and the ninth-grade students enrolled in Mr. Cohen's and Ms. Lattimer's co-taught physical science course are sewing stuffed-animal versions of endangered animals. They have been sewing for three straight class periods, and for many the end is finally in sight. Soft music from a student-generated playlist fills the room. Most students hunch over their stuffed animals, but a few early finishers work together on laptops, finding photos of their animals to print out and use to decorate the room during the upcoming exhibition.

Ms. Lattimer sits in the corner with a small group, demonstrating how to add embellishments such as buttons. Mr. Cohen circulates, talking with individuals and asking partners to explain how they have divided responsibilities. At some point, he makes an announcement to the whole group: "Before you sew everything closed, make sure that you'll be able to access the circuits to turn them on and off." He is referring to the circuit boards that students made the previous week by sewing LED lights to small circuits with conductive thread. The LEDs will become the stuffed animals' eyes.

Since the project is designed to draw together science and maker education, we ask students to talk about their learning across each of these domains. Students talk animatedly about how they got to choose their animals and about how they have never cared this deeply about making sure that a handmade artifact comes out just right. They are particularly excited about next week's exhibition, where they will sell their stuffed animals to visitors in order to raise money for animal advocacy organizations of their choice. When we ask about how the circuits inside the animals work, however, they falter. One admits, "I know how to make the LEDs light up, but I don't really know why—I just followed the teachers' directions." Similarly, when we ask what they learned about their animals, many of them have very little to say. "We have to choose pictures that will make people care about them and want to donate to help keep them from going extinct," a student explains. "We didn't really do much other than that."

This class was typical of some of the more "fun," "progressive" or "maker space" classrooms we encountered. Here the problem was confusing "hands-on" for "minds-on" and it involved doing in ways that did not help students see the underlying conceptual structures of their fields or disciplines. While, as we will see, good project-based learning can be very "deep," there was definitely a tendency among some teachers we observed to mistake student-centered or activity-heavy learning for deeper learning.

Bright Spots

The bad news coming out of our study, then, is that American high school education is not as far along as some accounts might suggest when it comes to enacting deeper learning at the whole-school level. The good news is that such learning is happening *somewhere* in virtually every school that we visited—including regular public schools that were not especially known for "deeper learning." This became a predictable dimension of our work: we knew that if we shadowed a given student over an entire six-period day, we inevitably would encounter one or perhaps two standout practitioners who had figured out how to infuse their classrooms with rigor and vitality. This finding is consistent with the Gates Foundation Measures of Effective Teaching study, which estimates that one out of every five middle-school classrooms features at least a moderate amount of critical thinking and analysis.[45] This statistic can be seen as disheartening—only one in five!—but it also can be construed as a source for hope. After all, if there are 3.7 million teachers working in the U.S. public schools, then there are more than 700,000 who have some degree of capacity to teach for deeper learning. It is also good news in that it suggests that these classrooms do not exist solely in schools that are somehow "special"—charters, private schools, magnets—but can and do occur in regular public schools throughout the United States.

Further, to categorize it this way—some teachers are offering deeper learning and some are not—invokes firm boundaries, whereas a continuum of skill would be a more accurate image. It also implies that teachers' level of skill is fixed rather than being a developmental journey from which we observed a particular moment. Another piece of good news, if you would consider it such, is that virtually all of the teachers we interviewed *aspired* to create classrooms that are intellectually lively places, where students make sense of complex questions and where there is spontaneous energy rather than forced compliance. Thus while there was a huge gap in realizing this vision, reflecting the absence of an important set of mechanisms in the field, the vast majority of teachers we interviewed were at least aspiring to desirable classroom qualities.

Relatedly, if, as is frequently posited, the new three Rs are "rigor, relevance, and relationships," while many teachers we observed were struggling with rigor and relevance, they were stronger on the relationships piece. Virtually all of the students we talked to said that at least one of their teachers cared about them, and they often defined their best teachers as "she is the one who took an interest in me; she is the one who will stay after school and help us." The HSSSE survey referred to earlier reflects similar findings—two out of three students believed that "most" or "all" of their teachers wanted them to do the best work they could; 88 percent said that there was at least one adult in the school who cared about them.[46] The classrooms that we visited were often friendly if not intellectually rigorous places—teachers not infrequently shared information about their own lives, sometimes inquired about students' lives, and often used humor to lighten the mood.[47] There was a class gradient to this—the more affluent the students, the looser and more relaxed the culture, with the no-excuses schools being the most disciplined and least relationship-oriented in our sample. Even in the no-excuses schools, though, students said that teachers cared about them, and that they displayed that care by putting in extra time planning their lessons and in other ways, such as trying to get them to college. On the whole, at least in this recommended sample of schools, students consistently reported that teachers cared quite a bit about them; those teachers were just struggling to find ways to translate that care into rigorous and engaging instruction.

If our overall story is about inconsistent patterns of deeper learning across different schools, we did find some departments and programs that consistently embodied some or all of its qualities. And among the thirty schools that we visited in total, we did encounter a few that were moving toward the consistent realization of deeper learning practices that we sought at the outset. We describe three of these schools in detail in Chapters 2, 3, and 4.

Visiting a range of schools also helped us to see that some schools were excelling on at least one corner of the mastery, identity, and creativity triangle, and thus could offer something to their students and to the field, even if they were struggling to bring all of the elements together. Such schools, we realized, can be clustered into rough groups that share a set of underlying values, as well as a theory of action about how these values can be instantiated through organizational structures and classroom pedagogy. For example, a number of the schools and networks in the Hewlett deeper learning network share an aspiration to support students in developing the general competencies that Tony Wagner describes as the "seven survival skills" necessary for the twenty-first century.[48] These schools emphasize the development of original work through engagement in interdisciplinary, collaborative, real-world-aligned projects—a model that often entails block scheduling, cross-subject teaching, and the use of performance or portfolio-based assessments. By making these changes to the grammar of schooling, these schools, we thought, were better able to give students opportunities to exercise creativity and to form deeper identities connected to their work. They were weaker on traditional forms of academic mastery as measured by tests or by the levels of intellectual power and academic fluency that we observed among their students.

A second group of schools sits much closer to the *mastery* node of the triangle, organizing themselves around the goal of supporting students in developing deep knowledge, skills, and competencies within the traditional academic disciplines. These schools, which include some that have adopted the Advanced Placement (AP) program, some that have adopted the International Baccalaureate (IB) program, and a few that have developed their own inquiry-based approaches, aspire to help students learn to do what David Perkins calls "playing the whole game" of the traditional academic disciplines—not just superficially learning about historical events, for example, but emulating the processes of historical inquiry through analyzing primary sources, debating competing interpretations, and conducting original research.[49] (Whether Advanced Placement courses constrain or support deeper learning is a complex question that we discuss in more detail in Chapter 5.)[50]

Schools organized around the International Baccalaureate program are trying to go even one step further, striving to help students understand how the core epistemologies ("ways of knowing") for each discipline compare to others. These processes could sometimes inspire students' creativity and help them develop academic identities, but they frequently did not result in the energy and vitality we observed in some of the project-based approaches described earlier.

A third group, which notably includes schools in the Big Picture Learning Network, focuses primarily on the *identity* node of the deeper learning triangle, striving to help students develop a stronger sense of themselves as learners, citizens, and soon-to-be professionals by offering them ongoing opportunities to learn from out-of-school mentors and to make extensive choices in their in-school course of study. These schools tend to bank heavily on structures that support individualized pathways to graduation: online courses, student-chosen internships, elective courses, and "looping" advisories. These schools, many of which were designed for students who had not fared well in traditional high schools, seemed to have succeeded in building warm, purposeful communities that had re-engaged students in their education. This was no small achievement. At the same time, they were lacking when it came to conventional academic mastery.

How to view these thematic schools is a matter of perspective. We choose to see the glass as half-full: schools in each of these three veins have understood something important about how to stimulate their charges. Part of the goal of this book is to think about how we might put these pieces together, and, in so doing, generate classrooms and schools that include all three corners of the deeper learning triangle.

The outlook gets brighter still if we widen the lens to include elective classes and extracurricular activities. Counterintuitively, at a number of the schools we visited the deepest learning seemed to be concentrated in these so-called "peripheral" contexts. Spanning the gamut from visual art and film scoring to theater and model United Nations, such contexts often harness the power of an apprenticeship model in which real-world domains of professional practice provide standards for good work, teachers model expertise and conviction, and students gradually are inducted into more and more complex aspects of the professional activity. This constellation of qualities infuses the learning with depth, meaning, and a palpable sense of momentum—the very qualities that are often lacking in mainstream academic classes. While we recognize that electives and extracurriculars are structurally "special"— students self-select into them based on interest and/or ability, there are rarely external pressures for coverage, and so on—we also think that there is something powerful to be learned from them about how to engage adolescents in deep learning. By extension, we believe that a critical question moving forward is how schools might be able to in-

fuse more of what happens at their "peripheries" into their core programs of academic study. We discuss in detail aspects of the relationship between the periphery and the core in Chapters 5 (electives) and
6 (extracurriculars), and again, from a wider perspective, in our concluding chapter.

Why Is There So Little Deeper Learning in Schools?

As David Cohen notes in his essay, "Plus ça change," the traditions that
promote knowledge as certain and given, teachers as tellers, and students
as passive recipients are millennia old. These assumptions continue
today, not only in American public schools, but also in public schools
around the world, in many private schools, and in universities, all of
which, despite their very different organizational contexts, fundamentally subscribe to the notion of teaching as knowledge transmission.
These assumptions emerged at a time when adult and religious
authority was gospel; very few people had the resources, time, or opportunity to participate in the construction of knowledge; and children
were expected to conform to the expectations of adults. The contrary
image offered by John Dewey and others—of the student as an active
sense-maker, and thus of teaching as an act that stimulates thinking and
helps students gradually unfold for themselves the mysteries of science,
literature, and other fields—is, as Cohen points out, only a little more
than a century old, a late and weak newcomer onto the educational
terrain.[51]

If the first part of the story is historical and epistemological, the
second part is structural. In the United States, the older conception of
teaching, knowledge, and learning was reinforced by the creation
of what David Tyack and Larry Cuban have called the "grammar of
schooling."[52] This grammar was established by bureaucrats who built
at the end of the nineteenth century the American school system that
persists to this day. Key elements of that grammar are age-graded classrooms, division of the curriculum into discrete academic subjects, the
creation of different academic tracks, and a teacher-centered pedagogy
that expects all students to absorb knowledge and skills in lockstep.[53]
Much of what we saw in classrooms in the early twenty-first century
still bears the heavy imprint of this century-old organizational design.

A third factor is the under-professionalization of American teaching. As one of us has argued in a previous book, one of the fateful decisions made when creating the American school system was to place power in a small, mostly male, administrative class, rather than to develop the mostly female teaching force as a full-fledged profession. Professional fields, like law, medicine, engineering, and many others, recognize that the work they are doing is complex and thus have developed professional value systems and structures appropriate to knowledge workers: they are selective in whom they recruit, develop a knowledge base that under-girds their work, provide lengthy training in that knowledge, and then require those who enter the field to demonstrate this knowledge and skill. By comparison, education in the United States took a different path by placing power in the administrative class and under-developing the needed professional mechanisms: teaching is an unselective field, featuring short training and low entry requirements, which are fre-quently waived altogether when there is a teacher shortage. The result of this non-system is wide variation across classrooms, just as we ob-served. Teaching in the United States also does not have a career ladder that includes opportunities for advancement and for the establishment of highly paid master teachers, which some other countries have. The consequence is that it is hard to draw a talented, capable, and diverse workforce into teaching, which, in turn, only exacerbates the desire for administrative control, perpetuating the downward spiral.[54]

The Hand of History

Observational studies of American classrooms from the 1880s to the present have repeatedly shown the ways in which these forces have pro-duced and reproduced a status quo of teaching as transmission, or what Paulo Freire called "banking" education. For example, in 1893, Joseph Mayer Rice, a pediatrician by training, conducted a tour of American school districts that in many ways paralleled the journey we took 120 years later. He found that the vast majority of classes focused on drilling facts into the minds of children and on recitations of what they read in textbooks. He found few examples of "new education," in the form of experiments, creative writing, or opportunities for students to think critically.[55] Larry Cuban's famous study of teaching from 1880 to 1980 found that similar patterns persisted across the twentieth century: while there was some softening of classroom practice toward becoming moderately more child-centered (especially in elementary schools), on the whole the pattern was subject over students, teacher talk over student talk, and most teaching from the textbook.[56] When researchers returned to high schools in the 1980s, they again found similar patterns. For example, John Goodlad's large-scale study of high schools in 1984 found that "75 percent of class time was spent on instruction and that nearly 70 percent of this was 'talk'—usually teachers to students. Teachers out-talked the class of students by a ratio of about three to one. . . . The bulk of this teacher talk was instructing in the sense of telling. Barely 5 percent of this instructional time was designed to create students' anticipation of needing to respond. Not even 1 percent required some kind of open response involving reasoning or perhaps an opinion from students."[57] As Dan Lortie famously argued, most teachers teach as they were taught, and thus the school system has a built-in mechanism for its own reproduction.[58]

There have been some exceptions to this dominant pattern, but they have been concentrated in "niches" and have been largely bastardized when tried across whole public systems.[59] For example, Dewey's rich vision of progressive education—an interdisciplinary hands-on curriculum that links theory to practice, and students to subjects—has been realized in full-throated ways in small private schools and occasionally in public elementary schools in affluent areas where there is sufficient parental support.[60] But when these ideas have been transported into public schools, particularly large high schools serving a more diverse array of students, they have tended to be radically watered down: home economics classes, life-adjustment education, and vocational education, all of which have drawn on the practical but eschewed the academic.[61] Schools have taken the part of it that was easier to do—offering more practical courses to less academically inclined students—but not the harder part: using the practical as a springboard to academic content. In many ways, the problems with life-adjustment education are the ancestors of the "fun-but-not-rigorous" progressive schools we described earlier.

Throughout this history, the dividing lines of race and class have played a critical role in determining who has had access to deeper learning experiences. Faced with massive immigration and a rapidly growing high school population at the beginning of the twentieth century, reformers built a school system that created separate pathways for students of different abilities and/or family backgrounds. Emboldened by the then new science of intelligence testing, these reformers created an explicitly differentiated school system that funneled more advantaged students into more conventionally academic tracks and poorer, immigrant, and working-class students into vocational or less demanding academic tracks. In the second half of the twentieth century, these inequalities were exacerbated by the growth of residential segregation and the deindustrialization of cities, developments that led to increasing disparities between city and suburban schools.[62] The result, according to both quantitative evidence and closely observed ethnographies of classrooms, is that schools and tracks that serve upper-middle-class students more frequently feature interactions in which students are given opportunities to express their thinking and grapple with complex or open-ended questions, whereas schools or classes serving working-class or high-poverty students tend to be dominated by teacher talk and to feature worksheets and other low-level tasks.[63] Some scholars have argued that there is a correspondence between the ways in which students are treated in school and the occupational positions they are expected to hold, with upper-middle-class students learning the managerial skills of assessing information, weighing options, and making decisions, and working-class and high-poverty students learning how to follow rules and comply.[64] In recent years, well-meaning efforts to close the achievement gap have sometimes unintentionally reified this divide, as disadvantaged students who are in danger of failing state tests get increasing amounts of test prep and a narrowing of the curriculum, whereas more advantaged students get a more varied and stimulating curriculum.[65]

Finally, this history also underscores perhaps the most important reason that there has not been more deep learning in American schools: limited public demand for it. The qualities associated with deep learning—thinking critically, grappling with nuance and complexity, reconsidering inherited assumptions, questioning authority, and embracing intellectual questions—are not widely embraced by the American people.[66] For example, the 1960s National Science Foundation curriculum, Man: A Course of Study (MACOS), which invited students to study another culture as part of an anthropological examination of what it means to be human, died at the hands of a fundamentalist backlash.[67] MACOS is just one example among many of the ways in which efforts to have students confront difficult questions have been rebuffed by the more conservative elements of our electorate. Thus creating deeper learning is not only about improving pedagogy but also about building demand for a different approach to learning.

Constraints and Omissions

Another way to understand the paucity of deeper learning is to think in terms of the negative forces that shape American high school classrooms today. We categorize these as *constraints* and *omissions*. To start with barriers at the school level, engaging students in sustained, authentic, high-cognitive-demand tasks requires structures and supports that many high school teachers simply do not have. Compared to their elementary-school counterparts, they teach many more students and see each student for many fewer hours each day, making it difficult to build relationships and to create opportunities for sustained inquiry.[68] As one eleventh-grade science teacher ruefully reported, "Forty-seven minutes is just enough time to get the kids really interested and engaged in whatever you want them to be learning, and then the bell rings and you have to start pretty much from scratch the next day." Organization into disciplinary subjects can compound this sense of fragmentation, limiting opportunities to support students in drawing connections and transferring knowledge across disciplines. Large classes and high teacher loads (the total number of students each teacher teaches across his or her classes) also work against individualized attention and substantial teacher feedback on student work. Beyond such systemic constraints, at a subtler level, high schools seem to reflect the profound dis-ease that characterizes our society's stance toward adolescents. Teenagers are expected to sit for hour after hour passively listening and following directions but are seldom engaged in tasks that involve real choice and latitude—likely, in part, because doing so would involve ceding some of the rigid control that often characterizes teacher-student relationships in secondary schools, especially secondary schools serving poor and/or minority populations.[69]

Another major structural constraint—the one most frequently cited by teachers themselves—is the pressure for content coverage associated with external assessments such as state tests, SAT IIs, and even some

Advanced Placement exams. This pressure has intensified in recent years, accruing particular urgency in low-performing schools, where administrators worry about making adequate yearly progress as measured by state standardized tests, but it is also being felt in upper-middle-class schools, where students are competing for acceptance to top-tier colleges. Similarly, district-mandated scope and sequence expectations emphasize breadth over depth, asking teachers to move quickly through large swaths of material with little opportunity to pause for more in-depth investigations. Finally, teacher evaluation systems can also constrain opportunities for deeper teaching by focusing on surface aspects of teaching—such as whether objectives are on the board—and, depending on the rubrics, can be misaligned with more inquiry-oriented teaching approaches.

The presence of these traditions and pressures is certainly a key reason that so few teachers even try to reorganize their practice around deeper learning goals. An equally powerful reason, however, is the *absence* of structures and processes that could help them to do so. Chief among these are sufficient time, resources, and professional learning opportunities to learn how to teach in new and different ways. For example, in the 1950s and 1960s, spurred by Sputnik, reformers, including Jerome Bruner and others from higher education, tried to retool the teaching of core subjects to align with how scholars in the disciplines actually investigated those subjects. Much of what they were attempting to do parallels our discussion of deeper learning. With support from the National Science Foundation, they developed new curricula to match. But accounts of this effort show that the reformers did not make a compelling enough case to teachers about why they should change, nor did they acknowledge that the shift would greatly increase the complexity of their work. There was also no sustained effort to build teacher capacity for the new ways of teaching.[70] The result: evaluations of the reforms a decade later showed that a small number of ambitious teachers were using the new math, the revised science, and the new social studies curricula, but, once again, most teachers were still teaching as they always had.[71]

Similar omissions plague the contemporary education sector as a whole. Essentially, current teacher practice is the product of a vicious cycle that has yet to be disrupted and reversed at any kind of scale. The realities that we described earlier in this chapter mean that, during their own experiences in high school, teachers were unlikely to have experienced much deep learning, especially in their core academic classes. Similarly, the widely acknowledged weakness and incoherence of American teacher-preparation programs mean that, as they begin their careers teachers are unlikely to have learned anything substantive about teaching for deep learning.[72] Finally, while we saw some progress in breaking down the isolation that historically has plagued teaching as a profession, we did not see much evidence that teacher collaborations were leading to more rigorous instruction.[73] On the whole, we observed that even if teachers yearn to infuse their classrooms with greater vitality and depth, they lack rich models for what these qualities might look like and what it might take to generate them—so they default to teaching in the ways that they themselves were taught.

How to Support Deeper Learning: A Preview

Against this backdrop, it becomes easier to understand what we witnessed in schools. Schools that were trying to create challenging, rigorous, purposeful education had to combat a series of historical and contemporary forces that were working directly against their objectives. That these forces included omissions as well as constraints meant that, in order to achieve their goals, schools had to supply themselves much of what was missing.

We develop our arguments in more detail in later chapters, but as a preview, we found that:

- *To close the gap between espoused values and enacted practices, schools need a specific and granular vision of deep learning and a carefully crafted organizational design that enables them to realize it.* Because teachers are not typically trained for deeper learning, schools have to organize much of this learning themselves if they are going to create consistent levels of quality across classrooms. Specifically, we found that the schools most successful at realizing their visions, while varied in their pedagogical approaches, had generated a specific and finely detailed vision of learning, developed extensive opportunities for adults to learn that vision, organized that adult learning in ways that were symmetrical to the ways in which they expected adults to teach students, made student and teacher work visible to create some accountability, developed a collective identity that engendered teacher and student ownership of the vision, and aligned organizational processes to support all of these efforts. Even for schools working within external systems, like International Baccalaureate, that could provide the external "exoskeleton" to support deep learning, a parallel internal "endoskeleton" with these features was required.

- *Achieving deeper learning is challenging because it requires significant unlearning.* For traditional teachers, moving toward giving their students deeper experiences in their domains entailed substantial loss: of some breadth in pursuit of depth, and of control, as teachers realized that being a teacher didn't always mean talking in front of the class. Making these shifts was difficult and painful, and even for our most successful teachers it often took many years. Thematically organized schools faced another version of this challenge at the organizational level: No Excuses High was trying to figure out how to reboot its culture of control to prepare students for the more open-ended environment of college; Dewey High was trying to find ways to continue to mount authentic and meaningful projects while integrating the building of foundational skills. For each of these schools, their core DNA, organizational processes, and culture were coherent and oriented in one direction. Integrating new goals was challenging because doing so would require undoing much of what had brought them success in the first place.

- *Powerful learning experiences integrate seemingly opposing virtues: mastery, identity, and creativity.* Whether in classes, extracurriculars, clubs, or elsewhere, students identified their most powerful learning experiences as those that gave them opportunities to develop knowledge and skill (mastery), become intensely connected to a domain (identity), and have an ability to enact their understandings by trying to make something meaningful to them (creativity). Apprenticeship models, in which students tried (and often failed) to do something under the watchful eye of more experienced teachers and students, were particularly well aligned with this integrated mode of learning.

- *The periphery is often more vital than the core; outside the core classes is a second "grammar of schooling" that is better aligned with powerful learning.* The so-called peripheral aspects of school—extracurriculars, clubs, and electives—had a very different grammar than core classes. Here students could make significant choices, they saw purpose in their work, learning by doing was common, depth was privileged over breadth, students were apprenticed to older students, and learning frequently integrated head, hands, and heart. While what happened to students during these peripheral activities was still dependent on the knowledge and skill of the people who led them, the core assumptions that guided these experiences seemed to support rather than constrain their efforts.

- *Some teachers were able to bring deeper learning to their core classes by taking a very different stance toward learning than most traditional teachers.* Because schools are loosely coupled organizations, even though the dominant patterns were grim, there were pockets of deeper learning in almost every school. The teachers who led these compelling classrooms differed from most of our teachers on a number of interrelated dimensions, which we call their *stance* toward teaching: they saw the purpose of what they were doing as less about covering material and more about inducting students into the work of their field; they privileged depth over breadth; they saw students as creators and not simply receivers of knowledge; they saw failure not as something to be avoided but as a necessary part of learning; and they tried to create an atmosphere of rigor and joy rather than compliance.

- *Those teachers who were able to provide deeper learning experiences for students had themselves had a "seminal learning experience" that had inspired them and helped them to see what it would entail to induct the next generation into their fields of study.* These teachers could each point to experiences during the latter part of college, in graduate school, or in the real world, when they had begun actually doing the work of the field or domain that they would teach. While they had had many mediocre learning experiences as students, they drew on these rare but powerful learning experiences to generate a different vision of their goals and practices. The implication for teacher preparation as well as for ongoing teacher learning is that more teachers need to have these kinds of experiences if they are going to create something similar for their students.

- *While some have posited that these methods are appropriate only for advantaged students, our research suggests that students who are most disaffected from school are the ones most in need of new approaches.* The teachers who were most effective at providing deeper learning experiences saw the approaches they were developing as particularly important for their most disadvantaged and disaffected students, because they were the ones who were least well served by traditional schooling. The teachers made sensible alterations for students with weaker skills—shorter texts, more careful scaffolding—but their core stance was the same for all students: inducting students into a domain by creating experiences that linked mastery, identity, and creativity.

- *The system is not oriented toward deeper learning; our most successful examples had to buffer themselves from external pressures. If we want more deep learning, we need to change the system.* Because the external environment—including testing, parental expectations, college pressures, and district scope and sequence—is not aligned toward deeper learning, our most successful classrooms, teachers, schools, and extracurriculars had to find ways to buffer themselves from these pressures in order to make space for the powerful learning environments they were trying to create. It is not a coincidence that electives, extracurriculars, and clubs—chosen and untested domains—were often these deeper spaces. If deeper learning is to move from the periphery into the core, the external environment will need to shift its assessments, culture, and other expectations to align with deeper learning.

2 ∽

The Progressive Frontier:
Project-Based Learning

IT IS ELEVEN O'CLOCK on a bright West Coast morning and Dewey High (a pseudonym) is humming with activity. It is June, a month that in many schools brings lethargy and distraction. Not here. Instead, the tone is one of focused anticipation as students finalize their spring projects and prepare to present them as "Transitional Presentations of Learning," the public presentations that are the school's version of final exams.

In a small classroom at one end of the building, Davon and Isabel are working at opposite corners of a rectangular wooden table. Isabel, a Mexican-American tenth grader with a round face and jet-black hair, leans over a magazine article. Her face registers something between interest and confusion as she pauses to reread a passage of text. "I think we should include this," she says softly. She barely lifts her eyes from the page. Davon, Isabel's project partner, appears at first not to hear. Black, tall, and wearing calf-high combat boots, he is as flamboyant as Isabel is soft-spoken. He sprawls in a metal chair and looks sidelong at an interview transcription on a laptop, glancing every few moments toward the glass that separates the classroom from the sunny "great room" beyond. After a moment, he trains his gaze on his partner. "What'd you find?" he asks. "We definitely need more statistics."

The two are making a video documentary that argues in favor of condom distribution at high schools, and they are trying to finish their script. The twelve-week project was developed by Mr. Quinn, an energetic young humanities teacher, in collaboration with his teaching partner, a Spanish teacher from El Salvador. At the beginning of the process, the students studied fear-based rhetoric, reading *The Communist Manifesto* and learning about McCarthyism during the Cold War. They then formed groups and began working on the project's performance task, documentary films that must make use of the "paranoid style" (a term famously coined by historian Richard Hofstadter) in order to make arguments about issues of current public concern. To fulfill the requirements, each group must choose and research a topic, write an informative memo and an argumentative essay about it, conduct filmed interviews with stakeholders, draft and revise a script that integrates these interviews with other sources, and produce the movie itself. Finally, each group has to add music and Spanish subtitles to their film before screening it for their teachers, parents, and peers at the class's exhibition night. Shortly after, they need to reflect on their work as part of their Transitional Presentations of Learning.

It is no accident that Isabel and Davon have chosen the topic of condom distribution for their project. Isabel has several teenaged peers who already have had children; Davon has a cousin who is HIV-positive. For both students, fear—along with sorrow, anger, and even tenderness—is an appropriate emotion to frame their film. It is also no accident that they have chosen to be partners. Their collaboration reflects the intimacy of close friends: periods of comfortable silence are punctuated by serious dialogue as well as by squabbles and play. When Davon comes back from an extended trip to the bathroom, Isabel chides him, warning him that they might need to work through lunch in order to meet the end-of-day deadline. "No way, girl," Davon counters. "I'm gonna get this done in a snap."

Around the room, other groups are working with similar fluidity and self-direction. Some students sit on top of tables discussing their ideas; others float in and out of the room carrying video cameras. A group of girls confers about the sequencing of images in their film, moving easily between working and socializing. For his part, Mr. Quinn is an energetic but understated presence in the room. He spends most of his time sitting with groups, listening to their conversations and asking probing questions. He allows students to make their own decisions about task division and time use, but when he senses that a group is getting off track, he directs them to useful resources. With one set of advanced students who are making a film about terrorism in the post-9/11 world, he reminds them in a wry tone that he expects "nothing less than perfection." With Isabel, he is gentler, affirming her decision to open the film with one of the statistics she discovered. He and his students seem profoundly comfortable with each other; there are few traces of the strained power relations that often characterize high school classrooms.

On the other side of the school, the forty students that comprise Ms. Johnson's and Mr. Davis's ninth-grade team are preparing to present their "20 percent" projects. Inspired by Google's practice of encouraging employees to spend a fifth of their time pursuing ideas of their choosing, these projects share a single core requirement: use the last ninety minutes of each day to design and create something that will benefit the Dewey High community. After exploring the idea of intrinsic motivation by reading Daniel Pink's *Drive*, students formed groups and began brainstorming, prototyping, refining, and then actualizing their products—a process that involved far less supervision than anything they had done earlier in the year. "The idea was that we wanted the kids to get a feel for what it will be like next year, when they have a lot more autonomy," Ms. Johnson explains. Tall, poised, and dressed in flowing clothes, her calm authority is well suited to the school's youngest students. "We figured if they made bad decisions, they would learn from those, too, so one of the main things on the presentation rubric is about being self-reflective," she adds.

In contrast to Mr. Quinn's classroom, the feeling of Ms. Johnson's room on this particular day is one of frenetic preparation. The project groups will present their work together, but individual members must each spend five minutes describing their specific contributions and reflecting on the lessons they learned in the process. This five minutes factors into their grades for both the project and the year. A number of students sit individually at tables around the room, looking over the presentation rubrics that Ms. Johnson handed out at the beginning of class. Others have already found a critique partner and are immersed in practicing their presentations. For the roughly half of students who did not attend one of Dewey High's middle schools, Transitional Presentations of Learning represent uncharted territory; they have had multiple opportunities to present publicly over the course of the year, but this is the first time that something as large as academic promotion is riding on their work. To compound this pressure, one of the project requirements was that all students had to invite at least three people from outside the school community to their presentation.

"When working on a darkroom, one of the most important things is to be preemptive," begins Kieran. "What I learned is to plan things out, to draw things out along the way." Tiny, intense, and dressed in tight black clothes that stand out against his white skin, he uses the open space outside of the classroom to practice his presentation in front of his friend Susan. He shifts his weight back and forth while he talks, gazing down intently at his notecards. For his project, he explains, he and his two partners constructed a moveable darkroom. He describes how the previous summer he had taken a film photography class, after which he and his friends "got really into it" and used a corner of his parents' garage to create a darkroom where they could develop images. With the start of school, however, they abandoned the hobby, until the 20 percent project came along and they decided that their contribution to the Dewey High community would be to create a darkroom, so that the school could have a film photography club. Unable to convince the principal to dedicate a permanent space for the purpose, they drafted and implemented a plan for a rolling wooden structure that is light-sealed and outfitted with the necessary supplies for film development, blogging about the process as they did so.

After a few more sentences, Kieran abruptly stops and crumples the notecards from which he has been reading. "When I have cards, I just look down at them nervously and they actually make me talk worse," he says. "I think I'm extra freaked out because I invited practically the whole school to come." Susan, a petite Asian student who transferred to the school halfway through the year, uses the pause as an opportunity to ask Kieran some general questions about the presentation process. "Is it more important to talk about what you did or what you learned?" she asks. "Both, really," Kieran responds. "They don't just want to know what you learned but how you learned it—and that's connected to what you did." He pauses, reflecting on what he had just said. Susan jots down some thoughts on her own notecards.

By noon, when the lunch hour begins, Kieran and Susan have each practiced their presentations twice, incorporating feedback from Ms. Johnson as well as from each other. Kieran has decided to talk openly about his tendency to take on too much of the work out of fear that his partners will not deliver; Susan has decided to emphasize how this project helped her to trust her own ability to contribute good ideas. They linger well past the point that most of their peers have spilled out of the building's open doors and into the ubiquitous sunshine. As he packs up, Kieran tells Susan that he is going to skip lunch in order to finish painting an image of a camera on one of the darkroom's external sides. "With this project, it's about taking something from inside yourself and saying, 'I want to get this done because I want to get this done, not I want to get this done because I want to get an A-plus,'" he explains. "Not all projects are like that, but this one definitely is."

∽

The Dewey High charter network, founded in the year 2000, serves in one region more than five thousand students across fourteen schools: six high schools, four middle schools, and four elementary schools. By relying on a zip-code-based lottery system, all of these schools serve racially, socioeconomically, and linguistically diverse populations. All follow a project-based model of instruction that strives to integrate technical and vocational elements with a liberal arts curriculum. The network's results on a variety of metrics are consistently impressive. On conventional measures, such as the state's standardized assessment, most of its schools outperform their district counterparts; in addition, 100 percent of Dewey High students graduate having completed the coursework required to enter the state-run university system in comparison to 57 percent in the surrounding district and 41 percent statewide. By other measures they do even better: 96 percent of graduates matriculate into two- and four-year colleges, with a third of these students being the first in their families to pursue higher degrees. Unlike at some high-achieving charter schools, these successes are not the result of "pushing out" students who do not perform well; more than 90 percent of entering ninth-graders graduate from Dewey High four years later. Locally, in communities spanning from blue-collar neighborhoods to some of the most affluent suburbs in America, Dewey High has become a household name, with many more students entering each school's admissions lottery than there are available seats. Nationally, and even internationally, the network has become a leader in the universe of public project-based progressive schools; the network hosts more than five thousand visitors a year, as well as many annual gatherings of national and international educators seeking to learn more about project-based learning.

The student work emerging from Dewey High also often has influence outside the walls of the school: a student-created field guide to the city's bay sells in local bookstores; a student-authored economics book—in which each spread features students defining an economic concept with a facing page illustrating that concept—was praised by President Clinton as one of the most lucid and incisive books on the subject that he had ever read. A feature-length movie about the school has played across the nation, often screened specifically with the aim of stimulating other communities to think about the possibilities of a twenty-first-century education. In addition to this external acclaim, another positive sign is that many teachers and administrators at Dewey (as well as the chief executive officer and chair of the board) have chosen to send their own children through the Dewey High system.

To many visitors' surprise and occasional dismay, however, those who flock to the school's original campus—ourselves included—often find that an initial tour leaves them feeling disoriented rather than enlightened. On the one hand, the school's innovative character is abundantly clear. The building is as impressive as it is striking: high ceilings with exposed piping offset concrete-and-glass walls that showcase a plethora of student-made artifacts. On the other hand, it is often very difficult for visitors to gauge the nature of the teaching and learning that is taking place. It is clear enough what is *not* happening in classrooms such as Mr. Quinn's and Ms. Johnson's: students are not sitting in rows taking notes, content is not organized along conventional disciplinary lines, standardized assessments are not guiding the curriculum, bells are not determining the flow of the work. Less immediately clear, however, are the principles and practices that have replaced the conventional grammar of schooling. This leads to a host of questions about the school's model—questions that connect to enduring debates about the promises and pitfalls of the more radical instantiations of progressive education. How did Dewey High come to have such distinctively different aspirations, and how does it achieve them? Why do similar schools struggle to do the same? What are the tradeoffs associated with this form of project-based learning? And, finally, would we as a society want schools like Dewey High for all students if we could manage to create them?

As we will see, the debates surrounding these questions date back at least to the beginning of the twentieth century. It is only recently, however, that these debates have involved nonselective urban public schools—because it is only recently that a number of such schools have taken up the cry of educational progressivism. We encountered many of these schools in our work: project-based schools, inquiry-based schools, even a Montessori high school. All were aspirational places striving to enact deep learning, but most tended to have the familiar "aspirations gap" with respect to achieving their visions. Among them, Dewey High stood out as the only system of public progressive schools we researched with not only a thick set of answers to the questions posed earlier, but also a powerful *design* that consistently translated these answers into the daily work of teaching and learning.

Origins

The way Chief Executive Officer Lorenzo Friedman tells it, Dewey High owes its existence to a series of serendipitous events. Slim, spry, and tirelessly talkative, Mr. Friedman—now in his mid-sixties—is the kind of leader who is best understood as a force of nature. Although he spends his days doing everything from overseeing day-to-day operations to fundraising and speaking at conferences, he always seems to have time to stop in the hallway to chat, and he always seems to know which projects are under way, which students have recently made breakthroughs in their work, and which topics teachers are gossiping about at lunch. Listening to him riff on these things as he tells the story of the school's evolution, it is clear that the character of the institution mirrors that of its creative and eclectic founder.

The first critical event in the birth of Dewey High, according to Mr. Friedman, was his unorthodox choice at the age of thirty-three to quit a nascent law career and take a series of positions teaching carpentry. What would become a life-changing shift of focus began as a side job: in order to support himself through law school, he had engaged in various carpentry projects, one of which involved constructing a darkroom in the attic of a settlement house serving low-income families. While he worked, the students who came to the house after school would come upstairs to chat and to learn how to use his tools. Initially, Mr. Friedman made little of this. As time wore on and an increasing number of students regularly showed up for carpentry lessons, however, he realized that there was something striking about the scenario. "It was a revelation for me: these kids were out of school for the day and they could do whatever they wanted, but making stuff was equivalent to, if not better than, play," he remembers. "I looked in the mirror one night and decided I wanted to teach."

Mr. Friedman's commitment both to teaching carpentry and to the field of education deepened as he learned the ropes during four years when he worked first at a psychiatric hospital's residential treatment program and then as a teacher at a newly created high school. In 1981, he was persuaded to take a position teaching vocational education in a large racially and socioeconomically diverse comprehensive school housed in a town with several highly regarded universities. Large, diverse, and heavily tracked, the school fell far short of actualizing the espoused progressive values of the community that it served:

> Back then, you had six schools within a school, five of them in a five-story building and then a separate building for the Technical Arts program. The kids of high socioeconomic status were on the fifth floor, the lowest on the ground floor. The Technical Arts building had the Cape Verdeans and the Haitians . . . all of whom were Gulagged there in a building which they not-so-ironically called "the island." So you had this stark social stratification which was architectural.

Mr. Friedman found himself increasingly frustrated by this de facto segregation. How could any school, much less one in such a progressive university community, systematically exclude poor and minority students from academically rigorous classes?

As the year passed, he began to believe that the inverse held true as well: elite students, except for a handful "pushed down" to him by friendly colleagues teaching on the school's upper floors, were being denied opportunities for the kind of powerful learning that can accompany hands-on work. After all, the experience of learning carpentry as it played out in his classroom was animated by a set of intangibly powerful forces—the same forces that had drawn the settlement house kids up to the attic. Students learned by doing, not just by listening. The artifacts that they produced had both utilitarian and aesthetic value. There was space for both routine practice and creative expression. Perhaps most importantly, these things occurred in the context of a potent form of apprenticeship. Mr. Friedman, an accomplished craftsman, modeled excellent work and helped students to add new skills to their repertoire as they engaged in increasingly difficult tasks. In turn, the more accomplished students modeled good work for newcomers and helped to induct them into the community.[1]

Within a few years, Mr. Friedman had begun to more vocally promote the power of hands-on work both in and out of the classroom. In 1990 he became head of the School for Technical Arts—a position from which he piloted new endeavors, such as an internship program, and advocated for greater integration of vocational and academic work. He also joined the faculty as a lecturer at a top education school in the same university town, where he taught courses on Dewey, the law, and the American high school.

The authorization of the School to Work Opportunities Act of 1994 set the stage for a second critical event in Dewey High's development. The policy, designed to lower the dropout rate by funding programs that incorporated career exploration curricula into "regular" academic programs, encouraged educators to reimagine the role of vocational training in high schools. In 1996, Mr. Friedman, as well as his colleague, friend, and collaborator Bill Sexton, accepted an invitation to work on a federally delegated committee tasked with identifying outstanding examples of such efforts. Alongside education philosopher Ted Sizer and progressive school reformer Deborah Meier, they traveled around the country observing schools and building a theory about the elements that made for success—a theory that featured design elements such as personalized learning, connections to the local community, and teacher-design curriculum. For Mr. Friedman, the experience served to consolidate and deepen his thinking, affirming the potential of bringing together "minds on" and "hands on" work. As the accountability movement began to gain momentum, however, the School to Work Opportunities Act lost steam. By the late 1990s, vocational education was decidedly out of fashion while the call to equip all students with basic skills in the core disciplines grew louder.

Against this backdrop, a coalition of forty local business leaders in the region that Dewey High now calls home began meeting to discuss their dissatisfaction with the quality of the local labor force. At heart the dilemma was a financial one: legislation prohibited their companies from hiring more than a fixed quota of international employees, but local hires almost always required intensive (and expensive) training.

After talking with several education experts from around the world, the group decided that the most promising way to address the problem would be to establish a school in the tradition of Danish *Erhvervsskoler:* upper secondary institutions that merged vocational apprenticeship with general education. Not knowing how to go about the task of opening a school, however, the group called in Mr. Friedman—who had recently moved west to work for a locally based philanthropist—to outline the options for governance structures. Within a few hours of Mr. Friedman's presentation, the group had decided that their new institution would take advantage of state charter legislation. Within a day, they had convinced Mr. Friedman to serve as the school's founding principal.

The vision for the new school was ambitious but nebulous, and the task of specifying a design fell almost entirely to Mr. Friedman. He turned to several longtime collaborators, including his friend Bill Sexton. Unassuming, humble, and more of a listener than a talker, Mr. Sexton made for a stark contrast to his gregarious colleague. Despite their temperamental differences, the two had long ago recognized that their skills and perspectives were deeply complementary. They quickly picked up where they had left off, drawing on their earlier work to come up with what they now refer to as Dewey High's three "integrations": integrating students from different racial and socioeconomic backgrounds, integrating school with the community beyond, and integrating technical and liberal arts studies. Fueled both by their own experiences in the classroom and by what they had seen during their travels five years earlier, they also arrived at the idea of "teacher as designer"; teachers, they believed, would best be able to actualize their potential if they were empowered to craft curricula that reflected their unique knowledge, skills, and passions.

The school's design principles were elegantly simple, but the process of planning an institution around them was complex. In the year leading up to the school's opening in 2000, Mr. Friedman, Mr. Sexton, and the founding team worked on assembling a group of teachers who had experience in their fields and would be willing to teach through projects; setting up a zip-code-based lottery system that would ensure a diverse student body; and forging partnerships with the local business community. The task was exhausting but energizing. "I realized then that all the work I had been doing for the last twenty years had been pointing in the same direction," Mr. Friedman says. "This was our chance to build a school around what we believed."

Dewey and Dewey High

Mr. Friedman and Mr. Sexton's vision was heavily foreshadowed, as well as influenced, by philosopher-educator John Dewey's vision of what schooling could be. Coming of age just as the second wave of industrialization was gaining momentum across the country, Dewey was deeply troubled by what he perceived to be the decay of American social and cultural life.[2] He looked nostalgically back to the country's agrarian past—a time when, in his eyes, even the most humble farming families had been engaged in work that was purposeful and cooperative. In the context of such families, Dewey believed, children organically learned how to be productive citizens: as they observed and increasingly participated in the routines of daily life, they developed practical skills and knowledge along with the ability to function interdependently. Now, in the age of urbanization and industrial capitalism, an ever-increasing number of adults spent their days completing rote tasks on the assembly line while their children sat in rows and recited their times tables in strict unison. How could the United States guarantee the survival of a cooperative and empowered populace in the face of such dehumanizing realities?

This, Dewey believed, is where the public schools came in. As the country's one truly common social institution, schools could serve to rebuild American culture, thereby insulating society from the dangers of industrial capitalism.[3] To do so, however, they would need to reject the factory-inspired model of organization and pedagogy that had become dominant. This model, which had emerged as rural one-room schoolhouses were consolidated into urban institutions serving large numbers of immigrant children, relied on several core "efficiencies": age-graded classrooms, separation of academic subjects by discipline, and an authoritarian pedagogy that required students to master knowledge—usually rote knowledge—in lockstep.[4] To the new class of bureaucrats whose job it was to run America's burgeoning city school-systems, these practices were the latest in cutting-edge design, drawing on popular principles of "scientific management" in order to streamline the process of educating the country's youth.[5] To Dewey, these practices were inhumane and undemocratic. Separating younger students from older ones, drawing artificial boundaries between subject areas, and allowing adults to predetermine the pace and substance of knowledge acquisition: in Dewey's view, these practices all but guaranteed that the learning process would be devoid of meaning and depth.

What Dewey proposed was not to re-form the schools that already existed, but to create a different kind of schooling entirely. His plan was counterintuitive: the "schools of to-morrow," rather than modeling themselves after modern factories, should look backward, emulating the values of agrarian households and artisans' workshops by adopting an interdisciplinary, hands-on, collaborative curriculum.[6] This would allow children and teachers to engage jointly in learning that was both practical and "adventurous"—learning that engaged mind, hands, and heart in equal measure and built important social skills as well.[7] In one of the lectures later published as *School and Society*, for example, Dewey described how children could build core understandings of history, culture, industry, and science, all by engaging in manual activities such as cooking and weaving. The teacher's role in this context would be to serve as a guide, posing questions and suggestions to ensure that the activities children chose to undertake served as platforms for deep inquiry rather than digressing into mere "utilitarian" exercises.[8] By adopting this model, Dewey argued, schools could become places where students completed *real* work—work that not only built the dispositions required for successful participation in the country's social, economic, and political life down the road, but also carried deep meaning for children in the here and now. "Much of present education fails because . . . the value of [the lessons learned in school] is conceived as lying largely in the remote future; the child must do these things for the sake of something else he is to do; they are mere preparation," he wrote.[9]

Despite Dewey's profound and lasting influence on educational thinking, his vision did not penetrate very deeply into the nation's schools. Throughout the twentieth century, the dominant mode of instruction, particularly in secondary schools, remained transmission of knowledge in teacher-centered classrooms. Portions of Dewey's vision took hold in pockets; for example, there were a number of independent schools that embraced the idea of students as capable sense-makers and positioned teachers more as guides than as knowledge dispensers, and in the 1980s Ted Sizer's Coalition of Essential Schools engaged in advocacy for organizational features such as portfolio assessments and internship programs. But many of these schools took up Dewey's ideas within the confines of traditional academic disciplines and college expectations; they left intact subjects, school walls as the boundaries of learning, and many other core efficiencies of modern schooling. Few schools have been audacious enough to draw on the more radical parts of Dewey's vision, integrating academic and vocational work, moving away from conventional disciplines, and making the world itself the laboratory for learning.

Dewey High aimed to get closer to Dewey's original vision. Mr. Friedman and Mr. Sexton wanted to extend their model beyond inquiry-based pedagogy—they wanted to build a school where students engaged in interdisciplinary projects in order simultaneously to develop core competencies, pursue their passions, and prepare for higher education. In these respects, there was no blueprint for the kind of institution that they aspired to build, and as a result there were more questions than answers when it came to organizing the school.

In trying to answer such questions, Dewey High had two key assets. First, it had the deep repository of practical wisdom that its leaders brought to the table. Mr. Friedman and Mr. Sexton may have had an unusually ambitious and even utopian vision of what school could be, but they were not mere dreamers; rather, their vision was rooted in years of experience working with non-elite public high school students. Second, the school had a clear and elegant design—the set of principles that the founding team had identified at the outset. It is this design, and the convictions in which it is grounded, to which the leaders of Dewey High have returned again and again in their endeavor to improve their school. And ultimately, it is this design that has helped them to resist the temptation to drift back toward more conventional practices.

A Difference in Kind

If John Dewey were to find himself wandering around the school that we have given his name, he might at first be perplexed by what he saw. There certainly are few traces of the preindustrial realities that he had remembered and drawn from as he outlined and refined his philosophy of education. Most of the student-created posters that adorn the hallways are digitally produced. Most of the school's classrooms have an array of computers, all of which are loaded with the latest versions of the Adobe Suite and are linked to a server that allows students and teachers to upload work onto their publicly accessible "digital portfolios." Toward the center of the school is a robotics lab. In the corner of a biology classroom is a genetics lab. Even the school's art classroom has a wall of desktops, which students use to work on tasks ranging from creating prototypes using computer-aided design software to blogging about their progress. There is decidedly little cooking and weaving.

What makes the school distinctive, however, is not the presence of twenty-first-century technology but rather the reimagining of schooling's purposes and processes—a reimagining that draws on deeply Deweyan ideas about how learning should be organized and what it should entail. Eschewing conventional notions about the roles of teachers and learners in relation to knowledge, the school draws on one of Dewey's primary models of inspiration—the artisan's workshop—and on one of the workshop's modern instantiations, the startup, in its attempt to support work that is creative, meaningful, and socially productive. Dewey High thus looks simultaneously backward and forward, bringing many of the key elements of progressive education into the present and demonstrating a model of schooling that represents a dramatic departure from convention.

A New Grammar of Schooling

One of the things that Mr. Friedman and Mr. Sexton carried into the planning process was the recognition that pursuing a different set of goals would require rethinking what Larry Cuban and David Tyack call schooling's core "grammar," the interrelated organizational features that characterize the vast majority of high schools around the country. Everything from lockers and bells to academic departments and final exams was on the table for reconsideration—and the vast majority of these features did not survive. Instead, the school is set up to support endeavors that are collaborative, interdisciplinary, flexibly structured, and sustained over long periods of time.

The most obvious sign of this reorganization is the school's physical plant, which has something close to an open floor-plan. The "commons" area at the center of the building serves by turns as a student lounge, a theater, a staging area for large projects, and an auditorium. Although most classrooms do have doors and walls, almost all have large glass windows on multiple sides, and it is not uncommon to find students, teachers, and administrators in rooms other than their own, observing each other at work or serving as impromptu audience members or critique partners. The fluidity with which students cross among spaces in the school sometimes results in a sense of disorder, but it is also important; combined with the more formal public exhibitions and presentations of learning, it helps to shape a shared culture and shared standards. Finally, the building's many doors are often propped open throughout the day, a visible sign of not only the school's commitment to integrating schoolwork with the broader world, but also the trust that it places in students.

The school's reorganization of human resources is not as immediately obvious as its reorganization of space, but it is equally important. For teachers, working at Dewey High means that instead of teaching alone and occasionally meeting in subject-specific departments, they enter into yearlong partnerships (sometimes trios) that bring together the disciplines: biology with media arts, humanities with Spanish, math with physics and carpentry, and so on. With ongoing support provided by colleagues, these teams design and teach semester-long projects that sit at the intersection of their interests and areas of expertise. In some cases, each member of a teaching team takes on distinct pieces of the project; in others, co-teachers choose to blend their roles more fully, taking the lead when it makes sense. Regardless of the form that the collaboration takes, the belief is that teachers together will create richer projects than they would on their own. To that end, teachers with more experience often partner with those newer to teaching or to the school, creating apprenticeship-style relationships where novices gain skill by working under the guidance of veterans. Students, for their part, are organized into grade-level teams of fifty and assigned to a primary set of collaborating teachers for the year. By design, each of these teams includes students of differing races, socioeconomic statuses, linguistic backgrounds, special needs, and prior achievements. In keeping with the first of the school's "three integrations," teachers treat this diversity as an asset and a source of learning, often assigning students to partners whom they would not have chosen themselves. Given the sustained nature of the projects, these assignments are no trivial matter.

Like their teachers, students have to learn to play to each other's strengths, to manage and persevere through conflict, and, ultimately, to produce work that represents a productive blend of their ideas and skills. In some cases this process results in surprising friendships—bonds, such as the one between Davon and Isabel, that transcend boundaries of race, class, geography, and personality. In other cases it is less successful, but, at least in the eyes of the school, this too results in important learning outcomes. As one eleventh-grader reflected, "Working with other people is something that is important not only because it can help build your character . . . but also because it prepares you for working with co-workers and other people later on."

Dewey High is organized differently from many conventional high schools in several other ways. Aside from traveling together in grade-level pods, students are placed into multi-age advisory groups that meet four times per week to build community and provide social and academic support; students stay with the same adviser for all four years. In addition, in the winter, regular instruction pauses for two weeks. During this period teachers lead groups of mixed-grade students in intensive explorations of topics outside the scope of regular instruction: nature photography, horror films, sailing, yoga and Eastern religions, mountaineering, and so on. In the spring, all eleventh-grade students complete a six-week internship that culminates in a high-stakes Transitional Presentation of Learning. On the adult side of the equation, rather than hiring in a piecemeal fashion, the school begins its hiring process with what it calls a "bonanza" day, during which new teaching candidates participate together in a project design challenge, then are vetted by panels of administrators, teachers, and students. Finally, many of the school's staff take advantage of (and in some cases teach in) the teacher credentialing, master's degree, and professional development programs offered by the school's associated Graduate School of Education, located a few blocks from the school's campus.

School as Workshop, School as Startup

In the traditional artisan's workshop, the goal of producing beautiful, unique, useable objects guides the structures and rhythms of the work. Master craftsmen conceptualize the artifacts to be produced, lay out detailed plans for making them, then oversee and/or participate in the process of doing so. Apprentices observe the goings-on, assist along the way, and, with gradually fading supervision, undertake their own projects. The work is methodical and sustained, with intense attention to detail and a communally held sense of what constitutes quality. Both the process and the products are public; everyone sees what everyone else is making in various stages of completeness, and the best work, which is judged not only by utility and customer satisfaction but also by its adherence to the aesthetic standards set by the field, serves as an example toward which others can aspire.[10]

In the startup environment, the goal is to produce something new in response to a gap in the market, or, in Dewey High's progressive version of this vision, to address a social problem. By definition, the designers of a given project cannot predict what they will produce before they have produced it. Long before they begin to draw up plans for the work, they engage in sustained "problem finding" to pinpoint the issue they are trying to tackle. Later, after brainstorming, they create prototypes and bring them to users, refining (and sometimes ditching) their concepts in response to feedback. The ethos of such work is playful, casual, and often irreverent. In theory, and often in practice, there is not an elaborate hierarchy of expertise; everyone is seen as capable of contributing a good idea. Failures are treated as normal and necessary parts of the process. Collaboration is integral. Ultimately, the artifacts that are created live and die based on their usefulness and marketability in the real world.

As these descriptions suggest, these two contexts are in some ways markedly different. The workshop looks backward toward a tradition of accumulated wisdom; the startup steers toward an uncertain future. The routines of the workshop are measured and rhythmic; those of the startup are breathless and ever-changing. Artisans find room for improvisation within frameworks that already exist; designers seek to "disrupt" existing realities. The learning that transpires in both spaces, however, hits on all three dimensions of the deeper learning triangle: the opportunity to develop something new (creativity), the imperative to build knowledge and skills while doing so (mastery), and the space for bringing one's unique experiences and vision to the process (identity). In this light it makes sense that Dewey High's vision of deeper learning draws on elements from both models—though in

the end, as with the other distinctive cases described in this book, the
school incorporates these elements into a model all its own.

Creating Products of Lasting Value

As with both the workshop and the startup, the vast majority of work at
Dewey High is organized around *production*. From documentary films
and the moveable darkroom to science museum exhibits, bentwood
furniture, and original historical plays, students at Dewey High are
consistently engaged in the process of designing, manufacturing, revising, exhibiting, and/or performing original work. The momentum
generated by such processes is a key part of what makes the school
distinctive. As Mr. Friedman discovered at the settlement house, there
is something inherently motivating about "the idea of making something that wasn't there before." Thanks to the impressive array of student work on display, new students and parents pick up on this energy
as soon as they enter the building. For their part, teachers talk about
how important it is to complete each new project themselves before
launching it with students—not only because doing so helps them to
identify key learning opportunities and potential pitfalls, but also
because it enables students to see right away a sample of what they are
working toward, which generates interest and purpose. Mr. Quinn,
the teacher of the documentary film project, learned this lesson the
hard way. Describing a project that his students completed during his
first year at the school, the aforementioned economics textbook with
linocut illustrations, he reflected on how his choice not to make an example that included a linocut had had some unfortunate consequences.
"Some of my best kids didn't end up with their work in the book because
they didn't do the linocuts," he said. "They were like, 'I didn't do it
because I didn't realize it would look so cool!'"

The school's emphasis on producing original work has cognitive
as well as affective advantages. After all, knowledge utilization and
creation—which are central to virtually all of the projects that students
complete—sit at the top of traditional learning taxonomies. By framing
instructional activities with the imperative to develop something new,
Dewey High insulates itself from the pitfall of teachers continually in-
tending to incorporate higher-order tasks into their instruction but
rarely delivering on that objective. At Dewey High, students are cre-

ating and using tools within their fields, and learning in a contextual way that creates thick and integrated knowledge. When students develop a field guide to the local bay, for example, they are learning about ecology, ornithology, and the local landscape; in addition, the act of synthesizing this learning for a real audience forces a kind of deep integrated understanding that a similar worksheet-based approach to the same topic would not achieve.

These projects are most powerful, in the eyes of the school's architects, when they are harnessed to the broader aspiration of making a positive contribution. It is no accident that Mr. Quinn's sophomores were creating films that made persuasive arguments about issues of public concern while Ms. Johnson's freshmen were striving to actualize ideas about how to improve the school community; in both cases, the key idea was to produce artifacts with real social utility. Mr. Sexton sees this vision as their contribution to building a democracy, "We're trying to create a context where people are collaborating together to create products of lasting value, which often morph into products of use to the community," he said. "That's what civil society is about."

This ethic—what we have come to think of as an *ethic of contribution*—is arguably the most distinctive and radical element of Dewey High's vision. As Michael Fullan and colleagues say, in reference to our work on the deeper learning triangle, "What gives humans meaning in life is a strong sense of identity around a purpose or passion, creativity and mastery in relation to a valued pursuit, and connectedness with the world and others."[11] These properties are not apparent in every classroom at every moment, but they suffuse the best projects and, as such, shape the aspirations of its teachers and students. They are also deeply Deweyan, reflecting the belief that schools should function as mini-societies where students engage not only in meaningful discourse but also in productive work. To ask teenagers to strive, with whatever degree of success, to create "products of lasting value," after all, is to communicate deep respect for who they are and what they can do—to honor what they can achieve in the present instead of focusing only on equipping them for the future. Of course, teenagers are still teenagers, and the school deals with occasional episodes of peer-group drama, illicit drug use, and student-teacher conflicts. In the broadest sense, however, the school's positive assumptions about students tend to be self-fulfilling; students are treated as people who can contribute and they respond mostly by striving to meet those positive expectations.[12] As one parent reflected, "There's just this tremendous amount of respect for the kids . . . and the kids respond by stepping up to the plate."

Divergence by Design

Dewey High's students are not the only ones afforded latitude and respect. Rather than trying to codify and disseminate a school- or system-wide curriculum, the school operates on the belief that teachers do their best work when they are conceptualized as craftsmen and designers: professionals whose work reflects their unique perspectives, passions, and skills. Teachers also are encouraged to involve students in the design process; it is standard practice at Dewey High for teachers to engage students as consultants who help to "tune" existing project plans, and in a few cases, teachers have used the first few weeks of each semester to gather and refine students' burning questions about the world as part of creating a unit plan. This emphasis on design and co-design leads to projects that are often startlingly different across classrooms. Students in one classroom might be learning genetic sequencing while those next door are rehearsing scenes from an original play. This also means that when teachers acquire new interests, new teaching partners, and / or new students, their projects change accordingly. While the most successful endeavors are sometimes repeated from year to year and / or adopted by teachers at other campuses, innovation is prized. In radical contrast to the mantra of most of American schooling, at Dewey High "standardized" is all but a dirty word when it comes to matters of curriculum.

As a jumping-off point for exploring this element of the school's model, it is worth returning to the two projects evoked at the beginning of this chapter: the "paranoid style" project and the "20 percent" project. In certain ways, the two endeavors are as distinct from each other as the teachers who planned them. The former, while its key outcome was a film, included a healthy dose of conventional humanities content: students read and analyzed a number of canonical historical texts including *The Communist Manifesto*, conducted original research, and worked on appealing to human "pathos" (in this case fear) to make persuasive arguments. In designing this kind of work, Mr. Quinn was playing to his strengths. As a self-described news junkie, he felt that his students should understand how fear-based rhetoric worked so they could avoid being manipulated by the media. On the skills front, he also wanted his students to practice synthesizing data from a range of sources and revising their ideas in response to counterarguments and critiques—desires grounded in intuitions he had developed during five years teaching English at a conventional middle school.

The "20 percent" project, by contrast, was much less recognizably academic. Although Ms. Johnson's classroom is a text-rich space, with a carefully curated library and a number of rituals around reading, this particular project involved comparatively little shared literacy content. Instead, the project's core focus was its *process*. By writing blog posts, conferring with their teachers, and revising their completion strategies at key junctures in the project, students began to develop both the executive functioning skills and the self-knowledge necessary to thrive under conditions of autonomy. Given Ms. Johnson's background working with juvenile delinquents in the context of wilderness therapy programs, it is no surprise that she co-created such a project; supporting the development of metacognitive skills reflects her strengths just as supporting the construction of paranoia-driven documentary films reflects Mr. Quinn's.

While Dewey High's teachers generally relish the latitude that the model gives them with respect to planning, it is easy to imagine the critiques that skeptics might level against it. Allowing for extreme differences in terms of curriculum is well and good, they might say, until the "clients" of such variety encounter a high-stakes exam, a college class, or an employment context that requires mastery of skills that they lack. Doesn't the school's model leave instruction too vulnerable to the idiosyncrasies of individual teachers? What guarantee is there that students will develop core literacies and numeracies?

In one sense, these questions cut to the heart of the tradeoffs that Dewey High chooses to accept in the course of pursuing its vision—tradeoffs to which we will return at the end of the chapter. The school does, however, have a number of features that are more conventional. Although projects constitute the main organizing structure for the curriculum, students all take discipline-specific (though untracked) math classes, and they all receive extensive one-on-one college counseling. Furthermore, as high-stakes assessments like the state test and the SAT approach, many teachers choose to devote some time to tested content.

The school's instructional leaders strive to make sure that all projects incorporate ongoing opportunities for reading across genres, writing across genres, revising work in response to critique, and giving oral presentations—skills that appear in virtually all state curriculum frameworks as well as in the Common Core State Standards. Finally, as we will elaborate at the end of the chapter, Dewey High's teachers and leaders recently have begun to use the tools of continuous improvement to ensure that deliberate and differentiated academic skill-building is integrated into all projects.

Steering into Uncertainty

Dewey High's model also requires teachers to embrace an underlying orientation that links together even the most apparently divergent projects. Reflecting the broader beliefs associated with one strand of educational progressivism, this orientation requires that teachers reject conventional ideas about what it means to teach. Traditionally, Americans have long thought of teachers as content experts who deliver knowledge to those who know less than they do.[13] To critics of that stance, taking seriously the proposition that the teacher should be "a guide, not task-master"—a proposition central to how early twentieth-century progressive educators talked about education—means asking teachers to abandon their primary responsibilities with respect to both content delivery and disciplinary control. Organizing instruction around open-ended tasks also risks exposing what teachers do not know, because, as one loosens controls, students are increasingly likely to venture into unfamiliar territory. At Dewey High, as in earlier experiments in progressive schooling, guiding students toward such territory is precisely the goal. Teachers are encouraged to draw on their areas of expertise, but the school's emphasis on creating original work means that one of their primary tasks is to help students explore the unknown, leaving behind the security of being the one who defines all the questions and knows all the answers.

While this orientation is a key element in empowering students to produce original work, it has its downsides. Without the certainty of predetermining the form and/or substance of what students pursue in their projects, teachers do not always have deep understanding of the content their students are exploring. They may have generally relevant expertise that allows them to guide the process and set standards for good work—in the case of the paranoid-style projects, for example, Mr. Quinn had thought a lot about what constitutes powerful rhetoric—but they are unlikely to be experts in everything that students choose to pursue in their projects, and thus they partially forgo the ability to employ pedagogical content knowledge.[14] When students venture too far from the domains that their teachers know, they must turn to others or fend for themselves. While this might help students to become more resourceful, it also can be construed as a failure to make use of teachers' carefully cultivated expertise. How, some might ask, could Ms. Johnson and Mr. Davis competently support Kieran, given their lack of knowledge about carpentry? And why weren't they making use of their respective understandings of how to engage students in the study of literature and physics?

Embracing Different Views of Knowledge

Taking this line of argument to its extreme would suggest that teachers who work within this progressive model need not have any content knowledge at all. This, however, is far from the truth. Dewey High's instructional vision does require teachers to accept a different view of knowledge from the one that tends to dominate the field: rather than seeing knowledge as something preexisting that can be transmitted as a whole, it holds knowledge to be provisional and imagines students to be active participants in its development. To teach with this view in mind, however, arguably requires more rather than less expertise. Teachers must be able to think not only *in* a given discipline but also *about* a given discipline—to think about how knowledge is created and to invite students into the process of doing that work. The stance of the paranoid-style project, for example, brought students into the world of historical interpretation; they learned not only about the Cold War, but also about a particular way in which Cold War rhetoric was mobilized by powerful stakeholders. Mr. Quinn needed to be willing to allow his students to venture into unknown territory as they worked on their films, but it was his rich understanding of historiography that gave a frame and shape to the endeavor.

Dewey High's teachers also have to rethink how students best can acquire basic knowledge and skills. In most high schools, the dominant paradigm dictates that students should master a large corpus of basic disciplinary knowledge before moving to more applied work. In a conventional physics class, for example, students might spend months mastering basic concepts around kinetic energy before being asked, as a "performance task," to design a mousetrap car. At Dewey High, however, this paradigm is inverted: the belief is that basic knowledge- and skill-building should happen *through* attempts at applying that knowledge and skill. When Mr. Quinn's students pored over articles about the topics they had chosen for their films, for example, they did so in the context of needing a knowledge base out of which to craft their central arguments. Reflecting its Deweyan roots, this "part to whole" paradigm of learning mirrors the world of the workshop, where apprentices, assigned to increasingly difficult projects, turn to their mentors when they run up against challenges that require skills they have not yet developed. It also maps onto the world of the startup and other contemporary job environments, where people acquire new skills as the need arises. This approach has significant advantages, because it puts students in the mode of seeking to produce real things from the start.

Adopting this stance presents a challenge for new hires at Dewey High because it requires them to unlearn deep-rooted instructional behaviors. As such, it is one of the things that Mr. Sexton, in his capacity as a staff developer, spends extensive time helping teachers to understand. "We try to caution teachers not to assume that kids have to have skills before they can embark upon a project—that, if skills are required to do a project, that they need to learn those skills before they embark," he says. "There's been a constant, ongoing conversation about that issue over the years." Mr. Sexton's work on this front is reinforced by the students, who over time become experts in their own right on Dewey High's vision of learning. As one articulate student noted, "There are some projects where you learn content for a long time and then you do a project to present it, and there are some where you learn *by* doing the project. When you are actually learning through the project-based methods, the learning is way deeper."

Trusting the Time

In his essay "The School and Social Progress," Dewey contrasts the rigid social control that characterizes traditional classrooms to the "confusion" and "bustle" that punctuate learning spaces that adopt a more hands-on approach.[15] "There is a certain disorder in any busy workshop," he writes.[16] Although this description predates Dewey High by almost a century, it could as easily have been included in the notebook of someone visiting the school. Among other things, the school's "disorder" takes shape as a constant ebb and flow of productivity that characterizes the days. At some points, students are working with intense focus, and at others they are just hanging out. Students affirm that this accurately represents their experience. "Some days we're doing projects and going psycho . . . other times we're just walking around the school talking to people," one freshman girl describes.

This is no accident. While teachers do not celebrate wasted time, they accept uneven productivity as the inevitable result of giving students real latitude. Mr. Sexton explicitly connects this stance to the rhythms of professional life. "Project time doesn't divide itself neatly into hours of the day," he says. "Deadlines loom and you see incredible bursts of energy and activity, and deadlines pass and there are lulls—just like you see with adults." He continues:

I think that schools now are in thrall of Taylor and efficiency—the more kids are on task for more time, the better; 100 percent is the goal. That's not the way adults work. If you walk around and look at the adults here, they're engaged in being adults and in adult conversations while getting their work done. Kids need that too.

Mr. Sexton is not the only one who explicitly connects the school's stance toward time use with its underlying humanism. Bob Eagle, an art teacher who was part of the school's founding team, talks about how his experiences working as a waiter helped him to recognize the counterproductive effects of micromanagement. "What adults have to remember is that kids want to be treated right," he says. The key to making sure that students do not systematically exploit the latitude that the school affords them, Mr. Eagle explains, is to set high expectations and to build in extensive grading structures along the way—to balance autonomy and accountability. He uses one of his endeavors, a project that combined "bent wood" carpentry with calculus, as a case in point. Every Wednesday each group had to complete a graded check-in, demonstrating what they had accomplished, reflecting on their process, and setting goals for the coming week. "I gave them flexibility but I let them know that not doing the project well wasn't an option," Mr. Eagle says.

Giving students so much flexibility in terms of time use sometimes backfires—especially when teachers fail to break projects into stages and provide interim deadlines. One student who attended the school in the years just after it opened remembers how his biology teacher took an entirely hands-off approach to a yearlong project:

> We had no instruction. We had no models for what her expectations were, and she didn't regulate us. We wasted about fourth-fifths of the entire year not doing a single thing. Then when it came crunch time—because we were so young, and we knew that this particular teacher would let us get away with it—we all pretended that we were incapable and didn't understand how to find different color rocks, or paint this, or how you do papier-mâché, when most of us were fully competent and capable of doing it. The teacher enabled us to work the system and not do anything.

This kind of spectacular failure happened more in the school's early years than it does now; veteran teachers help to make sure that novice teachers do not fall into the more easily avoided "traps" of project-based work. On a smaller scale, however, there are periodic debates among the faculty about whether giving students so much autonomy is worth the inevitable loss of productive time. "Most projects that take four months could take two months," one teacher admits. "But that would mean we were micromanaging the heck out of the kids, and part of the point is that we don't want to do that."

Normalizing Failure

Another result of giving students so much autonomy is that, despite the motivating power of graded check-ins and public exhibitions, some come up short in producing high-quality projects. This was especially apparent in the "20 percent" project. For some students, such as Kieran and his two partners, the unstructured nature of the process stimulated momentum and resulted in sophisticated work. In other cases, however, students floundered, making poor choices about which and how many peers to work with, struggling to organize their time, and failing outright to complete their projects by the deadline. The most exaggerated example was a group of eleven students—a mixed-sex clique of sorts. The idea for the project was solid: after hearing from administrators that the school was struggling to accommodate its many visitors, the group set out to create a self-guided tour of the school that would rely on smartphone "tag reader" technology. But after spending several weeks procrastinating and several more struggling to delegate responsibility for the various tasks involved, the group was unable to complete what they had set out to accomplish.

On the morning of their Presentation of Learning, the group's members had to stand in front of an audience of parents, peers, teachers, and community members, describing the project and reflecting on what had happened. The first student to present was Andrea, a high-achieving student who had become the group's de facto leader. Her father sat impassively in the front row; as she talked, she glanced tentatively toward him, at times appearing to be on the verge of tears.

> Eleven is a huge number, and it's really hard to give everybody a task and to get organized. For the first two weeks my group messed around. We thought we couldn't do anything because there was always "something else" to do. We should have just moved forward. We should have had group meetings twice a week to check in. We should have done a lot of stuff that we didn't do. Also, one of the problems is I'm a control freak; if I have to get something done, I feel like I have to do it all myself. This project taught me that I need to learn to be a leader but also let go of control and use my partners' skills.

After Andrea finished talking, Ms. Johnson and several other audience members asked her to talk about how she would approach the task differently if she could do it again. What strategies for role delegation would she use? How would she make sure that each group member was using time wisely? How would she keep herself honest about being truly collaborative? Andrea answered these questions thoughtfully and precisely, some of her confidence returning as she explained how she would come up with a detailed plan of action at the start.

This process is indicative of the school's broader stance toward students falling short of the expectations held for them. The teachers at

Dewey High do not relish such situations, but they also do not take them as evidence that the school's model is flawed. Instead, they treat failure as an inevitable part of engaging in tasks that are open-ended and uncertain—and, as the case of Andrea demonstrates, they treat such failures as opportunities for reflection and metacognition. In this, Dewey High explicitly shares an ethos with the world of the startup, where the importance of failure is almost a mantra. Industrial product designers talk about "failing faster" and "failing forward"; inexpensive prototypes are created in the belief that while the first version is unlikely to succeed, the process will force the inventor to develop a better product down the line. Related to this is the belief that innovation entails risk-taking—and the acknowledgment that real risks necessarily involve the possibility of real failures.

Teachers, encouraged as they are to experiment with developing new projects, experience periodic failures as well. Mr. Davis, the rangy and self-deprecating physics teacher who works with Ms. Johnson, talks about a project that the two of them attempted to lead in their first year at the school:

> The idea was to learn about circuitry by making the toys that were electric, and then we would donate them to the local children's hospital. We had it all set up, so that the hospital knew they were coming. Then it turns out that ninth graders can't solder! They were leaving the soldering iron on for too long, and some of these electronic components melted, and [the toys] didn't work anymore. It was so embarrassing.

Like Andrea and others, Mr. Davis and Ms. Johnson found the experience of failing to be a powerful source of learning: the disappointment that their students felt when their work could not be actualized, as well as the humiliation of having to renege on a public promise, motivated the teaching pair to think much more carefully about the skills that students would need to learn in order to complete a given project: the next year they exercised a good deal more foresight. Their ability to "fail forward" in this way reflects the powerful symmetry built into the school's design: just as teachers accept student failures and strive to help them learn from their mistakes, Dewey High's leaders take teachers' thwarted projects in stride, assuming that such failures (so long as they result in better work down the line) are a normal part of doing work that is original and uncertain.

Cultivating Playfulness and Joy

Another part of what allows Dewey High's teachers and students to be safe to fail is the school's broader ethos, which, like that of the tech startup, is infused with a spirit of playfulness. Students and teachers are frequently "playing around" and "trying stuff out," engaging in the kind of low-stakes improvisation that is known in the design world as ideation. As described earlier, this use of time might be construed by some as unproductive, but it also helps to create and sustain the palpable sense of joy that strikes so many visitors. The grim "sense of urgency" that characterizes so many schools serving high-poverty urban students is nowhere to be found; instead, the open-ended nature of the work, combined with the trust and latitude afforded to students, creates a platform for sustained positive engagement. As one parent recalled when describing her first time walking into the campus, "It was just so alive with creativity and energy and enthusiasm."

Students at all grade levels affirm that their experiences at Dewey High, while not devoid of tribulations, are overwhelmingly positive. They attribute this quality not only to the school's markedly inclusive social scene, but also to the experience of engaging with its unique curriculum. As one recent graduate remembers:

> My favorite memory of a project is junior year, when [our three teachers] set up a crime scene for us. And it included—for math, it was trajectory and ballistics. And then for biology, it was DNA. We did gel electrophoresis and we had to like match up whose DNA was at the crime scene. . . . I never really thought about [crime] in the terms that they'd given us. But also it was just really fun to walk into school one day and there'd be a crime scene set up with a fake body and blood, and the blood actually had DNA in it. And then we spent like a month trying to solve the crime.

The widespread reports of engagement that we heard in our interviews are substantiated by the school's performance on YouthTruth, a nationally validated survey that the school administers twice yearly to

students. Based on students' responses to the YouthTruth survey, Dewey
High is in the ninety-second percentile for student engagement, the
ninety-eighth percentile when it comes to relationships with teachers,
and the ninety-ninth percentile when it comes to relationships with
peers.

Of course, "fun" is not always a necessary ingredient in deep learning;
such learning can emerge out of experiences that are grueling and even
painful. The quality of pleasurable engagement that characterizes the
best work at Dewey High, however, is a key element in its distinctive
vision of what it means to learn deeply—a vision where the boundaries
between work and play are highly permeable. In some ways this vision
reflects the particular contribution made by Mr. Friedman, shaped
as he was by the experience of leaving the "serious" profession of law
in favor of teaching carpentry, the activity he had always treated as a
pleasurable hobby. In addition, however, it reflects enduring commitments associated with educational progressivism, which, in all of its
various instantiations, seeks to eliminate the boredom and anxiety associated with rigid adult control and to replace it with learning experiences that are "as real and vital to the child as the life which he carries
on in the home, in the neighborhood, or on the playground."[17]

The Pork Chop Dilemma

Reflecting on the wave of attempts to create "child centered" schools
in the second quarter of the twentieth century, historian Patricia
Graham likens the dilemmas of enacting educational progressivism to
those of making a pork chop—a dish that can be exquisite, but which
if even slightly undercooked (the lore goes) can lead to trichinosis poi-
soning.[18] "[The vision for progressive schooling] was a grand aspiration,
marvelous when fully realized, but catastrophic when only partially
achieved," she writes.[19] To put it differently, the joyfulness and depth
that characterized the learning in the most successful progressive
schools were mirrored by the chaos and intellectual barrenness of those
that tried but failed to organize along similar lines.

We learned firsthand that this dichotomy persists into the present
when we visited a number of schools that, like Dewey High, are striving
to enact educational progressivism with non-elite urban students. Many

of these schools had made a serious effort to organize their work around features such as interdisciplinary projects and performance assessments, but the results varied wildly from classroom to classroom, with a large amount of mediocre instruction and a small amount that was just plain awful. In one West Coast urban project-based charter high school, for example, history teachers had their students complete a "project" in which they conducted superficial internet research, copied a sampling of random facts onto posters, then read aloud from these posters as part of an "exhibition." Three thousand miles away, at a small alternative public high school in Manhattan, we observed a chemistry class where one student spent an hour experimenting with different ways to bake a cake while his peers lounged around and socialized. When we asked the student who was cooking to explain what he was doing, he was unable to articulate the thinking behind his decisions, much less to explain the concepts that the experiment presumably was intended to elucidate. Dewey would have cringed.

We did our share of cringing as well, not only because what we saw represented a distortion of progressive ideas, but also because the time we spent at Dewey High had showed us what project-based learning could look like at its best. There, the ratio of deep to shallow instruction was inverted from the one we encountered elsewhere: a few classrooms displayed the troubling patterns described above, but many were rigorous and joyful places to teach and learn. For us, as well as for other teachers and school leaders who aspire to engage their students in deep project-based learning, this raised one of the key questions posed at the beginning of this chapter. *What allows Dewey High to make good on the promises of project-based learning, while so many other urban public schools are struggling, with limited success, to do the same?*

The answer, skeptics argue, lies in Dewey High's "special" status as a socioeconomically diverse charter school fed by its own elementary and middle schools. But the many hours that we spent at other progressively inclined urban high schools suggest that the elements that set Dewey High apart transcend its surface-level organizational features. Few of these other schools were able to make good on a progressive vision with real consistency—and in many cases this was despite being small, semi-autonomous, socioeconomically diverse, and/or supported by linked middle and elementary schools. This underscores a key conclusion of our work: something else beyond factors such as size, autonomy, and socioeconomic diversity enables successful schools (pro-gressive or otherwise) to make headway toward their aspirations. In Dewey High's case, three factors were particularly relevant: (1) the way in which the school's standards for good work were highly visible, trans-parent, and laced through many of their processes, (2) the symmetry between how adults were socialized and apprenticed and how they ex-pected teachers to teach students, and (3) the school's willingness to say no to unaligned goals and priorities, in the interest of maintaining in all of its actions the necessary coherence, alignment, and collective identity.

Excellence by Example

Inspire Academy (a pseudonym), the school we described in the Intro-duction, is a small charter high school nestled atop a hill in a residen-tial section of the West Coast metropolis that it calls home. The school's vision is one in which students attempt to build twenty-first-century competencies by engaging in cross-curricular, collaborative, social-justice-oriented projects. Teachers have their own subject-specific classes, but they often work together to coordinate and / or co-plan the curriculum. Students participate in biannual exhibitions, as well as in two high-stakes performance assessments judged using schoolwide ru-brics. Administrators, for their part, seek to empower teachers and stu-dents to build core skills while connecting their work to the outside world. In short, the school is markedly similar to Dewey High in terms of its aspirations and theory of action.

In the state that we encountered it, however, Inspire was a place where the desire to leverage such structures into deep learning remained largely unrealized—the proverbial pork chop gone wrong. A few class-rooms were characterized by depth and passion, but most were lack-luster and chaotic places where teachers struggled to get students to engage in projects that involved little academic content. The school's students affirmed our diagnosis that the school lacked an essential di-mension of rigor. "I think [the teachers] should ask way more of us," one senior commented.

As we attempted to understand the Inspire community in more depth, it became clear that a key problem was that the school's vision of high-quality projects was almost entirely abstract, communicated to teachers and students only in the form of written rubrics. "The word rigor is thrown around a lot here, but we don't define it very well," one teacher reported. Other teachers echoed this sentiment, noting that they yearned for clearer examples of what they and their students should be aiming to produce. "I mean, I know I have to do a project or a research paper with the kids—but what does that mean at this school?" one asked. The school's vice principal, who serves as a de facto instructional coach, was painfully aware of the daily struggles that this lack of clarity produced. "I've totally changed my mind about project-based learning," he said, adding that he had come to the conclusion that he would rather run a school that was overly controlled and conventional than one which was as much of a "mess" as Inspire.

How did Dewey High avoid these pitfalls? It begins with the answer to a question that Dewey High's leaders insist is critical: *What do the walls say?* As described earlier, walking into Dewey High is a deeply aesthetic experience. It is barely an exaggeration to say that all available wall space, including that of the bathrooms, is covered in student-produced artifacts. During the time we spent at the school, these artifacts included a video exhibit that demonstrated the properties of light, functional "bentwood" chairs with accompanying posters that explained the calculus involved in their design, and a group of digitally produced posters exploring the causes of genocide—not to mention a playground-sized suspension bridge and other pieces that occupied space on the floor. These things fill the space with a sense of color and life, but they also communicate a great deal about the institution's distinctive qualities: the value placed on the production of original artifacts, the emphasis on making learning visible and public, and, perhaps most important in terms of learning, the standards of quality to which students are held. To newcomers, the effect is often immediate. As Ms. Johnson describes her initial interview for a teaching position, "I walked into the school knowing next to nothing about it, but then I saw the bridge. . . . Just seeing that these kids who were not gifted kids were making things like that was enough to make me want to work here." For students, the constant reminder of what their peers produce is a more powerful motivation to do their best work than any grading rubric; it communicates with unwavering clarity that they *can* and *are expected to* produce work that holds its own in the public eye.

Dewey High's distinctive walls are complemented by a number of other forms of transparency described earlier—which together create an interconnected system by which the school's standards of excellence are communicated. The glass walls and open-door policies throughout the building mean that members of the community often witness each other at work. Exhibitions and presentations of learning are staggered so that students, teachers, and staff can participate as audience members alongside invited guests. Digital portfolios, which staff and students are required to keep up-to-date with written, photographic, and/or video records of their work, allow community members (and other interested parties) to keep track of projects that are under way and help teachers to assess their students' progress. Teachers also get glimpses into each other's projects on Wednesday mornings, when they meet in groups to look together at student work and to help each other refine their project and lesson plans. Finally, teachers are encouraged to describe and reflect on their work in articles for the journal published by the school's Graduate School of Education, which often lies open on desks and in common areas.

These processes not only induct newcomers into the school; they also help maintain an ongoing commitment to quality work. As one veteran teacher reflected, "There's a very clear message that it's not okay to play the fool here. . . . Nobody wants to be the one with nothing to show when people are going to see your work." (The lack of a specific reference to "teachers" or "students" here is intentional.) The prospect of public embarrassment is particularly off-putting to adolescents, but teachers, too, find the realities of peer observation and public exhibition to be motivating—nobody wants to be the one whose students are presenting simplistic dioramas of the solar system when their colleagues' classes have published books or designed interactive exhibits for the local science museum. A friendly sense of competition, again true for students and teachers alike, helps to shore up this commitment to excellence. "There's this sense that you're always trying to design the most badass project," Mr. Quinn reports. The trace of ruefulness in his voice suggests that the pressure to raise the bar can sometimes feel burdensome. This pressure, however, is certainly better than the inverse: the apathy that sets in when teachers and learners toil in isolation, lacking clarity about what they are aiming to produce and the standards against which their work will be judged.

All good schools need a finely detailed vision of good instruction and ways to publicly communicate that vision. But it is doubly important at

progressive schools like Dewey High and Inspire because of the unconventional nature of the vision that they are trying to enact, an approach to schooling that few teachers are likely to have experienced as
students or learned in teacher training. Thus even with supportive
structures and detailed rubrics, they are unlikely to be able to instantiate it successfully unless they are surrounded by examples that can
serve as a compass for their work.

This is why Dewey High's multiple layers of transparency are so
important: they not only create universal standards that motivate
teachers and students to put their best foot forward, but also make visible and specific an endeavor that otherwise would remain impossibly
abstract. This is also one of the key reasons why Inspire may have failed
to gain traction; as a whole, the school lacked rich examples to which
teachers and students could anchor their aspirations. Reflecting on this
reality, Mr. Friedman likens the attempt to implement project-based
learning without having witnessed its end products to the act of panning for gold without knowing what the metal looks like. When the
school first opened, he says, it was critical that he and Mr. Sexton had
already seen glimmers of the kind of deep learning that they wanted
to produce. "[We were] saying, 'Now okay, we're panning and panning—
but at least we know what gold looks like because we found some
chunks,'" he says.

Robust Systems with Powerful Symmetry

Technical expertise, however, is only part of the story. Implementing
successful project-based instruction in the tradition of Dewey also requires a number of fairly radical shifts with respect to instructional
orientation. *How can teachers learn to embrace such a different notion of what
it means to teach, given the longstanding dominance of beliefs and practices that
run counter to it?* In addition to establishing a shared vision of what "gold"
looks like, this is a critical question for aspiring progressive, particularly project-based, schools to answer—and our observations suggest
that the strength and "thickness" of these answers can make all the
difference.

At Inspire, helping new hires to bring their beliefs and practices into
alignment with the school's vision is treated as less important than
hiring the right teachers in the first place. In part because it recently

responded to budget cuts by paring back its staff development program, the school comes down solidly on the "buy it" side of what some education reformers have called the "build it/buy it" debate: leaders try to hire their way into creating a staff that can make good on the school's vision. On a designated day in March, job candidates gather to spend a whole day at the school, delivering sample lessons to showcase their content and pedagogical content knowledge and participating in interviews where administrators, teachers, and students strive to ascertain their commitments to projects and performance assessments. But when those who make the cut begin their tenure in September, they often find themselves at sea with respect to translating the school's vision into practice. Grade-level and departmental teams meet periodically, but these meetings focus more on discussing students who are struggling and on aligning curricular goals, respectively, than on instructional practice. This reifies teachers' perception that strong project-based teaching is an inborn talent rather than something that can be learned. As one new teacher reported, "You see these other teachers who have done these amazing things [with their students], but you're like, 'I can't do that.' There's this stratified sense about those teachers who can do that and those who can't."

Dewey High, too, treats hiring as a critical part of its model. As at Inspire, teaching candidates attend a demanding daylong "bonanza" hiring event, but the criteria for selection differs. "We hire for disposition and train for skill," Mr. Friedman says. Expanding this point, he asserts that the school's best teachers are those whose areas of teaching expertise are deeply intertwined with their out-of-school identities. With job candidates, he notes:

> I want know what they're doing on weekends. If they have tools in their hands on a weekend, that's the engineering teacher I want. If they're a working artist, that's the art teacher I want. I don't want somebody who's just teaching it. I want someone who's *got* to do it.

Leveraging passion into skillful project-based teaching requires significant commitment to ongoing training, which, in contrast to Inspire, Dewey High zealously provides. All newcomers, be they recent college graduates or ten-year classroom veterans, participate in the "New

Teacher Odyssey," a two-week intensive summer institute where they practice designing projects under the guidance of the school's most skillful practitioners. When combined with the apprenticeship-style support created by co-teaching with veterans and weekly opportunities for collegial feedback throughout the year, new teachers are given the professional tools they need not only to build technical skills but also to internalize the school's core values.

Both hiring and formal teacher supports are critical, but they are reinforced by the *symmetry* built into the school's design—symmetry that links the experiences of teachers to those of their students, empowering them to draw on firsthand knowledge of what it means and what it feels like to learn deeply in the school's uniquely Deweyan mode.

To understand how this symmetry works, it is worth returning briefly to the various dimensions of the Dewey High model that were described at length earlier in the chapter. Each of these dimensions applies not only to the stance that teachers take toward students, but also to the stance that the administration takes toward teachers. Like students, teachers are encouraged to draw on their divergent experiences and passions, blurring the boundaries between who they are outside and inside of school in service of creating divergent work. Like students, teachers must learn to collaborate productively and to manage collaboration-based conflicts as they arise. Like students, teachers learn through the process of iteratively revising their plans and periodically "failing forward." Like students, teachers are afforded a large measure of autonomy that is framed by ongoing support and an overall culture of transparency. Finally, like students, teachers are treated as creative agents deserving of trust and respect.

Dewey High's symmetry may not translate into technical teaching skills, but it is an extraordinarily effective way to communicate the school's values and to help teachers release their more conventional orientations. After all, cognitive science research has demonstrated again and again that changes in beliefs tend to follow changes in experience; people are much more likely to shift their underlying mental frameworks when they repeatedly encounter "disruptive" phenomena than when they are simply told that their ideas are misguided or wrong.[20] Thus structuring the model so that teachers' experiences mirror those of their students adds critical energy and coherence to the school's work. Beyond this, the stance that the administration takes toward teachers, like that which teachers take toward students, contributes to the positive ethos that pervades the community as a whole. Many teachers cite the way in which Mr. Friedman and Mr. Sexton "walk their talk" as what enables teachers and administrators to be mutually respectful.

The Power of No

The final element that sets Dewey High apart from similarly organized progressive schools, as well as from the vast majority of the more conventional schools that we studied, is the willingness of its leaders to take off the table goals they regard as nonessential. Many schools are open to the vast array of goals that could be part of a good education, and the many providers who promise to deliver them. The result, however, is that most schools end up trying to do a little bit of everything—a tactic that often results in a whole lot of nothing. Finding themselves overwhelmed by the competing priorities and new initiatives that administrators foist on them, teachers lose focus or simply start selectively ignoring what they are asked to do.[21] One of this book's authors experienced this firsthand when her school's administration, impatient to see test-score gains and lacking confidence about the right thing to do, derailed a promising multiyear initiative focused on teaching literacy across the curriculum by piling on a number of unrelated priorities and programs.[22] The tactic proved self-defeating: achievement flat-lined, staff morale plummeted, and a number of talented teachers chose to seek employment elsewhere.

In the course of our research, we encountered a large network of progressive-leaning schools struggling with a version of this problem: meeting the disciplinary content coverage requirements posed by high-stakes exams while simultaneously engaging students in deep interdisciplinary inquiries similar to those at Dewey High. In a few of these schools—those that devoted the lion's share of their attention and time to the task—these two priorities were integrated seamlessly and powerfully. Most, however, struggled with a degree of bipolarity that was taxing for everyone involved. During most of the year, teachers would teach in a conventionally teacher-, subject-, and knowledge-centered mode; then, during a one-off week at the end of each semester, they would try to implement co-taught interdisciplinary projects where students led the way. The results were disappointing, with neither instructional mode fully actualized. Professional development time that could have been spent focusing on deepening daily instruction in the disciplines was taken up with project planning, but these projects were so brief that there was little opportunity to leverage what had been learned in order to do better the next time around. It did not surprise us that many of the leaders in these schools expressed ambivalence and a lack of clarity about what kind of learning they wanted students to experience.

The leaders of the Dewey High system, by contrast, are insistent and clear about downplaying or rejecting strategies that don't fit with its overall goals. To start, the schools in the network generally shake their head when it comes to contracting with external providers. Although teachers and students regularly venture into the world beyond the school's walls, partnering with community members and local organizations, Dewey High's leaders rarely bring in outside organizations to provide professional development or to run programs. Dewey High also downplays the pursuit of sky-high achievement on standardized tests. When it comes to offering Advanced Placement classes, the school simply says no; the AP program's emphasis on content coverage within the traditional academic disciplines runs directly counter to the vision of deep interdisciplinary projects. "We broadcast [our lack of AP classes] from the mountaintops," says the school's director. This public stance is critical because it means that families who choose to join the school are forewarned that AP will not be part of their adolescent's high school experience.

When it comes to state standardized tests, the system cannot afford to be quite so cavalier. Instead, its stance is one of resignation. As the administrator who serves as the testing coordinator says, "We basically tell everyone that they need to appease the state so they won't breathe down our neck." The idea, she says, is to prepare students do "well enough" on standardized tests that the school can maintain its autonomy, but to do so in a way that is minimally disruptive. This means integrating into projects instruction in literacy and numeracy skills— something that Dewey High is actively seeking to improve—then incorporating some last-minute content coverage. Many teachers accept this stance without ceremony. A few, however, flinch at even such a minimal nod to the state. Several years back, for example, Mr. Eagle assigned his students the task of demonstrating the low-level nature of the California physics standards by illustrating them all on a single poster. The result is a striking visual statement that occupies a prominent place on the wall of Mr. Friedman's office.

Tradeoffs and Tensions

Dewey High prides itself on embracing tradeoffs to preserve its approach to education. The first of these arises from the "part-to-whole" approach to knowledge development that is the hallmark of project-based learning. As described earlier in the chapter, teachers who successfully adapt to this mode must dispense with the idea that students need to master an integrated body of knowledge before making applied use of it; instead, students learn *through* their attempts at application, seeking out knowledge and skills as the need arises. This mode of learning is powerfully aligned with the problem-centered and frequently cross-disciplinary nature of modern professional work. It is also advantageous from a motivational standpoint because the acquisition of knowledge becomes "mission critical" rather than externally determined. Finally, it is compatible with cognitive science research suggesting that in-depth study is a more effective way to support learners in building robust mental frameworks than is superficial content coverage.[23]

Yet there are reasons one could be skeptical of this part-to-whole mode of learning. While it is true that many contemporary professionals are specialists whose work is focused around complex problems of some kind, many of them got where they are by first mastering a foundational body of skills and knowledge—working from whole to part. (Think, for example, of doctors and lawyers, whose educations famously include several years of textbook study; of classical musicians, who spend years mastering scales and working through canonical repertoire; or of academic scholars, who spend extensive time studying the foundational literature and mastering discipline-specific methods of analysis before specializing or innovating.) In this light, the idea that students' learning should develop exclusively in relation to projects has its limitations. In the humanities, perhaps, it is possible to imagine that students might be able practice core literacy and textual analysis skills in the context of making documentary films or staging original plays—but what about math, where certain concepts serve as critical gateways to others? Dewey High has no good answer to this question, which may help to explain why the schools in its network, as well as virtually all of the other project-based schools that we observed, chronically struggle when it comes to integrating math into their model.

There is also a compelling argument to be made for giving students access to the cultural and scholastic inheritance that shapes the society in which they live. Even if one doesn't embrace E. D. Hirsch's view of "core knowledge," it is possible to think that there should be more space for balancing breadth and depth in the study of subjects such as history and English, and to argue that to forgo a wide range of exposures is to deprive students of schemas by which they can understand the range of the English language and literature, interpret world events, and participate in democratic processes.[24] (In Chapter 8, we suggest what such a balance might look like.) Students at Dewey High, even those who have deeply bought into the idea of learning through projects, recognize that when it comes to subjects such as history their knowledge lacks breadth. As one student put it, "I feel like this school has a feel for the present rather than a feel for the past."

A related tradeoff is the absence of a "floor" for all students when it comes to literacy and numeracy. As is true of the vast majority of non-elite public schools, Dewey High serves a number of students with significant deficits in basic literacy and numeracy—some with special needs, some who are non-native English speakers, and some whose prior schools were particularly poor. The model's inclusive structure means that these students are treated as full participants in projects and integrated fully into the school's culture. This results in high levels of engagement and retention. There is no guarantee, however, that the school will help such students to close the "skills gap" by the time they graduate. While the campus has a fully functioning resource room staffed by several special education teachers, the model's emphasis on building shared dispositions rather than domain-specific skills, as well as its conscious choice not to seek sky-high achievement on tests of basic ability, mean that there will be unevenness in the development of students' basic skills.

Dewey High's leaders, however, are clear in their view that an attempt to reorganize around a guarantee of baseline academic achievement would undermine the school's core commitments. As Mr. Sexton says:

> Suppose you had standards for content and skills and understandings. You wanted everybody to be reading at a sixth-grade level or something like that, and you set that as your goal. Come the end of the year, not everybody's reading at a sixth-grade level. What do you do, then? What do you say to the kid who's not reading at a sixth-grade level? You say, "You haven't measured up." That's crazy, because development is not curricular. Development is individual and personal. Different kids develop at different rates and develop different skills at different times. The important thing is that those skills develop in relation to kids' passions and their willingness to try something new.

Given that almost all American schools focus on doing exactly what Mr. Sexton dismisses as crazy, this sentiment underscores Dewey High's essential radicalism. In a field relentlessly focused on raising the floor of achievement for all students, the school has set its sights on blowing open the ceiling, thus rejecting the logic that dominates the vast majority of American public schools.

The Turn to Continuous Improvement

In 2011, when we first conducted research at Dewey High, Mr. Sexton's denouncement of standards and micro-skill-building was the start and end of the story as far as most of its leaders were concerned. When we returned to Dewey High for a week in the spring of 2018, however, interviews revealed that a growing number of Dewey High's leaders and teachers had begun to question this logic. In particular, they recognized that the dogma of divergence—if taken to an extreme—can exacerbate inequities among their students. This recognition has led to a range of change efforts across the network, all of which focus in one way or another on ensuring a baseline of equity while preserving the school's core values.

Using Data to Confront Inequities

Dave Hughes, one of the longest-tenured leaders at Dewey High, is one of the model's fiercest defenders. His loping walk and sardonic wit are deeply familiar to teachers and principals, and he is a regular presence in meetings with board members, philanthropists, policymakers, and scholars. One of Dewey High's founding science teachers, Mr. Hughes moved quickly into leadership, serving for two years as the school's vice principal and four years as the school's principal before becoming its chief academic officer. Those new to the Dewey High network quickly learn that his opinions and ideas, which he tries to keep close to his chest, nevertheless carry a great deal of weight. Now in his mid-forties, Mr. Hughes is widely seen as one of Mr. Friedman's eventual successors.

When we interviewed Mr. Hughes in 2011, he had nothing but scorn for the idea of using quantitative data to guide the work of schools. As far as he was concerned, Mr. Hughes told us, "data" was a four-letter word—a tool used for control and micromanagement by the state. Standardized assessments, for their part, were a game to be played with the main goal of "keeping the state off our backs." In this, Mr. Hughes echoed much of what we heard from Mr. Friedman, Mr. Sexton, and other leaders at the time.

Seven years later, however, his perspective on data has changed dramatically. So has the nature of his work. Now serving as the provost of Dewey High's recently accredited and rapidly growing graduate school of education (GSE), Mr. Hughes is involved in leading multiple improvement efforts and networked improvement communities (NICs), all of which draw on the improvement science framework outlined by Anthony Bryk and colleagues at the Carnegie Foundation for the Advancement of Teaching. Several of these efforts—including a network of teachers and leaders seeking to improve and spread the use of student-centered literacy practices—are inward-facing, focused on problems of practice as they play out within Dewey High's thirteen schools. Others—such as improving math agency through the spread of constructivist, problem-based, high-cognitive-demand math instruction—originated at Dewey High but have grown to include educators from around the state. Hughes's dissertation, which he defended in the spring of 2017, focused on

Dewey High's efforts to improve college access for its most vulnerable students; a major donor recently awarded $10 million to the
GSE's research center to continue and spread this work. Unifying all
these efforts is a commitment to collecting and analyzing data in
systematic and disciplined ways.

"I wouldn't have guessed that I would have swung so sharply on this,"
Mr. Hughes acknowledges. As he tells it, he has always been "a data
guy" at heart. The problem was that during the decade following the
passage of No Child Left Behind—the decade during which Dewey
High was trying to establish and justify its radical design—he found
the myopic nature of the data that educators obsessed over, and the
punitive ways in which these data were used, deeply distasteful. Only
later, as the Dewey High network began to expand, opening elementary schools, and more explicitly focusing on equity, did he begin to
realize that his (and others') stance had given rise to unintended consequences: a culture that sometimes drew a false dichotomy between
designing authentic, engaging, student-centered projects and deploying
careful pedagogy to support foundational skill-building for all.
Mr. Hughes tells us:

> I was as hostile to test scores as almost anybody. At heart, though,
> I'm a quantitative person. When I was principal [of Dewey High],
> I would lead the school by saying things like, "Let's look at the
> percentage of kids getting Ds and Fs by race." But I was so mad
> when people said they had a laser focus on student achievement
> and it was actually all about tests, because the tests were just the
> most maddeningly moronic thing. I was like, I have a degree in
> physics, I'm not opposed to data, but this is crazy. So I had a narra-
> tive in my head that was blocking me. . . . But after awhile I started
> to notice that there was a crazy narrative that had sprung up, and
> it was especially bad in the elementary schools we had just opened.
> Teachers would be like, "We don't have time to work on literacy
> because we're working on projects." And I was like, "Do you hear
> yourself right now?" We had allowed this goofy innovation nar-
> rative to take hold, and that was poor leadership on my and
> others' part. Now that I think about it, I think what the [medi-
> ocre elementary school] test scores were showing was poor in-
> structional practice.

Mr. Hughes is not the only one for whom the task of running elementary schools served as a catalyst for new ways of thinking. Deborah Stiller, a founding teacher and former principal who now serves as the network's chief learning officer, agrees. She reports that growing into a K–12 network "has expanded our focus," adding that the most urgent question that has emerged is "How do we [approach schooling] in a balanced way that values projects and open-ended work and student voice, but also teaches kids to be literate as mathematicians, and as readers, and writers?"

Other Dewey High long-timers identify the turn to continuous improvement as originating less in the specific challenges of opening elementary schools and more in the generalized challenges of becoming a system. "When we started, we could fit all of the adults in one room," said Kyle McCormack, a former science teacher who now works at the GSE. "Now, we have seven hundred staff and faculty across thirteen schools. So the problem that [improvement] is trying to address is that we got big really quickly, and our ability to disseminate knowledge as an organization became more challenging." Mr. McCormack's colleague Eliza Dobbs, one of Mr. Sexton's protégés, agrees and elaborates: "When [Dewey High] started, it had very much an equity lens, but as we were expanding our schools that focus wasn't always funneling down as we were bringing new people on board." The work of continuous improvement, she adds, was appealing because it promised to become a mechanism to draw teachers into explicitly equity-oriented work, thus making clear that Dewey High sees project-based learning as a promising vehicle for pursuing equity rather than an end unto itself.

Improvement the Dewey Way

By the end of the 2014–2015 academic year, a small but critical group of leaders at Dewey High had spent time learning about what Anthony Bryk and his colleagues have called improvement science (IS), both by participating in events run by the Carnegie Foundation and by piloting a few small improvement projects within the network. One effort in particular, focused on a Dewey High school whose administration had started using the framework to tackle the problem of chronic absenteeism, had seen impressive success in a short amount of time—the kind of success that convinced leaders such as Ms. Stiller, Mr. McCormack, and Ms. Dobbs that IS was worth learning and spreading. The question then became how to get more teachers and leaders in the Dewey High network involved in improvement projects—and how to do it in a way that honored and sustained the network's existing values, rather than endangered them.

In a different kind of school, if the principal or superintendent decided that a certain strategy for school change was promising, it would become the law of the land by fiat. Dewey High's organizational DNA, however, excludes all forms of command-and-control leadership. For adults as well as for students, it is a profoundly democratic place—one that privileges passion, agency, choice, and individualization. As Mr. Sexton puts it: "We've always been about unleashing energy rather than controlling outcomes." Thus, to impose improvement science on leaders and teachers, or even to require that they join a NIC of their choice, would have doomed the effort from the start.

Recognizing this, those leading the charge were deliberately understated and careful as they began to engage members of Dewey High's community in improvement work. Drawing on personal relationships and knowledge about which teachers and leaders were already energized around certain issues, they began to bring small groups together for exploratory meetings—meetings designed not simply to introduce the tools of IS to participants, but also to engage participants in meaningful conversations about problems of practice that they were already passionate about tackling. These included ensuring that all students saw themselves as "math people," making sure that bilingual students felt a sense of belonging in their schools, and getting better at collaboratively solving problems with challenging students. The topics at hand were complex and nontechnical—unlike the more procedural problems featured in some of the IS literature. Nevertheless, Dewey High's leaders were clear that this was the right way to approach the work. As Ms. Dobbs explains:

> You have to start with people's passion—with what feels most kind of core, and most visionary, and most compelling to people—and go from there. People are not compelled by test scores; that's not where people's hearts are. We always knew that

when we started the improvement work, it could never work if it was viewed as making projects less student-led, or less authentic, or anything like that. We were going to die on the vine. It had to be in service of a more compelling vision. . . . We had to help people see that this would help them get better at doing what they already cared about.

As Mr. McCormack tells us, leaders were also clear that teachers should not feel pressured to join the work right away. "We had to change the conversation slowly, so at the beginning we followed the enthusiasm," he says. The initial improvement groups were small, growing organically as word began to spread. The facilitators deliberately began by "highlighting bright spots," so that the work felt energizing rather than suffocating. They also worked to tone down what they perceived as an overly rigid and technical orientation embedded in the IS methodology, taking out language that felt too formal and academic and striving instead to be clear that many of the tools of improvement simply were providing greater discipline to processes that were already intuitive to educators. Recently, in response to negative reactions from teachers provoked by the word "science," they started referring to the work as "continuous improvement" or simply "improvement."

Perhaps the most critical development was that those involved in the improvement work began to identify, and in some cases create, metrics and measures aligned with Dewey High's core values. As Ms. Dobbs tells us:

When we first started getting excited about improvement, the metrics and the measures that were being heralded were things like attendance and standardized test scores—all of these things that just didn't feel very inspiring, or very *us*. At this point, we're in our third year of getting clear about the data we actually care about: data that [are] related to deeper learning, data that teachers can gather in the course of their practice that feels authentic and useful to them. So we're not just talking about kind of elevating kids' test scores, but we're talking about questions like: "Who's in the game? What are you noticing about who participates in number talks? What are you noticing about the quality of questions that students are asking each other when they work in groups? What are you noticing about where students get stuck when they encounter a text, and the different kinds of scaffolds that they use, and who chooses which option when you give multiple options?"

Grounding Dewey High's improvement efforts in metrics that feel compatible with the existing priorities and values of the network, she says, has made the work not only more palatable but also more sustainable—allowing the network to make real headway toward addressing its own challenges without compromising its powerful and radical collective identity.

Beyond leaders' careful attention to launching the work in ways that resonated with Dewey High's culture, there are several reasons that the work gained traction so quickly. First, building a coalition of the willing requires that a number of "the willing" exist—and, as it turns out, there already were many teachers and principals in the Dewey High network who were troubled by the false dichotomy that some had drawn between authentic work and foundational skill-building. Even in 2011, when we first spent time at the school, a number of teachers voiced concern that the school's emphasis on "big picture" elements such as project design, authentic audiences, and visually stunning work sometimes overshadowed the importance of high-quality daily instruction. Others, including humanities teacher Mr. Quinn, complained that only a handful of his colleagues saw their work as being focused on equity; some worked at Dewey High simply because it was "awesome" to have so much freedom to design interesting projects. Thus although the problems of practice that the improvement groups proposed to tackle were very real, there was already a latent constituency ready—even impatient—to take them on.

Beyond this, improvement science fit well with many of Dewey High's existing values. Unlike other frameworks for school change, the IS framework is "problem-focused and user-centered." Rather than relying on scholars or other self-proclaimed experts to identify the goals of the work, it allows practitioners to dig into problems of practice that they themselves perceive to be important. In addition, it borrows from the tradition of design thinking (which is also popular at Dewey High) to emphasize the critical importance of *empathy interviewing*, a tool for exploring an individual's experiences and perspectives on a given topic, as a way to understand the causes and consequences of a given issue. Unsurprisingly, it is the empathy stage of the IS process that many teachers say "sold" them on the framework; it resonates deeply with Dewey High's humanistic values. Mr. Hughes tells us:

> Early on in the college access work we had an expert convening, and during that time we did empathy interviews with boys of color who were freshmen in college. We talked to maybe thirty kids, and that is still probably one of the most powerful things that ever happened in that work. People were hugging and crying, there were just so many powerful moments. It really got at the emotional and affective piece of it.

Thus, the "stickiness" that improvement work has had at Dewey High is not an accident—nor is it clear that a different framework for school change would have made as strong an imprint on the school.

Continuous Improvement: Promises and Tensions

As of the end of the 2017–2018 academic year, Dewey High has been using the continuous improvement framework for three years. The initiative is still relatively young; leaders are clear that they still have much to learn. In an organization with such strong traditions of autonomy and divergence, however, its spread is impressive: 60 percent of faculty and staff across the network's fourteen schools are involved in one or more long-term improvement projects. Most of these relate to the umbrella goal of strengthening the pedagogy deployed in Dewey High's classrooms so that all students—including the most vulnerable populations—develop a core of foundational skills and mindsets. The three largest and most longstanding groups are focused on, respectively, implementing the Next Generation Science Standards, empowering all students in experiencing math agency, and incorporating high-quality literacy routines into all projects. As noted earlier, the college access work has also gained strong traction, recently earning the network a large grant that will allow Dewey High to engage with other stakeholders from around the region.

Most involved in the work are cautiously optimistic about its impact on Dewey High's students. Reflecting on her decade working at the school, Ms. Stiller reports: "We're in a more coherent place than we were when I came. Back then, I almost felt like it was the Wild West; it was all about 'teacher autonomy, teacher autonomy, we design projects to passions.' Now I see a lot more projects attuned to *student* passions, and a lot more good instruction happening overall." Mr. Hughes agrees with this assessment, adding that the work has taken on a life of its own that he did not anticipate when he first began to get enthusiastic about improvement: "I have had many ideas in eighteen years, and a lot of time people are like that's really nice—but never mind. I never would have imagined in June 2014 that it would have had as much take-up as it has right now."

The adoption of continuous improvement, however, has not been without resistance—including at the top. Mr. Hughes tells us how his enthusism for the IS framework ran directly counter to Mr. Friedman's unwavering opposition to all things that smacked of conventional schooling. Mr. Friedman, however, is not one to quash the passions of people—especially people whom he trusts. Instead, when he heard that Mr. Hughes had received a small grant to pursue the college access work, he put on his door an oversized poster of Campbell's Law, which states that whenever a social indicator is emphasized, that indicator will become corrupted because people will seek to improve it rather than to address the underlying problem. Mr. Hughes forged ahead with the work anyway, and when later he presented to the board data showing impressive growth in the school's college matriculation numbers, Mr. Friedman's opposition grew quieter still. When we ask Mr. Friedman to reflect on the spread of improvement across the network, he admits, "It's helped more than I thought it would." Later in the same conversation, however, he makes sure we understand that he sees continuous improvement mainly as a tool for "keeping our schools open"—in other words, as a mechanism for convincing the powers that be of the legitimacy of Dewey High's work, rather than as a core process.

From one perspective, the continued disagreement between Mr. Friedman and Mr. Hughes is a sign of organizational dysfunction. Two leaders who take divergent stances on a highly visible initiative can, after all, lead to mixed messages and incoherence. From another perspective, however, the push and pull between the two men creates a healthy tension that helps to guarantee that Dewey High will continue to adapt new tools to its existing value system, rather than allowing the tools to pull it in the direction of conventional schooling. Hughes seems to agree with this second assessment. "[Mr. Friedman] is not a rigorous, disciplined, systematic thinker. He's a creative thinker. I never would have created anything like this place," he tells us. "My role is to push us to be more disciplined about doing the thing that he dreamed up."

Mr. Friedman is not the only one who remains skeptical of the improvement work. In pockets around the organization, most notably at the original Dewey High campus, teachers continue to voice their concerns about IS, to refrain from participating in NICs, and in some cases to actively resist the work. By this point, these folks are generally in the minority—but because many of them are among the network's most veteran teachers, they are a particularly vocal minority. As Ms. Dobbs put it:

I think for some folks, especially those that are part of that original vanguard, sometimes the worry is: "Oh, we're going to be all traditional now if we just focus on all of these things." So we're trying to get really clear and explicit about saying, "It's a false choice; it doesn't have to be either/or; we can do great math and great literacy practices all in service of really rich PBL [project-based learning]." But, that's kind of a tension we're grappling with as we're moving more into this.

The organization does not yet have an answer to the problem of those who continue to ignore and/or resist the work of continuous improvement. For now, professional development work grounded in continuous improvement still includes an "opt out" option for teachers who wish to go about their work differently; this makes sense given the school's general unwillingness to draw on the tools of command-and-control governance, but it does not illuminate a path forward. As Mr. Hughes tells us, "The easy part was getting 150 people doing this work; the 151st is the hardest one."

Stepping back, what is important to note is that the embrace of continuous improvement has not shifted the school's core values. As school leaders have been exploring ways to more consistently ensure that all students develop foundational skills, they have done so with a shared conviction that neither the goal nor the mechanism of such work should involve standardizing the curriculum. Instead, they have sought to imagine what it might mean to incorporate shared instructional practices in ways that continue to honor Dewey High's constructivist roots. This approach has allowed the school to engage in new learning, making headway toward new goals while continuing to resist being pushed off its center by competing priorities.

∽

Debating the Dewey High model unearths some of the most value-laden questions associated with American secondary schooling. Do we want high schools to be places where students look to the future by venturing into the unknown, or do we want them to be places where students master the timeless building blocks of disciplinary knowledge? Should we care more about cultivating passions and dispositions, or about building cultural literacy and a shared foundation of skills? Should the field empower teachers to be "adventurous" in their work, or, given that adventure entails the nontrivial possibility of failure, should it instead provide clear frameworks for what and how to teach as a hedge against inconsistency? Does the pursuit of divergence run counter to the pursuit of equity?

What we have tried to demonstrate in this chapter is that Dewey High has a firmly asserted set of answers to these questions—answers whose echo can be found in nearly every element of the school. In this, it is powerfully linked to the case that we explore in the next chapter: a school we call No Excuses High. No Excuses High is a design-driven institution led by impassioned leaders whose experience has shaped a clear vision of what good learning entails. Like Dewey High, No Excuses High has a set of thick processes by which this vision is communicated to teachers, students, parents, and visitors. Like Dewey High, No Excuses High harnesses the power of symmetry. This, however, is where the similarities end. As we will explore in the coming pages, No Excuses High's answers to these fundamental questions are profoundly different from the ones we have described in this chapter. Rather than embracing a Deweyan view, the school tries to make good on the promise of the last decades: to raise the floor of knowledge and skills as high as possible for all students, and in so doing to equip them for success in rigorous higher education contexts. To put Dewey High and No Excuses High next to each other is to consider two poles in the landscape of deeper learning, poles that can better orient our exploration of issues critical to the future of the system.

3 ⁓

No Excuses Schools:
Benefits and Tradeoffs

To some, "no excuses" schools are the antithesis of deeper learning. The images that these schools evoke—students working under regimes of tight discipline and control, completing teacher-directed tasks organized toward mastery of traditional academic goals—are not what comes to mind when one thinks about twenty-first-century skills or student-centered learning.

Yet as we have seen, student-centered learning is not necessarily deeper learning. Further, as our colleague David Cohen argued to us early in the project, progressive education is not the only route to deeper learning. What about the East Asian school systems in places like Shanghai, Singapore, and Korea, that take top honors in the Programme for International Student Assessment (PISA), a worldwide exam conducted every three years that measures higher-order thinking? Their students, he points out, seem to learn things, complicated things, but those schools are not cast in a Deweyan mode.

In our initial tour of schools, we went to visit a No Excuses school. Our experiences there suggest that there might be more to some of these schools than behavioral control. Consider this history class:

Students, all of whom appear to be black or Latinx, are given the following prompt:

"From the 1790s to the 1870s, state and national government intervened in the America economy mainly to aid private economic interests and promote economic growth. Between 1890 and 1929 government intervention was designed primarily to curb and regulate private economic activity in the public interest." Assess the validity of this statement, discussing for each of these periods at least two major areas of public economic policy.

Students are then directed to make a graphic organizer, with the columns reflecting the two periods, and the rows reflecting categories like people, government, and economic activities. Students are told to quickly fill in their grids with events that they know from history (they are given six minutes to finish), then discuss their findings with a partner. Meanwhile, the teacher, Ms. Franken, is writing her own organizer on a transparency, which looks like this:

	1790s–1870s	1890–1929	1930–1980
Promotion of private interests			
Promotion of public interests			

As the students move their attention back to Ms. Franken, she gradually fills in this organizer while asking them a series of questions. "Why would we push for trust busting?" "Do we agree that trust busting is entirely about promoting the public good?" "What do you think about the 1920s period?"

STUDENTS RESPOND: "The 1920s were a period that emphasized laissez-faire economics."
MS. FRANKEN: "Can you be more specific?"
STUDENT ONE: "Less of a focus on the public interest and more on promoting the private economy."
MS. FRANKEN: "What was their intention, what was the economic policy they were following in the 1920s and 1980s?"
STUDENT TWO: "Trickle-down economics. You start at the top and it trickles down."
MS. FRANKEN: "Who is 'you'? What do you mean 'you' start at the top?"
STUDENT TWO: "Through taxes, lowering taxes, especially on the rich."
MS. FRANKEN: "What's the opposite of that system, starting with the New Deal and FDR?"

STUDENT THREE: "Pump priming."

MS. FRANKEN: "What does that mean?"

STUDENT THREE: "Heavy intervention. It's when you put lots of money into social programs."

MS. FRANKEN: "So it's infusing money into the bottom of the social hierarchy?"

STUDENT FOUR: "If you add more taxes, wouldn't it hurt businesses? And wouldn't that affect the regular people?"

This was not the best history class we ever saw. Time was short; students did not examine primary documents; the teacher was leading much of the discussion. But the task was analytically complex, and the students, all of whom were high-poverty black and Latinx students from a severely depressed city, had the requisite background knowledge to engage in a real discussion of economics. Compared to many suburban classrooms we visited, where students were woefully ignorant of basic facts—and the absence of such knowledge precluded significant analysis and interpretation—this substantive discussion was impressive. Even more impressive: as we visited different classes—in biology, English, Spanish, and other subjects—we saw teachers present similar tasks that required analysis, and students who were up to the challenge. Further, as we learned certain statistics about the school—78 percent of students receive free or reduced-price lunch; scores on state tests, SAT IIs, APs, and even the PISA exceed those of their suburban counterparts; and 100 percent of graduates are accepted to four-year colleges—we became even more intrigued.

At the same time, we had real reservations about the model. If, as we discuss elsewhere in the book, "deeper learning" comes about when students' intrinsic interests are sparked, when students have large blocks of time to take on open-ended tasks, when students' identities (including their racial identities) are embraced, and when students have some agency and choice over the direction of their learning, then much of the no-excuses model is fundamentally antithetical to that vision of deeper learning. Intriguingly, during the time we spent at the school, the leaders of the school were beginning to reach similar conclusions— they, too, saw limits to what could be accomplished through intense behavioral control, particularly as they were finding that having gotten their students to college, those same students were frequently struggling with the open-ended nature of higher education. During our research, school leaders were trying to retool significant parts of their model, while at the same time keeping the strengths that had enabled their achievements.

All of this raised some significant questions. First, how had No Excuses High managed to consistently produce such classrooms and results, particularly given that they were working almost exclusively with high-poverty students and young teachers? Second, what were the strengths and weaknesses of this pedagogical model when it came to deeper learning? Third, what were the tradeoffs inherent in this vision of learning and social organization for both students and adults—what were the costs of control? And fourth, could the school find a way to retain its strengths while addressing its weaknesses? "No excuses" and deeper learning—building block or oxymoron?

Origins and Prospects of No Excuses Schools

Originating in 1994 with the founding of KIPP (Knowledge is Power Program) Houston, no-excuses schools have become increasingly central to the public debate around urban education reform. Including well-known charter networks like KIPP, Achievement First, and Uncommon Schools, these schools differ in their particulars but share a common set of precepts: strict discipline, which involves penalties for small infractions such as dress-code violations; high academic expectations, organized around state standardized tests and college preparatory exams; and strong norms of classroom control, including, famously, the requirement that students actively track speakers with their eyes in an effort to avoid distractions. More broadly, these schools seek to wall off what happens in the largely high-poverty communities they serve from what happens inside the schools themselves, minimizing external "excuses" for why students might not achieve at levels comparable to their more advantaged peers.

The school networks are also heavily shaped both by the policy context surrounding them and by the core beliefs that organize their work. As organizations founded on the goal of closing achievement gaps, they need to demonstrate measurable progress on state tests and other external exams. This goal was reinforced by the No Child Left Behind

Act, which made scores on state tests the critical marker for school quality. They have also been influenced by behaviorist models of instruction and social organization: incentives and consequences figure prominently for both students and staff, who work diligently toward the goal of mastering prespecified objectives.[1] Much of the school's behavioral approach to discipline is inherited from "broken windows" policing, which argues that permitting small infractions creates a gateway to more significant rule-breaking; thus the insistence on absolute behavioral compliance.[2] While the ends are arguably "liberal" (promoting social mobility for poor children), the philosophy of means is deeply conservative, in that discipline, order, and compliance to adult authority are seen as the keys to success.[3]

No-excuses schools have been the subject of considerable political and academic debate. For proponents, they represent an admirable effort to close achievement gaps and to put poor and largely minority students on the path to a middle-class life. Many of the schools send most or all of their graduates to four-year colleges, and studies that compare graduates of no-excuses charters with applicants who went elsewhere due to the results of school-placement lotteries have found the no excuses graduates to have significantly higher test scores.[4] For these reasons, no-excuses schools have grown in number and in visibility over the years, becoming a significant part of broader school reform strategies in a number of cities, including New Orleans, Washington, and New York.[5]

At the same time, critics have raised a number of objections to the model. They argue that the forms of behavioral control employed at no-excuses schools reinforce longstanding patterns of class bias: poor students are expected to comply with elaborate rules, mirroring the norms of factories and service work, whereas upper-middle-class students are given opportunities to self-direct and collaborate, echoing the values of skilled workplaces.[6] Critics also point to recent studies indicating that many of the students who graduate from no-excuses schools start college but do not graduate, which suggests that high levels of control and prescriptiveness do not necessarily serve students well in their postsecondary and adult lives.[7] Finally, many are troubled by the racial dynamics of these schools, which they see as imposing a new form of colonialism in which a largely white teaching force actively removes students from their communities and forces them to accept a new and "better" set of values.[8]

Despite the importance of this debate, there is a startling paucity of scholarly research on what happens inside no-excuses schools. Journalistic accounts such as Jay Mathews's *Work Hard. Be Nice* and David Whitman's *Sweating the Small Stuff* describe some of the core practices that characterize such schools, but they do not explore how these practices are experienced by faculty and students. A book from 2008 by Katherine Merseth and colleagues, together with recent dissertations by Joanne Golann and Seneca Rosenberg, represent the only serious scholarly accounts of these schools.[9] Finally, because many of the original no-excuses schools were middle schools, we know very little about what happens inside no-excuses high schools. There is also no research that looks carefully at the content of instruction against the criterion of "deeper learning," nor is there work that examines how such schools are striving to revise or change their models. For all of these reasons, we thought there was much to be learned from an examination of No Excuses High.

No Excuses High: A Case Study

We selected No Excuses High as a research site by asking leaders from a range of no-excuses networks which school we should study if we were looking for a high school committed not only to behavioral control but also to rigorous instruction. A wide array of these respondents agreed that No Excuses High was the most promising example. As such, No Excuses High should be seen as a best case for what the no-excuses model has achieved instructionally at the high school level. For the sake of context, we did visit several other no-excuses schools; in addition, Fine conducted a year of dissertation research in one. Based on these experiences, we share the impression that No Excuses High is particularly developed in the systems it has in place to guide instruction.

A few other contextual features of No Excuses High are important for understanding it. Its students are 82 percent African American and 15 percent Latinx; as stated earlier, 78 percent receive free or reduced-price lunch, and 76 percent would be the first in their families to attend college. The school is small, with roughly five hundred students across the four grades. As a charter school, it has the ability to hire and fire teachers at will, to set its own curriculum, and to use its budget as it sees fit. Another important feature of No Excuses High is that it is attached to a middle school (grades five through eight) that is part of the same network. This means that by the time they enter ninth grade, students are already accustomed to the philosophy and routines of school, and they enter with stronger basic skills than if they had attended local district-run middle schools. Finally, No Excuses High is located in a deeply depressed urban area located half an hour from a major city. This location means that there are a relatively large number of young teachers seeking work, but that, given the proximity of advantaged suburbs, it is challenging to hire experienced teachers.

No Excuses High performs extremely well by conventional performance metrics. The school has outpaced not only demographically similar schools but also much wealthier schools on state tests in math and reading. More than 50 percent of No Excuses High test-takers have passed AP tests in AP Biology, AP Calculus, AP Computer Science, AP English Language, AP U.S. History, or AP World History. No fewer than 100 percent of its graduating seniors are accepted to college, and 90 percent enroll in a four-year college. When we were collecting data, No Excuses High's tenth-grade students had recently taken the PISA test; the cohort outpaced the averages of all but nine other countries in reading, and its scores paralleled American wealthy suburbs in math. Thus, as a school that is seeking to close gaps in knowledge of conventional academic content for its students, No Excuses High seems to have succeeded across a variety of metrics.[10]

At the same time, like many similar schools, No Excuses High has significant trouble retaining its students. The school does not publish and would not provide us with figures about its retention rates, but one senior estimated that she had started with fifty students in her fifth-grade class and that only about half of them were still at the school in twelfth grade.[11] Lending credence to this story of attrition was the fact that class sizes for seniors are frequently much smaller than those for ninth graders. Conversations with students suggested that the most common reason students leave is that they can't or won't put up with the heavy workload and/or the regimen of strict behavioral control; these students seek traditional high schools where it is much easier to progress across the grades. We do not have any way of judging how many students left voluntarily as opposed to being "pushed" or "counseled" out by the school administration.[12]

How to read these figures is a matter of perspective. Critics would argue that if a school has a 50 percent retention rate, it is hard to call it successful. Proponents would say that No Excuses High is a school of choice, and that if it works well for half or more of its kids, then those students are getting a better education than they would have received otherwise. They might add that even if only half of high-poverty fifth graders graduate from the school and go to college, that figure is likely to be much higher than for a similar sample of fifth graders who did not have the opportunity to attend. They might also point out that students who leave the school may graduate from other high schools more academically prepared as the result of their time at No Excuses High. Either way, it is clear that No Excuses High benefits from the fact that everyone who is at the school has signed on to its vision and values. Even in a setting where 78 percent of the students receive free or reduced-price lunch, these clearly are not a typical cross-section of high-poverty students; rather, these are students whose parents have signed them up and who have chosen to stay.

As with other schools in the book, our goal in researching the school was to construct a case study grounded in rich ethnographic data. To that end, we conducted in-depth interviews with virtually all of the school's teachers and administrators; we also ran several focus groups with students. Because it was a small school, we were able to observe almost every class in the school at least once. In total, we spent 130 hours observing, and interviewed fifty people. This methodology does not allow us to determine the degree to which the school was "causing" the student outcomes described earlier. What it does allow us to do, given the existing evidence that shows the contribution of no-excuses schools to test score outcomes, is to explore the mechanisms through which these effects are achieved.

The Systems Engineering Approach

Everything at No Excuses High flows from the vision of its founder and principal, Peter Dewitt. Mr. Dewitt is tall, wiry, with angular features and pristinely slicked-back black hair. He is also always impeccably dressed. Mr. Dewitt has what one might think of as a "systems engineer" view of schooling. He has an almost visceral distaste for disorder of any kind; as one teacher told us: "It really sets the tone when Peter picks up even the smallest pieces of trash around the building."

Mr. Dewitt graduated from a top Ivy League university in 1991 with a determination to create social change, particularly for high-poverty and minority students. His undergraduate degree was in government, but he quickly decided that law, politics, and government were not the ways to create the most meaningful social change. Placing his bet on education, Mr. Dewitt taught in Washington, D.C., for three years, then obtained a master's degree from Harvard's Graduate School of Education. After graduating, he went to work at the Francis Parker School, a suburban charter school founded by the legendary progressive educators Ted and Nancy Sizer. The school featured a number of the core strategies of progressive schooling, such as involving students in collective decision-making and using gateway portfolios, as opposed to conventional exams, to mark passage from one "division" to the next.

Mr. Dewitt's experiences at Parker were formative to his perspectives as educator, but not in the way that the Sizers intended. As Mr. Dewitt perceived it, the school had "let its culture happen by happenstance," and as a result, this culture had turned "toxic"—students frequently were disrespectful and rude. More troubling still was that the general looseness of the school's structures seemed to be exacerbating inequalities. "The low-income students and the students with special needs really did not [get what they needed], even with two teachers in every classroom, which was the model. . . . [The leaders thought] we don't need any structures; we'll design it democratically." For Mr. Dewitt, the takeaway lesson was that even an enormously talented and thoughtful group of teachers and leaders could not make up for the absence of systems and structures.

It was with this perspective in mind that Mr. Dewitt joined the network of charter schools where he now works. He started by teaching for seven years at the network's flagship middle school. Although this campus was run by a leader whom Mr. Dewitt deeply respected, over time he began to perceive echoes of the same problems that he had experienced at Parker:

[The school leader's] charisma led him in the initial years to believe that he could hire just really good teachers and kind of let them go and things would be okay. . . . And what ended up happening, without a lot of systems in place, was that people would do really good work for a little while and then they would leave or there would be inconsistencies within the school, and then over time, like four or five years in, it seemed like we were back where we started again with brand new faculty struggling.

When Mr. Dewitt had the opportunity to open a companion middle school, and later a high school, he was determined not to replicate these mistakes. He knew himself well enough to know that charisma was not his strong suit; instead, he relied heavily on his commitment to detail and his orientation toward systems engineering, making these the linchpins of his work. Embracing what Weber calls "bureaucratic authority," Mr. Dewitt developed an approach to school leadership that is heavily focused on creating systems for controlling and guiding teacher and student work. "I had learned that . . . if you left it to chance, you could get really non-optimum results that were unchangeable," he reflected.

Systems are also essential for equity, in Mr. Dewitt's view. Unplanned variation among teachers will lead to variation in what students know and are able to do, which in turn will compromise the goal of creating better life opportunities for all students. Thus, it is most essential that an equity-oriented school leader minimize random variation and maximize consistency of experience across classrooms. "My greatest fear is randomness," Mr. Dewitt reflects.

The result of Mr. Dewitt's work, perhaps unsurprisingly, is the most developed set of systems that we have ever seen in a school. As we will detail in the coming pages, there are systems for everything at No Excuses High. For teachers, there is a centrally developed curriculum, templates for how lessons should be taught, weekly observation and feedback sessions that follow a prescribed form, weekly submission of lesson plans for feedback and approval, and video documentation of everything for the purposes of learning and improvement. Students operate in a similarly systematized environment, in which they need to pass in homework to baskets at the beginning of the day (to prevent them from working on it during classes), and, within classes, experience an extensive use of countdown timers to maximize time on task. All of this is backward mapped to support mastery of the goals laid out by the AP or SAT II tests.

Mr. Dewitt's personality, as well as his goals and values, shape the culture of the school. One prominent feature of this personality—and thus of No Excuses High as a whole—is its relentless emphasis on improvement. As Mr. Dewitt describes a conversation with a new teacher, let's call her Ms. Cristo: "At one point Ms. Cristo asked me in December, because she was part of this instructional leadership [process], 'When will this end?' And our response was—because she thought it was going to end after winter break. Like, 'Does this stop?' And we said, 'Never. It never ends. It is endless.'" The structures described earlier work in part because of the sheer determination with which they are applied; sewn into the fabric of No Excuses High is the narrative that it will take grueling work on everyone's part to close gaps in achievement.

Also central to the school's culture is a highly transactional approach to relationships, both among faculty members and between faculty and students. Mr. Dewitt acknowledges that at his middle school he consistently scored low on metrics such as "how much does this person know about you." He did not see this limitation, however, as getting in the way of creating a successful work environment. Teachers report that this belief serves as a model for how they organize relationships at No Excuses High. As one reflected:

> I find a lot of teachers a lot of times care too much about being liked, and that's something that Peter has never really cared about, not why he does what he does. And I think I take my cue from him as far as that goes. I want to be liked of course by people, but that's never going to be something that drives my interactions with students or anything like that. It's inappropriate, it's not what we're supposed to be about as educators.

This approach is also compatible with the broader no-excuses philosophy, because the school, like many among its ranks, takes the position that its primary responsibility is to equip its students with knowledge and skills; to "kill students with kindness" would be to neglect this responsibility and thus to disrespect their potential.

In sum, No Excuses High represents a somewhat extreme reaction to the perceived dangers of progressive schooling and untrammeled teacher autonomy. Deeply rooted in an equity-oriented mission, it seeks to achieve its values through extensively designed systems of hierarchical control that leaders hope will create upward mobility. The culture of the school is similarly instrumental in its approach; relationships are viewed as a means to creating better outcomes, but also as potential interference with the school's mission. Much of what follows, for good or ill, flows from these orienting assumptions.

Inside Classrooms

Depending on the perspective of the observer, what happens inside of No Excuses High's classrooms can be viewed either as highly conventional high school fare or as a radical experiment in remaking the contemporary high school.

The work is conventional in that the content, and the tasks that guide the teaching of it, will be familiar to anyone who has graduated from an American high school: analyzing *Julius Caesar*, exploring the impact of World War II, identifying equations that describe the trajectory of physical objects. These are the topics that American high school students have studied for generations; they are a deeply established part of the school canon.

What is distinctive is that these topics are superimposed onto a commitment that *all* students, particularly students from extremely impoverished backgrounds, will engage to the point of demonstrating mastery. If, as the authors of *The Shopping Mall High School* describe, contemporary American high schools are places where a tacit bargain exists between "teachers who pretend to teach" and "students who pretend to learn," the maxim at No Excuses High is the opposite: students will learn (whether they want to or not), and teachers will teach (whether they want to or not).[13]

To achieve that result, the classrooms at No Excuses High are long on four elements: intense behavioral control, which is used to maximize time on task; careful scaffolding, by which complex topics are broken into component parts and students are deliberately guided through them; frequent checks for understanding to see where students are in their learning; and backward mapping from SAT II and AP tests to ensure that the content aligns with expectations for college study. In contrast to traditional classrooms, where teachers talk for long periods of time while students listen passively, what we saw at No Excuses High was an extensive amount of *practice*—students working individually or in pairs to demonstrate their understandings of particular facts, concepts, and ideas. It is hardly an overstatement to say that students were exercising their brains virtually all of the time; No Excuses High had taken to heart the cognitive scientists' injunction that the person doing the mental work is the one who is learning. Many of the school's metaphors came from sports and the arts, in which guided practice, including detailed feedback on the smallest errors of form or technique, is central to the approach to learning.

Challenging Tasks, Carefully Scaffolded with Student as Producer

It is a sunny morning in late May and Mr. Moriarty's tenth-grade English class is about to begin. Mr. Moriarty, a slim young White man who is just finishing his first year of teaching, stands at the door of his classroom greeting students as they enter. All of his students are dressed in the school uniform—khakis, collared shirts tucked into belts—and all appear to be black or Latinx. Mr. Moriarty shakes their hands firmly and prompts them to sit down and get going, which they do without ceremony or side conversations. The class starts with a seven-minute "do now" task: an SAT-style vocabulary multiple-choice worksheet. When the students have completed it, they copy down their homework into their planners. Their homework involves reading the next chapters of Ann Petry's novel *The Street*, which is currently the focus of the class's shared work. In addition, they have to produce a rough draft of an essay.

Mr. Moriarty goes over the day's objectives, then asks a student volunteer to lead a review of the new vocabulary list. The student asks, "What part of speech is ___?" and "What other forms of the word do we know?" and other students raise their hands to answer. Then he gets to sentences that use the word, and when a student gives a simple sentence, Mr. Moriarty says, "We need something that highlights—show us the meaning of the word." The words themselves are SAT words: "specious," "constituent," "negligible," "arrogant."

After this review is over, sixteen minutes into the period, the class moves on to discussing the chapter of The Street that they had read the previous night. The students first spend three minutes completing a "reading check," a brief multiple-choice quiz that asks questions like "What does Min decide to do about her miserable life with Jones?" and "What can the reader conclude is the profession of a pushcart man?" When the quiz is over, Mr. Moriarty transitions into a discussion about the novel. He highlights the question that the class needs to answer today: "For what is the sky symbolic?" He explains that the group will read, then discuss what they've read, then write a full literary response to the question. Afterward, he prompts a volunteer to read out loud from the novel. At some point he takes over the reading "because you'll want to write during this part." About half of the twenty-one students appear to be taking notes while he reads.

Mr. Moriarty pauses and asks the students to take two minutes to write down thoughts about the discussion question, then two more to discuss their responses with a partner. When I walk around during the writing, most kids are copying down relevant quotations and a few are also writing sentences about what the symbolism might be. Afterward, during the "pair share," I listen to one group as they have a brief discussion about whether the sky might symbolize fate.

The class moves on to whole-group discussion. The students offer up a variety of interpretations, sometimes responding directly to each other and sometimes to Mr. Moriarty when he adds to or questions their ideas. They often use sentence-starters that allow them to directly connect to or build off each other's thinking. "I thought the sky was symbolic of the street and how everything on the street affects people," one student begins. Mr. Moriarty lets this student talk for a minute but then questions whether the street changes the same way the sky does. Another student offers: "I think Petry provides the symbolism of the skies to represent the loss of hope," evidencing this idea with a specific quote. In total, five students share their ideas, and there are about five other students with raised hands.

Mr. Moriarty asks another question: "If you were an author, why would you use the sky to represent the change in a person. . . . Why would it be a fitting representation for a gaining or a loss of hope?" After a pause, he adds: "There's no right or wrong answer here." Mr. Moriarty cold-calls a student who hasn't spoken yet. She begins to answer but then falters; another student offers: "In general, the sky and the weather portray how people feel, so she probably used the sky to symbolize the struggle in man's life in general." This discussion continues for about ten minutes, until the bell rings.

This excerpt illustrates many of the key elements that characterize the No Excuses High approach to instruction. The time was heavily divided—there were no fewer than nine distinct activity segments during the sixty-five-minute period. With the exception of the whole-group discussion at the end of the period, for each segment of the class there was a tangible deliverable (written or oral) that each student was accountable for producing. The tasks themselves involved a mixture of basic questions around vocabulary and text comprehension and higher-order questions that required students to identify symbols and themes. There were also questions for which students were asked to "think like a writer" by analyzing the reasoning behind the author's choices—a key part of engaging in the disciplinary thinking associated with English language arts. Virtually all of these tasks were backwardly mapped from external assessments: the vocabulary exercises are intended to prepare students for the SAT, and the literary analysis questions mirror those that students will face on the English SAT II or AP English in several years.

From a deeper-learning perspective, there are different ways of interpreting this lesson. A positive interpretation of this class would note that the questions the students grappled with in the second part of the class were difficult and meaningful, consistent with the kinds of questions that might be asked in an AP English class at an affluent school or in a college literature seminar. Students offered full-sentence thoughts as responses to these questions, and they made an effort to build on each other's ideas. The proportion of class time spent "on task" was very high, and students often were shouldering the cognitive load. Finally, it is worth remembering that Mr. Moriarty was a first-year teacher—a point to which we will return.

Conversely, critics would note that there was no essential question to help connect and lend meaning to the diverse elements. Students practiced vocabulary because they needed vocabulary for the SAT; there was no effort to incorporate the skill-building into a more meaningful arc. Only the second half of the class pushed students beyond the retrieval and comprehension stage. And, as we observed in our notes at the time, the short time for discussion compromised the energy in the classroom.

No Excuses High at Its Best

At their best, classrooms at No Excuses High were places where students engaged in deep disciplinary thinking, leveraging their considerable knowledge to tackle complex questions that required analysis and interpretation. For example, consider an eleventh-grade English class taught by Mr. Gregory, a short, energetic man in his thirties:

Mr. Gregory is wearing slacks and a zip-up sweatshirt that says, "The Messenger," which is the school's newspaper. Mr. Gregory was a journalist before he became a teacher. When I enter the classroom, there are thirteen students sitting in a semicircle. After an SAT-style grammar review sheet, they turn to the main task of the day.

Mr. Gregory asks the students to open to a featured debate in the newspaper, which is under the "He said, She said" column on the op-ed page. The heading is, "What should the role of a just person be in an unjust society?" and there are two students, Jaime and Hannah, whose ideas are featured. He gives the students seven minutes to write independently on a T-chart their summaries of what the two arguments are, then says that the students will be working in their "dream teams" to come up with their own answers to this question, which they will then debate in a hands-down discussion. He emphasizes that students "should use the stories you've read this year to make your case. . . . It's not an easily answerable question, at least not for me. I can see both sides, and I want to see if you can use what we've read this year to synthesize your ideas and see both sides too."

One of the girls in the trio closest to me starts, "I think that she's basically trying to say that if a government doesn't respect its people, then the people have the right to go against the government." Another girl talks about 1984, saying that "Winston—in a way he could support Jaime. Because didn't he try to kill the firefighter?—and that's violence. . . ." Then she adds that in Fahrenheit 451 "He [the protagonist] silently revolted against his government."

Then another girl talks about To Kill a Mockingbird: "Scout's father was going against society, but the way he was doing it was by going against the rules . . . and in Huckleberry Finn he moves away from society and he does violence, and in the end you see there is a change." A girl disagrees: "You're saying it as if Jim killed everybody but I don't think that book connects to Jaime's article." Mr. Gregory is sitting next to them at this point and he says, "This is good—this is an argument I want you to have. You don't have to agree." He throws out an idea about Atticus, and the girls start arguing against him, saying that Atticus Finch and Henry David Thoreau aren't opposite.

The timer goes off and the kids move back to their other seats. Mr. Gregory says that he will take notes on the board, and that "I'm looking at your broad ability to connect all of these different books to a broader theme—in part because that's what you will have to do in college, especially if you take English classes."

"Jaime thought that you had to make change by breaking unjust laws. Hannah took a more subtle approach—in order to make change you have to work within society," volunteers one group.

"An example my group used was from *Huck Finn*—he basically left and tried to get away from his society, which shows that violence is not always needed. I thought that his nonviolent ways and his ability to leave shows that you don't always need to break the law or be violent to make a change."

"But I have a question: so what change did that bring to society?"

"I was talking about Huck himself."

After a little more discussion of *Huck Finn*, Mr. Gregory asks the kids to refer to other books that they have read this year.

"I was going to refer to *1984*. . . . At first he does try to work with the system, and he does little things like developing relationships with the girl, and he's trying to slowly go against the system, but ultimately you could argue that the reason he wasn't successful was because he wasn't willing to fight for the cause."

Mr. Gregory asks, "If I forced you to pick, what would you pick?" and the girl makes a wry face, and then says that she thinks *1984* supports the violent side.

Mr. Gregory responds, "I understand your point, Rachel, but I have a different notion. . . . I want to know why everybody keeps connecting dystopia to fighting for change."

"I think that Hannah's form of rebellion is a less extreme case—Jamie isn't saying that you need to be violent, but that you shouldn't go along working within the rules. If you really want change, then you need to fight for what you believe in. In *1984*, the way he tried to rebel was too subtle, and so the society stifled his form of rebellion."

"I agree that the point of fighting and being rebellious has to be appropriate—you can't fight for petty things. I think racism is something that you need to rebel for, because it was basically started through violence. If something—like a bad principle or system—was implemented though violence, then you shouldn't use a passive way to fight it, because not much would be done."

"I think you're vilifying these characters who are trying to adjust to society. . . . Like in the instance with Winston, when he finally did start rebelling, he got tortured. You're making him seem like a hypocrite when really he's just trying to survive and live the good life—and that connects to our essential questions."

After a few more comments, Mr. Gregory stops the discussion and asks the students to write their exit ticket, which asks them to "take a stand" on the issue now that they have discussed it. The students hunch silently over their papers and write until time expires.

This session provides an example of No Excuses High at its best. The students are taking on a vital philosophical question—what is the role of a just person in an unjust society? Drawing on examples from a variety of classic texts, they are considering how under different scenarios it may or may not be justifiable to use violence against an oppressive regime. They consider different social change strategies and weigh the question of when, and under what circumstances, individuals have a collective responsibility to act for justice. Students are speaking in full sentences and accurately describing the books they have studied. Small groups and individual exit tickets are used to make sure that every student participates. To the degree that tasks of synthesis are meant to build on retrieval and comprehension, this task is a meta-level task that asks students to take what they've learned about particular texts and apply it in the context of a more general question.

A related example comes from Mr. Cunningham's eleventh-grade biology class:

As the twenty juniors enter the room, Mr. Cunningham greets them and prompts them to sit down and start reading the materials that will guide their seminar discussion today: a case study about an unusual variety of fish. "I want you to be pulling out important vocabulary words as you go," he says. The case study is in the form of a large packet, which includes an introduction to macroevolution, a "problem" section that describes how the three-spine stickleback fish has interesting variations in body armor, and a section with questions that students will be discussing. As the students read and annotate silently, Mr. Cunningham circulates and quietly affirms what he sees.

After five minutes, Mr. Cunningham draws the class together. He asks the students to articulate the central problem of the task. One student says, "Why morphological changes happen over time." Mr. Cunningham then asks the class to generate a list of vocabulary they can use that will "bring the discussion to the next level." Students volunteer a range of words and terms: natural selection, morphological, mutations, punctuated equilibrium, allopatric speciation. When Mr. Cunningham cold-calls a student and asks him to define the last term, the student responds without hesitation, "When species that are related develop different characteristics because they are in different environments."

The students who have been assigned to participate in the first inner-circle discussion move their desks into the center of the room and Mr. Cunningham starts the timer. The group has five minutes to tackle the packet's first question, which is whether the fish's traits are inherited. What experiment could the group design to test this question? After a short moment of silence, the students begin discussing the question earnestly and thoughtfully. As observers, we are struck that they know how to respond to each other, to disagree respectfully and substantively, to invite each other in, to ask questions of the others when confused.

> "One way we could test it is to breed the different populations of stickleback fish—use two fish from each population and cross the marine with the marine and the freshwater with the freshwater and you'd see which traits appear in the young."
> "I agree with you, but I thought that when you cross these fish you should cross the marines with the freshwater, because if it's like reversible then if that's the case, then the marine fish's babies would be sterile."
> "I wasn't sure you could even test this because yesterday we talked about how you can't eliminate an allele from a population because of carriers."
> "So it never actually stated whether or not the spines were coded for in the population, so you're assuming that it is inherited and it was lost in the freshwater population?"

"I have a question: [student name], you were talking about how the alleles could be lost as the result of the environment, but we don't even know if the allele was inherited. Do we all agree that the allele was inherited?"

Mr. Cunningham moves the group on to the next part of the case, which describes what the scientists did to design an experiment—it turns out to be similar to what the first student suggested—and lists the results in the form of a chart. For two minutes, the students have a discussion in which they clarify how to read the data listed on the chart:

"The diagram is showing that if you cross a marine and a freshwater you get C . . . [refers to the diagram]."
"What is C showing?"
"C is the offspring from crossing A and B."
"It has a partial spine."
"So based on that maybe it's like incomplete dominance?"
"I kind of disagree. I thought if you look at the ratios, it looks a lot like 9 / 3 or 3 / 1, which is the standard ratio for heterozygote cross. So I guess you can conclude that spines and body armor are linked genes."
"I wouldn't totally agree with that because of E and F—mostly E. Even though the fish only has partial body armor, you wouldn't—if they were linked, they would have to be shown together."
"Can somebody tell me what we just concluded? Did we come to a consensus? Like, what was [student name] saying? I understand the traits that the F2 generation had, but what does that mean?"
"I don't know if we really answered the question."
"I agree, because I thought di-hybrid crosses were different."
"The question is asking what you can conclude about the alleles, and we think it's a di-hybrid cross."

The group decides to move on to the next substantive question, which describes the results of the test and asks the kids to diagram what happened in this breeding test. One of the participants gets up to the board and starts drawing a chart with genes, but before he gets very far the timer is up. Mr. Cunningham asks them to summarize their ideas while the outside participants get ready to share feedback. Their comments suggest that they were following the process as well as the content of the conversation:

> "Whoever talked in the circle used a lot of vocab, and they used a lot of evidence from the case study itself. One criticism is that you guys never really decided what your conclusion was and what everyone thought, and if you agreed with [student name] nobody explained why."
>
> "I agree. In the first part you included more vocabulary and evidence. But the fact that some people were going back against what [student name] was saying—that was good too."
>
> "I like that [student name] looked at the ratios—I didn't initially think of looking at that but that helped me think about incomplete dominance."
>
> "I think that the use of questions was good, because it clarified—they didn't just move on when they were confused. But I didn't really understand what they were saying."

Mr. Cunningham jumps in. "There were lots of opinions, but there was a lot of hard, stone-firm evidence to support your claim—you got there at the end, but it took awhile to get there," he says. He affirms the student who asked the group to summarize the ideas that they had named, and then he asks the groups to switch so that the outsiders are now on the inside. A similar discussion to the one described above ensues, though with different questions this time—questions that progress from where the first group left off. The homework is on the last page of the handout. It asks students to cite three specific pieces of evidence from the seminar and define five key terms to answer the question: "Why have some freshwater populations of the three-spine stickleback fish lost their pelvic spines and body armor?"

This excerpt illustrates No Excuses High at its best, this time in the sciences. Here students draw on their background knowledge and skills to make sense of what happens in a new scenario—explaining the evolution of the stickleback fish. The task asked students to think about how biological reasoning works—students needed, in Jerome Bruner's words, to understand the underlying structure of the disciplinary knowledge in order to answer this question.[14] The students expressed no self-consciousness in using academic knowledge, and their conversation built on each other's points. They worked within established norms of how to conduct this kind of academic discussion, and they were given an opportunity to critique their performance and reasoning. The lesson concluded with homework that built on the seminar and provided individual accountability for processing what was developed as a group. Though stereotypes about no-excuses schools emphasize that students move in lockstep on fairly trivial tasks—for example, chanting multiplication tables—what was happening in this biology class shows what can happen when the disciplined accumulation of factual knowledge is used to tackle a significant analytic task.

No Excuses High at Its Worst

Not all classrooms at No Excuses High were as analytical as Mr. Cunningham's biology class. In classrooms that were not as strong, we identified a tendency toward breadth over depth, certainty over exploration, and control over passion. In some ways these problems mirror the challenges of American high schools as a whole; in other ways, however, they reflect the particular limitations of the No Excuses High model.

Consider the following ninth-grade math class:

Ms. Kilroy is a petite white woman in her late twenties or early thirties with dark blond hair pulled back in a ponytail. She's dressed in a no-frills kind of way in a tee shirt and long skirt, and her manner matches her appearance: when I introduce myself, she is neither warm nor off-putting. On the door of her classroom is a list of students who scored above a 90 percent on the most recent interim exam, ranked in order. Inside, one of the walls has a "student seminar wall of fame" with a number of accolades for students who have been nominated as the stars of "move it along," "wrap it up," and "best evidence."

The students, freshmen who are in the higher math track, start with a "do-now": writing the correct formula for some exponent problems. Ms. Kilroy hurries them through it, then prompts them to get out their binders and open to yesterday's exit ticket, which she has graded with checks. She hands out an answer key and gives the kids two minutes to write corrections on their problems. The girl next to me uses a red pen to copy down some of the work that is on the answer key. After the timer goes off, the students have two minutes to talk with each other about their answers.

"I only got two right," says one girl to her group. Ms. Kilroy comes over and one of the kids says to her, "I don't understand why you did it this way." Ms. Kilroy explains it to her, although we can't hear what she is saying.

The students take out their notebooks, and Ms. Kilroy thanks them for their professionalism. She notes that today was a "perfect homework day." She launches into the lesson, which is on a PowerPoint. She says, "We're going to learn about two kinds of rules: recursive and explicit sequence rules." She has the kids repeat the word "recursive" out loud multiple times. She then projects a table of values, saying that the task is to write the rule relating the x value to the y value. "$y = 2x + 3$," says the girl next to me within one second. When Ms. Kilroy asks how many got this, almost everyone raises their hands. One girl explains that the "shortcut" is to look at the y value when x is zero to get the intercept. Ms. Kilroy affirms this and says that this task is about writing explicit rules, which they can already do. "Now we're going to go over recursive rules," she says, and walks them through a different way of generating the equation, involving looking only at y compared to itself in the previous and next entries.

After a bit more direct instruction, Ms. Kilroy gives the students two minutes to try out one of these new problems with their groups. The students next to me talk about what to plug in where and do some calculations on paper. Next, the students silently do a similar problem on their own, which Ms. Kilroy then goes over with them. The format is much the same: students supply the answers; Ms. Kilroy clarifies and asks for some help along the way. She warns them that "sometimes when people learn how to write recursive rules they forget how to write explicit rules—so I'm going to have you write both each time for now."

This class offers a classic example of No Excuses High's guided practice lesson template: individual warmup to connect from yesterday; direct instruction that includes some opportunities for participation; time to practice in groups. Math experts would likely classify this lesson as focusing on procedures and algorithmic application rather than on conceptual understanding.[15] Students have learned some rules for how to identify algebraic equations from sets of data points, but they are not being asked to understand the underlying reasons that those rules work. If one thinks back to the now-famous contrast between American and Japanese math lessons, in which the Japanese approach features one difficult problem that students need to work together to solve, and the American features teaching a formula and then trying that formula across a range of examples, this lesson fits squarely into the American mode.[16]

What happened in this and other similar classes, we believe, was less a reflection of anything distinctive about No Excuses High and more a reflection of the broader milieu that shapes American instruction. As was true at many other schools we visited, there was an emphasis on procedural and algorithmic knowledge in math, and an emphasis on coverage over depth in science. Sometimes teachers were able to use building blocks to ask harder and more meaningful questions, as in the "just person in an unjust society" example in English and the stickleback fish lab in biology. But there were also times when the pressure to cover the topic completely and, in particular, the orientation toward what would be measured on the SAT IIs and AP tests, militated against deeper exploration.

The pace of classes also worked against qualities inherent in a certain vision of deep learning. If deeper learning emerges when students are given extended time to grapple with hard problems, to work and iterate solutions, and to do sustained work on meaningful products, there was not much learning of that sort at No Excuses High. In particular, the heavily scaffolded nature of the work, the desire to split it into small chunks in order to keep students on task, and the pressure to check frequently for understanding worked against longer, more open-ended, and more uncertain explorations. When we asked a number of students if they had done a piece of work that they were proud of, many could not name a single assignment.

The emphasis on extrinsic over intrinsic motivation also influenced the classes we observed. While students were almost always "on task," rarely did classes have high levels of energy, and rarely did we observe students volunteering ideas or questions that went beyond what was asked of them. We could count on one hand the instances where a genuine discussion or debate broke out that was not a direct response to the assigned task. If learning at its best takes on characteristics of "flow," of being "in task" rather than "on task," or of simply being genuinely intrinsically motivated, we saw few examples of that at No Excuses High.

Consider, for example, a drama class we observed. We wanted to explore what happened in elective spaces and the arts, because at other schools these were frequently arenas where authentic and impassioned work was happening.

When I enter, there are twenty students sitting in chairs in a large circle. The room feels oddly clean and empty; the walls are barren aside from a few simple masks on one wall and a few printed generic posters. Ms. Lopaz, a young Latina wearing a dress and very high heels, is pacing around talking and asking questions. After a couple of minutes, she transitions and hands out a worksheet. "We're going to work on learning how to do staged readings today," she says. She asks the students to take out their scripts. The class is silent. "Let me define for you what a staged reading is," Ms. Lopaz says, and reads out the definition, which the kids write down: "The opportunity for a playwright to workshop their play while it is in development."

Ms. Lopaz asks what a staged reading wouldn't have that a full production would have. The students answer: lighting, sound, costume. "I would have that in my notes," Ms. Lopaz says, as she repeats what they have said. The kids write. Ms. Lopaz then prompts them to flip to the front of the sheet and says that they are going to listen to a podcast and then answer the questions on the sheet: "What are the advantages of a staged reading?" "Name the physical and vocal skills you've been working on that will help you with a staged reading." The kids write notes as directed during the five-minute podcast; all but three are actively writing. When the podcast is over, the kids have three minutes to write answers to the questions. Afterward, Ms. Lopaz asks them to talk about what they wrote. A few students volunteer:

> "I would do a staged reading because there might be things I want to change, and the actors might evoke something that I want to add."
> "With a whole production you can't necessarily focus on the dialogue—you'd be paying attention to the lighting and design."
> "The person is still working, they're not finished, so a full production then they would have to make a book of your script."

The students are not responding directly to each other, and in almost each instance Ms. Lopaz responds to each comment with a comment of equal or longer length. Students are using theater vocabulary: they use terms like emphasis, voice projection, articulation, and body language. The conversation goes on through the other questions. At some point Ms. Lopaz alludes to the staged reading "lunch series" that they will do soon.

We can see in this class some of the tradeoffs of the No Excuses High approach. The students are again acquiring fairly sophisticated discipline-specific vocabulary in thinking about the nature of staged readings. But they do so devoid of context, unlinked to the staged reading of an actual play that they will be doing later in the year. In the absence of this animating purpose, students are following directions and dutifully learning the content, but without the energy that is usually associated with putting on, preparing, or even thinking about a production for a real audience.

Tradeoffs at No Excuses High

On balance, the amount of thinking required at No Excuses High was much more than one would see in most contemporary high schools. History teachers asked students to analyze historical cartoons and to research the impact of *Roe v. Wade*; physics teachers asked them to explore Newton's laws on the basis of data they had collected on a trip to a local amusement park; English classes featured discussions of "Recitatif" and *The Great Gatsby*; Spanish students were asked to conduct individual interviews with their teacher to demonstrate their proficiency in the language; and in their math classes, students were asked to develop a proof of the formula for the surface area of a sphere. The role of external assessments loomed large. Some portions of classes were given over to testing basic skill elements, and teachers, particularly in math, science, and history, worried that the external assessments were pushing them to trade depth for breadth, with imperatives to cover a certain amount of material limiting deeper explorations. Even so, on the whole, in twenty of the twenty-five classes we observed, at least some portion of the class was devoted to engaging students in higher-order thinking tasks that would be classified in the top half of Bloom's taxonomy—and most students actually could do these tasks.

At the same time, we saw only rare instances of genuine energy and engagement. The work was framed almost exclusively in terms of preparation for college or external assessments rather than as something of intrinsic interest or purpose; thus, students experienced academic work as something with which to comply rather than with which to engage. In addition, the constant scaffolding and frequent assessment meant that although students were acquiring a range of knowledge, skills, and content, they had few experiences where they directed their own learning or participated in sustained academic investigations.

The Big Picture

How does No Excuses High create these classrooms, which, if lacking in certain critical respects, were at least consistently asking high-poverty students to think about real subjects? We identify a number of dimensions that were critical for generating this consistency: the creation of a *specific* and *granular* instructional vision; a curricular *infrastructure* that supports teachers' work; extensive *feedback* mechanisms for adult learning; a *fierce culture*; and the *alignment* of all systems, structures, and incentives toward the school's objectives.

It all began with an unambiguous vision. As we described earlier, Mr. Dewitt's vision was that students would succeed on external benchmarks like state tests, SAT IIs, and APs . . . or else. Most schools we visited were what scholars have long described as loosely coupled systems, where the difficulty of monitoring teachers and the absence of a clear consensus on good practice meant that each teacher could, more or less, decide what his or her goals were and how to achieve them. No Excuses High was the opposite—crystal clear about goals, and equally unambiguous about how teachers would work within a hierarchical system that would show them exactly how they were expected to achieve those goals.

This detailed vision of what was expected from teachers was supported by a set of aligned structures and systems. At No Excuses High, the traditional subjects—math, science, English, and history—comprise the core part of each student's diet. Faculty are organized into departments, and the department chair is responsible for closely overseeing the work that his or her teachers undertake. A critical structural decision that Mr. Dewitt made when starting the school was to position these departmental chairs as key instructional leaders; they teach only two classes and use the rest of their time to observe and give feedback to newer teachers in their departments. "Even with my educational background, I was not going to be able to guide and lead and help make decisions [in every subject]," Mr. Dewitt says. "And so we decided if we really want alignment of the teachers and really want them to be developing, then we needed to do this department chair thing very aggressively."

One of the main responsibilities of department chairs is to develop common curricula, which the school sees as a key vehicle for making sure that classrooms are adequately rigorous and coherent across teachers. Accordingly, in each subject and grade level, an extremely detailed curriculum is created by the department chair and other experienced teachers, and is vetted and honed through use with actual students. As Mr. Dewitt says, "Once a curriculum is finished, it's pdf-ed. It's done. . . . We are happy with it." The development of such a curriculum aims to be what Seneca Rosenberg, in her study of Achievement First, calls a "safeguard": it seeks to ensure that what happens in a particular classroom matches the goals of the organization.[17]

In addition to developing curricula, department chairs are expected to oversee the learning of teachers in their areas. New teachers go through several days of summer training run by the instructional team at the network level; at this training they are introduced to the school's basic pedagogical approach and the set of strategies they are expected to use in the months and years to come. This induction experience is followed by weekly cycles of feedback. In a typical week, a novice teacher is observed by the department chair on Monday, debriefs that observation on Tuesday, and meets on Wednesday or Thursday to discuss lesson plans for the following week, drawing in part on feedback from the past week. Then on Sundays, all teachers who are not department chairs are required to send in the week's lesson plans by 2 p.m. to the department chair; they receive their plans back with comments and notes by 8 p.m. As Mr. Dewitt says, "We tell our teachers that the lesson plan has to be perfect." In addition, new instructors and department chairs often are assigned to the same room, which means that new teachers grade papers and prepare lessons at a desk in the back of the room while more experienced teachers in their subject areas are teaching, and, conversely, department chairs have informal opportunities to observe the novices in their charge.

The nature of this feedback process is also carefully structured and internally studied by the school. Feedback sessions are themselves videotaped and reviewed for ways to increase the efficacy of the feedback. When multifaceted problems are identified, they are broken into smaller parts so they can be worked on gradually. The sum total of these various processes means that teachers receive roughly twenty-five to thirty rounds of observation and feedback over the course of the year from experienced mentors who teach same-age students in the same subjects. The first- and second-year teachers who were part of this process almost uniformly described it as incredibly valuable. As Mr. Moriarty describes it, "Other schools of thought think that teaching is this thing that happens by osmosis. . . . We feel that you don't have time to waste and you can get better fast. Teaching isn't magic—at least not most of it. The way we do that is by codifying good teaching."

All of these features are part of what attracts teachers to the school. Teachers who had taught for a year or two in other schools really noticed the differences. One teacher who had taught for two years in rural North Carolina through Teach for America described the support at No Excuses High as one of the reasons for applying:

> Because of the professional development. My top goal was I wanted to become a good teacher. I felt like in my two years I was constantly failing. I didn't feel like I had developed . . . despite how hard I worked. And so, I was looking for a school that would help me achieve my potential. . . . [W]hen I heard about the development model here for teachers, [it] was way more ambitious than what other schools were promoting.

Selecting New Teachers

No Excuses High is distinctive not only for having remarkably organizationally coherent systems, but also for what happens inside these containers. The adults in the school, particularly the leadership, have strong standards for what constitutes rigorous learning, and it is the consistent application of those standards that enables them to enact their vision. One example: the school's teacher development processes, that is, how teachers are selected and coached.

Consider an interview with Mr. Henry, a prospective eleventh-grade history teacher. As is common at some private schools but rare in public school settings, all new teachers at No Excuses High have to teach a demonstration lesson. The lesson was observed by Mr. Allington, the history department chair, as well as by Mr. Dewitt.

Mr. Henry's lesson is divided into four parts, all focused on building understandings of the political and social dynamics of the United States during Reconstruction. In the first part, the "do now," he asked students to imagine that the ninth and tenth graders had tried to secede from the school but were unsuccessful. After getting some initial answers to this question, he moved to a factual set of questions about the period surrounding the Civil War and Reconstruction. Students could answer some of these factual questions and not others; Mr. Henry asked them to look up what they did not know in their textbook. In the third part of the lesson, Mr. Henry asked students to describe what they knew about Lincoln's and Johnson's Reconstruction plans and then to draw a Venn diagram with one circle for each man's plan.

After Mr. Henry finished, he, Mr. Allington, and Mr. Dewitt sit in the empty classroom for a lengthy debriefing.

MR. DEWITT: How did you think it went?

MR. HENRY: I was a little disappointed—didn't reach the thesis part, which came at the forty-minute mark. We didn't get to the comparison—the assessment was going to be a four-minute essay when they were going to write up each of Lincoln's and Johnson's plans and compare them.

MR. ALLINGTON: Why didn't you get to that point? If you could do it again, what would you do?

MR. HENRY: I would cut out the part about working with the categories without direction. Would have just gone straight from the brainstorm to the categories, rather than them making the categories. Also the direct instruction questions went on a little long. Maybe I could have cut off some of the student discussion and made it shorter.

MR. ALLINGTON: While we're on that topic of questioning with students— what were you listening for in student responses?

MR. HENRY: I wanted students to pull out the big questions—the superior question was going to be what do we do about freed slaves, punishing the South, and state / federal—those would have been the best answers. And they did get them.

MR. ALLINGTON: "What do we do with the slaves," one of the students said? That indicates some significant misunderstanding. That would have been a place for you to correct it or to let her correct it.

MR. HENRY: That's a good point—I wanted to hear something about slaves, so maybe I jumped on that too fast—you are right I should have corrected it.

MR. DEWITT: When you asked them central questions facing the nation at Reconstruction—it seemed big, but it didn't seem linked to part I. What was the payoff, why do that?

MR. HENRY: First the strips—then I wanted them to generate that knowledge without thinking about the categories. If we had talked about these big questions, they would have understood that these categories are related to the overall questions. Does that make sense?

MR. DEWITT: It makes sense if you get to the end product. But otherwise it feels like you are setting up the track and field and then not having the event.

MR. ALLINGTON: From the students' perspective, the question was what are we doing and where are we headed?

MR. DEWITT: Let's go back to Mr. Allington's question, knowing what we know now, if the goal is to get this big payoff in learning, and the ratio to be heavily on them. What I observed was a lot of moving the furniture around, and a lot of time to move things around, but not much payoff. So, if you were going to do it again, how would you do it differently?

MR. HENRY: I'm trying to bring Johnson and Lincoln into the lesson. These are pieces of the two men's plans—and then we are going to try to determine which goes into which category.

MR. DEWITT: They would ascertain that?

MR. HENRY: Yes, it's important for them to understand that Lincoln was pro freedmen's bureau.

MR. ALLINGTON: So that prior knowledge is important for the conclusion. They know nothing about Johnson; we haven't gotten to that yet. So if they know nothing, and you know they know nothing—how are you going to get to that point?

MR. HENRY: Fill in what you know about Lincoln. Then I'd lecture about Johnson.

MR. ALLINGTON: So perhaps they needed a short secondary reading.

MR. DEWITT: All I heard about Johnson was that he was a Southern slaveholder. And their knowledge about Lincoln is disparate. So the lesson itself is . . .

MR. ALLINGTON: Superficial.

MR. DEWITT: Which dooms the lesson to a level of superficiality. It needs to be seeded in something—in other schools we see lots of students just moving information around. What we've learned is that our students are capable of going deep, but it is entirely dependent on the circumstances we create.

MR. ALLINGTON: Trying to get to higher levels of interpretation, but they didn't get there. Moving information around.

In this excerpt, we see a number of aspects of what is distinctive about the No Excuses High approach. There is considerable attention to detail, as each part of the lesson is carefully probed and examined. There is no "hamburger" feedback (praise, critique, praise), but rather a deconstruction of what went wrong and forceful questioning about how to fix it. And there are real standards—watching what students know and can do, and trying to figure out how to help them get beyond the superficial and to the broader questions at stake.

Mr. Dewitt concludes the demonstration lesson with a final message to Mr. Henry about what it would look like to work at No Excuses High:

> Here, with the department chairs, we don't describe it as a mentoring program, which is why also the coach label in education circles, coach seemed to us too weak a term. We need our teachers to understand very clearly and I also need them not to either accidentally misunderstand or willfully misunderstand the relationship. . . . Mr. Allington is notorious for . . . finding himself in this situation, where the teacher doesn't understand that he is the decision maker.
>
> And so, I will have both of them [together] and I will say to the teacher, "You seem to misunderstand your relationship with Mr. Allington as your department chair. . . . [He is] giving you instructions that we expect everybody's going to follow. . . . That's not a suggestion."

Here we see the approach to hiring in a nutshell. Hiring is less about expertise than about malleability; they are looking for good young people who are eager to improve, open to feedback, and willing to learn the No Excuses High way.

Instructional Development

The school is confident that their young charges can be molded into good teachers through the instructional development process. We had a chance to observe some instructional sessions with practicing teachers, as well as to talk to both the department chair and the teacher who was being "developed." In one such pairing, between Mr. Allington, the history department chair, and a second-year history teacher, Mr. Cole, both described the ways in which the lessons shifted over the course of the year. They described three stages. Early in the year, they focused on what Mr. Allington called the "smallest lever we could fix." He started with how students should be organized as they entered the classroom:

> Here's a really good example: when students were coming into the classroom at the beginning of each class, there was often a lot of murmuring and side conversation of students who are slow to start that "do now" and get ready. And he couldn't figure out exactly how or why or what the problem was, and he was frustrated by it too. And the feedback I gave him was as simple as when they come in, you're not speaking, you're not intervening and working with students one-on-one yet. All you're doing for the first minute when they come in is you're standing in front of the room and observing them and just watching to see that everyone is sitting down, that they're silent, that the transition looks the way it wants—the way that you want it to.

From there, the next step was to focus on the instructional templates. Here, after trying a number of different strategies, Mr. Allington eventually decided that Mr. Cole was being overwhelmed with feedback in too many directions, and decided to narrow the focus to just repeating one instructional template. Part of the idea here was to reduce the cognitive load by focusing feedback on only one dimension. Mr. Cole describes what happened:

> I know I struggled at first. I know I was identified as one of the weakest teachers in school about a month in, particularly among the new teachers. Mr. Allington spent every day planning with me

and re-planning. We spent like probably a good hour and a half every day redoing the next day's lesson based upon that day's challenges and successes.

And then we realized by the month end that the students hadn't really—I wouldn't say hadn't learned anything, but they'd learned very little. They hadn't actually remembered much, they weren't able to recall anything in order to make some kind of statement. And so Mr. Allington identified that and tried to really simplify what I did in my class. So, I had the same structure in class every day, even if it was monotonous. We needed to make sure that the students were learning something.

So, we made what's called a standard history lesson. They were going to read for about 15 minutes, they're going to look at a document, and then they're going to answer some bigger question. And they're going to do that every day until you were able to get that done, and then we'll add more onto it. And so, although it may have been boring for students, it allowed me to focus on management, allowed me to focus on understanding the curriculum better, and so just really get control of the question and to make sure the students had been learning the basic facts about the earliest civilizations, for example, and then that way they could draw upon it once I had improved as a teacher.

By the end of the year, with Mr. Cole having gotten familiar with the standard history template, they were creating more variety in the lessons, and he was becoming more of a co-planner. As Mr. Allington describes it,

Now we are at the point in the year where the feedback I give in the discussions we have . . . [isn't] about getting students to come in and sit quietly and start the work. Now it's about, okay, 'What's the big idea? How can we—what's the best essential question to get at this idea? What's the best way we can organize this unit?' Now it's really content, it's about the actual content, it's about the actual curriculum, how we can improve it, how we can enrich it. So, the discussions have moved to a place that's a lot more intellectually stimulating for both of us, I think. And I think he feels pretty good about that at this point.

You can see in their description of their trajectory a number of elements that are characteristic of the No Excuses High approach, and parallel the school's vision of how students learn. The first is a view of how expertise develops, familiar from sports and the arts, which emphasizes working from part to whole: breaking down a large task into smaller elements. A second and related point that derives from a similar ethos is the importance of repetition and practice: the idea is that Mr. Cole would improve more by doing the same thing again and again than by cycling through different things. A third relates to comfort with hierarchy based on expertise; as emphasized earlier, Mr. Allington is clearly directing the operation and Mr. Cole is the novice. Finally, Mr. Allington seems to see no conflict between this view and a more expansive view of teaching—for example, the ultimate emphasis on organizing around essential questions—but he treats the more expansive tasks as something that develops slowly once one has mastered more basic parts of teaching.

A second instructional development interchange, between Mr. Tobbs, the English department chair, and Mr. Moriarty, the novice teacher described earlier, reveals a related set of dynamics. Mr. Tobbs's view of coaching strikes a balance between the need for systems and the need for teacher's individuality. He says that the risk of schools like No Excuses High is that teachers, particularly new teachers, think that they are supposed to be robots in a machine, whereas teaching requires some personal ownership to connect with kids. He says that Mr. Moriarty, for example, had a very "flat affect" initially, which was modeled on how Mr. Dewitt talks. But, Mr. Tobbs notes, Mr. Dewitt "when he's teaching, isn't like that all the time. He does weird things. He makes jokes or whatever. You can't be in a room with people, especially kids for hours every day, and be robotic." The challenge, then, is that teachers need to make the techniques work for them; to think otherwise, he adds, can be "a grave potential error in these kinds of 'no excuses' schools."

Consistent with this philosophy, Mr. Tobbs gave Mr. Moriarty extensive feedback, but also gave him some space to shape what he was learning. As Mr. Moriarty describes it:

> [Mr. Tobbs] has been very flexible in the sense of, yeah, this was my curriculum last year, but [you need to make your own decisions]. So the next year, I'm totally switching one book for the

next and just moving things around. And so he gives me that flexibility. But at the same time, he has been here for a number of years
and he also taught the course last year. So he's able to say, "All right.
You know. We need to focus on this." And he's taught me some
strategies to allow me to do that.

Between Mr. Tobbs and Mr. Moriarty, we see a coaching relationship that avoids either/ors and integrates multiple virtues. Mr. Tobbs
sees virtue in structures and systems, but also sees the importance of
ownership and individuality. He has the benefit of direct experience in
what Mr. Moriarty is teaching, but also recognizes the benefits of
letting Mr. Moriarty make adaptations. The result is that Mr. Tobbs
has the ability to advise and help Mr. Moriarty, but he is also taking
the longer view in wanting to give Mr. Moriarty a sense of ownership
over his work.

To be sure, not every coaching dyad was as effective as these two
pairings. There were situations where the mentee teachers felt that the
department chair was either not knowledgeable enough about content
or not as conscientious in giving feedback. But on the whole, it was clear
that much of the school's success could be attributed to the intensity of
the instructional development, which, on average, was much more frequent, detailed, and grounded in a clear vision of pedagogy than we saw
in other schools we visited.

A Fierce Culture

We struggled with which words to use to describe the nature of the enveloping systems, structures, and culture at No Excuses High. If we
called it "coherent" or "systemic" it implied a positive valence; if we said
it was like Foucault's "total institution" it would evoke a prison. The
truth was somewhere in the middle: the school's power derives in part
from a fierce culture in which both students and adults feel intense pressure to perform.

With respect to instructional development, for example, Mr. Dewitt
saw little value in the notion of "psychological safety" for learning. He
tells the story, for example, of a workshop that he and some of No Excuses High's staff attended, where the facilitators emphasized that mentors should never have an evaluative role. "Our question at the time

was, 'Well, why not?' Like, 'What is the big deal about this?'" Mr. De-witt says. Indeed, in his worldview, the job of the less experienced teacher is to do what the instructional developer says; giving this developer the job of evaluation is only natural since that person is the one who knows the work best. Again, there is a parallel here to the world of professional sports, where athletes are simultaneously coached and evaluated by their employers.

For the students as well, it is clear that behavioral compliance is a must. We saw an assembly where student videos were being projected on a big screen to say thanks to the operations staff. As we described it in our field notes:

> The room has a nice energy to it—kids are murmuring and chuckling at seeing one another on videos in front of the entire upper school. But then Mr. Dewitt gets up. "Track here," he says twice. "You are not being respectful," he adds, "and respect is one of our core values. I've already kicked out one ninth grader; you could be next. So we will listen quietly to the videos and then the choir will perform." The room looks hushed and cowed.

Similarly, we witnessed Mr. Dewitt admonishing a group of students for their behavior one day after lunch:

> We leave briefly to find another lunch spot, and failing to find one, we come back, and we discover that the principal is forcibly lecturing the ninth graders about their failings, particularly their not turning in homework and being late to class. I'm paraphrasing, but the general idea seems to be that you can choose to do something with your life or not, that there are people who are disciplined and move ahead in life and those who aren't who don't, and that they better shape up or they are going to face summer school. He says that he thinks that too few kids go to summer school as it is, and that he is ready to significantly increase the numbers, and that they shouldn't provoke him. A few teachers chime in with similar sentiments. The tone of this is fierce, and the kids are totally silent.

The teachers similarly described a culture where they knew that their jobs were on the line if they did not produce results on the interim assessments or if they crossed their department chairs. Mr. Dewitt was "your boss and not your friend," as one described it. Thus, while the coherence of the system was one part of what produced the school's results, for better or worse, the uncompromising force with which everyone was compelled to conform gave the system its backbone.

The Costs of Control

The same structural and cultural choices that produced high levels of consistency in teachers' practice across classrooms also came with significant tradeoffs. Below, we discuss three costs of the regimen of control. Because No Excuses High was such an aligned, mission-driven organization, these tradeoffs often ran in parallel for students and teachers, a parallelism that we have called symmetry.

Floors and Ceilings

One metaphor that became helpful in understanding No Excuses High was the idea of "floors" and "ceilings." We were introduced to this by a teacher whom we will call Ms. Carter, who had once worked at Dewey High and was now at No Excuses High. She began by praising the consistency of the "floors" at No Excuses High:

> At Dewey High a big problem I see is those kids sliding by and maybe the floor I feel was quite low. It's not too hard to pass by not doing very much. Here, I feel like the opposite is true. I feel like even those kids who are C, C minus students here are working extremely hard for those C's and C minuses. There is just no getting around the amount of work that every single student has to put in here. They cannot get around it. It's really unforgiving in every way.

At the same time, she saw limits to the approach:

> But I also feel that there's only so far the tests can push you. I mean the strongest students are not—they're gonna learn a lot of history by studying really hard for the AP U.S. History test, but there's a natural limit set by the test and by the College Board. . . . I

think that diminishes the importance of natural curiosity that is not driven by grades and the desire to do more and push yourself and explore.

Ms. Carter's concern that the highly controlled nature of No Excuses High was diminishing the intrinsic motivation and curiosity of students was shared by a number of other teachers. An English teacher noted, "We do control instruction so carefully that sometimes I worry that it doesn't provide enough opportunity for students to explore. I think our students sometimes don't have an intellectual curiosity, which to me can lead to higher-order thinking, or don't have the opportunity for intellectual curiosity, and that's definitely a challenge." As we will see, No Excuses High has become concerned with this "ceilings" problem in recent years; in particular, they have worried that the hyper-controlled learning they provide does not prepare students well for the more open-ended environment of college.

We saw a similar dynamic of "floors" and "ceilings" playing out in teachers' work. Teachers said that because of the extensive systems and structures, "It's nearly impossible to have a lesson that bombs," but it's also "more difficult to have an amazing lesson that inspires." Teachers developed a repertoire of lessons that fit within the No Excuses High prescribed direction, but had few opportunities to explore ideas that were of interest to them or to innovate. First- and second-year teachers greatly appreciated the level of infrastructure and guided feedback, but more experienced teachers often felt constrained by such high levels of direction. (Similarly, freshmen and sophomores were more positive about the school than juniors and seniors.) Structurally, No Excuses High's organizational structure offered only two roles—department chairs who developed and checked lesson plans and gave feedback, and teachers who were monitored and developed by those department chairs. That meant that "in between" faculty, for example, those who had a department chair in front of them who was not leaving, found themselves with few growth opportunities. In the year we did most of our research, many of the teachers who were leaving were in this middle group—no longer rookies, but with no space to move into instructional leadership roles.

Similarly, the school's view of teachers as essentially tabula rasa—blank slates awaiting No Excuses High's imprinting—held true for first-year teachers, but was not a good fit for certain more experienced ones. For example, one teacher came to the school after six years of teaching physics, chemistry, and math in three types of schools. She described her physics teaching at her previous school as somewhat more conceptually focused than at No Excuses High; also, with fewer pressures from tests, she facilitated more labs and spent less time working through calculations. Coming to No Excuses High, she adopted a hybrid style, squeezing in some labs amid a heavy dose of prep for the physics SAT II. She also described how not everything she wanted to do in physics fit within the standard lesson templates. Thus she faced a choice between changing her instruction, or writing lesson plans that conformed to the template and then changing them when teaching. Further complicating this dilemma was that some of her lessons were videotaped as part of the school's emphasis on documentation and accountability; she felt particular pressure to conform on taping days. She also had had some run-ins with the administration as she tried to consult with teachers across subject areas—which was not permitted in the strict vertical hierarchy of the school. When we spoke to her, she was planning to leave for a better opportunity at the end of the year.

A False Dichotomy between Rigor and Joy

Even for teachers who stayed, there were some persistent musings about the strengths and weaknesses of the model. We asked many of the teachers what the best day in their classroom would look like, and were surprised to find that their answers sounded much like those of teachers at any other school—they were looking for classrooms where students were energetic, engaged, and where the work was taking off without constant prodding. A concern that students were learning more about how to follow No Excuses High's directions than to take any joy in their learning troubled many of the teachers. Some asked whether we had come to the right place if we were searching for "deeper learning," which they themselves associated with more project- or problem-based curricula. As one longtime teacher described the dilemma:

> That tension is real. . . . I look at project-based learning schools. They seem like a ton of fun! I think one of the problems in education is that we've created this false dichotomy between rigor

and joy. . . . I do think that a school has to make choices—I wonder if closing the achievement gap means that you have to sacrifice exploration, discovery, or joy, and I don't buy that, but I think you have to solve the intellectual rigor of your work first.

Conversations with students affirmed this sense that they too saw the intensive work as necessary but not enjoyable. Many of them expressed appreciation for what No Excuses High was doing for them in the long run, but as one said, "No one actually likes it here."

A related point that many teachers made was the cost of not having deeper relationships with students:

> I think that No Excuses High is trying to get to a place where students feel more like humans than robots, and I think that that, in three to five years, [the school] needs to—it needs to continue to progress. They're trying to do that through the advisory system, but relationships are very professional at the school in a way that I think alienates some students from feeling truly part of the community that we are trying to build here. . . . I don't know exactly how to change that, given the demands of the school day, but creating some sort of emotional outlet for students would really, I think, benefit the number of students who are able to succeed all the way through.

Paralleling this concern for the students was a similar issue for the adults. A number of teachers reported struggling with the business-like approach to relationships, which precluded the building of adult friendships. In the words of one veteran teacher:

> I think that the typical twenty-something teacher also wants kind of a personal connection . . . we do need to think a little bit about how to support that, because they are looking for friendships in their workplace, and so just making sure that we can, you know, provide opportunity for those to grow and be productive. We are so centered on work sometimes and, you know, outcomes and student achievement and kind of like our purpose that sometimes, you know, we have to remember about how to take care of the adults, a little bit.

"Taking care of the adults" was not Mr. Dewitt's strong suit, as a number of teachers reported. Everyone at No Excuses High was working extremely hard: teachers consistently described working sixty, eighty, or even ninety hours a week, including coming in for long days on Saturdays, staying up very late, or getting up very early. Teachers described the work-life balance as "horrible" and/or nonexistent. In such an environment, teachers craved appreciation for their efforts, but said that the culture was so focused on problems and improvement that there was little time to celebrate the positive. One teacher said that No Excuses High was very much a "glass-half-empty" place:

> We're always looking at what's wrong and not frequently enough interested in being proud of what's right. I mean we talk about numbers, we talk about our performance in comparison to other schools with a lot of pride, and we speak in generalities about how amazing our teachers are, but it doesn't get to the personal level enough.

The absence of appreciation and community had real costs when it came to retaining staff. One very strong science teacher was leaving, in part, she said, because when she had been approached by other schools with leadership opportunities, No Excuses High had done nothing to show that it valued her. Teachers who were staying on suggested that this lack of appreciation was really costing the school when it came to retaining their strongest teachers. As one of them told us in an interview:

> We had a goodbye party yesterday for teachers who are leaving, and it was kind of like a funeral. I think everyone feels at a funeral, "Man, why don't we ever show appreciation to people when they're alive and say the best things about them when they're dead?" And we said the nicest things about teachers who are leaving, and I can guarantee that if we had said that stuff to them all along, three-quarters of them wouldn't be leaving.

Much as the school's joyless culture and absence of strong relationships contributed to significant student attrition, it similarly led teachers to continue their careers elsewhere.

Race and Bridging the School-Community Gap

A similar theme emerged in discussions with faculty members about the disconnect between the largely white staff and the largely African American community. Most faculty members lived outside the highly depressed urban area in which the school is located, and frequently felt that they were largely cut off from the community in which they were teaching and in which their students were being raised. Here one young history teacher describes his reaction to seeing parents at graduation:

> I was reminded of that at graduation last night, and you see parents who are acting in a way that's drastically different than how students and teachers act here, and just a reminder like kids are leaving a certain atmosphere and are coming here and they act in a completely different way. [When I taught in] North Carolina, you could see the connection between home and school, which I think is very good for learning. I think it promotes a healthy and productive learning environment, but I definitely don't feel like I could speak to a student's real character besides in an academic way.

Critics have been increasingly vociferous that no-excuses schools' racial stance—largely white teachers telling largely black and brown students that they need to conform to (white) middle-class norms if they want to get ahead—is problematic and rooted in deficit assumptions about black and Latinx communities.[18] Some within the school were beginning to reach the same conclusions. Mr. Tobbs, the veteran English teacher, who is white, forcefully argued that the school needs to adopt a more open stance toward the community it is based in:

> I think that the school needs to become more embedded in the community. And what I mean by that is it's—it is technically now here and obviously our kids are all from [the local city] and—but we need . . . the kind of relationship you have with an old friend or something, or you know, like a long-term friendship. The city—and the school needs that with the city, and right now it doesn't have it for two reasons. One, it's relatively young still. Two, there's no connection between the staff and the city. There's this like iron curtain up sometimes between us and parents.

Mr. Tobbs continued that acknowledging racial differences with his own students had been important in beginning to bridge that divide:

> I know for me, there was a big change in my sort of presence as a teacher when I acknowledged that to myself and acknowledged to students that I'm white and they're black. . . . I think schools need to train more in that issue, particularly because we seem to be only getting young, moderately wealthy white kids like myself, to teach.

Much like teachers had questioned what they felt was a false dichotomy regarding rigorous academics and students' joy for learning, they were also seeking to integrate the community and the school, to push forward academically but also to know their students.

Learning and Unlearning: Seeking Organizational Change

If we had ended this chapter after our time at No Excuses High in 2012, this would have been the whole story. In short, we would have reported about a well-developed organization that was taking very ambitious measures to shape the lives and practices of both its teachers and its students, following a model that has produced considerable achievements intertwined with significant tradeoffs. We would have explained that No Excuses High engaged mostly in what Chris Argyris famously called "single-loop learning," drawing on other no-excuses schools to improve its practices but not fundamentally questioning the core assumptions of its model.[19]

In the years since we first spent time at No Excuses High, however, the administration has been grappling with the shortcomings of its model. This effort has been prompted by several sources. First, and most important, there is the experience of their graduates in college. Like many similar schools, No Excuses High was having more success at getting their students *to* college then in getting them *through* college. Reports from the school's graduates suggested that they were academically prepared but that many were having considerable trouble navigating the open-ended environment of college.[20] This fact, more than any other, was driving the leaders of No Excuses High to rethink some of their practices. Second, the broader school-reform conversation was shifting in the direction of "deeper learning." Achievement First, a similar charter management organization, had partnered with the industrial design firm IDEO to design a new school model that they hoped would redefine their vision of schooling for the future. The air was rife with talk of twenty-first-century skills—collaboration, creativity, and innovation—raising the question of how these older school models could meet this challenge. Third, leaders at No Excuses High told us that our work had added fuel to the fire for them. We had published some shorter versions of our analysis, and, as Mr. Dewitt told us, "You were the only people who took us seriously and didn't just ideologically dismiss us, but still posed a critique. That was new for us."[21] In particular, that they were helping all of their students to reach floors but weren't creating opportunities for them to reach for ceilings was a galvanizing problem that they hoped to address. Finally, as all of this was happening, the racial awakening created by highly visible incidents of police shootings of unarmed black men and the subsequent Black Lives Matter movement began to infiltrate the language and thinking of No Excuses High.

As a result, No Excuses High spent some significant time venturing outside of no-excuses networks to look at other school models, including the school we call here "Dewey High," as well as a number of other high-profile schools that espouse more progressive visions of instruction. In the fall of 2015, one of the teachers who had been at the school the longest, Mr. Tobbs, was given the school's first-ever sabbatical to study deeper learning. Mr. Tobbs conducted his own tour of schools, read widely, and took a bus each week to Cambridge to take the course on deeper learning that we teach at the Harvard Graduate School of Education.

When we returned to No Excuses High in the spring of 2016, there was evidence of significant shifts. Two hours a week are now devoted to "project time," when all students are required to work on a project of their own choosing. Projects include making short films, studying and writing poetry, organizing an LBGTQ awareness day, and designing houses using cardboard box dioramas. Building on his sabbatical experience, Mr. Tobbs was given the freedom to organize his seniors to develop lengthy research projects and presentations on topics of their choosing, such as social media addiction and the history of hip hop. The school now partners with Project Lead the Way, a university-based group that offers a hands-on engineering program.[22] About a third of high school students are now choosing engineering as an elective because of the new program. Another initiative is a partnership with a local university whereby some of the school's seniors spend one afternoon a week working in college labs. The school also developed some of its extracurricular spaces as promising platforms for deep learning: the debate team, led by an experienced and highly skilled coach, was an activity the school saw as potentially combining the learning of debate techniques with student advocacy for causes they were passionate about; the literary magazine, led by a beloved English teacher, was similarly seen as a well-developed vehicle for capturing students' thinking while simultaneously training them in different genres of writing. The school was adding electives the following year in African American literature and Latin American history, electives that pre-enrollment numbers suggested were going to be highly popular with the school's population of black and Latinx students, who were eager for material outside of the traditional canon.

These shifts in curriculum have led to some shifts in hiring. Much as Dewey High sought to hire people who were knowledgeable and passionate about something and let them convey that enthusiasm to students, No Excuses High was finding that working in a different mode required hiring different people. The African American literature and Latin American studies courses will be taught by a former Ivy League university instructor who has recently come to the school; the courses will be modeled on those he had been teaching at the college level. The debate coach is himself a highly experienced debater; the journalism teacher had been editor of his college paper. To do more of this kind of work, Mr. Dewitt ruminated, would mean that they would need to find a different pool of people; their usual corps of highly malleable Teach for America graduates did not, for the most part, have the kind of experiences they would need to apprentice students into different fields.

Interviews with students suggested that the partial shift toward the project-based model had many of the same benefits as found at Dewey High. In particular, students appreciated not only the chance to choose their own topics, but also the trust and independence that came with being put in charge of their own learning. "I felt like this was the most adult feeling since I came to No Excuses High because I felt like we get babied a lot," said one student. "I just had to research everything on my own, I had to research the sources. I had to figure out what were the most important key points that I needed to pull out. I had to find an expert on my own, like who to talk to. So I felt that was just very adult . . . it was a very adult feeling, because it wasn't like everything is basically prepared for us." Students also said that they learned more from their peers than they did from teachers. As one student said, "I feel like it was different than most of our other classes because it was more hands-on, like we were the teachers instead of someone in the classroom teaching us. We learned from our peers. And I felt like that's what you should do when you really want to learn something, like we were responsible for our own education."

Our observations of student-led presentations in Mr. Tobbs's class supported this contention; students were highly engaged in their peers' presentations, responding quickly and enthusiastically when asked to identify contemporary songs or discuss the nature of social media addiction. Students also appreciated the chance to have their own interests recognized; one of the most powerful parts of the projects, several students reported, was that they got to share something they were passionate about with their peers. The students who had organized the LGBTQ awareness and support day said that they felt empowered to take an issue that mattered to them and try to influence the views of their peers. If the goal of the projects was to move closer to the identity and creativity parts of the deeper learning triangle, the interviews with students suggested that they felt this had been accomplished.

The projects also helped to break down the walls between the school and its outside environs. Students in Mr. Tobbs's class, for example, had to interview a real-world expert on their topic. They emailed and made phone appointments with college professors, music producers, journalists, and other professionals. Students described these interactions as a powerful part of the process. Much as at Dewey High, breaking down the walls between school and the world made the subjects more authentic to students, who were exposed to the perspectives of people who had spent years thinking and working in the arenas they were studying. Students also found it profoundly affirming that high-status people in the real world, like college professors, would respond to their emails and treat their interrogations as worthy of respect.

At the same time, Mr. Tobbs told us that he was worried that increases in agency and engagement were coming at the expense of rigor.

The social media presentation, for example, involved a mixture of statistics and videos drawn from the Internet, some participatory questions for the audience, a thesis about the problem, and a short discussion around the thesis. Mr. Tobbs said that he worried that the presentations were too much like a "really dynamic dinner party conversation"—someone throws out a provocative thesis and everyone adds a bit of what they know, but it doesn't really go anywhere. Judged by Bloom's taxonomy, we would agree: while some of the information presented was interesting, the level of analysis, both by the presenters and in the discussion, was fairly superficial. In particular, much of the information was presented without scrutiny of the statistics and of how they were derived; and the thesis statements took fairly simple positions—"social media is harmful; hip hop is derogatory whereas R & B was celebratory"—that masked complex underlying debates. More generally, if, as Dewey said, education is about linking the tree of knowledge in students' heads with the tree of knowledge that exists in the world, these presentations were tilted more toward bringing out students' existing knowledge and interests than toward using that spark to lead them to broader bodies of knowledge.

Interviews with the students affirmed this assessment. They thought that their presentations were not as strong as some of their other academic work, but they ascribed this having no previous experiences in the genre. We do everything else over and over, they said, and so we get better at it; this was our first time doing this kind of work, so naturally it wasn't as good as it could have been. But, they asked, why is this something we are only doing senior year, when school is almost over, rather than a core part of our educational diet from the beginning?

The Unlearning Challenge

We posed this question to Mr. Dewitt and to everyone else we talked to on the faculty. With one important exception, which we will discuss later, the steps that No Excuses High has taken to incorporate a different approach to learning have been *around* rather than *inside* their core disciplinary classes (what we describe in a later chapter as the *periphery* rather than the *core*). In particular, they have used electives to offer the new courses in engineering, African American literature, and Latin American history; they have used extracurriculars to encourage journalism, literary writing, and debate; they have used the period after seniors' college applications are in to let Mr. Tobbs develop student-driven presentations; and they have devoted two hours per week to developing projects. What they have not done is make many changes to their core disciplinary classes: most of the time, students still do lessons organized by the guided practice template; carefully subdivided chunks of time are still used to build proficiency in disciplinary content. Moreover, this "core" is where the school's emphasis continues to lie; teachers told us that there were few incentives to do well on the projects and they result in little feedback or professional development.

Why has more significant change proven so difficult? In short, we see the school as caught between competing sets of commitments: an older set, around which their structures are organized and which is embedded in their culture, identity, and epistemology; and a newer set, which would require undoing structures, rethinking their core identity and commitments, and risking the external markers on which much of their success and credibility rests.

The heart of the school's success rests on two structural elements: compelling student effort through use of timers, detention, homework bins, and other devices; and overseeing faculty work through lesson plans and extensive teacher feedback, mechanisms that together ensure department chairs and other instructional leaders retain tight control of daily instruction. Recently, the school has been charged with developing lesson plans for the other high schools in the charter network with which it is affiliated. In light of this reality, there is little appetite for redoing years' worth of curriculum and lesson planning, and, even if there were, the expectation to produce lessons not just for their own school but also for others would interfere. There are considerable sunk costs in what they have built to date, and making changes would require building something anew. Mr. Dewitt's response when we asked about shifting to the International Baccalaureate Program helps to illuminate this reality. "We have a lot to lose by not exploiting what we know works," he said.

A second barrier to change is the importance of existing external markers that affirm the school's quality. As Mr. Dewitt describes it, "I need the students to be taken seriously by outside observers, by outside evaluators, like admissions committees. So, a school in [No Excuses High's highly depressed home city]—unless we're riding on our reputation, which is not anything with admissions counselors who are one or two years out of college, who never heard of us, all they see is we're from [city]—we got to have credentials, we got to have like bona fide stuff we can point to." As we have seen, the school has aced such external metrics as AP exams, SAT IIs, and state tests; deemphasizing those tests risks much of what the school has achieved. That there is not a similar set of external mechanisms for judging the quality of project-based learning or other forms of inquiry-directed instruction means that the school would have no foundation from which it could anchor its instructional program, nor would it have a way to demonstrate the quality of its students' work to those outside the school.

In addition to these structural barriers and external incentives, the most fundamental obstacle to change is that giving students more agency would threaten core aspects of the school's values and commitments. If one vision of deeper learning is to give students more ability to direct their own learning, to assume greater agency, and to have opportunities to fail, the school was deeply conflicted about such a shift. This question was particularly salient in the context of readying students for the more open-ended environment of college. Consider the words of Mr. Allington, the history department chair, who is one of the school's longest tenured teachers:

> One of the things we definitely grapple with is sort of that gradual release of responsibilities and ownership for students. I mean that to me, that's probably the last step if you're talking about college readiness, right? There's not going to be anyone hovering over you to make sure you get your research paper done. . . . You want them to be college-ready, they need to have room to fail, but at the same time you can't allow them to fail because you're not doing the work of closing the achievement gap if you do that. So, where's the happy medium there, like figuring out exactly what that looks like? And a lot of the work we've done with college-readiness skills, and you know, the lesson plan types and all of that has been kind of geared towards addressing that concern, but [I] don't know if we're 100 percent there yet, probably not.

A similar view was voiced by Ms. Carter, the teacher who had moved from Dewey High to No Excuses High, who reflected, "Even if we loosen those surface level structures, we are not going to let them fail. In college, they very well could fail. So I think it's important to let them semi-fail in a place that's not going to let them completely fail before they completely fail in a less supportive environment."

These comments illuminate the dilemma that faces No Excuses High as it considers moving toward more open-ended learning. At one level, the school's teachers and leaders are aware that students will need to take more responsibility for their own learning if they are going to succeed in college; at a more fundamental level, however, they worry that giving students more rope risks letting them fail to learn key content. Hence, moving in the direction of more student-directed learning potentially threatens core aspects of the school's raison d'être.

A similar dilemma exists at the teacher level. In theory, giving teachers greater ownership of their lessons would make them feel more invested in their work, which in turn would make them, especially experienced teachers, more likely to stay. At the same time, however, allowing teachers to make revisions to lessons potentially compromises the school's consistent level of rigor. An experienced history teacher describes this conundrum: "We've talked a lot about creating safe places for students to fail and to take risks. I don't think it is there for teachers. . . . Failures amongst teachers become very public." This veteran went on to say that what was routinely assessed for teachers was student progress on interim assessments, state tests, SAT IIs, and Advanced Placement tests, and in such a climate, success is expected and failure is not tolerated.

For Ms. Carter, who moved from Dewey High to No Excuses High, the contrast was stark.

> At Dewey High, they were okay with me trying something and it failing. When you're doing a project or an inquiry-based lesson and something is just a little bit messy . . . no matter how much time you spend planning, there's some non-trivial probability that it is going to fail, that the students are not going to learn, that there's going to be some disaster that the experiment doesn't work, whatever it is. Here, there's not that forgiveness. There's this sense of urgency that you don't have time for a bad lesson. . . . Here it's different. I mean I think there's intentionally a little bit of the culture of fear. At the beginning of the year, before I knew any

better, I was always afraid that if I gave a bad lesson, I was gonna get fired. I think that's a little bit my paranoia, but there was definitely a little bit of that.

The absence of this room for experimentation is not a coincidence; it is baked into Mr. Dewitt's vision of the school and his hierarchical view of expertise. In his view, only a few senior people should be innovating; the rest should be implementing their innovations:

> Our metaphor is kind of like the nation and a frontier. We only have some people on the frontier and they're the ones who should be exploring, and the other ones should be building the country. So, teachers like [Mr. Allington] we want on the frontier exploring the new fringes, and then everybody else we want in the building.

What Mr. Dewitt refers to here is equivalent to what organizational theorists Michael Tushman and Charles O'Reilly call the "ambidextrous organization," a descriptor of organizations that simultaneously seek to meet the challenges of the present while designating subunits to plan for the future. Work in this vein has emphasized how difficult it is to become an ambidextrous organization, in particular because the cultural and structural requirements of "exploration"—discovering new possibilities—are very different from what is needed for "exploitation"— getting more people to do what is already known. As Justin Jansen and colleagues describe it, "Exploration and exploitation require fundamentally different and inconsistent architectures and competencies that create paradoxical challenges. Whereas exploration has been associated with flexibility, decentralization, and loose cultures, exploitation has been related to efficiency, centralization, and tight cultures."[23] From this perspective, No Excuses High is fundamentally organized to promote exploitation, and thus creating significant innovation within its current structure is a particular challenge.

The College Challenge: Innovation Within Existing Grooves

All of these questions came to a head around the question of what it would take to help students succeed in college. Interviews that the school conducted with their alumni suggested that the problem was less in academic preparation than in dealing with the more general shift that came with moving to an open-ended college environment. Ms. Whitman, who was the guidance counselor during our first research trip in 2012, characterized the challenge for its students this way, "They need to learn time management, how to advocate for yourself, work in study groups, and lead your peers in discussion." The current guidance counselor, Mr. Pickford, describes the challenges similarly:

> I think our students struggle with becoming the drivers of their learning more than anything because when they are here, they are in really intentional—intentionally planned classes, right? Their teachers are super intentional with every move that they make in terms of their lesson planning, in terms of how they teach the content. And so, when they get into a classroom setting where they're not being given as much structure, they suddenly start to realize they have to change their practices, they have to spend more time studying, forming study groups, leveraging their peers more.

Mr. Dewitt describes the impetus for some of the recent changes that No Excuses High has made:

> The impetus was that all we did was guided practice. It's, "You know, here's what we want you to do, let's do it together. Now, you do it, I'm going to monitor you." And we would do that over, and over, and over again because it was very effective in teaching discrete skills and content. But it wasn't representative of what our alumni were telling us they were encountering in college. And so, our alumni are so unprepared for college, and you name it, they are unprepared in that way. So, in addition to all the race stuff, and leaving [their home city], and feeling unprepared, and entering a society which doesn't look like theirs, and overt racism, on top of it then, they came from a very controlling high school which gave them no choices and didn't prepare them to make choices, didn't even let them not do their homework to face that consequence, and didn't prepare them for college lectures, didn't prepare them for shitty college instruction, which is the vast majority of what's going on in colleges.

In response to these challenges, No Excuses High has made some adjustments. One was to extend into college the kind of enveloping support it had provided for students in high school. The school had counselors call students to ask them how they were faring in college and what they were struggling with, and to encourage them to go to office hours and seek out on-campus resources like writing centers and student support offices. Belying its strict image, the school also sent care packages to students during finals, including, as one alum told us, "candy, popcorn, lipsticks, lotions, toothbrush, like all of that. And it was just really good, and the feeling was like 'Oh, No Excuses High is still thinking about us.'"

A more substantial change was the development of two new lesson templates: "college lecture" and "student seminar." These templates deliberately mapped onto two of the largest academic challenges that students reported facing in college. College lecture is a template in which teachers show students how to take notes on longer lectures, including how to spot the main ideas and how to organize their notes. Mr. Dewitt notes, ruefully, that this has been hard for the teachers because it requires them to stop their usual practice of frequently checking for understanding, and to move toward a model of delivery with no regard for whether what is being delivered is being understood.

Student seminar, as the name implies, is a template in which students are expected to discuss a text or a question, responding and building on each other's comments. As would be expected, this template was developed by a few of No Excuses High's most experienced teachers and includes a detailed rubric that specifies how students are expected to talk. Seminars have been videotaped and presented to students as models. In several seminars we saw, students were asked to evaluate the quality of the comments that the class had made and to think about steps for improvement. All of these strategies were refined as leaders and teachers tried to build their own best version of the student seminar.

The student seminars were popular with teachers and students because they provided a break from the guided practice template and gave students a chance to interact with each other. At the same time, the emphasis on objective-driven learning did constrain some of the potentially free-flowing discussion that one might think of as constitutive of this mode of learning. As Ms. Kilroy describes it,

I do think that we still think there's kind of a right answer, you know, when I do a student seminar and it's supposed to sort of predict all the possible answers that students could come up with. In my lesson plans, I should script out my questions and all the possible answers that students should potentially come to with those, and there's not really room for questions that I don't have answers to.

The reasons for these choices come directly from Mr. Dewitt's vision of learning, and the dangers he sees of freelancing on the part of both students and teachers. As he says, "We don't want our lesson templates to be interpreted in thirty-one different ways or twenty-eight different ways by our teachers. That will be a disaster. We're trying to avoid the wishy-washy outcomes and have it be specific."

Thus we see in No Excuses High's response to the college challenge a set of choices that is consistent with its overall value orientation. In particular, while they adopted the idea of a college seminar, they did so in a way that was highly structured and pre-planned, thus making the "college seminar" more like a No Excuses High class than an actual college seminar. The school also maintained tight control of the change process, with a small number of people innovating and a larger group executing these lessons. In ways big and small, the response to this challenge was very much within the contours of the school's overall approach, values, and epistemology.

No Excuses and Deeper Learning?

How should we assess No Excuses High? In a nutshell, what we observed is that the school and its feeder middle school have taken students who lack dominant social and cultural capital, and, through intensive regimes of behavioral control and controlled courses of study, enabled those students who stay at the school to acquire knowledge and skill in disciplinary subjects. As measured by a range of external assessments, including state tests, AP exams, and the PISA, students do very well, outpacing many from more affluent suburbs on these exams. At the same time, the school's design choices come with corresponding tradeoffs—students report little intrinsic interest in their studies, many choose to leave the school, and those who graduate report being prepared academically but often unprepared psychologically to deal with the open-ended nature of college and adult life.

Put another way, the school has, through an extensive set of processes, created a certain "floor" of achievement for all of its students, but these same systems have constrained their "ceilings." In particular, centralized lesson planning and micro-timed lessons are effective in making sure that students acquire particular pieces of knowledge, but are less well suited to the sustained and open-ended explorations that deeper inquiry often requires. At its best, we might compare what the school does to the early stages of learning a classical instrument—since successful music students often begin their learning in small chunks, with repetition and discipline guiding their learning habits and structuring the learning process. At its worst, we might say that what happens in the school is a poor facsimile of what actually happens in the disciplines—in part because of the limits imposed by the external assessments but also in large part because of the school's instructional model, since students, for example, learn about what professional historians and biologists have done rather than themselves learning to engage in the messy and uncertain explorations that are characteristic of doing history and biology.

We see a symmetrical pattern for teachers. Teachers at the beginning of their careers find the scaffolded approach to instructional development immensely rewarding and appreciate its intentionality. More experienced teachers, or teachers with contrasting philosophies, are less enthusiastic; many wish there were more opportunities for them to share ideas and to develop new types of lessons. The result: few lessons that do not meet a minimum standard, but also few lessons that really fly. In many ways, these contrasts are a mirror image of what we saw at Dewey High, where there were a number of examples of truly exceptional work, but not a floor, for all students, of foundational knowledge and skill.

Part of the challenge is that the school's systems and structures are targeted at first- and second-year teachers who have been the organization's bread and butter. Like many other no-excuses schools, No Excuses High is staffed primarily by very young teachers working very long hours. It is an open question whether, if the school created a more positive and sustainable adult culture and more opportunities for adult growth, it could retain more of its teachers or recruit more experienced teachers. As the model currently stands, systems and structures that are set up to train young teachers often burn them out, which, in a self-fulfilling prophecy, requires more young teachers, which makes it hard to change the structures.[24]

No Excuses High is aware of some these tradeoffs and has worked to address them. With respect to raising the ceilings for students, in particular, it has made significant changes in the elective and extracurricular arenas to give students opportunities to do more extended work and to give teachers more flexibility to teach subjects they are passionate about. But these changes have not yet penetrated core instruction, because the school is afraid to risk what it has achieved, because it has huge sunk costs poured into its existing lessons and structures, and because it is unclear how to externally assess other modes of learning. There is a central tension between the school leaders' desire to close achievement gaps using methods of control it thinks are necessary, and the goal of giving students more open-ended and student-directed experiences. This tension limits the scope of the experimentation the school is willing to try. Thus, the school has made significant progress toward the mastery end of the deeper learning triangle, but has done so at the expense of identity and creativity. It is the mirror image of Dewey High: both can point to considerable accomplishments; both are still searching for the sweet spot. Achieving this integration would require undoing as much as adding; the unwillingness to change what has gotten them as far as they have limits their ability to reach the next level of work.

We began this chapter with David Cohen's admonition that a look at those Eastern countries that top the PISA rankings might suggest there is more than one route to deeper learning. As it happens, while we were working on this chapter, one of us, Mehta, was given an opportunity to conduct a site visit to Shanghai as part of an international educational summit. As classes unfolded with the help of a translator, the scene looked remarkably familiar. In one upper elementary math class, for example, students were sitting in groups of four, facing forward, with the teacher at the front of the room. Attention was complete—every student was focused on the task. The task itself was a fairly difficult one—students were being asked about different ways of bisecting a rectangle—but it was split into parts. As each part was introduced, students were asked to work on it, first individually, then in their fours, and then in front of the whole class. One part did not give way to the next until it was clear that everyone had done the previous part. The class proceeded in this way—teacher-directed but with students doing most of the mental work—for an hour, at which point homework that built on the work from the day was distributed.

The parallels to what we had seen in No Excuses High were considerable. The core values and the core practices were similar. With respect to values, there was respect for adult authority and a strong belief that carefully designed teacher-directed lessons were the surest way to produce consistent learning. In terms of practice, both systems were organized around a set of external exams that governed much of what happened inside the schools. Both had high levels of behavioral control and thus high levels of time on task—in No Excuses High's case, produced by their systems of detentions and consequences, and in Shanghai's case, produced by parental pressure, Confucian culture, and, for older students, college entrance exams. The results, in both cases, were students who, over time, accumulated considerable amounts of disciplinary knowledge, which enabled them to fare well on international assessments, including the PISA.

At the same time, teachers, administrators, and ministry officials we talked with in Shanghai were struggling with many of the same challenges that we saw at No Excuses High. While the American contingent had come to find out how Shanghai topped the PISA, many of the Shanghai members grilled the Americans about how they promoted independent thinking and creativity. In particular, Shanghai teachers and administrators were worried that their students and parents were too fixated on the external exams, and were frustrated at their inability to cultivate more intrinsic interest in learning and more independent thinking. But, again similar to No Excuses High, while they had formed working groups on twenty-first-century skills and had introduced some electives that moved in this direction, they were unwilling to make core changes to their basic patterns of instruction or to the external assessments around which their system is oriented. For them as well, unlearning and undoing may be critical if they want to move from their current strengths to becoming the kind of schools they aspire to be.

Ironically, in Shanghai a number of our interviewees told us that many of the most interesting and creative schools were ones where the external exams were not the be all and end all. These were either private schools, public schools that served students who were so advantaged or skilled that they were likely to do well on the exams in any case, or public schools where the leader had publicly argued that lower exam scores were worth it in order to produce well-rounded human beings. This observation carries distinct parallels to the United States, where many of the best schools also in one way or another stay outside of or transcend the dominant system—either as private schools, highly advantaged public schools, or schools with leaders possessing unusual courage of their convictions.

The problem, of course, is that while these particular schools are good for their students, without systemic guidance and support it seems unlikely that there will be very many of them or that they will be sustained over time. Could there be a system of schools that creates clear external guidance and expectations, but does so in a way that is more oriented toward deeper learning? International Baccalaureate aspires to be that system; we turn to it next.

4 ∾

International Baccalaureate: A System for Deeper Learning?

WITH THE WINTER solstice rapidly approaching, the morning sunlight that filters through the windows of Ms. Walsh's classroom is weak and almost gray. Outside, the scrubby conifers that surround the south campus of IB High (a pseudonym) brace and bend in a frigid coastal wind. Only three days remain until winter vacation; as a result, conversations in the faculty room and cafeteria are about holiday plans and the possibility of an upcoming snowstorm rather than about what is happening in classrooms.

As the twenty mixed-ability juniors in Ms. Walsh's "Theory of Knowledge I" course take their seats, however, the energy in the room feels studious and focused. Several students open laptops and read over the comments that Ms. Walsh has added to their in-progress essay drafts. Others pull up their outlines and commiserate about their writing woes. This is their first attempt at producing the kind of essay that they will write at the end of next year when they sit for the International Baccalaureate Theory of Knowledge exam, and for many it is a daunting task. In line with the heady content of the course, the two essay prompts ask, "Are some ways of knowledge more or less likely to lead to truth?" and "Can a machine know?" To respond to these questions, students must explore and evaluate the four "ways of knowing" that they have studied in the course thus far: sense perception, imagination, memory, and intuition.

Without apparent prompting, the students quiet down to allow Ms. Walsh to address them. She is dressed casually, in jeans and a sweater, and she opens the class informally. "I see little fingers communicating in the

Google doc," she says. "If you opened your essay and you saw so much blue, don't panic! We're on the same team, I promise. I'm just trying to make you better thinkers and writers." She flashes an encouraging smile at her students. Her fluid movements and deep voice seem to belong as much on the athletic field as in the classroom—not surprising given that she has doubled as a coach for most of her twenty-year teaching career.

As Ms. Walsh continues talking, her language too seems to take on a coaching stance. She reminds students that they should think of this essay as "the ToK season opener": an important effort to make use of what they have learned, but also a task that is more about growth than about "getting it right." After clarifying a few questions, she prompts the students to get to work. "I don't want to talk too much," she says. "This is your time."

The students turn their attention to their essays. Some of them move their desks into loose clusters so they can consult with their peers as they work. As with many of the classes at IB High, the ethos of the room is simultaneously studious and relaxed; students stay focused on their work but do so in a variety of ways: by listening to music on headphones as they write, by "chatting" back and forth on Google documents, or by bouncing ideas off their peers. Ms. Walsh moves easily around the room, conferring in a low voice with individuals and clusters. Sometimes she mainly listens and asks questions; other times she makes suggestions or posits counter-claims in order to push her students' thinking. The room fills with a productive hum.

In a corner near the windows, two students—Daniel and Nancy—pause from their own work to help their friend Sydney as she puzzles through her response to the second essay prompt: "Can a machine know?" Sydney, a dark-haired white student wearing army pants and a long-sleeved cotton shirt, says that in her mind she has substituted the word "computer" for the word "machine" because it helps her to make the question more concrete. Yet although she spent time at home before class brainstorming, she is still having trouble articulating her thesis statement. As the three of them talk things through, Ms. Walsh joins them to listen and help.

DANIEL: "Can a computer know? I mean, I guess computers do memory very, very well, but humans can only remember a very small sequence of numbers. But I'm like 100 percent certain that they can't feel like we do. I guess that they can remember keystrokes, though? Does that count as memory?"

SYDNEY (PAUSES BEFORE SHE RESPONDS): "I guess. But if you have a computer, it doesn't remember it was dropped—it only has memories that we programmed into it."

MS. WALSH: "Hmmm. But with artificial intelligence, it learns from its experiences." She looks at Sydney with an expression that hovers between encouragement and challenge.

SYDNEY: "But computers don't have experiences, not like we do."

NANCY: "So what are you arguing?"

SYDNEY: "I guess that it depends . . ."

MS. WALSH: "How does it depend?"

SYDNEY: "It depends because human beings are conscious thinkers, and machines are not. We can make sense of what we're experiencing, we can put two ideas together—machines can't do that."

Ms. Walsh breaks into a wide smile. "Ding ding ding! Now you're starting to get somewhere. Now stop talking and try to get your ideas on paper."

Sydney returns the smile but continues to look slightly anxious. As she starts to type, she says, "This class makes my brain hurt."

Brief as it is, this conversation epitomizes the quality of deep cognitive engagement that Ms. Walsh's Theory of Knowledge course supports students in developing. Invited for the first time into the world of epistemology, students grapple with content that is deliberately abstract, in order to consider a range of issues that relate to the course's overarching essential question: "How do we know what we know?" Along the way, they learn to think across disciplinary boundaries, to engage with and critique each other's logic, and to construct multidimensional arguments. Ms. Walsh serves as a guide in the process, breaking down complex concepts into component parts, encouraging students to steer into perplexity, and, as she does with Sydney, modeling the kinds of "thinking moves" that enable rich discussion.

Intriguingly, the work that these students are doing is a requirement of the International Baccalaureate program, which we were interested in as having potentially created a *system* for deeper learning. The IB program, founded in 1968, was created by a group of Swiss-based private school educators with a particular goal in mind: to design a comprehensive set of assessments that would allow globally mobile students to certify their readiness to attend top-tier universities.[1] IB unapologetically asks students to do "deep" thinking—to ponder questions of epistemology, write extended historical essays, and grapple with complex questions in math and science—and so has set itself apart from the low-level state multiple-choice tests that are so common in American education. While for much of the program's history the International Baccalaureate Diploma Program (IBDP) was an unequivocally privileged one for global elites, in recent decades a growing group of American educators has begun to experiment with broadening the program to provide more equitable access to deeper learning. Lynn Walsh's school, which we call IB High, is part of this movement: it embraces an "IB for All" mission for its untracked, socioeconomically diverse group of learners.

For all of these reasons, we wanted to investigate IB as a potential system for deeper learning. As we visited a half-dozen IB schools—all of which were non-elite public schools—we came to think of IB as a very useful resource for promoting deeper learning, but one that needs to be paired with a set of school-level mechanisms to achieve its promise consistently across classrooms. For reasons we will discuss later, in many of these IB schools we saw practices similar to those we had seen in other schools, namely much teaching from the textbook and few opportunities for students to engage in complex sense-making. In contrast, the school we call IB High had found a way to build upon the IB framework to create classrooms that were frequently challenging and rigorous, where student thinking and questioning were the sine qua non of daily instruction. This motivated us to take a deep dive at IB High to understand exactly how they had managed to build on this external framework to create a powerful intellectual community within their school. In particular, we asked: How does the IBDP framework function and what are its beliefs about deep learning? What internal qualities do schools need to cultivate in order to make good on IB's potential? What are the promises and challenges of offering IB courses to a wider range of learners than historically have had access to them? And, finally, what does the IBDP tell us about the possibility of erecting an external system to support deeper learning at scale?

History and Goals

In their book about the history of the International Baccalaureate Organization (IBO), Jay Mathews and Ian Hill refer to the IB as a "supertest." Given that the IBO has developed curricular programs for the "primary years" (ages three to twelve) and "middle years" (ages eleven to sixteen) that do not center on external assessments, the term is in some ways a misnomer. Yet the International Baccalaureate Diploma Program (IBDP), offered to students in their final two years of secondary school, is the original and most fully specified of the IBO's programs, and is, in fact, a kind of test.

To be specific, the IBDP comprises an extensive set of academic and extracurricular performance tasks on which students must demonstrate mastery in order to gain enough points to earn the prestigious IB diploma. These tasks include both more and less conventional forms of assessment. Like the more widely known Advanced Placement program, each subject taken concludes with a criterion-referenced written exam. But in contrast to AP, which began as an effort to give high school students the content of college-freshman survey courses, and thus has traditionally emphasized breadth over depth, IB exams do not use multiple-choice questions and instead ask students to engage in open-ended analytic tasks.[2] For the literature exam, for example, students are required to craft several essays—one in which they read, and write an analytical essay about, a previously unseen text, and one in which they draw on works they have studied in order to respond to genre-specific questions such as: "Considering two or three plays you have studied, compare the impact on meaning of some arrivals and departures from the stage." For the math exam, students complete a series of free-response problems, showing their thinking and calculations as they go. For the music exam, students listen to an unidentified piece of music and then write an essay in which they develop an evidence-based hypothesis about its historical, geographic, and stylistic characteristics. Once students have completed these exams, they are mailed out to highly trained "IB examiners" all over the world, who score and comment on them according to exam-specific rubrics that use a common scoring scale from one to seven.

The marks that students earn on these tests, however, count as only a portion of the overall credits that students can earn over the course of each subject's two-year arc. In each subject, students also engage in a series of "internal assessments" (IAs) designed to support and capture their learning across a range of modalities. In IB Literature, for example, students must complete an audio-recorded "interactive oral" exam in which they respond extemporaneously to analytic questions about a course text; they also must lead a class discussion, produce multiple drafts of both analytic and persuasive essays, and craft original pieces of creative writing that demonstrate their understanding of certain genres. In IB Math Studies—the IBDP's non-calculus math option—students must craft a mathematical question related to their interests, collect and analyze relevant quantitative data, and write up their results in the form of a formal research paper. In IB Music, students participate in solo and group performances as well as produce original compositions that demonstrate their understanding of music theory. Teachers grade these IAs internally using IBO-provided rubrics, but they also send the IBO a random subset of provisionally graded work for each task. If there are consistent differences between internal and external evaluations, the teachers are required to adjust their grading schemes accordingly. Thus, the assessments that constitute the backbone of the IBDP are *externally guided, internally executed, and then externally moderated*—features that distinguish the program from those that rely on highly scripted curricula, as well as from those that revolve entirely around summative end-of-course tests.

In all of these respects, the approach of IB is consistent with one vision of deeper learning, which we might call *disciplinary authenticity*.[3] The requirements of the program ask students not only to learn content, but also to develop enough facility with the tools of the discipline to produce work similar to that of scholars in the field. In contrast to the traditional pattern in American secondary education, wherein students are primarily asked to assimilate content, the IB consistently requires students to discover knowledge, produce original work, and reflect on the processes critical to doing the work of the disciplines. This vision is more classically academic than that of Dewey High; there is less emphasis on projects and forays into the community, and more on connection to universities and the kind of work that scholars do. This is not a coincidence—in a program designed to prepare youth from

around the world for admission to elite colleges, the IB's designers en-
listed a number of elite university scholars from around the world as
thought partners, and university faculty continue to play important roles
today as content consultants and senior examiners. Thus the IB quite
intentionally breaks down secondary-to-postsecondary boundaries,
supporting a vision of deeper learning that is aligned with university
approaches to the concept.

The IBDP also encourages depth through its structural requirements. In order to earn the diploma, students take at least three but no
more than four "high level" courses, which involve more extensive content and a greater number of instructional hours than their "standard
level" counterparts. This allows the program to chart a course between
the extremes of breadth and specialization: while the "at least three"
requirement encourages students to dive into some subjects more
intensively, the "no more than four" mandate tries to ensure that they
do not stretch themselves so thin that their focus suffers. To further
emphasize this goal of balance, the two types of courses are weighted
equally, each affording students a maximum total of seven points toward
the twenty-four-point minimum required to receive the diploma.

While many of these courses and exams are within the disciplines,
the IB program also seeks to create connections across them. The most
robust of these requirements is the two-year Theory of Knowledge
course, in which, as Ms. Walsh's class illustrates, students are asked to
analyze and compare the epistemological assumptions associated with
each discipline. Students draw on what they have learned in other
courses to consider questions such as, "How does making a valid argument in the physical sciences differ from making a valid argument in
history?" or "What do science, history, and art tell us, respectively,
about the limits of human empathy?"

Additionally, the IB Learner Profile—one of the program's foundational documents—specifies a number of cross-cutting dispositions that
all components of the program reinforce. A one-pager intended to
capture the essence of the program's aspirations, the Learner Profile
states that "the aim of all IB programmes is to develop internationally
minded people who, recognizing their common humanity and shared
guardianship of the planet, help to create a better and more peaceful
world"; it then elaborates that participants in the program should strive
to be "inquirers," "thinkers," "communicators," and "risk-takers" who are

"knowledgeable," "principled," "open-minded," "caring," "balanced," and "reflective." As we will discuss later, the extent to which this document helps to create connections and coherencies across subjects is largely a function of how individual schools execute the program. But it is clear that one of the program's core aspirations is not only to develop disciplinary thinkers, but also to cultivate a range of humanistic dispositions for the young people under its guidance.

Two other requirements seek to help realize the broader ambitions of the program. First, students must produce an "extended essay": a self-directed piece of research on a topic of their choosing, culminating in a four-thousand-word paper. The topics that students choose are in many cases interdisciplinary and / or related to interests that lie beyond the content of their core academic courses: the promises and pitfalls of artificial intelligence, the cultural function of spectator sports, the role of community organizers in sparking social change, and so on. Second, students must complete a 150-hour "creativity, action, and service" project in which they undertake self-chosen extracurricular activities (including sports, arts, and volunteer opportunities) and reflect on the growth that these experiences support. The IBO provides extensive guidance on what kinds of activities and reflections might fulfill this component of the program's vision, but, unlike IAs, decisions about credit are reached internally by each school's administration. Finally, the arts—music, theater, and visual art—constitute one of the program's six required subject groups; IBDP courses in these areas are weighted equally to courses in disciplines such as math and science.

Stepping back, the design of the IBDP reflects a clear desire to chart a middle ground between extremes—to balance breadth and depth of study, to engage in disciplinary traditions while also encouraging cross-disciplinary comparisons, to honor the canon without overlooking lesser-known work, to emphasize intellectual development without neglecting social-emotional and physical development, and, throughout, to allow for school- and teacher-specific adaptations while maintaining rigorous external standards. IB scholar Jerusha Conner argues that it is this balanced and amalgamated quality that accounts for the spread of the program among U.S. high schools:

It is perhaps because the IB represents a compromise between the traditionally polarized camps of the standards-based reformers and the progressive educators that it has attracted such widespread attention in the United States; each group can find within it an appealing feature or a philosophical premise. Not only does the IB represent a deliberate synthesis of divergent [European] national educational traditions. . . . It also stands as an unintentional and innovative amalgam of competing [American] educational traditions.[4]

Indeed, given the program's elite European origins, its rapid spread within the U.S. public school system is fairly remarkable. As of 2015, 30 percent of the nearly three thousand secondary schools worldwide that offer the IBDP were located in the United States, with most of these being public schools. The initial surge of adoption occurred in the 1990s, but the past five years have seen a second wave of interest in the program, grounded mainly in the desire to use it as a tool to expand access to rigorous learning experiences.[5] In Chicago, for example, promising findings linking local student participation in the IBDP to perseverance in higher education contexts prompted Mayor Rahm Emanuel to call for a strategic expansion of the program, with the goal that all district high schools become fully accredited "wall to wall IB" institutions.[6]

Despite such developments, however, IBDP still represents a small niche in the landscape of American high school curricular reform: only 2 percent of U.S. public schools offer the program, compared to the almost 78 percent that offer AP classes.[7] As a result, comparatively few American educators or parents know much about the program. Matthews and Hill argue that this unfamiliarity accounts for the lack of more widespread adoption, especially in high-income communities where parents tend to worry—albeit without grounds—that choosing the IBDP over the more widely recognized AP program might hurt their children's competitive advantage in college admission.[8] Others, citing instances of suburban communities where parents have organized to reject the program, credit a strain of "paleo-conservative sentiment" that sees the IB's emphasis on multiculturalism and global peace as "anti-Christian, un-American, and Marxist."[9] Still others point to the program's comparatively resource- and time-intensive nature; in contrast to AP, which can be implemented in a modular way and imposes fairly minimal costs on schools, the process of gaining full IB accreditation takes three years, expensive IBO-provided training for all participating teachers, and significant documentation, as well as an annual fee of $11,000 to support the process of external moderation. We would add a fourth interpretation to the mix: while the IBDP may indeed resonate with a number of different American educational philosophies, its deeply intellectual nature runs counter to certain mainstream American values and traditions.

As comparatively small a niche as the IBDP represents, however, we believe that it is worth taking seriously as a framework that can support high schools in organizing to provide deep learning consistently across classrooms. Like all externally developed programs, however, the vision, guidance, and materials that the IBDP provides are no guarantee that consistently deep learning will occur.[10] We need, then, to understand what kinds of school-level characteristics and practices are needed to maximize the program's potential.

A Closer Look at IB High

We chose IB High for in-depth investigation because it stood out among the non-elite IB schools we visited as a place where instruction was consistently achieving the aspirations of the IB program. Across ninety hours of classroom observation at the two campuses, we found that three-quarters of the classes featured tasks that asked students to think, inquire, and develop ideas, while only one-quarter were more conventional teacher-directed classes.

Demographically, IB High falls solidly in the middle of the socio-economic spectrum. Founded in 1998, the school serves a total of eight hundred students across two campuses ("North" and "South"), both of which are located in a former shipping town about eighty miles from a major East Coast city. Reflecting the working-class and middle-class population of the surrounding region, 90 percent of the school's students identify as white, 7 percent qualify for free or reduced lunch, and only a handful are English language learners. These official classifications mask a great deal of variation with respect to motivation, skill level, academic background, and class. Like other public charter high schools in the state, students gain admission by entering a randomized lottery prior to their ninth-grade year—and their reasons for doing so are highly varied. As one longtime teacher reports: "Some of our kids are the academic *crème de la crème*, and some of them are here because they were bullied because they're lesbian or gay, some are here because the school has a good reputation and mom and dad wanted them here . . . and then some are kids who failed at everything at their previous junior high schools." IB High's students affirm this range of characterizations. Many talk about being "C" students in their previous schools; others, especially those who identify as being among the 16 percent of the school's population with diagnosed special needs, describe coming from places where they felt both academically and socially marginalized. "At my old school, they 'accommodated' my dyslexia by putting me into the lowest classes possible," one such student reveals. While some of the students are from professional-class families, the school also has a large population of working-class students, as well as many students who are dealing with the ravages of alcoholism and the opioid crisis. Statistics show that the region where the school is located has the highest death rate in the state due to opioids.

It is this backdrop, as well as the IB's history as a program designed by and for the intellectual elite, that make IB High's approach so distinctive. Since receiving its IB accreditation in 2004, the school has proudly defined itself as an "IB for all" institution, which means that all students take a full roster of pre-IB courses in their ninth- and tenth-grade years and an equally full roster of IBDP courses in their junior and senior years. While students can choose to sit for selected IB exams rather than to pursue the full IB diploma, there are no non-IB courses offered; everyone completes the full curriculum in order to graduate, and almost all students who enter the school ultimately do graduate from it. This ambitious approach has yielded impressive results that corroborate our observations. In *Newsweek*'s 2015 ranking of U.S. high schools, IB High ranked among the top ten charters in the country as well as among the top fifty U.S. high schools overall. The school's results on the 2015 PISA test confirm that its students achieve at high levels compared to both domestic and international peers. If IB High's students were a country, they would score second in the world, behind Shanghai, in reading and science, and fifth in the world in math, slightly ahead of South Korea.[11] IB High also scores well above domestic averages on such items as "most of my teachers are interested in my well-being" (90 percent of IB High students agree) and "most of my teachers really listen to what I have to say" (95 percent of IB High students agree).[12] In terms of achievement on the IB, all students take at least three exams and almost 80 percent pursue the full diploma, with 43 percent of the overall school population attaining it and virtually every student in the school earning at least one course-specific certificate.

As a charter school, IB High has certain advantages over traditional public schools. Like Dewey High and No Excuses High, it is considerably smaller than most comprehensive high schools, with four hundred students on each of its campuses. Students (or their parents) have chosen to attend the school, and teachers have chosen to teach there. These factors enable it to create a more unified mission than is often possible in traditional public schools. It also has more flexibility than do district schools over how to use its resources, and, as we will see, it has made some different decisions about how to use them. At the same time, in our travels we saw many charters that had the same struggles as traditional public schools, which is consistent with national evidence that shows that charters, on average, are no better than regular public schools. Thus a key part of the question is what IB High is doing with these flexibilities that enables it to achieve what it does.

At IB High, we observed ninety hours of classes, which enabled us to see the large majority of classes across the two campuses at least once. We interviewed forty teachers, administrators, and students. We were particularly interested in the consistency of inquiry-oriented instruction across classrooms, so we shaped our investigation to understand how this came to be. We gave particular credence to instances where different actors gave similar accounts or where our observations confirmed interview data. As we describe later, we also investigated a struggling IB school; understanding this "negative case" helped us to see what was distinctive about IB High.

IB High: External Guidance, Internal Coherence

"What does explaining your thinking look like and sound like when you're translating something? And what's the benefit of explaining your thinking process in Latin class anyway?" asks Mr. Lowe, looking quizzically around the classroom. He pauses for a moment to let his questions register. With his boyish face and eager smile he could almost be mistaken for a high schooler himself, but his twenty pre-IB Latin students—tenth graders at IB High North—listen attentively. "I want us to talk about those questions because I realized that you spend a lot of time up at the board going over translations you've done, but we haven't been very explicit about what we want that process to look like or why we do it in the first place," Mr. Lowe adds. He prompts the students to prepare for a class discussion on these topics by talking about them in groups for a few minutes.

The room erupts into conversation. It's halfway through last period on the Thursday before winter break, but, as with Ms. Walsh's Theory of Knowledge class, the ethos is clearly one of focused engagement. Walking around, however, we see that the students are in different places in terms of their ability to tackle the questions at hand. Some of them struggle to offer thoughts that move beyond vague generalizations; others immediately jump into analytic conversations about why it might be useful to think out loud for each other when translating. Mr. Lowe circulates from group to group, listening in and pairing words of encouragement with follow-up questions that seek to spur students to deepen their thinking. When one girl asks whether her group has the "right answer" to the second question, he smiles but doesn't respond directly. "There are a lot of ways you could think about it," he says. "Keep talking—see if you can come up with some other ideas."

After ten minutes, Mr. Lowe draws the class back together and asks students to share ideas that have emerged. As the students speak, he writes their thoughts on the board, using their exact words when possible and interrupting only occasionally to ask questions or to invite those who haven't spoken to do so. The students, for their part, listen to each other actively, some of them jotting down key points in their open notebooks.

STUDENT 1: "So for the first question, you should be pointing to what you're talking about in the translation with hand gestures."
STUDENT 2: "Yeah, like using your hand to guide people through physically. Like at the board you [looks at Mr. Lowe] make us point at the words we're talking about, so people know what word we're on."
STUDENT 3: "It helps people with sequence."
MR. LOWE: "Can you say more about what you mean by that?"

STUDENT 3: "Um ... [pause] ... like it helps you communicate your grammar, like the grammar that goes with each word and the correct order."

STUDENT 5: "It looks like you're teaching the class. You're ... explaining what's going on and that's what teachers do. Like in a translation—let's say a paragraph—you have to go up and teach the class what's going on through your head."

STUDENT 6: "It's one thing to point to each thing and explain what it is, but you have to explain how you know. Like, you have to touch on all of your prior knowledge—this is what it is and this is how I know. You have to explain what you're thinking as you're talking."

STUDENT 7: "Yeah, and to add to what [student 6] said, we have to explain how we could have otherwise translated it, and why it doesn't work to do it that way."

MR. LOWE: "I can hear some of you connecting number one to number two—why is sharing your thinking useful in the first place? Who else has thoughts on that?"

STUDENT 8: "I guess you can improve your way of thinking from other people."

STUDENT 9: "Yeah, like if you don't know the concept very well and you have it incorrectly, the teacher can clarify it because then the teacher can know what you don't understand."

MR. LOWE: "Is the teacher the only person who can know that?"

STUDENT 9: "Maybe yourself?"

STUDENT 10: "Or each other—if we're explaining our thinking we can help each other when we get confused or if we get it wrong."

STUDENT 5: "You can almost gain a different perspective by explaining your process. That can kind of cause a good discussion, and you can gain a lot of knowledge from that."

STUDENT 11: "When you learn how someone thinks, arguably that's a way to get to know someone."

MR. LOWE: "So there's a social component to sharing our thinking—I've never thought about that before! I'm going to keep thinking about that. That's really interesting."

As the conversation continues, Mr. Lowe invites those who haven't participated to help synthesize what others have said. In the last few minutes of the period, he asks students to silently journal about how their thinking has changed or deepened based on this conversation—and he invites them to address a third question: "How is sharing your thinking with others useful more generally?" He tells the students that they will return to this topic at the start of tomorrow's class before diving back into the work of translation with a renewed sense of purpose and a more specific sense of process. "I look forward to reading what you've written," he tells the students. "You shared a lot of interesting ideas today—you really got me thinking!"

The IBDP as a Scaffold and Anchor

Like epistemology, Latin makes for a pretty heady subject—and perhaps not one immediately fascinating to twenty-first-century teenagers. This class session, however, exemplifies how Mr. Lowe, like Ms. Walsh, manages to invite students into the content at hand in ways that produce layers of cognitive engagement. To start, he frames the day's task as one rooted in a question that students themselves likely have about the course. Then, as the task unfolds, he makes a number of moves that position his students as the key sense-makers in the room: giving them time to consider the questions at hand before launching a formal discussion; making their thinking visible by writing notes on the board; and encouraging them to respond to and build on each other's ideas rather than to seek his affirmation. His gentle refusal to accept single answers to his prompts helps to ensure that the discussion deepens as it progresses, generating intellectual rigor. Finally, his stance communicates genuine interest in what his students have to say. In aggregate, these practices form a foundation for the kind of student-centered, constructivist "deeper teaching" that Magdalene Lampert and others have described.[13]

How did Mr. Lowe learn to teach like this, and how much of his learning can be traced back to the IB? As a recent college graduate who joined IB High's faculty two years ago after spending the first few years of his career in a nearby district school, Mr. Lowe is among the school's novice teachers. In conversations, he emphasizes that he still has a lot to learn about both the particulars of the IBDP and instructional practice more generally. The deeply intellectual and skills-focused nature of his course, however, is no accident. Using the IB Latin assessments and the IB Learner Profile as a compass for his work, he organizes his curriculum so that everything connects back to essential questions related to the study and translation of classical languages: To what extent can we connect with the words of someone who lived two thousand years ago? What is lost when we try to translate texts across language, time, and space? Can we ever truly understand what somebody else means to convey? As a result, his course is an intentional mix of vocabulary and grammar acquisition on the one hand and rich conversations about philosophical and epistemological "Theory-of-Knowledge-type questions" on the other. Along the way, he tries to support students in becoming more aware of the "hows" and "whys" associated with what they are doing—key metacognitive understandings.

Mr. Lowe openly credits the IBDP as one of the key sources of guidance for his curricular choices. With unqualified enthusiasm, he describes how the IB Latin assessments have helped him to determine the skills, understandings, and dispositions around which to organize his ninth-grade course:

> Yeah, the IB Latin test is a test, but getting kids to the point where they're prepared for it is the best way that I can imagine to teach Latin. It says right in the IB curriculum guide that the goal is not just about learning content, but learning skills that are going to be cross-class skills, thinking skills. . . . so with translation, it's not just about what the Latin says, but it's really about what it *means*. . . . Students are treated as the stewards of the language because they'll encounter a word that can mean four quite different things, and then the question is: how do you make that decision?

Mr. Lowe's endorsement of the IB framework is echoed by a majority of IB High's teachers, who similarly view the structure, content, and values of the IBDP as useful anchors for their work. Even those who are much further along in their careers seem enthusiastic about the program, spending much more time describing the ways that the IB has pushed them to expand their practice than dwelling on the ways that it constrains them. For example, Ms. Walsh spent a long time explaining how recent shifts in the Theory of Knowledge curriculum and assessment have pushed her to expand her own practice:

The course is set up with ways of knowing and areas of knowledge. [The previous version of the IB curriculum] used to treat them as independent units. Now, the push of the course is really to just introduce the ways of knowing, and then to integrate them. . . . also, they added all of these fun ways of knowing that you could teach. They used to be language, emotion, reason, and sense perception; they added memory and intuition and imagination and faith. I was like, "Wow, these are all ones that I've always wanted to talk about," so I did *all* of the new ones.

One way to understand these positive experiences is to recognize that the assessment tasks that lie at the core of the IBDP specify a *granular vision of deeper learning outcomes*—that is, they paint a detailed picture of the kinds of knowledge, skills, and dispositions that are worth developing and the kinds of subject-specific activities that can support their development, as well as provide rich models of what proficiency looks and sounds like. In so doing, the IB is solving a problem that we witnessed time and time again in non-IB schools—much talk about "deeper learning" and "twenty-first-century skills," but no clear picture of what such concepts mean in terms of actual classroom instruction or student outcomes. We therefore describe IB as an "anchor" and a "scaffold" that guides the work of its teachers.

The scaffolding function of the IBDP holds true at the school level as well. Essentially, IB frees up the organizational equivalent of cognitive space, allowing stakeholders to work on implementation (the "how") rather than to spend all of their energy trying to specify and agree on the logic (the "why") and content (the "what") of their goals. Mr. Stone, the principal of IB High North, draws on a recent experience of observing classrooms—including Mr. Lowe's tenth-grade Latin classroom—to affirm this point:

I was in IB Math Studies yesterday. I can see a connection between what is being taught there . . . and what is being taught in the sophomore Latin class I saw today: really both classes are explicitly teaching metacognition. And it wasn't my or [the system leader's] flavor of the month that now we're going to teach metacognition. It's built in. Kids are going from classroom to classroom, asking: How do I think about this? How do others think about this? Those habits are built into the curriculum. Without that, we'd have to engineer it, and that means that you're not spending time actualizing it.[14]

Similar sentiments are voiced by one of the school's English teachers, who asserts that "it's still possible that deep learning is going to happen without IB, but I think IB is a structure that has it built in, so it makes it easier for the school and for the individual teacher alike."

Such observations resonate with a burgeoning literature that highlights the role of what David Cohen and his colleagues have called "infrastructure" in helping schools to achieve their goals.[15] At the core of this literature lies the argument that in order to create more consistently desirable learning outcomes from classroom to classroom, schools need to reach agreements about what kinds of problems teachers can reasonably tackle and what kinds of results should be expected; furthermore, to support the enactment of these agreements, they must possess materials and technology that guide the work as well as codified standards and norms that can inform judgments about quality. In this light, the IBDP's power comes from the fact that it provides one version of such infrastructure—a version that has at its heart an unusually ambitious view of what students should know and be able to do by the time they graduate, and thus can help to jumpstart efforts to pursue deep learning of a certain type.

At the same time, our research at IB High suggests some of the limits of implementing an external "infrastructure" when corresponding school-level supports are not provided. Mr. Stone's comment that IB High devotes its energy to "actualizing" the vision and values of the IBDP makes a critically important point. No matter how well-specified and/or compelling a set of instructional materials or design for schooling might be, the burden still ultimately falls on leaders, teachers, and students to leverage it in consistently powerful and context-sensitive ways. As we alluded to earlier, our experiences in other IB schools illustrate this point. In all of these places, we encountered classrooms that embody the program's signature features: disciplinary authenticity, cross-disciplinary thinking, and an emphasis on applying knowledge in service of producing original academic work. In none of them, however, was there the same level of program-wide coherence and depth as at IB High. In several of them, for example, the Theory of Knowledge course is treated as a survey of Western philosophy rather than as a platform for making connections across disciplines; the Learner Profile, for its part, functions less as a living document than as an unnoticed poster on classroom walls. Moreover, across all of these schools, many teachers continue to rely heavily on textbooks and lectures, despite the emphasis of the IB assessments on active student engagement. As a result, students described their experiences of the IBDP in decidedly more varied and ambivalent ways than did students we interviewed at IB High. What, then, is IB High doing differently?

Feedback, Hiring, and Cultural Transmission

If one part of the puzzle is the anchoring and scaffolding function played by IB, another critical part is the set of mechanisms the school has developed to support deeper teaching. Mr. Lowe describes his ongoing feedback cycles with Mr. Stone, the campus principal, as critical to his ongoing development. Such cycles, in which all IB High faculty participate several times a year, have a three-part structure: a brief pre-conversation where the teacher outlines a current problem of practice, a period-long observation, and a debriefing conversation in which the teacher reflects and the participating administrator helps to sharpen or deepen the teacher's thinking. In Mr. Lowe's case, he had been working on finding ways to draw out his students' thinking and to get them to engage deeply with each other's ideas—a goal aligned with the Learner Profile's emphasis on developing "inquirers" who are "open-minded." Accordingly, this was the focus of his recent work with Mr. Stone. The big "aha" of the debrief, Mr. Lowe tells us, came when Mr. Stone asked him to articulate what he wanted students to learn from watching each other translate sentences at the board, which in turn made him realize that he had never broached this topic explicitly. As a result of this conversation, Mr. Lowe designed a series of lessons to get students to talk about the how and why of sharing their thinking—lessons that he hoped would both make the norms for translation clearer and foreground students' thought processes. In so doing, the feedback process moved instruction from what was already a student-centered mode—having students learn from each other's work—to a metacognitive level—asking students to reflect on the purpose of their shared communication.

Mr. Lowe is what many administrators consider to be the human-capital equivalent of gold: a highly reflective teacher with both the inclination and ability to adjust his practice in response to feedback, as well as a willingness to set aside his own role as a "sage" in order to focus on student learning. For a number of reasons, however, these characteristics are not solely a function of Mr. Lowe's individual strengths. That teachers like him end up at IB High reflects a highly intentional hiring process. Overseen by the school's executive director, Mr. Weber, this process is far less time-intensive than those at Dewey High and No Excuses High; in fact, after the initial vetting process, face-to-face time often includes only a single interview conducted via Skype. Mr. Weber, however, is clear about the types of candidates he seeks: candidates who model "passionate engagement" with their subjects, who are "super reflective" about their practice, and who "don't use 'I' very often" when describing their classrooms. While the first quality aligns with the IBDP vision of disciplinary authenticity, the second and third qualities help to ensure that new teachers will be receptive to IB High's emphasis on student-centered instruction. This emphasis is communicated not only through regular individual feedback sessions but also through carefully structured peer observations, the placement of newer teachers with same-subject mentors, and department meetings that focus on the instructional implications of the IB Learner Profile. New teachers with less experience are also assigned a lightened course load in order to free up time for planning and coaching. Thus IB High, like Dewey High, adopts a "buy it *and* build it" strategy with respect to its teachers.[16]

The "build it" dimensions of this strategy are particularly important because one of the critical limitations of the IBDP is that it does not in and of itself force a disruption of teacher-centered instructional practices. Essentially, while the IBDP specifies in granular detail what content and skills are worth learning and how learners should demonstrate mastery, it does not specify with similar richness the kinds of teaching practices will best support progress toward these outcomes.[17] This omission, paired with the fact that—unlike project-based learning—IB's vision represents a subtle rather than a radical shift away from conventional thinking about the goals of high school education, means that without robust school-level supports it is all too easy for teachers to continue seeing themselves as content experts whose role is to "profess" fixed bodies of knowledge to their students. The history and reputation of the IB as a program aimed at preparing students to thrive in elite universities, where skillful lecturing is celebrated, exacerbates the problem. As one seasoned IB teacher wryly notes, some teachers who are new to the program see it as a mandate to become *more* teacher-centered:

[A lot of teachers who are new to IB] are like, "Oh, now I'm what I always wanted to be, ever since . . . [local] State Teachers College: I'm now a *college* teacher! And God help these little buggers because I'm gonna make it a college course!" So then they lecture and do all kinds of other things that are non-IB.

Of course, as noted earlier, the nature of the IB assessments does encourage deep study and a wide range of activity types—but this alone is not sufficient to support teachers in accomplishing the shifts in stance and in practice that allow for a deep focus on student thinking and reasoning. Ms. Walsh, the Theory of Knowledge teacher, notes that this limitation is particularly problematic when it comes to offering the program to learners who may not be ready or able to learn mainly from lectures and/or to be fully self-directed in their work. "IB is really difficult to do well with all students without good teaching practice," she says. The school's leaders echo this sentiment, noting that while the school's robust model of professional learning and consistent emphasis on student-centered instructional techniques have resulted over the years in "a significant shift towards students at the center," IB High still has a number of teachers who rely too much on techniques such as lecturing. Our ninety hours of classroom observations across the two campuses confirm this reality; while many teachers display a deep commitment to supporting student thinking and to assessing and responding to their students' progress in dynamic ways, roughly a quarter remain largely teacher-centered in their practices.

Sticking points notwithstanding, IB High's ability to focus so many of its efforts around student-centered instruction reflects the school's cultivation of deep institutional knowledge about the IBDP itself. The program, after all, is far from self-explanatory; it encompasses a highly particular set of expectations, assessments, and rubrics that can take teachers many years to understand fully. (At one of the recently accredited IBDP schools that we studied—a school with very few teachers previously familiar with the program—we encountered a number of teachers who described the subject-specific IA requirements by turns as "esoteric," "complicated," and "super-technical.") Given this reality, having a core group of teachers who understand and can communicate the ins and outs of the program as instantiated across different subjects, and who know how to interpret the IB's numerous assessment rubrics, spares the school substantial effort. Compared to the other IBDP schools that we studied, IB High's core in this respect is particularly robust: of the school's eighty-three-person teaching staff, nearly a third have taught in other IB programs—many of them at schools abroad—and seventeen are certified as IB examiners or assistant examiners.

Mr. Weber serves as the guardian of this reality, filling some open positions with new teachers who "have the right attitude and haven't been spoiled by another system," but also aggressively recruiting mid-career candidates from IB schools abroad. This all but guarantees that newcomers to the school are able to hit the ground running with respect to curriculum- and assessment-related support. The approach to hiring also plays a critical role in establishing and maintaining the way that IB High's teachers learn to think about the program's vision and goals as an integrated whole. As one IB High veteran explains:

> It's very, very difficult to get teachers' mindsets into what the IB is really about unless they've had contact with other IB teachers. Schools that are starting fresh have a very difficult time. When I came here, [Mr. Weber] had seeded each department with at least one person who had taught overseas in another IB program, who understood the cultural milieu, who understood what IB really means: that it's not AP, that it's not just a series of courses, that it's a whole way of approaching kids. That's what's hard to replicate—the culture—unless you know what it is you're trying to get to.

Strikingly, this assertion echoes the emphasis of Dewey High's founder on the importance of "knowing what gold looks like" with respect to a school's aims. In both cases, apprenticeship and cultural transmission—having people steeped in the model guiding newer people who are learning it—are critically important for maintaining the school's values and practices.

Stepping back, the net result of IB High's emphasis on student-centered teaching in the context of the IBDP is a level of shared practice and shared expectation from classroom to classroom that, while far from perfectly consistent, creates an unusually strong platform for deep learning. As one teacher who recently joined the faculty after having spent many years teaching AP calculus in various other public schools says:

> It didn't take a month and a half for kids to be like, "Okay, yeah, [the way this guy teaches math] is pretty awesome." It took two days. For me, a lot of that is because they're used to being challenged. They're used to being asked to think, and that's really, really nice. It's really nice to not be the one teacher doing that, or one of five teachers doing that, or even one of ten teachers doing that, but to actually have an entire school of teachers doing that. It makes it so much easier to do.

An Inclusive Culture

"I said it before and I'll say it again: the IB is a chameleon," Mr. Costa tells us for the third time. He retreats into silence. With his thick glasses, grizzled beard, and poker-faced expression, it is hard to tell whether he is amused or annoyed by our many queries. Still, given his status as the most knowledgeable and seasoned IB teacher at IB High— over the course of his forty-year career he has taught, led, and helped to establish the IBDP in four different schools around the globe—we persevere in our questioning. "What makes you use the word chameleon?" we ask. "And how, exactly, is IB so different here than at other schools where you've worked?"

Our persistence seems to convince Mr. Costa that our desire to understand the school is genuine. Suddenly becoming more animated, he launches into a lively description of the experience of joining the IB High community a decade ago, shortly after the school had received its IBO accreditation and Mr. Weber had been hired to lead the charge. At all of the schools where he worked prior to IB High, Mr. Costa says, there was enormous pressure for students to excel on the exams—pressure that often threatened to distort the core values of the program. "By shooting just for high scores, you may, in fact, be sabotaging the essence of what the program is about—the combination of intellectual excellence, thinking carefully, an international perspective, understanding the other, and focusing on kids and their development instead of on *stuff*," he says. It became clear to him right away, he continues, that Mr. Weber shared this humanistic view of IB. It was this view, for example, that prompted the executive director to insist from the start that all students participate in IB classes—and to make it abundantly clear to everyone that meaningful participation should be valued above raw achievement. This message, Mr. Costa tells us, has allowed the school to avoid the overly achievement-oriented tenor that the program often takes on in more elite contexts. "When teachers start teaching IB, they're afraid they're gonna be judged about their teaching abilities if the kids don't do well. We have to spend a lot of time building morale. . . . telling them that [the kids] may not all be getting sixes. It doesn't matter. What counts is they've been through this experience," he says. His colleagues, even those who know far less about the range of ways that the IBDP plays out in other contexts, clearly have processed this message. "We don't focus on saying we're trying to get everyone to achieve at this one level—our administrators especially are very opposed to any language or policies that might reflect that sort of thinking," one math teacher says. "Rather, we measure success largely through participation."

As we talk with other IB High leaders, teachers, and students, it becomes clear that this emphasis on inclusivity is central to the school's culture—and that it is manifested in a rich variety of ways. The most obvious of these is the element that Mr. Costa emphasizes: the absence of tracking paired with the valuing of participation over achievement. Teachers, in particular, are keenly aware of how this affects the social dynamics of their classes. One math teacher, describing a girl in his IB math studies class who has a significant cognitive disability, says that her case illustrates the school's philosophy:

I don't think every kid's going to get an IB diploma, but I think that every kid's going to get an IB education. In the end, I think that's really the most important thing. . . . just that philos-

ophy of kindness and inclusion ... I think because it's an IB-
for-all program, you have that. That's what lets me not worry
about [this girl] getting mocked.

Beyond the school's baseline "IB for all" strategy, the faculty is encouraged to let students make their own choices about which high-level
and standard-level courses to take once they reach eleventh grade. "We
have students who have chosen to take a higher-level course that maybe
we wouldn't describe as being 'higher-level material,'" the same math
teacher says, noting that these students may not be earning high scores
on the IAs or exams but are still benefiting from the experience of
delving more deeply into course content. He adds that the school's leadership encourages teachers to celebrate students' growth over time regardless of their actual achievement levels—and that some, though not
all, of his colleagues take this idea of cultivating a "growth mindset"
very seriously.[18]

IB High's students, too, comment on the impact of the school's culture of inclusion, with many of them emphasizing that because of this
culture they end up accomplishing much more than they ever expected.
One student, for example, talks about how both he and his parents were
skeptical that he could participate in the IBDP's immersion-model
foreign language classes, given that he has dyslexia; however, after en-
rolling in Spanish because the school gave him no other choice, he realized that, with extensive support, he not only was able to learn a
second language but also could enjoy the process of doing so. Others
talk about how prior to matriculating to IB High they never identified
themselves as "the kind of person who would do a super-intense program like IB," but how over time they began to see themselves as serious and intellectually engaged learners. IB High's students also note
other ways in which the school communicates the value of inclusion,
often emphasizing the school's unusual policy that nobody gets cut from
sports teams, regardless of background or skill.[19] A few also talk about
how even the student government reflects an inclusive spirit: rather than
letting the election process become a schoolwide popularity contest,
each advisory group chooses two students to represent its interests to
the campus principals, and to report back during advisory sessions.

IB High's emphasis on inclusion might in fact be likened to that of a
large and high-functioning family: the adults at the helm do not ignore

the inevitable variation in their children's inclinations, abilities, and temperaments, but they do not use this variation as an excuse for excluding anyone from group activities deemed inherently worthwhile. Instead, they offer encouragement, support, and nonjudgmental acceptance of a range of outcomes—and they cultivate opportunities for different children to excel in different ways. With this in mind, it comes as no surprise that at IB High, students and teachers alike frequently describe the school as feeling like a "family" or "team."

The school's inclusive stance, however, is not in and of itself a guarantee of consistent deep learning for all. It is hardly a stretch, after all, to imagine that a school with an emphasis on inclusive participation could unintentionally devolve into a place where low expectations dominate. Recall, for example, the case from Chapter 2 of Inspire Academy—a largely untracked school in which, although students reported feeling welcomed and at least somewhat engaged in the projects their teachers designed, cognitive rigor was often absent. How does IB High avoid this pitfall?

High External Expectations, Support for Students

One of the answers to this question lies in the high cognitive demand associated with the IB assessments and in the semi-external nature of the IBO's grading system. As the IB coordinator at IB High North says, "I think sending the assessments overseas or to other schools is very powerful both for the teacher and for the student. . . . It decreases subjectivity." Another teacher, echoing this sentiment, notes that that IB "allows us to tell students that they've succeeded because of their efforts and their participation and their growth, but also not to give them false praise. There's still an external benchmark . . . and the top of the scale is very high." In addition, since students receive feedback and externally moderated grades at various points during each two-year course, both they and their teachers are more motivated to seek improved outcomes over time than they might be if, as with the Advanced Placement program or other culminating exams, scores were released only following final exams or graduation. Finally, although IB High manages to avoid the kind of cutthroat achievement culture found in some affluent suburban schools, it is hard to imagine that the middle- and upper-middle-class families that are part of this socioeconomically diverse school would tolerate having few students actually receive the IB diploma. Thus, the school's internally cultivated emphasis on inclusion is balanced by various external forces that help to ensure a baseline of rigor and externally certified achievement.

Out of their commitment to all learners, IB High also has developed a series of supports to help all of their students participate fully and meaningfully in the IB curriculum. At the instructional level, this means that departments spend a significant portion of their bi-weekly meeting time thinking about how to differentiate and scaffold the curriculum. Referring to the many years that he spent teaching in IB High's English department before becoming the campus principal at North, Mr. Stone says, "We know that we can't just say, 'All right, kids, go home and think about these things.' Instead [what we think about is] how are we going to make graphic organizers? How are we going to develop a common language? How do we find books that are short and [of] high interest so we can develop students' thinking and reading and communication abilities?" Mr. Lowe's class, with its emphasis on making visible the reasoning and expectations associated with translation, and Ms. Walsh's class, with its frequent opportunities for students to develop their thinking orally before starting to write, both exemplify this collective commitment to scaffolding the curriculum. For their part, students pick up on their teachers' commitment to supporting them. As one student says, "I can ask my history teacher for help and he'll never look at me funny—it's extra work for my teachers, but if I ask them for it, they're excited that I want to know, which I love."

IB High also has a number of structures to help students develop the more general "student skills" needed to participate meaningfully in the IBDP. As Mr. Costa puts it, the school treats the program as one that specifies "college-like work with high school-like supervision." This means that students who lack the organization, executive function, and/or academic background to handle the rigors of the program independently receive large amounts of personalized support. Lunch period, for example, doubles as "make-up learning time," an administrator-supervised study period for students who have fallen behind and/or need extra tutoring. Most teachers also offer frequent afterschool office hours and study sessions, which a large number of students report attending. More globally, the school's response to students who are in danger of what Mr. Stone calls "big mess-ups" is to intervene compassionately, rather than to penalize them. Mr. Steedman, Mr. Stone's counterpart at IB High South, sees this practice as not only allowing more students to meet the program's many requirements but also facilitating long-term learning and growth:

> I don't think that people who don't hand things in on time are failures in life. Yes, you have deadlines in the IB, but you try to keep [students] in the game as long as possible. . . . So, for example, the extended essay is due October 31st but some kids are not going to have it done by October 31st, and when you realize that, that's when you really surround that kid and say, "Okay, what's really getting in the way, why don't you stay in for lunch, why don't you meet the teacher?" And you give them a pathway to access. So there are some students here who wrote their extended essay in about a month's time, because we sat together and helped them navigate the library and things like that, and in the end they got a D and it wasn't a great essay, but they had that experience—and now they're at [the state university's flagship campus] and doing just fine. So with IB for all, you're trying to give students experiences that they learn from . . . and hopefully they'll make all kinds of mistakes and then when they get to college and they're faced with their first major paper, they're like, "Oh, I made those mistakes in high school, I'm not going to do that again."

The process of identifying students who need these "pathways to access" is facilitated by the advisory program, the special education and guidance departments, and regular grade-team meetings where faculty identify and strategize about students who are struggling. The small size of most classes—Mr. Weber insists that spending money to keep classes at or below twenty is well worth tradeoffs such as the lack of a cafeteria or gymnasium at each campus—also means that teachers are able to keep close tabs on individual progress so that they can intervene early when students are struggling or falling behind. IB High thus strikes a middle ground between Dewey High, where student failures are fully normalized as opportunities for reflection and growth, and No Excuses High, where failures of any kind are avoided at all costs.

An Intellectual Community

IB High's final buttress against the encroachment of low expectations is less structural but equally powerful: its overall culture of intellectual seriousness. Described by teachers and students alike, this culture is one where deep engagement with academic content is a central and celebrated communal value. As one student says, "You have to learn to embrace your nerdiness here. . . . At [my previous school] I didn't realize that I could *know* something but not *understand* it—now I really want to understand." Echoing this sentiment, a veteran math teacher compares IB High to the various schools where he had taught previously, emphasizing his sense that "[here] there is a natural intellectual curiosity and it's an intellectual community. That's what so many schools don't have—they have a community, but it's not an *intellectual* community." He goes on to note that this characterization applies not only to the students but also to the faculty, citing as an example how a colleague in the history department recently approached him and, knowing that he used to teach economics, revealed that she wanted to know more about the stock market in order to be able to teach the 1929 crash more deeply. "She was. . . . 'I don't get the stock market' . . . so we sat down in the faculty room and for about thirty minutes I walked her through it." That this interaction happened in the campus faculty room—a public space that at many schools is the domain of small-talk and gossip—speaks to the pervasive culture of curiosity and self-initiated learning that extends to IB High's adults.

What creates this culture? Certainly it is in part supported and sustained by the deliberate selection of teachers who care deeply about the subjects that they teach. The IB itself is a contributor, in the questions it asks and the work it requires. As Ms. Walsh, who teaches IB history as well as Theory of Knowledge, says: "I felt . . . high school honors U.S. History was an exercise in trivia—like, 'Okay, I'll make flashcards.' Here, you really put a microscope on it. You really look at the details. That, I think, leads to a level of intellectualism." Beyond this, two of the program's three core requirements—the Theory of Knowledge course and the extended essay—reflect a belief that adolescents can and should engage in sustained conceptual inquiry. This belief is one that many of IB High's faculty and staff seem to have internalized. As one summarizes it, "Adults treat students like they have a brain. . . . there's a real respect for student ideas, and they rise to that."

School Pride Based on Learning and Equity

At once overused and undertheorized, the term "school pride" refers to a phenomenon that popular representations of high school mainly link to domains beyond the classroom: sports teams, glee clubs, and other competitive extracurricular groups. At IB High, however, a feeling of collective identity emerges directly from the school's "IB for all" mission. For students, this feeling stems from knowing that they and their peers are contending with similar challenges. As one diploma-seeking senior describes it, "There's this sense of community with people, even if they're not [pursuing the] full IB [diploma], because you still have to take these difficult classes where we're all going through the same thing. If you've never talked to someone, your first word with them is like, 'Ah, how are you doing on your math? I'm really struggling.'" Teachers too describe a sense of shared purpose linked to the conviction that supporting "regular kids" through a program designed for the intellectual elite is incredibly difficult. To this end, many faculty members use language that evokes the experience of perseverance in the face of adversity; they talk about feeling solidarity with students in a common "quest" to "conquer" the IB. Mr. Lowe takes this line of thinking a step further, explaining that the school's distinctive mission makes it especially important that students see their teachers modeling intense effort:

> You have to remember that these kids are attempting a curriculum that in most situations they would never be allowed to attempt. It's difficult. It's really difficult. [The students] really need you on their team. . . . If I'm asking them to work as hard as they are, then I need to be working as hard as they are. Otherwise, it's unbalanced. In asking them to do these things, I've got to make sure that I'm doing that sort of stuff, too, that's pushing me. The kids know that. They see that.

Thus, for Mr. Lowe, the school's emphasis on cultivating collective identity is directly tied to his instructional practice.

Mr. Lowe is not alone in seeing the school's mission as giving broader meaning to his work. Almost without exception, the school's teachers are hyper-aware that their school represents a frontier with respect to engaging "ordinary" students in a program that was designed for the privileged few. For some, namely those coming from elite international schools, the desire to bring the IBDP to a broader array of learners is what attracted them to the school in the first place. For others, their original commitment lay with engaging historically marginalized groups in deeper learning, and IB High's "IB for all" model offered a way to do so. Regardless of their backgrounds, teachers express a sense of collective pride about the school's work, as well as a shared belief that this work transcends any given set of students. Many are involved in running regional and national training sessions focused on expanding access to the IBDP; several members of the school's special education staff also recently collaborated with counterparts from around the globe to create "The IB Guide to Inclusive Education," a strategic planning resource for schools. Even those who are newer to the program and to the school express a sense of purpose rooted in the school's enactment of its mission. As one teacher reports, "I think that one of the best things we have going here is that we are successful. We see the success every day in our students' faces, in their conversations, in our classrooms, in the hallway. That just feeds on itself. You just know that it's a great honor to be part of this experiment."

IB for All? Access, Equity, and Scale

At first sight, the Benjamin Franklin Upper School—a non-selective middle and high school serving roughly five hundred high-poverty students in an immigrant-heavy section of a Northeast city—appears stately. The campus is housed in a century-old brick building with an arching entryway and all of the features that one imagines in a venerable institution of secondary learning—high-ceilinged hallways, leaded-glass windows, built-in bookshelves, hardwood floors. A closer look, however, reveals a state of disrepair that speaks to the district's tight budget as well as to a general lack of attentiveness to the space. In the hallways, locker doors hang loose. In the classrooms, light fixtures dangle precariously and the windows are permanently clouded with dust and age. Throughout, there is a conspicuous absence of books and technology, and only a few rooms have any kind of student work displayed on the walls. "We say [this school] is a prison because there's broken stuff everywhere and there's no supplies," one eleventh-grader reports.[20]

Despite this state of dilapidation, the school—known locally as "the Franklin"—has a growing local reputation for its academic rigor. Since receiving accreditation in 2010, it has functioned as an IBO world school, offering the IBDP to its upperclass students and, more recently, the IB Middle Years Programme to its younger students. Not coincidentally, given IB High's location only ninety miles south and its status as the most successful unscreened IB school in the region, Franklin's leadership team has been in ongoing conversations with IB High's administrators, and, accordingly, the parallels between the strategies that the two schools employ are striking. Like at IB High, students at Franklin can choose whether or not to pursue the full IB diploma but all are required to take IBDP classes. Mirroring IB High, students with special needs (19 percent), as well as those with limited English proficiency (16 percent), are given extra support but still included in IB programming. And as at IB High, virtually all teachers at Franklin have attended at least one IBO-sponsored training—which in Franklin's case has cost the school upward of $100,000, since few of its teachers had prior exposure to the program. The *Washington Post* recognized Franklin's as one of the "most challenging high schools in the United States," an honor that recognized the school's commitment to having a school of high-poverty students exclusively enrolled in an IB curriculum.

One only has to spend a few hours in the hallways and classrooms of Franklin, however, to realize just how much work lies ahead if the school is to actualize the promises of the IB as a framework for deep learning. One April afternoon, for example, a group of diploma-seeking seniors gathers in a downstairs classroom to serve as an audience for each other's Theory of Knowledge presentations. The structure and goals of these presentations are common across all schools offering the IBDP: in order to support each other in consolidating their learning prior to the end-of-course written examination, groups of students present for roughly twenty minutes on one disciplinary area (for example the natural sciences or the arts), giving examples to illustrate the epistemological structures that characterize the discipline, then fielding questions from the audience. As one might imagine, the outcomes of this task can vary enormously depending on the students' skill levels and degree of preparation, as well as on the broader culture of the class and the school. In this case, there are roughly twenty students in the room, as well as their Theory of Knowledge teacher and two invited panelists: the school's co-headmaster and the IB math coordinator. As we observe, the first presentation unfolds.

The presenters are six twelfth-grade boys—three black, two Asian, and one Latino—who stand in a loose semi-circle facing the audience. They have handed out a sheet labeled "The Human Sciences" with some bullet-pointed definitions on it. There is no projection technology; instead, the presenter on the far left holds an open laptop in front of him like a book. After the teachers engage in some shushing, the room quiets down and the group members introduce themselves. The presenter holding the laptop begins: "So I know that you guys may be thinking: what are the human sciences? Is it the science of humans? Definitely not." He reads the definition of the human sciences verbatim, crouching slightly to see the screen. "It's [a] pretty clear difference between the natural sciences and the human sciences," he says. "In the natural sciences it's much easier to come up with laws and rules. Human behavior can't be studied like that, you can't actually prove things. . . . like depression: through natural sciences you can show that a certain chemical is activated in the brain, but in the human sciences you might see someone walking around smiling but the next week they committed suicide and you had no idea. It's not as observable."

The next group-member takes the laptop from his peer and reads about the history of the human sciences verbatim from the screen. He slouches and mumbles as he speaks, and within a minute various side conversations erupt. He looks enormously relieved when his section is over. The presenter standing next to him says that he is going to give an example of activity that involves the human sciences. He asks one of the other presenters to smile and asks, rhetorically, "Do we know if he's really happy? No . . . there's no way that we can tell for sure." He then asks the students in the audience to make faces at each other and to guess how the person they're looking at is feeling. The noise level in the room immediately bubbles up; audience members leer at each other and generally goof around for a couple of minutes while the presenters remain standing at the front of the room, occasionally flashing each other a sheepish grin. The math coordinator appears to be jotting down some thoughts on a sheet of paper but neither she nor the other adults have a formal rubric that they are using to evaluate the presentations.

After a few minutes have passed, the Theory of Knowledge teacher calls the group together and says that it's time for the presenters to field questions from the panelists. The co-headmaster, a middle-aged Asian man who has been observing the goings-on with arms folded, asks why the word "science" is in the term "human science." None of the group members answer; an awkward silence descends. Eventually, the Theory of Knowledge teacher intervenes with another question. "How could you operationalize happiness in a way that's not self-reported?" he asks. One of the presenters says that he might draw different faces and ask a subject to point out the one that best represents their mood. The teacher shakes his head and says, "I want you to give me an example of how you could measure happiness in a way that isn't self-reported." A different student says that you could measure blood pressure or heart rate. The teacher says, "Right!" He goes on to give a number of other examples of how to measure emotions using physiology, talking for almost the entirety of the remaining five minutes in the presentation. A few of the audience members nod as he speaks; others are looking out the windows or doodling on the presentation handouts. The presenters shift their weight around, appearing relieved to let the teacher take the reins. One of the students at the back of the room mutters to a friend, "Why do we even have to do IB? We're not, like, European."

There are certainly some glimmers of depth to be found in this assignment, especially when framed in terms of its aspirations. Students were tasked with the collective responsibility to take on a conceptually complex topic; their presentation included an illustration of one of the core dilemmas associated with what it might mean to ascertain "truth" in a particular discipline; there were opportunities for interactive engagement by audience members; and the presence of the two panelists attempted to raise the stakes for the assignment. All of these components are highly aligned with the vision of deep learning specified by the IBDP. But the reality didn't come close to meeting the ideal of the program.

Most striking, perhaps, the presenters' lack of basic academic skills undermined their ability to do what had been asked of them. Given that most of the presenters read verbatim from a secondary source, for example, it is unclear to what extent any of them had engaged in the independent synthesis and cross-disciplinary comparisons that the task was intended to support. Furthermore, the simplicity of the experiment they designed and their inability to tackle the questions posed by the panelists suggest that their understanding of the subject lacked conceptual depth. All of these limitations were exacerbated by their obvious—even painful—lack of comfort and fluency when it came to presenting publicly.

These problems were by no means limited to this particular task. Our observations, as well as our conversations with teachers and leaders, suggest that they play out in a variety of ways throughout the school. In particular, teachers at Franklin find themselves thwarted by the question of how to ensure that students with significant skill and knowledge gaps—a group that comprises a majority of the school's population—can be meaningfully engaged in the high-level tasks that IBDP coursework demands. When tackling an IA task, for example, how should one think about trying to offer appropriate support to eleventh-graders who read at the equivalent of a fourth-grade level, and / or who have not yet mastered basic mathematical concepts? What should they do with students who are unable and / or unwilling to work independently on academic tasks in the sustained way that many of the IBDP assessments require? More broadly, how might they convince students, many of whom do not come from English-speaking or college-educated families, that the academic intensity of the IBDP is worth the effort when compared to the less ambitious curricula offered at neighboring high schools— especially since only a small fraction of Franklin students who seek the diploma are able to earn it?

The school's leaders, for their part, share these concerns. They also describe their bafflement about how to change what they acknowledge to be a pattern of teacher-centered, "worksheet-centered" instructional practices, especially given that the school's budget and time for professional learning are extremely limited. One of the co-principals is particularly focused on the instructional issue, emphasizing that while the shift to becoming an IB school has encouraged some changes in teaching practice, especially within the math department, it has not penetrated as widely or as deeply as he had anticipated. Students, too, pick up on this pattern. As one insightful senior reports:

> In tenth grade we didn't learn anything new, but when we got to eleventh grade the teachers went to this IB training over the summer and so then they started pushing the students to know more. The biggest shift was the way teachers communicated. When we were sophomores our teachers didn't really communicate, but after the training they started to get to know us better and began asking us what we thought sometimes. . . . They still talk a lot but [at least] they want us to know the stuff.

These sentiments, along with our observations, suggest that one of the key missing elements at Franklin is the unusual and important *stance* that a large number of teachers at IB High seem to share—a stance that couples a real interest in who students are and how they think with a genuine belief in what they can do when given adequate support.

Franklin is also missing a number of the other mechanisms present at IB High. It did not have a cadre of teachers with existing knowledge of IB to guide newer teachers in understanding the program. It did not have built-in response mechanisms through which teachers could carefully unpack their lessons and receive feedback from more knowledgeable others. It had not developed a specific set of supports for students who were struggling with the IB requirements. Without these mechanisms, "IB for All" became more of an aspiration than a reality, which in turn made it hard to sustain a culture of equity.

IB High also had some structural characteristics that gave it a significant leg up over Franklin. IB High is a socioeconomically diverse school, which means that some students come from professional-class homes. IB High is also a charter school, which means that both students and teachers have chosen to be there. As a nonselective, high-poverty district school, Franklin has fewer financial resources, less control over hiring processes, a dramatically more limited set of professional learning programs, an inferior facility, and far less ability to attract and retain middle-class families than does its counterpart down the coast. That Franklin has to compete with highly selective local magnet schools, which serve as a "brain drain" for the area's more motivated and highly skilled middle-school students, puts it at a further disadvantage. Finally, and perhaps most importantly, the severity of the skill gaps and language barriers that characterize a large number of its students intensifies the question of how to embed remediation and scaffolding opportunities into ambitious academic tasks—a question that, as we explore in Chapters 7 and 8, the field has yet to answer with any kind of systemic coherence.

In this context, IB High can be seen as a living illustration of the field's "learning edge" in terms of using the IBDP as a tool to create and equitably distribute opportunities for deep learning. The school demonstrates the viability of bringing the IBDP to a broader range of learners than historically have had access to it, and it reveals the school-level characteristics that can help leaders and teachers to actualize the potential of the program. What it does not as yet answer is the question of how to overcome the tangle of problems that plague the most disadvantaged pockets of the K–12 system. To put it differently, the school does not reveal what it might take to offer IB successfully for *all*; rather, it tells a compelling story about what it might take to offer IB successfully for *more*.

A System for Deep Learning?

Can International Baccalaureate create a system for deeper learning? The research in this chapter suggests that it should be viewed as an important resource in meeting that aspiration, but is not a cure-all in and of itself. As an "anchor" it offers a rich, detailed vision of what it would mean for students to think complexly in different subjects and across them. As a scaffold it can help to guide teacher learning toward these outcomes. It also serves as a safeguard against low expectations through its creation of a series of externally moderated assessments. All of these assets that the program brings reinforce the arguments about the importance of building an infrastructure to support deep learning. But infrastructure is not self-enacting. Like any other external policy tool, it will achieve its aspirations only if paired with internal school supports and mechanisms that help teachers realize its vision. These mechanisms include frequent feedback from lead teachers who have previous experience with IB, a cultural commitment to equity, and a willingness to provide additional support to students who need help

meeting the IB requirements. IB High is also distinctive in the equitable and humanistic stance it takes toward students: it does not track,
and it foregrounds participation in IB over results on the exams to
avoid the danger of IB becoming yet another form of test prep.[21] The
IB creates the opportunity to work toward deeper learning, but it is
still the adults in the building who create the culture, tone, and stance
toward students that make the school what it is.

From the perspective of scale, there are pessimistic and optimistic
ways to read this conclusion. The pessimistic view is that if the
knowledge and skill of the teachers and the culture of the school are
what shape the outcomes, and IB can achieve its promise only once
those school-level factors are in place, then it is still really the people
in the school who count. The optimistic view would acknowledge the
importance of local talent and skill, but assert that IB plays three critical functions. First, by setting clear and highly specific set of expectations for students, it lessens the load on the school, creating a clear sense
of the "what" and freeing the school to work on the "how." Second, by
creating a system that is externally moderated and has high standards,
it creates pressure to create and maintain rigorous learning and helps
schools see where they stand in helping their students accomplish complex disciplinary tasks. And third, by creating a shared framework of
what is to be learned, it serves as a platform for teacher learning around
common content and objectives—learning that accumulates over the
years as teachers gain practice teaching, receiving and later giving feedback, and eventually serving as IB examiners. Thus while it is fair to
say that no externally derived system can be successfully utilized without
a corresponding level of knowledge, skill, culture, and internal coherence in the school in which it is employed, IB can play an important
role in helping schools to build those critical qualities.

IB is also intriguing because it strikes a middle ground between more
radical and more traditional visions of deep learning. To this end, the
IBDP came up in our conversations with leaders at both Dewey High
and No Excuses High—and, as it turns out, both schools view the program in a positive light. At Dewey High, outward-facing network
leaders have connected as critical friends with leaders at several IB high
schools abroad; their view is that the diploma program, while more
conventional than Dewey High in how it organizes the "what" of academic learning, provides a platform for richly constructivist and glob-

ally oriented classrooms that have much in common with their own. At No Excuses High, leaders view the program with admiration; they even have considered adopting the IBDP as a more rigorous and integrated alternative to their current curricular programs, deciding against this option only because it would require abandoning the extensive infrastructure that they have built around the SAT IIs and the APs. That two such dramatically different schools take the IBDP seriously as an approach to creating deep learning says a great deal about the program's potential as a mechanism by which to deepen what happens in many American high school classrooms.

5 ∿

The Comprehensive High School:
Performance versus Learning

So FAR, we have explored approaches to deeper learning in three relatively small schools, each organized around a particular theme: project-based learning, no excuses, and International Baccalaureate. These schools show us what is possible in environments where students have chosen to be there and are oriented around a shared mission. But what about the comprehensive public high school, where the vast majority of American teenagers are educated?

In this chapter, we visit one such school, which shows the possibilities but also the limits of pursuing deeper learning within a large comprehensive public high school. The school, which we call Attainment High, has slightly more than two thousand students and is located in an affluent suburb outside of a Northeastern city. Its student body is 66 percent white, 14 percent Asian, 9 percent Latinx, 7 percent African American, and 4 percent Other; 16 percent of its students are eligible for free or reduced-price lunch. A busing program that brings students from the city contributes to the school's racial and socioeconomic diversity. A full 92 percent of its students go directly to college from high school, with 84 percent attending four-year colleges. Top students routinely attend Ivy League universities or highly competitive liberal arts colleges; a full college acceptance list shows institutions at varying levels of selectivity, from local colleges that admit nearly all applicants to highly selective universities like Stanford. Attainment High is housed in a beautiful brick and glass building, completed in 2010. It routinely appears in lists of top schools in the city's magazine and other ranking systems, and the suburb it is housed in is a highly desirable residential area.

Attainment High is thus, in one sense, a best case scenario for apprising the possibilities of the comprehensive high school. The school has a significant base of highly educated parents, is financially well endowed, and has experienced teachers, many of whom describe Attainment High as their dream job. It also has some racial and socioeconomic diversity, which enables us to explore questions of diversity and difference within an advantaged context.

As in other cases in this book, our picture of the school comes by way of immersion in the school and its activities. In total, we visited forty classes, attended club meetings and extracurricular events, went to whole faculty and department team meetings, and interviewed thirty faculty and administrators, as well as twenty students. Since this was a much larger school than the ones profiled in previous chapters, we could not see every classroom or talk to every teacher, so we had to take another approach to make sure our research had both breadth and depth. In our first few days, we shadowed a variety of students, across grades and tracks, throughout their days. This gave us a sense of the instructional patterns and their distribution at the school. Then, based on those observations, and conversations with students, faculty, and administrators, we conducted deep dives into places identified as particularly powerful learning spaces, seeking to understand what made those places tick and how or why they were different from the norm. Finally, toward the end of our research visit, we returned to the question of the whole, asking how the principal, department chairs, and teachers were seeking to expand the rigor, relevance, and equity of learning in core classes, and the barriers they faced in doing so.

While there are many stories one could tell about this school from the perspective of powerful learning—learning that is challenging, engaging, and invites students to create as well as receive knowledge—we found an institution that features pockets of such learning against a backdrop of largely conventional instruction. There are many forces that work against deeper learning at Attainment High. Teaching as transmission remains the dominant pedagogical mode. Students are adept at playing the "game of school." The desire for credentials, including APs, militates against opportunities for more genuine engagement. State tests emphasize floors over ceilings. Inherited

structures, like classes that run for fifty-minute blocks, limit opportunities for deeper exploration. Community pressure to play the attainment game reinforces a "performance" as opposed to "learning"
orientation. Tracking preserves differences in opportunities for
higher-order thinking across levels. Particularly striking is the mismatch between the school's treatment of adolescents as passive learners
in core classes and the school's empowering stance toward students in
clubs and extracurriculars.

At the same time, there are exceptions to the dominant academic pattern, particularly in electives and non-AP honors courses, where the
combination of mutual choice, freedom from external constraints, depth
over breadth, shared teacher and student passion, and, in some cases,
hands-on learning, yield more powerful learning experiences. Some
administrators and teachers are challenging the dominant academic
conventions by trying to reduce curricular differentiation, embrace
inquiry-oriented instruction, deemphasize AP scores, and directly address issues of racial inequality, but change has been slow and piecemeal.
The implication is that steering even leading public schools toward
deeper learning and equity is politically difficult, both within schools
and with respect to external expectations. What are some of these barriers to deeper learning?

The Grammar of Instruction

Scholars Larry Cuban and David Tyack have suggested that elements
of a certain "grammar of schooling"—age-graded classrooms, learning
divided into conventional subjects, and teachers in classrooms with
twenty-five students at a time—are such baked-in aspects of how schools
are conceived and organized that they are impervious to change. While
the grammar of schooling focuses on structural aspects of schools, we
see an accompanying "grammar of instruction" that lays out the pedagogical rationale for traditional classrooms. The pattern here is that
there is a prespecified body of knowledge to be covered, students spend
some period of time learning to remember some key attributes of this
body of knowledge, there is an assessment (either a test or a writing assignment), and then the process repeats with a new topic. At its best,
this process builds some knowledge in a domain; at its worst, it becomes

a game of "cover-remember-test-forget-repeat" that occupies students' and teachers' time but produces little sustained understanding.

Unlike at No Excuses High, there was no single template that dictated what happened in all classes. Core classes were more teacher-centered than not, but the specific modes varied by discipline and by teacher. History classes featured a mix of lecture and some opportunities to deal with document-based questions or offer opinions on historical events. English classes featured a mix of student discussion of text and teacher mini-lectures on elements of writing. Science classes featured a mix of lecture and student labs. Math classes were in the process of being reformed when we investigated them, and thus we will return to them in more depth later. One administrator estimated that he had seen almost 90 percent of the classes at the school, and in almost all cases the class featured the teacher standing in front of the room. The standards and pacing guides in science, history, and math were set by the state and district, and the combination of the textbooks and those standards set a course that emphasized breadth over depth. Almost all of the core disciplinary classes worked within a "batch processing" model, where the whole class moved through the same content, took an assessment, and moved on to the next. All of these core classes were based in single traditional academic disciplines, with no opportunities for the disciplines to connect or interact. With the exception of the labs in science, students were mostly sitting in these classes, using their brains to remember and decipher texts and problems, with little use of their bodies or voices. Thus, while there was some alternating between lecture and more active student experiences, there was little hands-on, individualized, interdisciplinary, apprenticeship, or project-based learning in core academic classes.

The success of this approach varied. This mode could work well for academically inclined students in subjects they were interested in. A number of students reported having good experiences in at least one of the academic disciplines, ascribing those positive experiences to their interest in the subject or the ability of the teacher to get them invested in those subjects. At the same time, many students said that they were not interested in much of their academic diet, which they said they had not chosen, was not useful, and was largely an exercise in doing what needed to be done to get to college and beyond.

Two governing assumptions were particularly limiting. The first was expectations for coverage, which meant that classes needed to move quickly across a variety of topics. Laboratory experiments were usually squeezed into one class period. The Crusades got a week; the Cold War got two days. Consequently, deeper historical or scientific investigations were scrapped in favor of moving across more content, and the quantity of material covered was so great that students had significant trouble remembering it. One teacher told us that when she tried to refer to material that students had successfully answered questions about on a state science exam only three months earlier, the students not only didn't know the content but argued that they had never seen it before!

A second set of assumptions is that a student's job is to assimilate knowledge that has already been discovered and organized into disciplinary buckets. Because of this assumption, teachers had little incentive to incorporate ideas or events that were live in society or in students' minds; the necessity of pouring more content into students' brains reigned supreme. It also meant that connections across fields or disciplines—literature on the Cold War, film about the Cold War, the lived experience of the Cold War—could not be accommodated. And it meant that students spent much more time learning what other people had learned about the disciplines—these are the causes of the Cold War; these are Newton's laws—than actually doing the work of the disciplines themselves. As a science teacher who had a Ph.D. from MIT told us, the problem with science in school is that you are mostly demonstrating to yourself what is already known; real science, she said, is all about the unknown.

The result was that students were sometimes surprised when they were given real-world opportunities to immerse themselves in the same disciplines they had studied in school. For example, Edward, a high-achieving student at Attainment High, had a chance to work with a history professor over the summer between junior and senior years. He described the project—an archival investigation into the work of artisans and craftspeople in Germany in the eighteenth century—as totally different from how he had learned history in class. The junior research paper he completed in school, for example, was, "It's a lot of 'this is what your textbook says,' 'here are four [web]sites you should use, they will have stuff on it.' It's a very structured way of doing research, which makes it a lot easier to do a project," but, he says, "it isn't the environment you will find" when you actually do research. In contrast, he says, research with the professor was much more uncertain: there was an initial question and some sources to consult, but beyond that, the research evolved based on the sources that he found. Not only did the experience change his conception of what it is that historians actually do; the fact that it would lead to an actual published product greatly increased his motivation for doing the research. "I had a lot more fun doing it . . . with the professor, because I felt that what I'm doing isn't just doing what thousands of other students have done," he said. "I'm not just writing this formulaic paper, but I'm actually finding information that he will use in a paper he writes in the future. I had a lot more fun with that."

Playing the Game: Learning versus Performance

As befitted a community that had high levels of cultural and social capital, students were good at playing the "game of school." Students mostly did the assignments and homework required of them, although they told us that there was considerable copying of answers from one another. In return, the atmosphere in classes was not authoritarian but rather loose—there was a constant buzz of students chattering with one another as they worked on math problems or conducted science labs. These were what previous scholars have called treaties: students agree to basically do what teachers ask, and, in return, teachers do not micromanage every aspect of students' existence.[1] The combination of the shared class and racial background of most students and teachers, and students' desire to do well in school for college, meant that a more cooperative atmosphere prevailed than was the case in many higher-poverty schools that we visited.

While there was clearly some learning going on in these classes—as measured by students' passing of AP and Sat II tests and acceptance into selective colleges—this approach also bred considerable cynicism among students, who were very aware of the difference between doing what teachers wanted in order to get good grades and actually engaging in the subjects. From the students' viewpoint, the problem was that teachers presented their subjects as being open-ended, but in practice, each question had a right answer that they expected students to deliver. We saw this, for example, in an AP psychology class, where students had taken a multiple choice quiz, adapted from the AP test, on a series of psychological terms (operant conditioning, behavioral conditioning, and so on). The teacher was calling on students to volunteer which options they had chosen on the quiz: "Connie—what did you get on this? A? That wouldn't be the best choice," the teacher responds. And then she called on someone else who gave the answer she was looking for. While one might argue that building such factual knowledge can form the basis for deeper investigations, conversations with students suggested that this subsequent day never came—it was just off to the next unit and the next set of definitions. Students were particularly critical of this mode when it seemed incompatible with the subject matter. For example, a unit on transcendentalism conjured up Thoreau and Emerson breaking from convention but the mode of delivery was a PowerPoint summarizing the key points of the movement. A student cited another example: "We were watching *Dead Poets Society* in English class . . . and then the teacher is like, 'This is what you're supposed to infer from this movie,' which is, like, the complete opposite of the point of the movie."

A chemistry teacher and a physics teacher argued that the consequence of years of socialization in this approach was that students in their classes were now trying to "read" the teacher to guess the right answer. They discussed this dynamic in reference to a chemistry chromatography lab that yielded ambiguous results about whether five or six dyes were present in the sample:

> *Interviewer:* Are students comfortable with the idea that there could be five or six, and it depends on how you measured it, or how you look at it? Do they think there should be an answer?
> *Chemistry teacher:* No. They think there should be—
> *Physics teacher:* Yes, there should be a right answer.
> *Chemistry teacher:* They wanna know what we want. I mean I think I learned early on that a poker face is really important. I mean I don't know, I haven't been in elementary or middle school classrooms. It seems to me like there's a lot of students who just learn to read teachers' faces, and that's what they do. They give a response and—
> *Physics teacher:* It's sort of like with a question at the end.

Chemistry teacher: —look for the teacher's face. They have this sense, and I don't know where it comes from, but they have this sense that there's always a right answer, and that's always what I wanna try and give. The teacher will have "a tell" that will give it away.

Physics teacher: We're teaching kids to play poker in elementary and middle schools.

Chemistry teacher: Yeah. I feel like students get frustrated a lot, cuz they give me an answer, I just kinda look at them, or ask them to explain, or why. Then they change their answer . . . Yeah.

Physics teacher: Yeah.

Chemistry teacher: Yeah, I think they're more comfortable with the idea that there is an answer, and I have it, and they're just supposed to find it and deliver it to me.

Scholars have distinguished between "learning" and "performance" orientations: learning orientation emphasizes that learning is a process, that failure is part of learning, and that getting the right answer is not as important as struggling with the question. Performance orientation is the opposite—focusing on whether one is right, potentially to the neglect of what one is learning.[2] At Attainment High, there were posters everywhere about the importance of a learning orientation, but in practice, for both students and teachers, performance orientation was king. Students needed to get right answers to get good grades to get into good colleges. Teachers needed students to pass state, SAT II, and AP tests if they were going to stay in good standing with their students, parents, and colleagues. The result was that in most classes the long-standing model of teaching as transmission prevailed. While there might be some active student processing, as students experimented in a lab or worked out a math problem, the ultimate goal was less for students to explore a subject area than for them to be able do what these external metrics required.

AP: Credentials versus Engagement

This tension between performance and learning orientations was brought to the fore in the school's Advanced Placement classes. In a recent year, 395 students at Attainment High sat for 766 AP exams in twenty-one subjects, with 92 percent scoring three or higher. Much of what happened inside the AP track was structured by forces that lay far outside of it. In particular, the increasingly competitive college landscape, and the parental pressure that accompanied it, meant that students felt considerable pressure to take AP classes and do well in them. As one teacher described it, "A big source of stress for our students is that their parents all did very well in school and went to elite colleges and that's how they can afford to buy a house in this district." The result was an ethos that was both "super high performing" and "super competitive," which the teachers described as frequently inhibiting the kind of learning they were seeking to promote. As an AP physics teacher described it, "Competition is a serious obstacle to deeper learning; collaboration is crucial and when students have the feeling that they're being evaluated as individuals, that's at cross-purposes to collaboration."

Over the past few years, between Attainment High and the other high school in the same district, three suicides took place. While the causes of these suicides were specific to each of the students, they provoked widespread discussion among faculty, students, and parents about how to mitigate the culture of achievement and competitiveness. As one physics teacher described his changing stance, "A big part of me teaching AP this year is explicitly talking about anxiety and lessening anxiety—in the past there was this emphasis on 'this is a hard course and you're going to work very hard for me and that's what you get when you sign up for an AP course.' Changing the tone of it a little bit and talking with them about putting less pressure and stress on themselves." But the teachers, while they were seeking to lessen some of the pressure, were also aware that they were not the primary sources of the stress. As one said, "We're not going to get rid of the competition—they put immense pressure on themselves, they've internalized the pressure coming from the community, and they're not thinking about mental health and finances and other stuff."

If one source of the pressure is parents, the other is the expectation of colleges. Like many schools, Attainment High uses a weighted grade-point average system, in which AP courses can help push one's GPA over four and potentially toward the maximum of five. As one observer described it, "I find that the majority are very caught up in credentialing and very eager to gather as many fours and fives on as many AP tests as possible. . . . Students perceive that their applications to elite colleges are invalid without them." The result is that top students load up on APs, trying to take as many as they can. The consequence, says one teacher, is that they are so busy "loading up their plate with stuff to do . . . they don't have the time to engage in deeper learning." A second echoes the sentiment: "The kids take so many high-level courses that they don't have time to develop passion or dig deeper." This problem is so pervasive that the school recommends that students take no more than three AP courses, but, given college and community pressures, it is hard to make that recommendation stick.

The emphasis on AP and the AP exams is particularly troubling to some of the AP teachers because the content of the tests has histori-cally emphasized breadth over depth. There is some variety across sub-ject areas, but particularly in history and the sciences, teachers felt that the push for coverage was interfering with deeper investigations. As an AP history teacher said, "It's a lot more lecture in AP, it's a lot more push to get through content." Said another, "AP includes more lecturing than I would like, there's lots of plowing through material—you sacri-fice something there. The College Board claims that there will be more depth and less ridiculous material but I'll believe it when I see it."

One significant reason that APs have this emphasis is their history. Advanced Placement was created after World War II by a small group of private schools and elite universities in collaboration with the Ford Foundation and was opened to public high schools in the mid-1950s. Its goal was to meet the demand for academically ambitious study and to certify this learning for selective colleges. Its solution was to offer faster-paced, more demanding courses, but it did not seek to radically change instruction or make it more student-centered. As David Cohen and Jal Mehta have written elsewhere, "AP was a subject-centered rather than student-centered reform. . . . AP teachers still lectured, students still took notes," and most classrooms were still teacher-centered. Unlike International Baccalaureate, Advanced Placement does not offer a vision of what kinds of people it is hoping that students will become; only a roadmap for the content they hope students will assimilate. So in several ways it is both congruent with and reinforces many of the tendencies of Attainment High: first, it is compatible with the dominant pedagogical orientation of teaching as transmission; and second, it pro-vides a high-status credential, which is a huge part of what parents and students are seeking from the school. As one astute observer of the credentialing process commented to us, "AP is fundamentally about making the attainment structure of secondary education work; if it didn't exist, we would have to invent it."[3]

Teachers who were dissatisfied with the APs also told us how APs interfered with opportunities to develop project-based curricula. For example, in biology, students used to conduct a lengthy research project as part of their AP biology course. Here the biology teacher describes what happened:

> It was a year-long project that had four phases. It had to incorporate . . . something out in the community. A lot of them would work on . . . [a river watershed], or some ecology application was pretty common. Some would work in labs. The challenge became that our AP biology course was primarily taken by juniors, and they were also taking AP U.S. history, and they were also writing their junior thesis, which is the big paper at [Attainment High]. The workload was unbearable.
>
> The students told us that [the project] was, by far, the best part of the course. When we transitioned to the new AP bio curriculum, we made the decision to drop the project. It was also unbearable for the teachers to handle—one of our teachers teaching AP bio this year has four sections of twenty-seven students each. That many independent research projects is unbearable to manage. One of the things we've talked about is do we care about the College Board? Do we care about AP? We could do those projects if we weren't so confined by some of the College Board constraints. What we've heard from students is that [it] was a really powerful experience.

A number of the teachers openly wondered whether they would do better to simply drop the APs and offer rigorous capstone courses that didn't culminate in the exams. As one teacher argued, "If the courses weren't labeled AP—you can make it be what you wanted it to be and you can set the parameters. You could say we're going to teach an honors senior biology course and it could still be the toughest course in the school, but you might make it so that the grading isn't just about what you might get on the exam." A number of private schools have taken the step of moving away from APs, and Attainment High was exploring the possibility of cutting back on such courses. The previous principal took a number of senior teachers to visit a school organized around IB, but Attainment High did not take any definite steps in that direction.

The way in which teachers approached AP also had significant implications for how students experienced it. In a number of AP classes we saw, the test was clearly ruling the roost. Unit tests were taken from or deliberately modeled on AP tests, and teachers made frequent mention during class of what sort of questions were likely to be asked on the exam and what kinds of answers were likely to please the AP examiners. Some teachers did so in a spirit of earnest helpfulness, while others did so while badmouthing AP or expressing resignation to their fate. Each of these choices effectively deadened the atmosphere of these classes, since the stance from the teacher was not enthusiasm for the subject but rather submission to the requirements of the College Board.

A few skilled teachers took a different stance toward the exam. Adult developmental psychologist Robert Kegan describes what he calls a "subject to object shift" in which people take some aspect of the belief system that has ruled them, and make it "object," meaning that it becomes something they stand apart from and make decisions about.[4] In a similar fashion, some teachers had made a subject to object shift with respect to the AP exam: while they covered the key material that students needed for the exam, they also promoted their own goals for the course. For example, the AP comparative government teacher had been drawn to the subject because of her own experience as an immigrant and her commitment to helping students de-center their American perspectives. But she found that the AP comparative government test was quite a dry, mostly multiple-choice affair that simply asked students to remember features of six different countries, but did little to ask them to understand the social and economic realities of those different nations. She therefore organized parts of the course around student presentations about pressing issues in different countries. In one class we witnessed, we saw a heated debate about how to address the U.S.-Mexico drug corridor, a discussion that integrated political, cultural, economic, and moral perspectives. Not surprisingly, students were highly engaged in that class and spoke enthusiastically about it, because it was grounded not in a distant exam but rather in live issues and a variety of lenses through which they could be investigated.

Perhaps because of the potential opportunity that AP afforded—a chance to work with a select group of students on high-level content—teachers were particularly frustrated when students used that opportunity to "play the game of school." Teachers across subject areas reported that students frequently played the "what did you get?" game, competing with one another to score points on quizzes, tests, and even in discussions. One English teacher described how, in group discussions, honors students were frequently caught up in "performing" for her and for other students: "I do think honor students are really sensitive to this idea—and it's a myth, to some extent, of when you're participating in class discussion, you're performing in some ways. You're performing for the teacher. 'Look. I really know this.' You're performing for your peers."

Teachers believed that these classroom dynamics could be altered by adopting new pedagogical strategies—but these steps went only so far. The English teacher found that in small groups, rather than the larger group, students were more willing to take risks and offer partially developed ideas. The chemistry and physics teachers quoted earlier had flipped their classrooms and given students more time to work on problems together in class. They had also stopped grading weekly problem sets—to avoid the problem of policing whether students were copying each other—and instead put the stakes exclusively on the final exam. They found that in this atmosphere, students were increasingly likely to see the weekly work as something that would benefit them—or cost them if they chose not to do it—rather than as a game being policed by a teacher.

Even though these pedagogical changes could partially mitigate problems, the teachers described the more fundamental issue as arising from the student, parent, and community expectations for credentialing. One AP teacher described what she sees, referencing the educational theorist David Labaree, who has been critical of the credentialing race:

My cynicism is influenced by David Labaree—a lot of what he writes explains my experience and my frustration. My frustration many times is I feel like I'm trying to engage with students around a common purpose but I feel like I am being received as an opponent—that my goal of educating students is at cross-purposes with students' goals and perhaps the community's goals, which is to gather credentials.

I would like to engage with students in what you are calling deeper learning: students would ask the questions and answer their own questions, with me providing guidance to resources and posing counter-arguments and engaging intellectually. And many of our students are quite capable of functioning in an environment like that, but I think the students want another stamp on their passport and move on to the next. I think partly it comes from anxiety about the acceptance rate to the competitive colleges, which is dropping—it's promoting a paranoia about the process.

Labaree argues that education has both intrinsic value (what is gained from learning) and exchange value (what someone will give you for that learning). In his view, as the competition for elite credentials intensifies, students, quite rationally, begin to pursue the credentials rather than the underlying knowledge and skill. As he writes, "When they see education through the lens of [its exchange value], students at all levels quickly come to the conclusion that what matters most is not the knowledge they learn in school but the credentials they acquire there. Grades, credits, and degrees—these become the objects to be pursued. . . . The effect on education is to emphasize form over content—to promote an educational system that is willing to reward students for formal compliance with modest performance requirements rather than for demonstrating operational mastery of skills."[5] Or as, one particularly insightful student said, "But the thing is I feel like most of the time we have to choose between getting a good grade and actually learning. And like I'm going to choose a good grade, because learning doesn't help me get into college, right?" While this might be quite rational from the point of the arms race that is now college admissions, it is not surprising that teachers feel as if it undermines the fundamental purposes of teaching and learning.[6]

What we see in these top tracks also sheds a cautionary light on Annette Lareau's well-known work on "concerted cultivation." Lareau argues that more advantaged parents both socialize their children to take on more assertive styles with adults and spend much more time arranging their children's schedules to build resumes that will serve them well in the competition for college and beyond. Poorer and working-class parents engage in more "natural growth" in which they give their children more time to play and are less cognizant of how to play the game of climbing the status ladder. What we see at Attainment High is the logical outgrowth of concerted cultivation—students who are very accomplished at generating the many credentials they need for college. But their teachers are telling us that while this strategy may be effective from the point of view of retaining social status and privilege, it frequently undermines the engagement in learning that school is supposed to produce.

The Persistent Significance of Tracking

While AP classes may have had a faster rather than deeper quality to them, most did ask students to engage in at least some higher-order thinking. In English, this meant analyzing the author's choices; in physics it meant looking at data about projectiles and seeking to make sense of how objects moved and why; in history it meant developing a fifteen-page research paper. While in each of these domains one could imagine a deeper level of work—in English, tying one's analysis of a story to a long-term effort to write one's own; in physics, designing one's own experiment rather than replicating an existing one; in history, drawing on more original sources and developing one's own investigation—these classes did at least ask students to produce some original work and to engage in some analysis.

In lower track courses, which Attainment High calls college prep (CP)—the lowest track—and advanced college prep (ACP), which is the middle track, there were fewer opportunities for this kind of analysis and thinking. The expected assignments were shorter, teachers talked more and students talked less, class time was split into shorter segments, and the work was generally more structured in terms of what students were asked to do.

Reba Page's book *Lower Track Classrooms* can help us to understand these classes. Page's research suggests that lower track classes generally assume three patterns: the "skeleton" pattern, in which a superficial version of upper-track material is covered at a slower pace; a "relevance" pattern, in which fun, timely, or real-world content is used to try to interest the students; and a "skills" pattern, in which students are drilled in basic skills.[7] We saw all three patterns in our data, both at Attainment High and at other schools we visited. At Attainment High, teachers said that they tried to cover the same material but did so more slowly: "In lower tracks you're spending three times as much amount of time working on the same task as you are with the honors kids." Another teacher, speaking to the relevance point, said that as the curriculum level goes down, "The more nurturing I become as a teacher, and it's less about the content and more about trying to keep them from shutting down."

Inequalities across tracks were not specific to Attainment High; we saw these differences at every comprehensive high school we visited. We chose one school in a major Midwestern city for investigation precisely because it was a large comprehensive high school that was racially and socioeconomically diverse and housed one of the nation's first International Baccalaureate programs. But when we arrived, we found almost exclusively advantaged, white, and Asian-American students in the IB classes, while mostly poorer black and Latinx students were in the regular, non-IB classes. On one December morning, we watched two English classes, back to back. In the advanced/honors one, students were being asked to analyze the author's choices; in the regular class, students were laboriously just reading the story out loud, with no effort made to make sense of the story, nor of why the author might have structured it as she did. Differences across tracks have been documented again and again in the literature, but they are still important to attend to in a deeper learning study because tracking is a critical means by which learning opportunities are distributed across the student body.

Attainment High also had racial inequality across the different curricular levels. The school's internal data show that while the school's population is 7 percent black and 9 percent Latinx, the average enrollments in upper-level courses are 2.4 percent black and 5 percent Latinx. Asian students are overrepresented in advanced courses: they comprise 14 percent of the school's students but make up 19 percent of the average enrollments in advanced courses. These overall distributions include art, music, and career and technical courses; in the core academic subjects, black and Latinx students have even lower representations: advanced English classes are 4.2 percent Latinx and 2.1 percent black; advanced math classes are 5 percent Latinx and 2.9 percent black; advanced science classes are 3.4 percent Latinx and 2.0 percent black; advanced language classes are 8.2 percent Latinx and 1.5 percent black (see Table 5.1).[8]

Table 5.1 Percentage of Students Taking Honors or AP Courses, by Race

	School demographics	History and Social Studies	English	Math	Science	Language
White	66	71.5	72.4	68.7	65.5	66.7
Asian	14	17.7	16.6	19.3	24.2	19.1
Latinx	9	3.9	4.2	5.0	3.4	8.2
Black	7	1.8	2.1	2.9	2.0	1.5
Other	4	5	4.7	4	5	4.5

While students could and did take advanced classes in some subjects and not others, they perceived that they mostly saw the same students as they went through their days. This was particularly true of the AP/honors students, who took many of their classes together, and the CP students, who did as well. Says one upper-track student, "It's pretty like—I mean it's kind of divided. By the time you enter high school, you almost have the levels of classes set, like you have the highest performing students. And then, it's sort of like two or three other levels that don't really change that much. Like I see the same kids in all my classes, and there are some people who I was friends with in middle school who I only see at a football game or something, because they just won't be in any of my classes." The exceptions to this pattern were in sports, which drew a mix of students, as well as in some other extracurriculars, and some electives, as we will discuss more later.

That differences across tracks were highly correlated with race and class could also create unhealthy dynamics across curricular levels. One teacher described a fire drill where "my CP kids and my honors kids ended up in one room, and I'm like oh my god, I could see the looks between them exchanging." When she talked with the CP kids afterward about the hostility in the room, "I'm like, 'What happened?' and one student said, 'Well, those honors kids think they are better than us, that we're stupid, they're all rich.' And I said, 'This is nothing to do with money.' And another student said, 'Well, they sure make it look like that.'" This teacher said she was against tracking, because "it's basically segregation" within the school.

Teachers also perceived that students in the lower curricular tracks tended to internalize their positions in the academic hierarchy. One teacher said that he felt that students in the lower tracks "have more embarrassment" when they are wrong in class, and that there is "more shame with low-level kids." A second teacher told a story of a student who had been mostly in CP and ACP classes but was placed into a mixed English class with honors students. He continually questioned whether as an "ACP" he belonged with the honors students, and "I'm like, oh honey, you got to let it go. You're in the right place. You really are." A third teacher compared the challenges in the AP track to the lower-level tracks. With the "honors kids," she says, "we're up against credentialing," but at least, "they kind of want to know stuff," whereas "these other kids are like, 'When I'm a grown-up, I hope I don't have to go to a job I hate as much as I hate the job of showing up to school.'"

Given these differences across curricular levels, which classes students were placed into was a critical question. Formally, the criteria for placing students varied across departments, but generally students were initially placed into tracks based on the recommendations of their eighth-grade teachers. From there, moving up a level would be recommended for students who were getting good grades (A range) and were completing assignments without needing extra help from teachers. While in the past there had been more test-based approaches, on the whole the school felt that in-school performance was a better predictor and also gave faculty the flexibility to move students up even if they didn't test well. Recommendations for moving up or down came from the teachers, with department chairs having the final say. There was also wiggle room in the process; that is, determined parents and students could push for higher-level classes.

Teachers and students offered a range of explanations for racial differences across curricular levels. Some saw it as evidence of bias. On a panel the school had organized about racial and gender bias, one Latina girl said, "I always wanted to be in honors classes. Sometimes I got the same grade as a student who was white, and they got put in honors and AP and I didn't. It's all white or all Asian in the APs and Honors—I believe that blacks and Latinas could be in those classes if we supported them more." A related point was made by an English teacher who taught across tracks: "As much as we hate to admit it, we move kids up more on behavioral criteria than their actual talent level." By behavioral criteria, he says, he means that "Everything is on time, they're not causing us—you know, you don't have to redirect them all the time." He finds that these behavioral criteria disfavor the minority students and also sometimes white males whose work is strong but behavior is shaky. One data point that does not support the interpretation that bias leads to fewer black students being placed in honors or AP courses is that while 93 percent or more of Latinx, white, and Asian students received As or Bs in those courses, 79 percent of black students did so. (Of course, grades themselves could be racially biased.)

Teachers and students offered three other explanations for racial differences across tracks. One was differences in family background and in preparation from previous schooling. From this vantage point, the curricular levels were a response to different levels of skill and knowledge that students brought to various subjects. Some saw this as just a reality that came with a school that served some of the most affluent families in the metro areas as well as students in foster homes. Teachers who taught in the CP track had a number of stories about how families of students in this track did not have nearly the resources to support their children as did those with children in the higher tracks. A related explanation was that initial differences in academic background were compounded by grouping practices and other teacher/school choices in elementary and middle schools. From this perspective, what were initially small differences in school preparation are exacerbated by the ways in which elementary and middle schools respond to these differences; over time, the white, economically advantaged students come to think of themselves as high achievers, and the minority, higher-poverty students come to think of themselves as not. One teacher said that the perception among students in the CP track was that "once you were placed in a support class in middle school, you would be in all the dumb classes until you graduate high school."

Teachers and students offered one other explanation: the placement process gave parents and students the ability to agitate for more upper-level classes, and more white and Asian parents took advantage of this opportunity to push their children into honors and AP. For example, in science, the department chair, in an effort to broaden access to opportunity, had decided that she would approve any petition by parents or students to move to a higher-level class. With this new policy in place, 126 white and Asian students and parents asked to move up from the regular track to the honors track in science between ninth and tenth grade; one black student and one Latinx student did the same. Similarly, between tenth and eleventh grade, nineteen white and Asian

Table 5.2 Students Shifting from Regular (R) to Honors (H) Science, by Race

	9th-grade R to 10th-grade H	10th-grade R to 11th-grade H	11th-grade R to 12th-grade H
White and Asian	126	19	30
Black	1	1	3
Latinx	1	1	2

students asked to move up from regular to honors, compared to one black and one Latinx student; between eleventh and twelfth grade it was thirty white and Asian students asking to move from regular to honors, compared to three black and two Latinx students (see Table 5.2). The school, out of concern for students' mental health, recommended that students not take more than three AP classes, but some parents and students ignored that recommendation in the hopes of making themselves more competitive in the race to get into a "better" college. As advantaged white and Asian students took more and more APs, often to the neglect of their mental health, faculty and administrators despaired of closing the racial gap in advanced placement courses.

The school had struggled to address these discrepancies for years without much success. The previous principal, Karen Stein, had been at the school for seven years, and her primary focus had been closing racial and socioeconomic gaps in achievement and attainment. This effort had borne some fruit, including some real progress on standardized tests. But with respect to placement of students, while the departments had reexamined their criteria to try to ensure that they were accurately correlated with students' ability to do the work in higher-level courses, this had not led to significant changes in placement rates. We attended one meeting where a group of faculty discussed this issue, and all of this and more came up. They come with different levels of preparation, said one. But is there something about how we are placing them? asked another. Let's look at success cases, said a third—are there things we could learn from those cases? We also don't want to over-place kids, said a fourth; sometimes when we try to move kids up for the sake of moving them up, they are not ready. Observing this from the outside, what we saw was a group of well-intentioned people who cared deeply about students but were faced with a large problem they didn't know how to solve.

State Testing: Progress on Floors, Concern about Ceilings

In direct contrast to the stasis on class placement, the school had made significant progress in closing gaps on the state tests in English language arts, math, and science. In physics, for example, the percentage of low-income students proficient or above increased from 50 percent in 2008 to 92.2 percent in 2016; for black students the increase was from 36.6 percent proficient or above in 2008 to 80 percent in 2016. Large gains were also achieved in math and English language arts, and for economically disadvantaged students. Table 5.3 summarizes the changes.

This effort was led by Ms. Stein, who had joined the school with an agenda organized around using data to promote equity. One of her mantras was that there were more low-income students at the school than in almost any charter school in the state (which was true, given the size of the school), and that they had an obligation to serve those students well. The focus on data was fairly new for the school; as one department chair said, the initial reaction was a bit like "What are these graphs that you're speaking of?" Over time, however, "sharing the data with people helped . . . make an argument that you really can't say no to. When you see the gap mapped out visually, it's not just empty words, it's not just a person who's spewing their own ideas for the sake of being a dictator, but we all can sort of rally behind that." Using a combination of force of personality, data, the push from an external environment that highly incentivized progress on these tests, and a strategy of giving departments some latitude to figure out how best to close the gaps in their individual contexts, Ms. Stein was able to create significant progress on the state assessment.

Table 5.3 Percentage of Students Proficient and Above on State Tests, 2008–2016

	Black students, 2008	Black students, 2016	Low-income students, 2008	Low-income students, 2016
Math	45.4	82.6	63.2	89.8
English Language Arts	64.2	100	68.0	98.0
Physics	36.6	80.0	50	92.2

Once the vision had been established, the school took a series of steps to improve performance and particularly to close gaps. The school oriented a considerable part of its curriculum, particularly in science, to the topics that would be covered on the state test. It examined how its students were faring on the tests and gave students practice tests. It created extra blocks of test prep for students who were in danger of failing it. And, especially as the test got nearer, they coached students on what sorts of questions to expect and what sort of answers to give.

As sometimes has been true of standards-based reform elsewhere, a significant part of the story was that a common goal and set of metrics enabled more collaboration than in the past. One science teacher compared teaching chemistry, for which the school did not participate in state tests, to physics, for which it did. "There's a lot more freedom in what you can teach in chemistry. I find what's nice in physics is that kids will have common experiences. As much as I don't like the [state test], it makes sure that you're holding all students to some level of understanding." While the teacher felt a bit as if he was betraying his tribe by supporting the state testing, he did think that having an external standard to work toward had created more equity in what students were exposed to and what they could demonstrate they had learned. Standards-based reformers who argued that No Child Left Behind would push even "good" schools to attend to data on performance gaps for low-income and minority students would see the developments at Attainment High as validation of their view.

At the same time, there were significant questions about whether the state test prep fundamentally undermined deeper instruction in the disciplines. Consistent with external analyses that find that state tests are low in cognitive rigor, many teachers thought that orienting toward the state test was fundamentally limiting.[9] Said one science teacher, "I feel like at least in the physics department, what we teach. . . . the goal is to pass the state test really, even though we won't necessarily admit that. It is how everything is framed. We skirt the issue of deep learning. I think we do students a disservice. And we are very, very shallow in what we expect the students to be able to do, and understand." How does surface learning differ from deep learning? "Deep learning in physics would be something where you could really take time to grapple with the problem, and come to a way to model it, and understand it in a way that makes sense to you." He continued that deep understanding would come if one could show multiple ways of representing the same idea, which would reveal that you understood not only the formula but also the underlying concept.

The longtime chair of the science department, while more positive about the progress in closing the gap on the state test, also felt that the pace and the emphasis on breadth over depth undermined deep understanding. She gave the example of acceleration as something that was hard for freshmen to understand, because it is the rate of change of the rate of change. She said that in the past, "we would spend two weeks with kids doing all kinds of worksheets with problems, trying to understand acceleration." But then a new teacher had come up with the idea, drawn from a British TV show, *Top Gear*, of having "students figure out the acceleration of an object, you know, a cheetah, Usain Bolt, the space shuttle. And the kids had to do the research to get all the data, distance, time, velocity, all the information they were going to need to actually . . . figure out some acceleration information about this one object, do all the unit conversions to get it into meters per second squared, and really kind of own that object. And so, instead of doing lots of acceleration problems, they only did one, but they did it really deeply."

The consequence, she said, was a very different understanding of physics. "And what the teachers found was for the first time, kids understood what fifteen meters per second squared meant versus two thousand meters per second squared, because they'd be doing a problem like on another worksheet, and they would get a number, and say, 'Well, that doesn't make sense, because the space shuttle has that acceleration, and we're talking about a car.' They were able to own it in a way that they had never been able to own it before. So I would rather kids own it, and be able to walk away with something. But when they have to perform on the state test and be able to do a variety of kinds of acceleration problems, it's a difficult balance. So we try to insert some projects like that one into the curriculum, but we've never felt like we could say, 'We're going to do all of ninth grade physics in that way.'"

Finally, while the school had closed gaps in "proficiency" on the state test, it had not made nearly as much progress on the "advanced" standard. In physics, for example, 62 percent of all students had scored "advanced" on the physics exam, but only 35 percent of economically disadvantaged students and 32 percent of black students had scored similarly. While scoring "advanced" on the state test simply meant getting more questions right, and thus was not actually a sign of a qualitatively different kind of understanding, it did signal that there were still race and class differences in what students knew and could do.

Equity and the Ecosystem

While gaps on "advanced" scores persisted and there were legitimate concerns about the depth of learning in preparing for the state test, there had been significantly more progress in generating equity across test scores than in addressing racial inequalities in course-taking patterns. The school also seemed highly efficacious when it came to the state test; faculty and administrators worked together, used data, took collective responsibility, and made reliable progress over time. In contrast, with respect to minority students in upper-level courses, they had no similar collective strategy except to cluster the few minority students who were there. Rather, they were much more likely to assign responsibility for inequalities to factors outside of their control, such as students' home culture and previous school preparation. Why the difference?

We think that the answer lies in the external ecosystem. Improving state test scores was strongly incentivized by the state. Students needed to pass to graduate, and the passage rates were reported in local magazines and other sources that ranked the schools. The tests also measured more floors than ceilings: the ability to do basic math, comprehend reading passages, and apply moderately complex algorithms in science. The school had conviction that everyone could and should be able to pass these tests. Prepping for such tests led to some parent complaints that such a high-powered district shouldn't focus on basic test prep and may have led some parents to choose private schools, but the effort did not fundamentally disrupt the bargain that the school would serve as a conveyer belt to top colleges.

In contrast, the school was much more ambivalent when it came to the allocation of students across curricular levels. The very existence of the curricular tracks was itself a solution to two problems: the problem of academic differentiation, and the problem of signaling to colleges who are the most highly skilled students. Any efforts to de-track or lessen tracking at the school thus ran into opposition from parents: for example, when the school had moved to having just two levels of ninth-grade physics, with 85 percent of the students together, and 15 percent in a lower track, some parents complained, asking why, if their child was in the highest math level, he or she should take physics in what they saw as an unleveled class. Similarly, while the school recommended for mental health reasons that students take no more than three AP classes, it did not create a firm limit, because doing so would have been in direct opposition to parents' and students' efforts to win the college arms race. Teachers also expressed ambivalence: while on the one hand they would have liked to see more diversity in upper-level classes, on the other, they believed that upper-level classes were for students who had shown they were ready for that standard of work, and so were not inclined to push to open the doors wide to additional students. One newcomer to the school said that she was told in interviews by teachers that "AP and honors weren't what they used to be," meaning that as sections were added to accommodate more students, the overall level of preparation and interest in the subjects had gone down. The teachers were also similarly committed to counterbalancing some of the stress-inducing aspects of the school, and thus saw their role in part to resist parents' and students' drive to take as many honors classes as possible.

Administrators did try to tackle these equity issues, by creating an afterschool "homework club" and a "legacy scholars" program, both of which supported minority students academically by creating structures, time, and support. The district created a calculus project that helped minority students learn calculus over the summer and so make it easier for them to enroll in upper-level math programs. School administrators also created a "clustering" program, which placed the few minority students who did take AP in the same classes in order to create social support and avoid having students feel like they had to serve as representatives of their race. While these programs were widely praised, they did not appreciably change the enrollment patterns or the structure of curricular differentiation at the school. Overall, while the school had wholeheartedly embraced the goal of increasing the performance of minority and low-income students on state tests, it remained more ambivalent about creating racial equity in course-taking patterns.

A Different World: Clubs and Student Leadership

Classes were not the only places for learning at Attainment High. The school was also home to more than eighty-five student clubs, as well as an array of sports, arts, dance, music, and literary groups. These were, in many ways, the lifeblood of the school. We asked one student what Attainment High would be like without its clubs and extracurriculars, and his expression became pained. "They wouldn't do that to us," he said, unwilling to even contemplate the possibility.

These clubs met in the same places as core classes were taught, but they operated under a different logic. The logic of core classes was fundamentally teacher-centered: the teacher determined the objectives, organized the learning, and assessed whether students had met their expectations. The student's role was mainly to do what teachers asked. This model resulted in some learning, but the hidden curriculum underlying it rewarded students for complying with teachers' wishes.

In contrast, the logic that governed clubs and extracurriculars was very different. We discuss extracurriculars in depth in Chapter 6, so here we will focus on clubs. In clubs, the idea is that students can determine what they are interested in, and the faculty's job is to support that learning. There was no preset direction that this learning or work should take; each year both the array of clubs changed and what happened inside them changed, based on the ideas of the students who ran them. In core classes, students were segregated by age and by track, but in clubs there was much more mixing across grades and there were no tracks. Clubs also differed from core classes in that students chose to be a part of them; no one had forced them to be there.

From a deeper learning perspective, what particularly caught our eye were the clubs that were involved in political causes, civic work, or leadership at the school. These interested us because the logic that governed them was so different from the assumptions of the traditional grammar of schooling described earlier, where teachers are the experts, and students are receptacles who need to be filled with knowledge. In contrast, with clubs the school embraced a very different view—that students were capable leaders whose knowledge, judgment, leadership, and organizing ability could be major assets to the school, the community, and the wider world.

This was never more apparent than when the school was confronted by a series of incidents that challenged its image of itself as an inclusive haven. On a day meant to celebrate black culture, some students asked openly racist questions. The feminism club had put up some posters in bathrooms, asking "What does feminism mean to you?" and in the boys' bathroom students had drawn penises on the posters and written "I hate girls," "fuck the matriarchy" and other anti-feminist messages. At a basketball game with a Catholic school, the team was taunted with chants of "you killed Jesus" (referring to the substantial Jewish population at Attainment High). Two swastikas were drawn in the boys' bathroom. And finally, in an incident that was captured on video and heavily reported in the city's major newspapers, two students drove a truck with a confederate flag in circles around the schools' main entrance about two months before the 2016 presidential election.

In response to these events, the students formed a club, Voice, that brought together a variety of groups representing different races, ethnicities, and sexualities in order to organize events, propose policy changes, and argue for a vision of inclusion and equity. In response to the confederate flag incident, which had rocked the school, the club organized a "blackout" event in the cafeteria. Though held during a normal class block, the principal agreed that interested students could go to the assembly, which drew 250 students. All the attendees wore black in solidarity with African American students. Several black students spoke, explaining what life was like for them at Attainment High, provoking a further series of conversations among students about race and privilege. The students also took charge of aspects of the anti-bullying curriculum; describing what the adults had done on this issue as "super cheesy," they designed a set of interactive activities to help students reflect on the nature of bullying in the school.

The principal, himself a person of color, called on Voice to help organize an anti-bias professional development for *faculty*, too. The group met several times and created a panel representing a range of racial and ethnic groups to talk about race on campus. They also helped to develop an eight-minute video that featured a number of students talking about homophobia, anti-transgender sentiment, and gender bias at the school. These two prompts—first the video on gender and sexuality bias, then the student panel on racial bias—comprised the first hour of a half-day professional development session for faculty. After these prompts, the adults, without students, held their own discussion of the nature or extent of bias at the school. Many faculty members said that the video and testimonials from students had been the most powerful part of the day; seeing the school through the students' eyes had helped reveal some institutional blind spots. But even while the school was struggling with its own transgressions, it was notable that it trusted students to contribute to efforts to address them.

For the students involved, while their stated purpose was to educate others, taking part in Voice had also stimulated significant learning for themselves. Jacob, the leader of the group, described himself as initially a moderate liberal Jew with South African parents, but that "hearing experiences from black students and non-dominant groups and the way they had been treated at Attainment High—I had never felt the similar pain that they felt." He described this awakening as life-changing in the way he viewed his own skin color and privilege. With the exception of leadership class, an elective discussed in more detail later, he said he had never had an academic experience as powerful as his experience in Voice. While in some ways one could view this as a predictable trajectory—liberal young white people in 2016 gradually coming to a racial awakening was the story of the nation, not just Attainment High—it still represents a significant shift for Jacob and others involved in Voice. And it is not a coincidence that this happened in a club and not as part of the formal curriculum; the openness and fluidity of the club space allowed for learning that was connected to ongoing developments in the outside world.

Electives: Innovation in the Periphery

If one space that offered a different "grammar" of schooling was clubs, another such space was electives. Outside of the core curriculum and disproportionately taken by seniors, electives at Attainment High are free from many of the pressures and requirements that govern other classes. Ranging from engineering to theater to philosophy to leadership to oceanography to hip hop, they cover a wide spectrum of subjects and teaching modalities, none of which leads directly to an AP, state, or SAT II test. When we asked teachers and administrators to point us toward places where "deeper learning" was going on, they frequently suggested that we look at the elective curricula.

If the logic that organized the core curriculum was statist in its key assumptions—there are certain things that the state and district think that students need to know; the teachers' job is to implement that vision—the logic of electives was that of regulated market, driven by both teacher and student choice. Teachers could propose electives, first to department chairs, who would evaluate whether they fit within the department's overall offerings, had academic merit, and would draw student interest. Supported proposals would then go to the academic standards committee, comprised of department chairs and administrators, which would make the final decisions. While occasionally proposals were turned down, the more common process involved a series of conversations that would help an idea evolve until it seemed likely to succeed. If clubs offered a different vision of students from the core curriculum, electives offered a different vision of faculty, seeing them less as implementers of the will of district and state, and more as capable people designing courses of interest to themselves and their students.

As in any market process, there was some variation in the quality of these offerings, but on the whole electives featured student engagement and interest, and, often, faculty passion. A primary reason was simply mutual choice: faculty and students had chosen to be there. This ensured both interest in the subject and a higher level of commitment to the enterprise; since students had volunteered rather than being conscripted, they felt more on the hook to produce. That mutual choice is a significant part of the power of electives is perhaps not surprising; a big part of "electives" is that people "elect" to be there.

More intriguingly, as we investigated these electives, we realized that each had altered at least one dimension of the conventional grammar of schooling. Electives frequently made a different choice from core classes about breadth and depth. Rather than marching students through large chunks of content, electives often focused on studying one thing, investigating it from a variety of angles rather than just moving from one thing to the next. Many courses moved away from the batch-processing model, instead creating ways for students to work at the different paces that suited their talents and skill levels. Some were more hands-on, creating opportunities for students to integrate making or performing with thinking; that is, students used their bodies as well as their minds. Some broke down the walls between school and the world by creating projects for real-world clients or devoting chunks of curriculum to events dominating the news. Others broke down the walls between object and self, exploring how different academic lenses could help students penetrate their own identities. Many were student-driven, giving students opportunities to develop sustained projects within a broadly defined content area. Some were interdisciplinary, for example, they brought together a history and a science teacher to offer a history of science course. And even the ones that were most academic and structurally familiar—a philosophy class run as a year-long Socratic seminar—took a fresh slant on students and knowledge, treating philosophy not as something that needed to be assimilated but rather as something that students could use as a tool to investigate ageless questions about the purpose of life and the nature of existence.

Of course, any container is only as good as what people do inside it. Not every elective is a good elective: especially since seniors took a disproportionate number of electives, there were some that had a pronounced case of senioritis. But on the whole, our observations were consistent with teachers' and students' sense that the elective curriculum provided more opportunities for depth and higher levels of student engagement than did the core curriculum. We describe a few courses here that show, in different ways, what is possible within an elective curriculum.

Self-Paced Organic Chemistry and Film Scoring

One pillar of conventional schooling challenged by some electives was batch processing: the idea that all students need to move through a similar body of material at a similar pace, take an assessment, and move on to the next. Adam Simmons, the chemistry teacher who had lamented that students were trying to "read" teachers for the right answer, created an elective in organic chemistry that upends this idea. The course features a series of modules, written by Mr. Simmons, that present increasingly complex problems on the structure of molecules. Students move through these modules at different paces, meaning that one student might be on module one or two and another on module six or seven. Class starts with students working in pairs to answer a common question posed by Mr. Simmons, but most of the class time is spent on students working individually on their modules. They draw on a variety of resources as they work, including lectures that Mr. Simmons has filmed of himself explaining the material, Khan Academy videos, textbooks, and other resources. Mr. Simmons circulates, answers questions, and talks with students about how they are progressing. At the end of each module they take an open-note test—as Mr. Simmons says, "it's not what they've memorized, but what they can do with the knowledge that counts"—and they have to solve every problem before they can move on to the next module. If they do not achieve a perfect score on a test, they study some more and take another test, which assesses the same content but with different problems.

This approach has advantages over the traditional batch-processing model. Because each student needs to earn a perfect score before moving on, the role of assessment shifts from a way of sorting students to incentivizing mastery of content. It takes as long as it takes to complete module one, but once you've completed it, you really have demonstrated that you know that material. Mr. Simmons says that the normal approach to studying is that "it's like a game, I've just got to get this stuff in my head in order to get through this one milestone, and then I can move on to the next one." He continues, "In the Orgo class, I have to break them out of that, because they do the quiz, it's not perfect, that's fine with me. I give it back to them. But they've got to keep going until they really know it." Students corroborated this account, saying that in this class they felt the "thought process doesn't seem as manipulated" as in other classes, because the object was less to please the teacher and more to draw on a variety of resources to master the material.

The competency-based model also enables a different approach to differentiation. All of the students in the class were eleventh and twelfth graders who had taken one year of chemistry, but they varied widely in their curricular tracks. Both the students and Mr. Simmons described the course as working particularly well for students at both the upper and lower skill levels: advanced chemistry students who wanted to go deeper and faster appreciated being able to move at their own pace through the modules, and students who had struggled with chemistry liked the variety of different resources available, the chance to move more slowly through the material, and the opportunity for one-on-one tutoring with Mr. Simmons when they got stuck. Initially, finding themselves with students from different curricular levels was unsettling. As Mr. Simmons describes it: "Students who come from a CP level course, and they walk into a room at the beginning of the year and see a bunch of students who just came from AP chemistry—that can be really intimidating." But over the course of the term they realized that the structure of the course could work for very different students. Part of the key to the class's success is a different approach to assessment: Mr. Simmons grades for effort rather than speed of advancement. Students need to show that they are taking notes, that they are using the resources, that they are setting goals and meeting them—and it is this process, rather than the number of modules they complete, that is reflected in their grades.

Students also said that the course made a different demand of them. They were asked to be more responsible, more in charge of their own learning. Students described this as both empowering and sometimes challenging—good to be responsible for their own education, but sometimes hard to motivate and organize a course of self-directed study. One African American student we interviewed said that "some people like the traditional course because it has more structure," but that "it is great for students [like him] who always feel held down by the curriculum." Another white student, listening to the conversation, added, "I dropped out of AP U.S. History because it didn't allow you to explore interesting topics that you like." This course, he said, because of the flexible pacing, allowed you to go deep on things as you got interested in them. Here the first student chimed back in and said that he had gotten really interested in "fourteen molecules that changed history" and this course had allowed him to explore it in more depth. He added that "it's good prep for college; you just have to rewire yourself."

Finally, the design of self-paced organic chemistry was a good fit with the course's designer. Mr. Simmons was a self-described chemistry dork who had always been drawn to chemistry and was a bit of a local legend as a summer teaching assistant for organic chemistry at a nearby top university. Mr. Simmons loved chemistry: making up problems, exploring the underlying structure of modules. And he liked to invite students into this world of organic chemistry and help them make sense of it. But he did not like policing whether students were copying homework, had no desire to be the sage on the stage, and had no need for the adulation that comes with the performance aspects of teaching. By shifting the mode into one where students were just doing chemistry, and his role was to write modules, circulate among students, and help them move at their own pace through the material, he had found a way to organize a class that was consistent with the best of what he could offer as a teacher.

228 IN SEARCH OF DEEPER LEARNING

A similar approach prevailed in a course on film scoring. Film scoring is choosing or creating music to accompany a video. The course was taught by a teacher, James Nelson, who was the chair of the performing arts department, had a degree in film scoring, and taught classes on it at a local community college. He had a stance toward his field that was similar to Mr. Simmons's—wanting students to "learn through music" and not "about music" and to induct them into a realm that he was passionate about. Each student sat at a computer with a program that enabled them to match music to video. They worked largely independently, with occasional mini lessons from Mr. Nelson. From his perspective, the essence of film scoring is to look at a scene, understand the emotions of the character or the events, and then develop musical choices that reflect those emotions. While in one sense this was an applied task, Mr. Nelson had a liberal arts vision of what he was trying to accomplish. "I just think the more you know, the more beautiful life is," he said. He described attending a concert with a well-educated family member, and the family member asking at the end, "Was it any good?" His goal was for students to develop a vocabulary so that they could answer that for themselves.

To achieve that goal, he embedded mini lessons about music within a project-oriented mode. Students had a series of assignments to complete over the course of the year—projects of growing size and complexity—beginning with a car commercial and moving toward longer and more self-designed work. Like Mr. Simmons's role in organic chemistry, Mr. Nelson's role was to set the overall arc of the course and build the culture and tone of the class. With that done, he often spent his days circulating, helping students with features of the program, and offering feedback on their developing ideas. Also like organic chemistry, the course could be accessed by students with very different levels of prior preparation: some students could read and even compose music, while others were learning what notes are. The program that the students used, Logic, enabled this differentiation, because it was possible to write music from scratch but also to play with the electronic instruments and create music that way. The course also drew students from across curricular tracks. As Mr. Nelson described it, pointing to two students sitting next to each other, "There you see student 1 and student 480 . . . almost nowhere else in the building would that be true." In terms of levels of engagement, this was one of the most committed classes we saw in our time at Attainment High;

on several of the days we attended, the students came in and just started working with little direction, or none at all, from Mr. Nelson. Students said that they appreciated the class because, as one said, it was "freer" than regular classes; another said, "We had an opportunity to be creative and make things, to use my imagination, rather than simply following along." With a very light touch, Mr. Nelson had created an environment in which students could drive their own learning.

The Leadership Elective

It is 7:50 a.m. on the day after the 2016 presidential election. Donald Trump had defeated Hillary Clinton only seven hours earlier. I make my way into "Leadership class," a course that brings together fifty nominated leaders from across the school to learn about race, social justice, and leadership. There are students from all tracks and interest groups: athletes and artists; white, black, Asian, and Latinx students; AP kids and CP kids. One of the two co-teachers, an Asian American woman whom we will call Ann Wang, had been fighting back tears in the hallway, but composes herself as she opens the class with these words: "We are going to deviate from our curriculum, but the world is our curriculum. It has been a hard night in our families, and we love each and every one of you. There may be people in this room with a whole range of emotions. We come from a place where we believe that everybody has a place to live with dignity. Every fucking body. We want to use this as a space to think about what we will do to move forward together." The other teacher, a white man married to a black woman, gives some prompts, which he asks students to write about, then discuss in fours: "1. What is working? 2. What needs to be fixed? 3. What will you do to take action?"

The students begin to write. A number of the students are in tears. Some of the students of color look absolutely shell-shocked, as if they have been run over by a truck. After a few minutes of small group discussion, a larger group discussion commences. Here are just some of the comments we heard:

- *White boy*: "If we were back in World War II, we would think Hitler was a great leader."
- *Black girl*: "I feel like I don't have a president to be honest. Obama was our hope. I feel like a whole country went off on us—we don't

have any support for the next four years, we don't have any representation, we don't have a president who acknowledges us."

- *Black and Latina girl*: "In my opinion we're naïve if we believe that anything is working."
- *Black girl*: "The first thing I thought of was my skin and being a black female, how many more times am I going to be violated because someone like Donald Trump has been elected president. A little child today is growing up and thinking he's the president and I should look up to him. David Duke endorsed Trump. I feel really uncomfortable knowing that this happened; it's just shocking."
- *White girl*: "As a white female I know it's not affecting me the way it affects the person of color. The vote we did [at Attainment High the previous day] is 70-plus percent for Clinton. And there are people who voted for Trump, and that's fine. And they're happy today. We always talk about how we are open as a community—when people have a view that's different from the majority, we all become defensive."
- *White boy*: "I saw a poll last night. How would you feel if Trump were elected? 54 percent were concerned or scared. It's scary for me as someone in the majority in all categories—you can say what you want about Hillary, but we wouldn't be scared. You could be pissed off but you wouldn't be afraid."
- *Transgendered white boy*: "There is a lot of language of everyone is equal. When your opinions are specifically about demonizing other people, those views should not be tolerated. Voting for Trump is homophobic, classist, ableist, racist."
- *Latina girl*: "I believe in this country no matter what. I cried this morning. We're the home of the brave. We're not afraid of Donald Trump. I look around this room and I see leaders. It's not over here. Time for us to come together, but I don't think this is the end."
- *White girl*: "I am very scared. Hitler said I alone can fix it. We are going to scapegoat a group of people. He used the fear and the hatred, and he used that to rise to power. We are seeing a whitelash against a black presidency. People don't want to move past white supremacy. We have a majority of people who are subliminally racist, he is using racism and sexism. What is going to stop him from literally building a wall around our border? And displacing Muslim Americans. His running mate supports conversion therapy."
- *Black boy, forcefully*: "How the fuck did this happen?"

Over the course of almost an hour (this is a long block), the discussion continues. By the end of the hour, almost all of the fifty students have said something. The teachers occasionally interject to try to bring some context to the discussion—offering a thumbnail history of the way in which the Republican Party has evolved, for example. But mostly they just let the students talk. At a school that is 80 percent for Clinton (as shown by the mock vote the day before), no one says anything explicitly in favor of Trump. As the discussion goes on, the raw emotions in the room dissipate somewhat—the hurt and shock felt by many of the students at Trump's election is mitigated to a degree by discussion. As the class is moving toward its conclusion, one boy says, "We woke up this morning and moved from a black president to a white supremacist." "Orange," another boy jokes. And the class cracks up in laughter, a modest release after an earth-shaking night.

Despite Ms. Wang's initial proviso that today they were going to "deviate" from the curriculum, in Leadership class, the world is always the curriculum. The class, which has been running for several decades with different teachers, was conceived of as a time when a cross-section of the school would come together to learn about issues confronting their school and their world. Students learn about implicit bias, segregation, race, politics, privilege, and many other strands tied to the social justice curriculum through a mix of sociological readings, critical texts, poems, documentaries, and other resources. These readings and activities include some classics but also some highly contemporary works: Ta-Nehisi Coates is on the syllabus; students do the implicit association test that Mazarin Banajee developed at Harvard; a PBS documentary—*Race: The Power of Illusion*—is shown. Discussions generally move among the texts, the students' lives, and current events. The atmosphere is generally loose, grades are deemphasized, and students are free to say what they want. While the day after the election was the only day we heard profanity, it was frequently a space where the emotional and the cognitive intersected, because talking about real issues often led to powerful emotions. Intended to help students understand the forces of structural and institutional racism, the course skews to the Left and could certainly be critiqued for not challenging the liberal consensus shared by many students in the class. Adding more conservative thinkers would have broadened the conversation in interesting ways. At the same time, it explores the many layers that create inequalities in society, and students gradually become familiar with the range of ways that such issues have been understood in a variety of fields and disciplines.

Students prized the class as one of the very few at Attainment High that allowed them to talk about contemporary issues in a classroom setting. As was true of Jacob's experience in Voice, white students in the class frequently began to see things about their own advantages that they hadn't previously considered. Asian American students, many of whom had thrived at Attainment High, experienced a different kind of awakening, beginning to learn about model minority narratives and the ways in which Asian Americans have faced discrimination in America. This point was particularly important to Ms. Wang, who had grown up in a majority Asian society in Hawaii, only to come to the states and have white professors question whether English was her first language. For black and Latinx students, the course offered a chance to talk directly about race and discrimination, moving their experiences to center stage when they were largely at the margins of the mainstream history curriculum. And it was also the rare place where students from different tracks and different races got to talk to each other. As one white student who took mostly honors track classes said, "I mean when I walked into Leadership, the first day I was like, I know like ten kids out of the fifty-five kids in this room, and they were all seniors. And it's also like my friend group is white . . . , you surround yourself with people that you feel most comfortable, whether or not you want to admit it or not." He added that while conversations about race usually take place among self-selected groups, what was distinctive about the Leadership class was that everyone was having the conversation: "There are kids who may have never thought about these things that are nominated, and they come to this class, and they're like, 'Wow, I never thought about this before.' And in my ideal world, everyone will have to take a class like that."

Science Electives for the Real World

Another set of classes that students described as particularly powerful were the design, engineering, and green engineering electives. In the design and green engineering classes, students used design processes to develop real-world projects for real-world clients. One of the most celebrated examples was the creation of a pedestrian alert system in Ethiopia. The goal of this project was to reduce the number of road traffic incidents; the group chose to focus on Ethiopia because it had one of the highest road-fatality rates in the world. One of the students had also been born in Ethiopia; he helped to broker a connection with a school in Addis Ababa to gain a greater understanding of the local conditions and context. With the help of an initial $10,000 grant from a nearby university, the students built a machine that could sense the speed of an oncoming car and tell pedestrians whether it would be safe to cross. The machine works on solar power and can be created with recyclable parts. To develop this work, the students found mentors at two prestigious universities, as well as among professional engineers and designers. These mentors helped them through many rounds of critique and iteration, including an extended critique session at a design firm in the city. Their teacher also had spent sixteen years as a designer before teaching high school, an experience that shaped her knowledge and sensibilities. The project was eventually featured in a White House science fair and the students were recognized by President Obama. Obama, one said, "has surprisingly soft hands but his handshake has a firm grip."[10] Not all projects were this successful, but it was a remarkable example of what high school students can produce when given the opportunity.

The design and engineering courses took a different approach to knowledge and its acquisition. If the logic of most core classes was "here is a body of material that you need to learn because it might be useful later," the logic of these electives was "figure out what you are trying to build, then acquire the knowledge that you need to make it." Engineering did have a sequenced course of study, and the earlier courses were more organized around content (with applications); later courses were more project-driven on the assumption that students already knew much of the basic content. Overall, though, the people running the engineering program took the stance that what you know is less important than what you can do with what you know. The engineering teachers, Mr. Baker and Ms. Peterson, recalled introducing an instrument, a caliper, and asking students to figure out how to use it. Students went to YouTube, traded ideas with each other, and eventually figured out how to use it. Here we ask about the purpose of this inductive approach:

Interviewer: Wouldn't it be more efficient for you just to show them how to do it?

Mr. Baker: It would be, but that's not what I want them to know.

Interviewer: Why not?

Ms. Peterson: And they don't remember it. So, what's the point? And you can tell somebody a whole lot of information, but our goal isn't that they hear it; our goal is that they learn it. There's a difference.

Interviewer: What's the difference between hearing it and learning it?

Ms. Peterson: Because if I tell it to them, they heard it. Next week, it's not still in their brain. That's not useful to me.

Part of this approach grew out of the very different backgrounds of the engineering teachers. Mr. Baker, who invariably could be found wearing a gray football hoodie and faded jeans, had attended a local state college and majored in manufacturing. His own experiences in school had not been positive: "I was that special needs kid. I didn't learn the standard way," he said. "You know, I'd be sitting in the back waiting till the teacher stops, and then I'd open up the book and try to figure it out myself, right? Go behind the scenes, try it eighteen times until I could figure it out, and I had to teach myself how to do these things." The result was that Mr. Baker had no reservations about moving away from the conventional teacher-led model; he prized giving students opportunities to mess around and figure things out. Ms. Peterson had taken a different route to arrive at the same point. After college, she had earned a masters' degree at Northwestern, and a Ph.D. at MIT. But when she arrived at MIT for her first year of graduate school, she found that the kind of learning she had done up to that point hadn't prepared her well for real science: "I actually was a very good traditional student. I did well [until] I got to grad school, and like there were no instructions anymore. There's a bunch of crap in the lab, and you've got to figure out how to make it do what you want to do. And there's not—the whole point of doing research is that it hasn't been done before, so there's no instructions for how to do it. So, you've got to figure it out. And it was painful." After graduate school, she joined a startup created by one of her professors and found in that environment as well that open-ended problem-solving and persistence were a lot more important than any specific piece of existing knowledge. Thus Ms. Peterson and Mr. Baker were united in their desire to teach students to "futz" their way through, valuing this persistence over quick facility with the right answer.

As was true for teachers of other electives, these goals also changed their approach to assessment. Much as IB is designed to assess what you *do* know rather than assess what you *don't* know, Mr. Baker had adopted a similar approach, in which he had students report less on their results and more on the process they had used to get the results and on how they had improved that process over time. He pointed out to students that there was a lot of research out there on how to create effective teams, and he asked students to look into that research if they were having trouble managing their groups or their process. The teachers' goal was to incentivize effort. As Mr. Baker said, "What I see as success is if the student tried to solve a problem seventeen times, and failed every time, great. It's much more successful than a student that tried to solve once, and just got the right answer the first time." In their emphasis on rewarding a learning over a performance orientation, Mr. Baker and Ms. Peterson said that their stance ran counter to much of how the rest of the school operated. As such, their class could be something of a culture shock for students. Particularly for high-achieving ones, they said, it could initially be a considerable challenge to shift from "here's how to do it to get a good grade" to "figure it out." In the longer run, however, they said that only rarely did students leave their courses for this reason; more often, they adapted to the different expectations and approach.

These courses also broke down the walls between school and the world in a way that most academic classes did not. Not only did many of the projects have real-world clients; the developers of the engineering sequence had formed an advisory council with businesses, college engineering programs, and former students. This council, in turn, had guided the school in selecting which skills to emphasize and why. This process sometimes led to surprises. Mr. Baker describes a startling early piece of guidance from this committee: "When I pulled in the advisory committee, I started asking, what skills do you want our students to know when you get them? And I was expecting specific technical skills. And one of the shocking things that I found out was, it wasn't that. It had more to do with work ethics—working within teams and presentation skills were huge. . . . And it was like, if you give me somebody who can do that, we can teach them the technical things that they need. . . . So, we built that into everything that we do." As a result, projects were all completed in teams, and students had to present their projects when they were completed.

These programs also had a strong social mission that was important to the founders and the students. After completing the Ethiopian pedestrian design project, some of the students who had led the project partnered with a high-poverty middle school in the city to teach a weekly class on design and engineering to seventh graders. Students in the carpentry class had partnered with the leadership class for several years to go on a week-long trip to New Orleans to rebuild houses for families after Hurricane Katrina. As one of the teachers running the program described it, "For the students to be in an environment that's been so devastated, to get to know somebody in another part of our country, to experience that person's story, to be a part of that person's life, to work on a home, is so transformative." During their time in New Orleans, the students not only rebuilt houses; they also talked with community members about the political aftermath of the storm and the lives of the people whose homes they were rebuilding. The teacher continued, "The transformation in these young people in that short period of time is just—it's so moving for me. That experience and what they felt stays with them. It resonates with them. It changes the way they see things from that point on."

Electing to Study Philosophy as Literature

One of the schools' prized gems was an elective called "Philosophy as Literature." We will discuss this class and the man who teaches it in more depth in Chapter 7, where we describe how the best teachers we observed transformed ordinary academic subjects into topics for deep investigation. But we include it briefly here to show that electives can create powerful learning environments even when they are not self-paced, project-based, hands-on, or exploring contemporary issues. In this class, taught by a man we will call Mr. Fields, about twenty students sat in a semi-circle and discussed philosophical texts. Mr. Fields would lead off with a question, "How does Descartes establish that we exist?" and students would gradually unpack the question, drawing on quotations from the text. Over time, the discussion might shift to whether the students believed Descartes—does the fact that we think imply that we exist?—and students would bring up counter-examples (Do you exist as a vegetable, even if you can't think? Computers can think, but do they exist?), each of which would be entertained and debated. Students were so excited about this class that discussions often continued after the bell rang; one student recounted to us that he had repeatedly tried to explain to his carpool his thinking about Descartes and free will.

As we will detail in Chapter 7, what made Mr. Fields special was his stance, both toward students and toward knowledge. Students were not passive vessels in need of filling, but active sense-makers whose ideas and developing opinions were worthy of respect. Knowledge was not something that was passed down; rather, the best questions were ones about which students could develop differing and even original interpretations. Students responded passionately to this approach, saying that Mr. Fields was the rare teacher who meant it when he said there wasn't a right answer. Much as was true in the Leadership class, students also seemed developmentally primed for his course's content: for skeptical adolescents the idea that the world is not as it seems—a chair might not really be a chair—is a powerful elixir that offers the possibility of pulling back the mask on the world as it has been presented to them.

Much of what Mr. Fields did in his Philosophy of Literature class he could and did do in his regular disciplinary classes. Yet the fact that this was an elective made the learning environment more powerful here than in his English I classes, which we also witnessed. That students had chosen to be here was key—there was a kind of rapt, shared attention in this class that we did not see to the same degree in his regular classes. There were no questions about how many points one would get for this or that, which were sometimes raised, much to Mr. Fields's frustration, in English I. And the absence of any pacing expectations meant that there was no rush in Philosophy as Literature—time seemed suspended, and a given discussion or set of ideas could unwind over as long a time as students needed them to. When we asked students about the value of this pacing, they responded with a passionate defense of exactly the intellectual virtues Mr. Fields was trying to inculcate. We asked, "Wouldn't it be more efficient for him to guide you through Descartes?" "No," responded a student. "Why not?" we asked. "Because I feel like understanding Descartes is not the point of reading Descartes. It's not to give us the information; it's learning how to understand the information. What he does is what makes us think, and thinking is the point."

Electives: The Power of a Different Grammar

In different ways, these electives were able to open up alternative possibilities for schooling, and so unleash an energy and level of student interest that was often absent from core classes. They were able to do so in part because they were buffered from many of the demands and expectations that controlled the rest of the school's curricula. Because many of the students in electives were seniors, the college pressure was lessened, and there were more opportunities to engage in a learning rather than a performance orientation. Similarly, given that most students had taken the state test, their SAT IIs, and their APs, they had already created external markers of their knowledge, freeing time and energy to be more about learning than performing. Electives were also mostly not part of the vertically aligned sequences that existed in core disciplinary subjects, which meant that individual teachers and students felt free to follow their passions. Because students already had met— or were meeting—the demands of convention, history, and external authorities by completing the required sequences in core subjects, they were free to experiment and explore in the elective space.

From the perspective of equity, it is clearly true that in electives, as in the rest of the curriculum, there is some vertical differentiation. In particular, it has long been true that the more vocational electives are more frequently taken by working-class students, and courses like Philosophy as Literature are more frequently taken by students in the honors tracks. At the same time, some electives were the only academic spaces in the school that brought together students from different tracks. Sometimes this integration was an intentional choice in terms of who was admitted (such as in the Leadership class), but sometimes it arose as a byproduct of changing the conventional grammar of schooling: in classes that were more project-driven, self-paced, or student-centered, it was possible to have students with different levels of skill working side by side or together.

There are complicated normative questions in thinking about electives, questions that relate to both horizontal and vertical differentiation. If classes like Leadership and Film Scoring made up all of students' academic learning, most people—including us—would think that something important was being lost. But might there be ways to inject the qualities we saw in these electives, such as more depth, more choice, and more student-directed learning, into the teaching of core subjects? And does the subject matter itself make a difference? For while it is true that poorer and working-class students often chose vocational electives, it is far from clear that if these electives were eliminated and the students took purely academic courses, things would be better for them. Students were much more engaged in these arenas than they were in lower-level academic courses, in part because of the differences in pedagogy, but also because the vocational electives had a clear purpose and had the prospect of leading to real-world employment. The likely answer is not to eliminate vocational courses but to update them, to connect them more closely to the real demands of employment, and to equip students with more generalizable skills than such courses have taught in the past.

Departmental Efforts to Revise the Core

While the most significant innovation at Attainment High occurred in the electives, there also had been some efforts to revamp core disciplinary classes. The key unit for driving these changes was the department. As previous scholars of high schools, such as Leslie Siskin and others, have emphasized, in large comprehensive high schools it is departments where teachers form cultures and do much of their work.[11] This was particularly so at Attainment High, a large, newly constructed building where faculty offices were organized by departments, often with a fridge and some shared long tables in one room, and individual offices off that common area. The result was that faculty frequently ate lunch or worked with colleagues in the shared departmental space, almost by default, but had to make an active effort to talk with teachers in other departments.

The size of the school and the strength of the departments also mitigated against centralized efforts to improve instruction led by the principal and his or her administrative team. In previous chapters, we showed that the success of those schools in realizing their disparate visions came from aligning a number of key elements with a definitive conception of teaching and learning. Whether it was projects at Dewey High, IB assessments at IB High, or schoolwide instructional templates at No Excuses High, the leaders of each of these institutions had begun with a granular vision of good instruction. They then developed robust mechanisms for adult learning, made collectively visible what students were doing and learning, treated adults the way that they hoped adults would treat students (symmetry), built a collective identity around their vision of instruction, and organized all aspects of their structures to support that vision. None of that was possible schoolwide at Attainment High. There were too many faculty, there were longstanding traditions of faculty as "thoroughbreds" (hire the best and let them teach), faculty were resistant to having other teachers observe their classes, and there was comparatively limited time for adult learning.

Different leaders had handled these constraints in different ways. The former principal, Karen Stein, had by force of personality and with support from the external environment pushed hard on a schoolwide equity agenda. She had been able to increase the focus on state tests and improve minority students' outcomes on those tests by getting small groups of faculty to focus closely on them. She had also been able to create new *programs* to assist struggling and disadvantaged students— programs that helped students work on homework after school or that created high expectations with high levels of support for students of color. But the hardest nut to crack had been actually changing *instruction*, because that would have required more directly challenging many of the longstanding norms and practices of the school.

The new principal, Jack Dixon, and his associate principal, Wendy Parker, the former science department chair, were interested in directly taking on the challenge of improving instruction. They wanted to improve instruction not only within departments but also across them, creating opportunities for teachers in various departments to visit each other's classes. Ms. Parker described the challenge of breaking the disciplinary culture as one of symmetry: "So, I think our students think in very siloed ways right now because our teachers think in very siloed ways. [If] we want kids to be able to see the connections, and make connections, and carry skills from one to the other, I think we have to get the teachers to be doing some of that first." Mr. Dixon and Ms. Parker were enthusiastic about many of the same electives that we spotlighted, in part because these courses were able to break the boundaries that constrained many disciplinary classes. But they knew they had to tread carefully in seeking to broker more regular connections across departments, because doing so violated the strongly held vision of disciplines as the key holders of instruction.

Within the disciplines, they were also seeking change, but here they faced powerful resistance from a culture in which department chairs exercised power over the thinking in their disciplines and had organized many of the developments surrounding instruction. What happened in each of these departments reflected a mixture of the interests of the chair, shifts in the external environment, and the views of the departmental faculty. The result was that different departments had moved in different directions: some had emphasized equity, others identity, and others rigor in the conventional sense. They also varied in the degree to which department chairs were seeking uniformity and in which dimension they were seeking it (content or skills). To illustrate, we will briefly look at developments in science, History, English, and math.

Ms. Parker had been head of the science department for nearly a decade before moving to a role in the central administration. She believed strongly in equity and in inquiry-oriented instruction. The biggest shift, which had started under the previous department chair but had fallen to her to implement, was changing the sequence of science courses for all students. In the previous iteration, "We used to have kind of a bimodal system in science where some kids got to take biology in ninth grade, and they were the accelerated kids, and they were on this track to take biology, and chemistry, and physics. And then, other kids, about 40 percent, took physical science in ninth grade, and they went down a different track. So, it was like complete divergence in ninth grade." The department shifted to a system where everyone took physics in ninth grade, chemistry in tenth grade, and biology in eleventh grade. This both created more equity in that all students were taking the same sequence of courses, and made more sense substantively because "you need to understand physics before you can understand chemistry, and you need to understand chemistry before you can understand bio." This change also reflected a national shift in the sequence of science courses, as more and more schools across the country were making similar decisions about the relationships among the science disciplines. The department also made the decision to offer only two ninth-grade physics courses (no honors): an ACP course that served 85 percent of the students, and a CP course that served the other 15 percent. In tenth-grade chemistry, where there were three levels (honors, ACP, and CP), they had also found a curriculum, *Living by Chemistry*, that could be used by all three levels, replacing the previous pattern in which the higher tracks covered much more chemistry. While higher-level classes might have more variations on a given concept or connect them to higher-level math, the goal was that core concepts of the disciplines would be similar across tracks. In all of these respects, the science department felt it had made progress in its mission to educate all students.

All of this happened within fairly standard ideas of what should happen in physics, chemistry, and biology, replicating the dominant patterns of instruction described earlier—more breadth, less depth, batch processing, labs to demonstrate existing principles rather than labs as opportunities to investigate the unknown. But the new science department chair, Ms. Campbell, a woman in her early thirties, had herself gone to high school at Midwestern Math and Science Academy (a pseudonym), a statewide exam school that we will discuss further in Chapter 7. In that school, students spent a month figuring out what explained the trajectory of the moon, were released from school on Wednesday afternoons to work in labs on college campuses, and did final presentations of scientific research that they hoped to publish in journals. To Ms. Campbell, carrying this vision of what high school science could be, Attainment High looked like a pale imitation. And while the department had some innovative faculty, particularly in engineering, many of the science teachers had never experienced a different view of what science instruction could be. To change this situation, in a department with many experienced teachers much older than she, in a school with a strong reputation and no external impetus for change, was a daunting challenge.

History was the most traditional of the disciplines at Attainment High. In fact, our observations here and at other schools suggest that it is, in general, perhaps the most conservative of the major disciplines. The chair, Mr. Thomas, very explicitly defined the work he was doing as opposed to progressive schooling in all its manifestations. He favored lecture and thought that content was at least as important as skills: "Our students come to us, they don't know anything. When they leave, the majority of them will never take another history course. So, what we actually have to do, I think, to prepare, you know, reasonably competent citizens, is to give them a narrative survey of important things, important stories in history." He argued that there was a sharp distinction between universities, where both teachers and students were free to study what they pleased, and high schools, which were intended to implement the will of the people: "We're not hired to be scholars. We're hired to teach what the city of [Attainmentville] wants us to teach, not what we want to teach. And you know, you talk to university people . . . there's this notion like 'how can teachers do a good job with content they're not passionate about?' Complete bullshit. We're not hired to talk about what we think is interesting; that's what university people are hired for. And you know, [at universities] you can file courses with the deans, and be like, 'I want to teach course on, you know, Victorian pantaloons and their significance.' Knock yourself out man. That's not what we're hired to do. We're not hired for our content expertise or interest. We're hired for our pedagogical expertise and interest." Mr. Thomas's views were grounded in his own powerful experience with Columbia's core curriculum, his view of the role of schools in a democracy, and his reading of E. D. Hirsch, who, he argued, made a compelling case for the importance of core knowledge as foundational for both democracy and equity. He argued that "progressivism is a luxury of the rich" and that covering major aspects of American and world history was critical for equalizing the playing field for students with uneven background knowledge.

Mr. Thomas had been the department chair for more than fifteen years and had hired almost all of the teachers in the department. He wanted all of them to teach around a four-question template he had developed: (1) What happened? (2) How did people who were there understand it? (3) Why did it happen? And (4) What do you think about what happened? As at No Excuses High, Mr. Thomas had a granular vision of what good instruction looked like and was willing to use his power as department chair to achieve it. Through a combination of selection at the hiring phase, observations and feedback, and the development of the four-question template, Mr. Thomas was doing his best to realize a particular conception of history instruction at Attainment High.

Jack Dixon, the new principal, had a quite different vision of history instruction. He, too, had been a history teacher, and he preferred a much more active, less lecture-heavy approach. He thought that while Mr. Thomas's method was strong in covering key topics, it did less to develop students' ability to think like historians, nor did it give many students much of a reason to become interested in history. Some teachers in the department also resented the standardization that Mr. Thomas's approach required. Because he wanted to ensure that every student had covered every key topic in American and world history, there was not much room for teachers to develop units or ideas that were of interest to them. He also had developed a common question bank for each course that all teachers would draw from for their finals. Some of the newer and younger teachers were also interested in rethinking the core to include more non-Western history, social history, and history from the perspectives of marginalized peoples around the world. But despite these critiques from above and below, there was little real impetus for change: Mr. Thomas had a developed vision of what history should be, it was congruent with district and parental expectations, and it was well suited to the content-heavy AP and SAT II tests that the students would take. In the absence of some metric or external constituency that would challenge Mr. Thomas's approach, Mr. Dixon was not having much luck in budging the longstanding history department chair.

The English department chair, Ms. Morgan, had a very different vision than Mr. Thomas had in history. Ms. Morgan's vision had been shaped in part by her own experiences in high school, where she had been a straight A student. But then things went downhill in her family life: her parents were getting divorced, and then her mother got cancer. "Then nothing became relevant to me, and nobody noticed. Nobody had conversations with me. It was all just like, 'Well, why aren't you, you know, reading *Ulysses?* This paper on *Ulysses* is late.' And, you know, like I don't care about that." After a stint in film studies in graduate school at a major research university, where again she felt the institution cared little about its students, she decided to return to high school, where she wanted to create the caring environment that had been absent in her own educational experiences. She vowed that she would always "see students first as people" and she went out of her way to talk to students, to attend their performances and games, and to show them in little ways and big ones that she cared about them.

As department chair, she married this student-centered vision with a sense that the purpose of teaching literature was to help students see what literature could do and to build their skills in reading texts and writing about them. Her task was complicated by the fact that when she joined the department fifteen years ago there was a strong tradition of teachers as "thoroughbreds"; at the time, she says, all you got was a list of books and one vague page about English department goals. She says that English teachers did and do cherish this autonomy; they liked being in a high-functioning suburban school in large part because it gave them the freedom to teach as they wished. They were ferociously skeptical of common district mandates, which they viewed as emanating from out-of-touch bureaucrats. The tradeoffs, from Ms. Morgan's perspective, were that some classrooms were much better than others, and that it was difficult for the department as a whole to move collectively toward any goal.

To manage these dilemmas, Ms. Morgan spent a lot of time talking with teachers individually, building trust. Then she tried to strike a series of balances. She emphasized the importance of commonly building particular skills, but gave teachers considerable flexibility in the texts they chose to develop those skills. In part this is because, unlike Mr. Thomas, she didn't see her teachers as people "implementing the will of the district," but rather as people whose passion for books could be contagious: "You know, if you're passionate about *Of Mice and Men*, and that brings you joy, that will translate to your teaching, and then the students will feel passionate. But, if I'm making you teach *Of Mice and Men* just because. . . . Some people are [made] really uncomfortable by that book. They don't know what to do when they get to the character of Crooks. They don't know how to handle the relationship between Lennie and George. They hate the book. Is that good for kids?" At the same time, she said, she was trying to move away from teachers picking books *only* because they liked them; she wanted teachers to articulate why a particular book would be useful in developing a particular skill that they had commonly agreed was important.

A related dilemma existed around the "core" texts that would be read by all students. One contingent of faculty in the department thought that all students should read Shakespeare and many other core texts of the canon. A smaller group thought that the canon, while important, could be trimmed to create opportunities for non-Western texts and texts featuring minority authors. This group also thought that the usual texts were not reaching well their minority students, who rarely saw people like themselves represented in the books they were reading.

Ms. Morgan patiently hosted this debate, honoring the importance of both positions, encouraging everyone to listen more closely to their students and very gently exploring whether a few items from the traditional list could be eliminated to make room for new authors. She also used the flexibility offered by electives to create a "Diverse Perspectives in Literature" class, developed in part in response to concerns expressed by a number of minority students. Thus, in her approach, Ms. Morgan was the rare figure in our research who was trying to balance the different corners of the deeper learning triangle: honoring teacher passion and student choice, while also maintaining respect for common knowledge and, particularly, skills; recognizing the importance of the traditional texts of the discipline, while also introducing new texts and courses to stimulate student engagement and affirm identity.

Math was the discipline undergoing the most significant transformation during our time at the school. Until five years ago, math teaching at Attainment High had looked very much like traditional math: students sitting in rows, working individually on problems; teachers moving through textbooks, using in-class time to explain problems; and homework devoted to practicing algorithms. In recent years, sparked by the Common Core, the math department had gradually undertaken a significant shift in its math instruction. The Common Core focuses on a variety of "mathematical practices"—for example, "make sense of problems and persevere in solving them," "model with mathematics," "reason abstractly and quantitatively"—all of which emphasize that education in mathematics is less about remembering algorithms and more about beginning to think like mathematicians. Central to this approach is the importance of "productive struggle"—teachers present a multi-step problem and, rather than walking the students through the steps, ask them to think about the pieces that would be important in solving the problem. There is an emphasis on group work. Finally, there is a shift of focus from getting the answer to a problem to thinking about the variety of ways through which any given mathematical problem can be attacked. While there was variance in teachers' comfort with the new approach, observations and interviews suggested that teachers were trying to teach in the new way and were excited about the shift.

How had this change been accomplished? The key elements here were akin to what was described in the previous chapter on school-level instructional change, but this time the department level was centrally involved. Much as at IB High, the new standards of mathematical practice provided an "anchor" for the departmental effort. Then the teachers worked collectively to think about what this vision would mean concretely—in terms of curricular units and pedagogical practices. Critically, they did not expect each individual teacher to figure out how to integrate the new approach into his or her teaching (and to figure out how to solve accompanying dilemmas presented by pacing guides and other constraints); rather, they worked together to develop a common way of integrating old and new. Since math is sequential, the work started with ninth grade: they tried to re-envision what ninth-grade math would look like under the new approach. Subsequent years led to phased-in changes in tenth grade and then in eleventh. Piloting the work with the ninth grade, and having success, as demonstrated both by performance assessments and by students' increased engagement with math, made it easier to convince holdouts that making the change was worthwhile. Since many of the teachers taught across grade levels, those who had done the work in the ninth grade were able to champion the work at other levels. As they did this work, it also gave them a way to talk about math across curricular tracks. As in science, these teachers were looking for ways to explore the same content at different levels in the hope of making it more viable for students to move up levels. Finally, external circumstances were also favorable: the coming shift toward the Common Core provided an external impetus for the work, but the state had not yet chosen an assessment that would replace the existing state test. This meant that while there was some motivation for change, the department was able to affirmatively build its own momentum and design for math without feeling it was teaching to a new test.

The response of individual teachers was, not surprisingly, varied. Some teachers took to it right away, particularly teachers whose own vision of math was to see it less as an algorithmic discipline with clear right answers and more as a multifaceted way of investigating and making sense of the world. These teachers were already seeking out resources and taking online courses with leading purveyors of the new math like Dan Meyer and Jo Boaler, and using these inputs to deepen their practice. Other teachers had more trouble with the shift, particularly with the way it asked students to move to the role of central problem-solvers and teachers to become guides of student work. In the

CP classes, the idea of removing scaffolds and letting students take on more complicated problems ran counter to the more structured approaches that were common at lower levels. Trying to draw the line between "productive struggle" and students just floundering was another dilemma that teachers sometimes found difficult to manage. These issues were live during our time at the school.

Overall, the math department example shows how significant incremental change can happen within departments in large comprehensive high schools. When the circumstances are just right—external impetus, internal support, time to work on re-envisioning curriculum and pedagogy, stable and experienced faculty—it is possible to move collectively in the direction of learning that is less algorithmic and more like real work in the discipline. The example also shows the constraints imposed by the grammar of schooling—the department did not change the system of curricular differentiation or make math more interdisciplinary or project-based, and teachers continued to be frustrated by the limits of the AP and SAT II exams. Yet despite these constraints, the department was able to make meaningful changes in the nature of math instruction.

As Mr. Dixon looked across his school and contemplated his end goal—that every class be one in which students were asking authentic questions and were engaged in their learning—he reflected that he knew that such a widespread shift would be a heavy lift: "So, I think my experience in [a similar district] taught me that slow change that's focused on sustainable change is better than [a] sort of overhaul. And so, that may have kind of weakened my perspective. . . . I think the impact that I can have is not as overhauling as I think I once did when I was going through the principalship." Looking at a large institution created before he was born, with many inherited structures and assumptions, he knew that change would be a long process.

The "Shopping Mall High School" Revisited

Our account of the contemporary high school both builds on, and differs from, other writings about similar high schools. *The Shopping Mall High School*, the 1985 classic about large comprehensive schools, argued that the problem was that students could choose across a variety of different electives, which diminished academic coherence and adult responsibility for students' education.[12] Perhaps because of academic reforms over the past thirty years, this is no longer the case—students are now taking a full diet of academic core courses, and electives are restricted to the periphery. There may have been some positive consequences to this shift: when one of the authors of *The Shopping Mall High School*, David Cohen, read our account, he was struck by the fact that while we may often have found academic classes lifeless, at least something academic was happening; conversely, he says, thirty years ago, there were many classes that were perfectly pleasant but had little content. At the same time, there are still some significant limits to the current mode of instruction. The core grammar of schooling, the tradition of teaching as transmission, state and district demands for breadth over depth, and pressures for external credentialing have frequently resulted in a core education that involves racing through a mass of information with few opportunities for choice or for exploring a subject in depth. Conversely, the electives were where we found much of the significant innovation happening: freed from the constraints of traditional core classes, teachers were developing interdisciplinary courses that were student-driven, that privileged depth over breadth, and that were much more meaningfully connected to the world and to students' lives. Not surprisingly, these classes featured much higher levels of student engagement. They were also where students and faculty pointed us when we asked about "deeper learning." This suggests an inversion of the argument from thirty years ago: the periphery is in many ways more vital than the core.

A re-reading of *The Shopping Mall High School* suggests that while the authors' top-line conclusions are contrary to what we argue here, their underlying data support many of the same conclusions. They, too, found that many core academic classes were dull and unchallenging places, with bored students and an array of classroom treaties that preserved a status quo that did not ask too much from students or teachers. And they, too, found many bright spots in what they called "specialty shops," which were spaces within the school notable for a shared mission—student choice and commitment coupled with teacher passion for inducting students into their fields. These were among the most powerful learning environments in their study. In the concluding chapter, they ask whether there might be ways to inculcate these same qualities in core disciplinary classes, a question that we continue to ask today.

Our account also differs from writings that depict students at places like Attainment High as "organization kids" (David Brooks) or "excellent sheep" (William Deresiewicz).[13] These authors have argued that some of our top students have become better at jumping through hoops than in defining their core purposes and orientations. While there is some merit to this critique, our investigation suggests that students respond in different ways to the different worlds that are presented to them. In many core classes, the world is presented instrumentally—do what we ask, "read" the teacher for the answer, do what the College Board demands—and you will be able to go to college and fulfill the expectations of your parents and community members. Such environments can produce learning, especially for students who are particularly interested in a domain, but they also produce cynicism and a good deal of playing the "game of school." In contrast, in clubs and extracurriculars, as well as in many elective classes, the world is presented very differently: as an induction into a self-chosen domain of learning, and as a place where formal assessment is deemphasized; where intrinsic motivation is central; and, frequently, where the subject is clearly connected to the world, the self, or some broad domain of human activity. In these spaces, there was much more student enthusiasm, persistence, willingness to be wrong, curiosity, and general enthusiasm for learning. Much as Dorothy Holland and her colleagues have argued that people assume different identities in response to the different "figured worlds" presented to them, we find that as different corners of Attainment High expect very different things from students, students respond to those various demands and often even develop distinct identities in those domains.[14]

The school, particularly a subset of faculty and administrators, recognizes the challenges imposed by the conventional grammar of schooling but is quite constrained in its ability to address them. Unlike the mission-driven environments described in previous chapters, this comprehensive high school is a longstanding entity with deeply rooted traditions and powerful external expectations. Internally, many faculty had themselves been socialized in similar schools and had neither the vision of what something different might look like, nor the appetite, in a conventionally high-performing school, for significant changes.

Externally, parents did not demand such changes and were largely sat-isfied with the current arrangements, particularly their assurance of students' college prospects. As one reformer told us about a proposal to change a similar high school in another town, parental reaction was, "Do whatever you want, but whatever you do, make sure that after four years I'm going to have that [college] bumper sticker on my car." As a result, while there were some reforms to the core curriculum, they were more often alterations in degree rather than in kind, single-loop rather than double-loop learning, or changes intended to incremen-tally improve rather than to fundamentally reimagine the approach. (Math was a partial exception.) With respect to race and equity, sim-ilarly, the school had made progress in closing gaps on state tests and had programs designed to increase the number of students of color in upper-level tracks, but the core structures of tracking, which were baked into the grammar of schooling at Attainment High, preserved these fundamental inequalities and remained largely unchallenged.

While there were other powerful forces preserving the status quo, it did seem that the traditional grammar of schooling was at odds with the school's more enlivening impulses. To put it starkly, the school was in some ways divided against itself—the assumptions enculturated in the traditional grammar of schooling were in conflict with the way the school otherwise wanted to treat its students. Relationships between faculty and students were generally warm and highly respectful. Faculty lamented the way in which students would ask what would be on the test. Many faculty hated the rushed pace and craved time for more projects and opportunities to explore their subjects in more depth. A critical question, then, is whether it is possible to create a different grammar of schooling, one that would align the way faculty wants to treat students with the mode in which they are working. We argue that this grammar already exists—just in the extracurricular domain. We turn to this next.

6 ～

Deeper Learning at the Margins: Why the Periphery Is More Vital than the Core

IT'S A COOL, fall, Monday in New England, as I continue my visit to Attainment High. I have been attending classes throughout the day, and the last one is a senior English class. It is about two weeks before the 2016 presidential election, and, as I walk in, the students are, with teacher encouragement, Googling on their phones which countries have the highest voter turnout. Belgium, says one. I think it's Uzbekistan, says another. Roughly the first seven minutes of class pass this way.

Then attention turns to me. I'm a visitor, and students are searching for anything to take attention away from the proposed task of the day. "Where are you from?" asks the teacher. I explain I'm from Harvard, which prompts a number of questions about Harvard and the purposes of my study. We talk for about five minutes, and then twelve minutes into the period, the actual class begins.

This is a senior English class. The course, it turns out, is on hip hop, but all seniors have to read *Hamlet*, so this is a class on hip hop where the task for the day is *Hamlet*. The teacher, a white man in his late thirties, speaks in a kind of street slang to a group of students, half of whom are white and half of whom are black and Latinx. He starts by explaining that if you are writing an analytical paper, you need quotations, textual quotations, and explains the format for a text quotation. He tells them that not all essays need to be five-paragraph essays; if you have more to say, feel free to go longer. He tells them to put titles on their work. The students are listless and seem bored.

Then they turn to *Hamlet*. "What is the difference between being a coward and being cautious?" the teacher asks. "Whatcha got, Logan? Whatcha got, Amanda?" he calls, trying to draw out some responses. After a few perfunctory responses, he turns to Hamlet. Is Hamlet a coward? A student responds, "He talks about doing all of these things but didn't follow through on any of them." The teacher summarizes, "We've all been there, talked crap and not backed it up." About five minutes for this mini-discussion.

They turn to watching three different film versions of *Hamlet*. The students are supposed to be looking at how different actors played Hamlet and judge how believable he is as a "man of action." After twenty minutes of watching the film, a five-minute discussion ensues. Mel Gibson is emotional; Kenneth Branagh more measured.

The teacher tells them that they haven't been up all day, so they should walk around. They walk to the back of the room, look at some of the posters on the wall, and sit back down.

The final task is to look at modern English versions of some of the Shakespeare lines, and, in pairs, to try to figure out which scene in the play it matches with. They do this, without much enthusiasm, for about ten minutes, when the bell rings. Students hurriedly get up and begin to file out. The teacher plays some hip hop as the exit music. As they are leaving, he writes the scenes of *Hamlet* on the board that they need to read for next time.

As class ends, one girl, Emily, approaches the teacher. She says that she isn't going to be able to read Act IV of *Hamlet* for later this week; she is the stage manager of a show, *The Servant of Two Masters*, which is going up next week, and she has some late nights in front of her in the theater. The teacher says, "Don't worry about it, you know what's important," as she heads out.

About an hour later, I'm at theater rehearsal for the aforementioned show. The energy is entirely different than the class I have just left. Students bound in and begin chatting with their friends. The crew is buzzing around the stage, putting some finishing touches on a railing that has just been attached to the upper deck. Emily is reading through the script and preparing for the day. Ben DiSalvo, the adult director of the show, calls them to order and offers a brief agenda of the scenes that they are going to be working on that day. Students quiet down and listen attentively.

The action begins with warmups—first physical, then mental. The actors form a circle. Today's physical warmup is going to be led by Matt, one of the senior actors in the show. "All I want is a proper cup of coffee," he intones, and they repeat it back to him. "Made in a proper copper coffee pot. I may be off my dot. But I want a cup of coffee. From a proper coffee pot." As they work through this tongue twister, which they use at the beginning of almost every rehearsal, the atmosphere is light. They repeat it, faster, with laughter when there are the inevitable slip-ups. From there it is onto some stretching: rolling the shoulders, windmilling the arms.

Ben then moves to the mental warmup. I know, he says, as they close their eyes, still spread around the stage, that you may have had stressful days. But leave that behind. Forget that test, that problem set, the things that are giving you stress, and let it go. Be here, be present. Get yourself into your character. Begin to think about the world from the perspective of your character. Feel the emotions of your character.

And then it is on to rehearsal. For two hours, they rehearse, stopping for feedback and notes. Today is a full run. It is not necessarily their best run, since they have recently dropped their scripts and thus the actors, who are struggling to remember their lines, have lost some of the fluidity of movement that characterized some of their earlier rehearsals. But as they get further into the play, the energy is better, and by the end, they are proud to have at least done a full run-through, which can serve as the basis for the work tomorrow. Rehearsal ends, students reconnect with each other, and they head slowly into the parking lot, some lingering a bit to talk with Ben or debrief the day's rehearsal with a friend.

It may seem counterintuitive, but in many high schools there is more deep learning happening in "peripheral" activities than in "core" disciplinary classes. We've already seen that elective classes often create more powerful experiences for their students than core disciplinary classes. Here we extend that argument to extracurricular activities such as theater, music, debate, newspaper, athletics, dance, Model United Nations, and many more, which students tell us have the depth, authenticity, and creative ethos that their core disciplinary classes tend to lack. These extracurricular spaces are not only more fun and engaging, but also are actually more consistent with what we know makes for good platforms for learning.

Although extracurricular settings vary widely in their particulars, they share key features that provide a platform for depth. First, they provide opportunities for students to connect their identities to real-world domains of professional practice, to build knowledge and skills over time, and to create authentic products and performances. Second, learning in these settings happens through an *apprenticeship model* in which real-world domains of professional practice provide standards for good work, teachers model expertise and conviction, and students are gradually inducted into more complex aspects of the field. Apprenticeship scenarios also have the advantage of exposing learners to what scholar David Perkins calls the "whole game," inducting them as junior members into a functioning and integrated domain.[1] Finally, the element of choice empowers students both to explore new identities and to play to their strengths—a developmentally appropriate balance of risk and security. Taken as a whole, we argue, these qualities explain why peripheral school settings are so often where the deepest learning occurs.

Elevating the virtues of the periphery inverts some traditional assumptions about how to view the American high school. Some have argued that the development of extracurriculars and electives have diluted the proper academic mission of high schools.[2] We argue here something close to the inverse—that these peripheral spaces have some distinctive advantages in fostering serious learning that could make them a model for more traditionally academic spaces within the school. In making this argument, we will tie in research on how out-of-school settings can promote positive youth development, research that emphasizes the importance of many of the same qualities we identify in electives and extracurriculars.

We did not plan to make this argument when we started the research for this book. Our intent was to focus on core disciplinary classes. But as we spent more time in schools, we were struck by the contrast between the student passivity, boredom, and apathy that was too often found in teacher-controlled core classes and the energy, vitality, teacher passion, and student leadership we saw in the elective and extracurricular spaces.[3] Having repeatedly observed this pattern, we decided to focus on one extracurricular activity in order to understand in more detail how different features of these spaces can come together to create powerful learning environments. Later we will consider how the key elements we identified in theater are also present in other extracurriculars, and whether there are some broader lessons that might be carried from the periphery to the core.

A Brief History of Extracurriculars and Electives

The growth of extracurriculars and electives is highly intertwined with the expansion of the American high school. Until 1900, high schools served only a small fraction of elite American students, and the curriculum was largely classical subjects—Latin, Greek, ancient and foreign history, and philosophy. Over the next thirty years, the high school crystallized into the form it has today—a mass institution serving the vast majority of youth ages thirteen to eighteen. The main spur was economic. As the economy shifted from an agrarian economy to an industrial one, and child labor was increasingly prohibited, more and more youth were now expected to acquire a general education rather than going directly into the labor force.

As the school expanded, it needed ways to engage the many charges that were now under its roof. This led to a significant shift in the activities of school, including changes made to the formal curriculum and in the development of extracurricular activities. With respect to the formal curriculum, more and more modern subjects were added. A debate ensued about the nature of this changing curriculum. One faction, led by Charles Eliot, Harvard president and chair of the renowned Committee of Ten, argued that the curriculum should be expanded to include more modern subjects—including French, physics, and chemistry—but remain academic in its foundations, and that this curriculum should serve all students. A second group, whose views were influentially put forward in the Cardinal Principles document of 1918, argued that schools needed to be more relevant to meet the interests of their students, which would require a much wider array of subjects, including bookkeeping, stenography, home economics, and others. While the first group was successful in setting much of the formal curriculum, particularly for higher-track students, the second was successful in greatly expanding the range of subjects that could be studied in school. A big part of how these changes were reconciled was through the creation of different tracks—students in the academic track would study the curriculum prescribed by the Committee of Ten, those in the commercial tracks would learn the skills for low-level white-collar jobs, the vocational track would have more hands-on courses that would prepare students for manufacturing, and the general track would include a smattering of all three. The newly emerging science of intelligence testing was used to buttress this system of tracking, because it seemed to provide objective assessments of who belonged where.[4]

During this period the extracurricular panoply that we see today was also developed. In the first wave were boys' sports, including baseball, football, and track and field, followed later by basketball and soccer. Other early activities included debate, drama, yearbooks, and newspapers. Between 1910 and 1930, schools developed many other activities, including student council, band, orchestra, and glee, as well as a variety of clubs and hobbies, including some connected to disciplinary subjects.[5]

Critics raised two large objections to these shifts. The first was that the promotion of these elective, practical, and extracurricular subjects diluted the focus on academic subjects. The Lynds' classic 1929 book *Middletown* portrayed both students and adults as more interested in these various clubs than in actual academic work.[6] The Lynds quoted principals as complaining that "hardly a week passes that they do not have to take time from class work in preparation for a contest, the special concern of some organization."[7] They quoted students as saying they had figured out how to skate by in their classes doing minimal work to free up time for more participation in these clubs and activities.[8] The Lynds saw these early clubs, particularly the social clubs (which even included chapters of sororities and fraternities), as having "canons not dictated by academic standards of the world of teachers and textbooks" and as being more about "getting on" socially rather than "learning and the things of the mind."[9]

James Coleman extended this critique in his 1961 classic *The Adolescent Society*. Coleman argued that the elongation of adolescence as a separate period of life had given rise to an adolescent society that was largely separate from either the world of adults or the stated purposes of schooling.[10] Status was allocated in this society not by one's ability to do well in the formal curriculum of school, but rather by virtue of one's performance in this extracurricular realm, with athletics being the surest path to adolescent glory (especially for boys). Again, this treatment could be read to mean that schools were losing control of their fundamental academic purposes, and that social and athletic concerns were exerting disproportionate influence. More recent accounts, such as *The Shopping Mall High School*, have taken a similar tack, arguing that schools have succeeded institutionally by developing an array of electives, tracks, and extracurricular offerings that meet the desires of all of their highly varied students, but in so doing have forsaken their responsibility to develop a coherent educational approach that will make significant academic demands on all of their students. The second, and related, objection offered by a number of scholars of the American high school is that these developments have created and maintained a heavily stratified system of schooling.[11] From the beginning and continuing to the present day, more advantaged students have been slotted into the academic track where they are exposed to core academic subjects, while less advantaged students are put into commercial, vocational, and practical courses that direct them away from college and the middle-class jobs that can follow from a college education.

This criticism was most pointed in reaction to figures, events, and movements that sought to make education less academic and more practical. One familiar target is Stanley Hall, a romantic progressive whose thinking was critical in the development of the Cardinal Principles. Hall argued that schools should be less about training in esoteric subjects and should be oriented to preparing the vast majority of students for life rather than college.[12] Another target was Life Adjustment Education, a 1940s movement that combined the idea that students valued the immediate over the abstract with extremely bourgeois sensibilities over what was worth learning, resulting in an education that taught girls how to sew and go on dates and boys how to manage the family finances. Hall, the Cardinal Principles, and Life Adjustment Education have been lumped together by critics who saw all of these efforts as both dumbing down schooling and denying to less advantaged students the kind of academic education that remained for the most advantaged students.[13] From this vantage point, adding more "periphery" into the "core" dumbed down education and reified stratification.

These are important critiques and not without merit. But they also miss some inconvenient facts and conflate several distinct issues. One inconvenient fact is that the most closely observed studies of classroom life clearly show that there never was a golden age of academic education, even for the most advantaged students. Joseph Mayer Rice's 1893 study of classrooms found that students were mostly simply reading textbooks and reciting the material back to their teachers.[14] There was little evidence of independent thought, and few opportunities for students to investigate questions, develop ideas, examine primary sources, or any of the other hallmarks of what we would today consider a good education. The accounts of the Lynds, Hollingshead's *Elmstown*, and Coleman did not reveal any significant intellectual engagement, even among the upper-track students; for all students, it seemed, the formal part of schooling was largely something to be endured. As we reviewed in more detail in Chapter 1, careful classroom studies at different points across American history again and again have documented much of what we see today—largely lifeless teacher-centered classrooms, devoid of intellectual vitality, that favor close-ended transmission of information over more open-ended investigations. Thus while it is true that students in the academic curriculum have been exposed to more substantial subjects than those in the general, commercial, and vocational tracks, the ways in which those subjects have been taught have been unlikely to incite their intellects or imagination.[15]

Conversely, there were glimmers from the start that some of the most interesting action was in these extracurricular and elective spaces. In the Lynds' account, students "hated Latin"; it was the clubs where students expressed "keen interest," and the vocational courses were the "darling of Middletown's eye."[16] A 1915 article quoted a high school principal arguing that the extracurricular activities "pulsate with life and purpose" while the formal curriculum "owes its existence to a coercive regime, loosely connected and highly artificial."[17] Coleman's account is perhaps the most intriguing. While he is remembered for describing the influence of athletics and the emergence of the self-enclosed adolescent society, his remedy was not a return to some bygone age of formal schooling, but rather an expansion of the interscholastic competitions to include more academic arenas. The major advantage that sports had over academics, Coleman argued, was that performance in sports represented the school, whereas academics represented the individual; thus students and parents idolized star athletes but envied star students. If physics and chemistry became part of academic competitions, it followed that they would both be more motivating to students and become higher-status activities within adolescent society.[18]

There is a way to reconcile these views, and it was provided, perhaps not surprisingly, by John Dewey. As David Cohen has described it, the distinctive contribution of Dewey was that he took Rousseau's romanticism about what education could become outside of formal schooling, and suggested that it could happen within the walls of a school.[19] Dewey also rejected what he saw as a series of false dichotomies: between the practical and the academic, between school and society, between the interests of the child and the centrality of the subject. Dewey argued that all of these seeming gaps could be fused by skilled teachers: for instance, understanding how a car works can and should be integrated with understanding physics and chemistry. He also maintained that it is worthwhile for all students—no matter their eventual destinations—to understand both the practical mechanics of the car and the underlying scientific disciplines. Dewey was horrified by both the stilted teaching that to him produced superficial understanding in formal schooling and the bastardization of his ideas by progressives who emphasized the practical to the neglect of the academic.

What Dewey foretold, but what is still frequently missed, is that the standard account conflates two dimensions into one. It pits education that is academic and rigorous against education that is relevant and not rigorous. But whether education is academically focused has no relation to whether it is rigorous: education can be academic but not rigorous, and, critically, it can also be both relevant and rigorous. Table 6.1, which we've labeled Dewey's Quadrant, shows the possibilities. Many interpreters of the American high school have focused on the contrast between the top right (academic and rigorous) and the bottom left (relevant and not rigorous). The problem with this contrast is that it exists more at the level of policy talk than practice—while Eliot and the Committee of Ten championed the kind of rigorous academic education that they were seeking to provide at the university level, most studies show that this was rarely achieved within American secondary education. Rather, what was much more common was the top left, where students were exposed to academic material, but, for a variety of reasons, were exposed in ways that emphasized transmission of information over substantive engagement with it. Also common is the bottom left, where practical courses may have been more engaging to students, but did not push those students to connect more deeply with a domain of study. Social clubs, sororities, and fraternities also belong here.

Table 6.1 Dewey's Quadrant

	Not rigorous	Rigorous
Academic	Most American high schools, academic track	Charles Eliot (rarely achieved in practice)
Relevant	Stanley Hall; Cardinal Principles	John Dewey
	Most American high schools, lower tracks	Best of progressive education
	Social clubs, fraternities, purely practical electives	Many extracurriculars and electives

Largely absent from this account is the possibility of the bottom right quadrant, where learning is both rigorous and relevant. This is the kind of education that Dewey championed and that has been exceedingly difficult to realize in regular public schools within the formal curriculum, though skilled teachers can make it happen. There are also substantial reasons to think that many extracurriculars and electives qualify as examples of this approach.

There are some limits to this heuristic. As we have noted, there are many ways to make something "relevant" to students, and skilled teachers find ways to interest their charges in traditional academic subjects. But even then, they often do so by finding some broader hook or narrative in which to enmesh their subjects, as when, for instance, a biology teacher motivates the study of the cell as a way to understand human disease. Thus, in the spirit of Dewey, we might say that the best education is clearly in the right column, but collapses the distinctions between the rows, moving seamlessly between theory and practice, academic study and relevance to students.

A Fresh Look at Extracurriculars

What would happen if we took extracurriculars on their own terms, rather than comparing them to their academic counterparts?

Studies have consistently found a positive association between participation in a variety of extracurriculars and subsequent academic, social, and psychological outcomes, including grades, test scores, mental health, and civic engagement.[20] Participation in extracurriculars is also associated with lower dropout rates, and is negatively related to drug use and other delinquency outcomes. The associations between partici-pation and lower rates of problem behavior are particularly strong for high-risk youth.[21] While it is not entirely clear that these associations are causal as opposed to being produced by self-selection, it is clear that there is not a zero sum game in which participation in extracurriculars crowds out the ability to perform well academically.[22] Rather, partici-pation in the extracurricular arena is positively correlated with good grades and other indicators of school success.

There are also reasons to think that the internal states that are aroused during extracurriculars and other activities organized outside of school are more conducive to learning than what happens in tradi-tional school. This question has been of particular interest to Mihaly Csikszentmihalyi, who developed the theory of "flow" to understand the conditions that promote the kind of rapt attention and concentra-tion that characterize work and play at its best. In an ingenious series of studies, Csikszentmihalyi and his colleagues beeped students at dif-ferent points during the day to gauge how they were feeling at that mo-ment. They found that students consistently reported low levels of intrinsic motivation and high levels of boredom while doing their schoolwork. Lower levels of engagement were found when students were listening to lectures, taking notes, or doing individual work; higher levels of engagement were found in group work, labs, and talking indi-vidually with the teacher. But, on average, the beeper studies confirmed the broader trends of research on engagement, which is that students are, more often than not, disengaged with school.[23] In contrast, when they beeped students during extracurricular or organized after-school activities, they found that, on average, students showed higher levels of intrinsic motivation, concentrated effort, and positive mood states than during the rest of the day—including during leisure time (such as hanging out with friends or watching TV), when students had high levels of intrinsic motivation but low levels of concentration.[24]

Sociological research on out-of-school contexts also shows why they can be such promising platforms for development and learning.[25] A study by Milbrey McLaughlin of 120 youth-based organizations in thirty-four cities found that these are places where youth feel known and supported, where they have opportunities to take responsibility and ownership over their learning, and where they create products and engage in public performances that they see as meaningful. Students in the study said that they were frequently treated as "problems" in school and in the neighborhood but that these community-based organizations took the time to get to know them and build on their strengths. McLaughlin's work also stresses that the best of these community-based organizations were "intentional learning environments" centered around some domain they were trying to teach, featuring a progression of knowledge over time as well as formative feedback as students gradually improved as ballet dancers, basketball players, or community-service organizers.[26] Research by Sam Intrator and Don Siegel, which considers a range of out-of-school programs, reaches similar conclusions.[27]

Robert Halpern's work builds toward a more theoretically informed vision of why this approach can be particularly powerful. Halpern's framework is grounded in notions of apprenticeship. He notes that there is abundant evidence that human beings, starting with babies, learn by imitation and watching the models of their elders. He synthesizes the work of Dewey, Maria Montessori, and Lev Vygotsky to argue that learning occurs when the head and the hands work together, that the role of the teacher is to scaffold tasks just out of the reach of the learner, and that learning is a fundamentally social act that happens within communities of knowledgeable people. He points out that Dewey and Montessori were bullish on learning but somewhat skeptical of traditional school, precisely because its grammar of learning created artificial barriers between theory and practice, head and hands, in school and out. Paralleling Jean Lave and Etienne Wenger's work on legitimate peripheral participation, he argues that people learn by becoming gradually inducted into a community of people who know how to do a particular skill or discipline, and that they become increasingly central members and engage with the field in deeper ways over time. Halpern also argues that this form is particularly well suited to adolescents, who are seeking to develop their own identities but are still seeking some adult guidance. Giving them structured opportunities to work with adults but also to take considerable responsibility and initiative for their work meets them where they are developmentally. And, he argues, opportunities to work alongside adults are particularly important for youth who have had hard upbringings, because they need opportunities to connect with well-meaning adults, to experience success, and to achieve some public recognition.[28]

Theater as a "Powerful Learning Ecology"

We chose theater as a domain to investigate in more depth. Theater seemed a particularly intriguing arena because it is closely connected to an academic domain (English language arts), but in most schools is organized primarily as an extracurricular activity. Hence it seemed a promising place to investigate how the "periphery" might approach a similar subject as the "core."

Attainment High has a thriving theater program. The school, which has more than two thousand students, puts on eleven shows a year, including freshman cabaret, a large musical, several modest-sized nonmusical shows, and a playwrights' festival featuring student-authored work. More than two hundred students participate in some aspect of theater annually, including by attending classes or taking on jobs in crew, costumes, lighting, music, acting, and student directing. Theater is the largest activity at Attainment High other than athletics, with four full-time employees (the director, a lighting designer, a costumes designer, and a technical manager). The large size of the program is itself evidence of the program's success in attracting students and securing community support.

We focused our research on one show, *The Servant of Two Masters*, which went up in the fall of 2016. We attended ten rehearsals and the show itself, went to production meetings, spent time with actors and directors while they were off stage, and followed along as students worked on costumes, lighting, and running crew. We interviewed almost all of the actors in the show, as well as the director and assistant director, stage manager, lighting designer, costume designer, and props lead. We also interviewed all but one of the adults involved in the show.

While theater is not unfamiliar to us or our readers, we aimed to see it with fresh eyes. We wanted to identify the key elements of it as a platform for learning and to see how those features compare to typical classroom experiences. We found that theater provides a strong platform for learning by bringing together a powerful blend of purpose, passion, and precision. Students described theater, as opposed to school, as a place that they had chosen to be, one where there was a clear public product that created purpose for their work; a place where they could develop not only their minds but also their bodies and their emotions; a place where people assumed defined roles and became part of a highly interdependent community; a place that offered an arc of learning, beginning with creative exploration and ending with careful refinement; a place that was part of a much larger enterprise (theater), which they identified with and aspired to; and a place where they were never bored but rather alternately terrified, exhilarated, and finally proud of what they created.

Purpose

Perhaps the most striking contrast between theater rehearsals and regular classes at Attainment High was the sense of *purpose* that pervaded rehearsals, in comparison to the apathy or dutiful compliance we saw in many regular classes. Each day's rehearsal had a clearly described arc to it: some initial time to mingle with fellow castmates, a physical warmup, a mental warmup, and then rehearsal, with frequent stops for feedback from the directors. The schedule of rehearsals was emailed out by the stage manager at two-week intervals, so that only those who were part of the rehearsed scenes needed to be present for a particular rehearsal. The result was a transparency of purpose that is rarely achieved in regular classes; everyone knew who needed to be there, when, and why. Rehearsals ran from 3:00 to 6:00 p.m. daily (later during tech week and dress rehearsals).

With this purpose clearly in mind and the show date getting ever nearer, the kind of behavioral monitoring that is so frequently a feature of regular classes was eliminated. At rehearsal, there were no hall passes, and no one asked if they could use the bathroom, get a drink of water, or have a bite of food. Students ate and drank when they weren't on stage, went to the bathroom when they needed to, and checked their phones or did their homework when they weren't called. In comparison, when they were on stage, they were fully present, rehearsing scenes and taking feedback, often for several hours on end.

The work of the set design crew and those working on the costumes, props, and lights was even less closely structured. In addition to attending the main work time after school, students showed up—at the theater, in the several rooms that held props and materials, in the tech crew workshop, and in the costume-making room—at all times of day, during their free blocks or at lunch. All of these spaces were almost always unlocked. A student might spend a free block hanging a light, sewing a piece of a costume, or painting one part of the set. Students often came in pairs or would chat with one of the adults in the theater program while they worked. And although there was an overall plan for the coordination of these tasks, the day-to-day work often happened with high degrees of independence.

Jean Lave, who has studied the work of Liberian tailors, describes the overall trajectory of work as loose in the day-to-day, but tight on the overall sequence of activities and final expectations of learning.[29] A similar pattern prevailed for the crew and designers, who were being held to high final standards but were granted considerable day-to-day autonomy. This pattern contrasted sharply with what we observed in most traditional classrooms: there the daily work is closely monitored, but the overall arc and purpose are fuzzy to the students. One of our interviewees brought this point home to us: why, she asked, do I have a schedule of what is going to happen in my rehearsals, but not in my classes?

With the purpose established, the atmosphere was often quite playful. Students and adults had less formal and often closer relationships than was usually true between students and teachers. Cody Black, the chair of the theater department, was "Black"; Ben DiSalvo was "DiSalvo." Students made fun of Cody's (absence of) hair, Ben's always highly posh attire, and Ross (the gruff but beloved crew director) for the way that his bark was worse than his bite.[30] In one rehearsal, the male and female leads, Truffaldino and Smeraldina, were struggling in their efforts to flirt with each other. My notes read, "She goes for a hug from the side; it looks awkward. Talia, the student assistant director, walks over to Ben, the adult director, faces him, takes his hands in her hands, and says, 'Would it work to try it this way?'" While this kind of physical contact would be unthinkable in class, in theater, a female student taking a male teacher's hands in her hands is simply an accepted part of the rehearsal process.

Similarly, for the adults in the theater program, the space afforded opportunities for different kinds of relationships with students. Ben, the director of the show, was a Spanish teacher by day. He describes the differences between the two settings: "I feel like I know these [theater] kids in a totally different way. In Spanish we keep it 90 percent in the target language. Down here, we are in an environment where we are talking about a character's emotions, we get real and personal. They are also here of their own volition. And we have three hours instead of forty-five minutes." Adults on the production side also spent long periods of time working alongside the students—giving some instruction, but also just working in parallel as they built a platform or sewed some fabric. Especially over multiple productions, over several years, they got to know students in ways that would not have been possible during the time crunch of regular school. The costume director, a warm middle-aged woman named Naomi, said that several of her apprentices were like her own children.

Another feature of theater that differentiated it from most traditional classroom experiences was its approach to time. In most traditional classes, credit is still accrued from seat time—students need to spend a certain number of hours in class to receive a credit. The result is that, from the students' perspective, time can pass very slowly in class, and disengaged students have strong incentives to doze off or stir up trouble. In contrast, in theater, time is, in one sense, very luxuriously allotted (three hours a day) but in another it is a very scarce resource, because it never feels like there is enough of it to get everything ready before the show goes up. Students are also willing to put in extra time— staying until 8:00 p.m. or later during tech week, and until 11:00 p.m. for the three dress rehearsals before the show. The production team worked in project rhythms that resembled what we saw at Dewey High—less intensive work early in the process, and then an all-out effort, including some weekend days, as the show neared. In all of these respects, time in the theater was less like factory-model schooling and more like time in a modern workplace—alternating between work and rest, with the project deadline hovering over everything.

Purpose can also create flow, Mihaly Csikszentmihalyi's term for what happens when people are totally immersed in an activity. As the costume designer, Rosalind, describes the difference between theater and class: "A lot of the time in class I'll be like, 'Okay, fifty-five minutes,' I'm checking the clock every ten minutes. In costumes, I'll get there at 3:00. It'll suddenly be six o'clock."

Education writer Parker Palmer argues that the best classrooms are dominated neither by teachers nor students, but rather by a "Great Thing," which is the subject that demands attention.[31] The theater is like that—the presence of the show and the expectations of the audience are always there just out of sight, organizing the use of space, time, and attention. It puts the students and adults on the same side—when working collectively toward a goal, time is the enemy (because it passes too quickly), and any action that might potentially promote the goal is entertained. And it eliminates the need for grades, and other forms of management, because the production is what organizes the action.

Choice

A big part of what characterizes theater, other extracurriculars, and electives is that students choose to attend. When we interviewed students after the show, again and again they returned to the fact that it differed from core classes in school because they had chosen to be there:

- I am always excited to go there, because I love doing it. And I mean school, you have to do it. Whereas with theater, you can choose to do it or not.
- I'm happier to be at rehearsal than at school, because it is, something I want to do, love to do, with people who want to do it.

Even Ben, the show's adult director, acknowledged that he was able to bring more of his full self to directing than to Spanish class, because of the shared choice people had made to be there:

I think it's easier to open yourself up when you feel like you're surrounded by people who have the same level of motivation that you do, or the same things at stake that you do. And in the theater, everyone is kind of on the same page. And so, they're kind of opening themselves up naturally as well. And in a Spanish classroom, I feel like I've got kids who want to be a Spanish teacher, kids who want to travel abroad, and kids who would rather be in, you know, a dungeon.

Electing to take part in a show also created a heightened level of accountability. Actors said that the combination of choosing to be in the show, the interdependent nature of the work, and the public nature of the final product meant that they felt more onus to be intellectually engaged in rehearsal than in class. As Matt, a senior in the show, describes it, "I feel like there's definitely much more of an expectation for effort in a rehearsal than in a class." Why is that? "Obviously, because you chose to be in rehearsal, you didn't necessarily choose to be in a class. On top of that, there were other people that auditioned for the show that also wanted to be there that didn't end up getting to be there, and because you were chosen . . . you need to be giving it your all . . . you need to prove them right." Another actor, June, put it this way: "I feel like I need to be present more in rehearsal because it's not just about me and my education. It's also just about the show and my team-mates, whereas in class—also in class, if you're kind of zoned out during the class, you can always, you know, ask your friends or ask the teacher."

The actors also felt that there was something special about being part of a community that had mutually chosen to participate in theater. Several described fond memories of summer theater camps where they had put on productions with other kids who shared a similar passion for the stage. Mutual commitment legitimated forthright passion for theater—here was a space where it was okay to be into Shakespeare, or to talk about acting as a craft. Acting also entails vulnerability, which was easier among people who were similarly committed to the same end goal. Laura says that because everyone had chosen to be there, "you're really free to be onstage"; Ben describes it as "easier to open yourself up" among people with similar motivations. Here Sage explains the difference between theater camp and regular English class, beginning with the fact that all seniors are required to study *Hamlet*:

All seniors have to do *Hamlet*. And I really enjoy Shakespeare, but I don't always really enjoy it with that class, or at this school in general just because a lot of the kids don't really want to be doing it. . . . That indifference sort of ends up rubbing off on everyone else. And then, if you are really enthusiastic about it, you just feel awkward, and weird.

She contrasts this to Shakespeare in summer camp:

And so, the thing about the Shakespeare is—I mean the first time I started doing it actually [was] at this camp up in Vermont called *Get Thee to the Funnery*, which Renee [another student in the show] also has gone to. And it was a really phenomenal experience. . . .

We played improv games, and did acting exercises, and we'd perform an abridged version of a Shakespeare play every summer. And that was really, really, really great.

Why was it great?

You were surrounded by people that were also enthusiastic about the same thing that you were enthusiastic about. . . . So many of the people have gone there that were in the years above me, I just admire so much still. And we just read through, and for each scene. And whenever anyone has a question—you stop, and you talk about it. And it was fantastic, because I think the first time I went, the summer before seventh grade, it was great, because suddenly you notice of all of the inappropriate jokes, and all of the foul language, and all of the really beautiful poetic language too. Because I was one of the younger kids there at least my first years, I had older teenagers to look up to, and people who . . . a lot of them have helped me out a lot.

How does that compare to reading *Hamlet* in school?

Oh gosh, people don't acknowledge the dick jokes, or if someone does, no one laughs at it, because it's not funny, it's just, I "Oh, wow, this is awkward, I don't really care about anyone in this class. So, I'm not going to laugh at something that's funny, because I don't want them to think that I'm a nerd," and stuff like that. And it's also—I don't know, I feel a lot of the time, people are kind of scared to say that they actually like Shakespeare at least at school, especially at this school.

Community

As Sage's account indicates, part of what made theater powerful for students was not only choice but also community. Community was the most frequently appearing code in our field notes, indicating that students had talked about it more than any other element of theater. At best, theater created a way for students to find friends with similar interests and passions; at a minimum, it gave them a place to go and a community that accepted them. We were surprised at the number of students who simply appreciated that they didn't have to go home and be by themselves after school and liked knowing that there was a place they could go and hang. Much like former professional athletes who say that the thing they miss most in retirement is the camaraderie of the locker room, students reported that the best part of theater was the chance to be with their friends.

Formal and informal mechanisms were used to support the creation of a theater community. Formally, shows featured cast bonding, where the cast would go to someone's house, hang out, eat pizza, or build a fire pit. There is also a tradition of the cast playing laser tag against the cast of another show. Students clearly valued these opportunities, and spoke fondly of cast bonding. But perhaps the more powerful mechanism for forging community was just the nature of the daily work. Spending three hours together every day to produce something that was collectively made, where some time was scheduled for specific tasks but there was also some free time, created a recipe for building such a community. Here Olive answers a question about the difference between school and theater:

> I think the sense of community is different. I think when you're in a classroom, you might not know everyone's name, but when you're in a show, you learn everyone's name. You have a relationship with everyone. . . . If I'm talking to you in the scene, I should talk to you outside of this, because I kind of want to know who you are as a person. Whereas in class, you raise your hand, and [sometimes] you work in groups, and it's "oh you sound interesting," but then you're back in your rows, and you forget about it.

Theater also created a way for students to find a niche and define their identities in a large high school. Students in the program described themselves as "theater kids," which they saw as a recognized identity within the high school ecosystem. Part of the power of theater was that it was not only an activity but also an identity. Theater kids generally hung out at the end of the school where the theater was, not only after school, but also over lunch and during the day. Theater kids frequently defined themselves in opposition to "sports kids," who hung out at the other end of the school. In a signal of how prominent sports are in

American society, several actors, when asked how they got into theater, began with "well, I wasn't a sports kid" or "I cannot do any sports; I cannot; I don't even know what a football is." More affirmatively, the theater kids defined a collective identity around the arts, liberal political and social values, inclusion of minorities and gay students, and love of theater. Raven, one of two African American students in the show, said that she had found a home among the theater kids in part because of their racial awareness:

> I mean I would come into the girls dressing room, and they would be talking about "Oh, did you hear about what happened with Trayvon Martin, or Tamir Rice," or—well, not exactly those, but instances like those, and they were "Oh yes, it's awful,—and did you hear about, you know, what's happening at the protest?" And these were things that I wasn't even aware of at first. So, the fact that kids with a different ethnic background that weren't—pretty much that weren't minorities, and they were diving more into it, and being [more] open to these topics than I was, that was really surprising. And that really made me happy, and hopeful.

Students who did not necessarily fit that well into other social groups often found a home in the theater program. One lesbian actress describes the nature of the theater community:

> Well, I definitely think that a lot of weirdos end up in theater. And . . . in sixth, seventh, eighth grade, middle school years, it was, "Oh, it's the theater kids it's—they're possibly gay, they're kind of awkward, they're quiet, unless they're screaming about Stephen Sondheim." I don't know. But now it's kind of, "Oh, it's the theater kids. They have a pretty good control of speaking with people, their words, their emotions, they know how to hold a crowd, and they're pretty interesting people."

While "weirdos" seems unflattering to the many delightful people we met in theater program, it does capture the way in which it prioritizes embracing non-conformists, including non-athletes.

It would be unrealistic to suggest that it was always roses and honey in the theater program. Students said that other actors could be catty and cliquey, and that, in particular, there were often tensions among friends when they auditioned for the same parts and some got them and others did not. Some said that there also were divisions between people who were regulars in almost every show and those who were more peripheral to the program. As with any enterprise involving teenagers, friendship and community were the most powerful draws, but forces of jealousy and exclusion could also rear their ugly heads.

On the whole, however, the balance was heavily tilted toward the creation of an open, inclusive, and warm community. While that community was built and sustained by everyone in the theater program, it originated with the program's founder, Cody Black, who, Ben says, has "kind of the magic touch." Cody was a Jewish kid who was born in Detroit and grew up in Queens. Cody's parents were divorced, and his home life was, in his own words, "dysfunctional." Theater and sports were his respite, the places where he went to find the kind of community that was missing at home. These were special places because "you're working with people to achieve something. You know, I look back, it gave me joy, and it made me feel good about myself. And I think that was important, because I wasn't getting that at home. And I think working with like-minded people for the most part, whether it's a sports team, or a play production, and having teachers who cared about that."

Cody was particularly shaped by a few teachers, who were distinctive in that they really trusted their students. The critical symbolic act that Cody remembers was when teachers would give students their keys: "There's always that teacher that give you their keys. 'Hey, go get this,' hey—and it's this ring of keys. And those keys meant to me they're trusting me with this. They're giving me their keys for God's sake. So, they're trusting me, and they're giving me ownership—not power, but . . . they were giving me what they had . . . I had to take care of those keys, and treat them as if they were my own." Cody embraces this approach in his attitude toward his own students: "So, I feel like it's important to give these kids the key to the kingdom."

Cody gives the students the keys to the kingdom in the form of access to his "office," a place unlike any other at the school. Theater kids hang in this ten-feet-by-ten-feet space seemingly 24/7, sprawled across the couch, sitting on the floor, doing homework, or just shooting the breeze. Particularly at lunch or right before rehearsal, you'll find students strumming a guitar, eating, or lounging. Cody is sometimes there, sometimes not. When he is there, he often sits toward the back working on his computer, occasionally joining the conversation with a joke or a gentle teasing comment, but mostly just letting the students be. Cody's office is a judgment-free zone—you can unload about your day, complain about homework or other teachers—no topic is off-limits, and there is none of the self-censoring that students usually engage in around adults. Students *own* the space, in a way that this school, which has lots of hallways but few benches or other places to sit, permits few opportunities for. Some of our best interview data came from Black's office, because students seemed freer to say what they really thought. One student said it had been "overrun by teenagers" and was now "less like an office" and more like a "communal space." Another said, "That's a place where you can go, and you can get like pretty much anything off your chest. You can just get with friends, and talk about some chick that was being really annoying today. So, to other people, probably people who aren't in theater, it's like, 'Oh, it's another group of kids, you know, just talking in some teacher's office,' but to us, it's like a secret club."

In addition to running the theater program and directing the musical each year, Cody also teaches a Theater I class. In the class, the culminating assignment is for students to write a letter to a friend or family member communicating something that they always wanted to say but haven't been able to voice. Then they perform it for the class. In these monologues, students have come out as gay, shared about alcoholic mothers and abusive fathers, and described friendships and relationships that have gone south. Cody describes what happens next: "And the point is, is that they look at each other, 'Wow, we all have our story, and we all have places we come from, or things that are going on in our lives that we can relate to, or connect with'. . . . And then it's always the same thing in the end, 'Oh my god, you know, like we know each other even better,' you know, and then when they see each other out in the hall, they understand they have this special connection." Since many of the actors in the program have been through Cody's class, they have had this experience together, which creates opportunities for deeper relationships with one another. Says one actor in the cast, "I've been in his theater arts class, and it was raw. I mean the content we were learning in terms of like the monologues, and discovering characters, it was a really raw process. So, once you've gotten [through] those monologues, you feel pretty comfortable with saying anything."

While building a trusting community makes for better theater, Cody's view is more that theater is a mechanism for building community. Cody has a master's in educational counseling, and for his thesis he developed an improv troupe that took on issues like homophobia and date rape, and by dramatizing them, tried to help adolescents talk about them. When we asked him what his primary goal is for the program—people first? subject first? people through subject?—he responded, "People, I think it's people. . . . You know, I think it comes down to this human experience that I think we all crave—humans—even animals, we crave to be connected. I mean I'll be honest with you. When I meet somebody, and they're a Jewish person from Queens, I feel connected. Hey, where are you from? Did you go to Waldbaum's? And I think we all feel that, in my mind, we want to be connected." Particularly when working with young people, who are actively trying to develop their identities, take risks, and figure out how to relate to one another, Cody sees theater, and the community that it builds, as integral to not only developing students' acting skills but also helping them become more confident and connected young adults.

Interdependent Roles

EMILY (THE STAGE MANAGER): If anyone is out or sick, it puts a damper on the whole process. No matter who it is. You can function, but it's not going to be the best, if someone is sick or not there.

INTERVIEWER: Interesting. Why is that?

EMILY: Because every part is crucial—every person is there for a reason, and we don't have extra people just hanging around. If you look at a stage crew or lights or stuff, everyone is always doing something, because they have to. Because they have deadlines. And these deadlines aren't flexible. So, it's integral that everyone is where they need to be, always . . .

BEN (THE DIRECTOR): In theater, it is a community because everyone has a part to do. Whereas if Billy is asleep in the corner of my Spanish class, it doesn't really affect my performance in the class. We're co-constructing something together in theater, but in Spanish class [we're not].

One way in which the theater production differed from regular classes was the presence of roles. While most classes have just two roles—teacher and student—the production had as many roles as there were people, thirty in all. These included all of the different acting roles in the show, as well as the director, assistant director, lighting designer, assistant lighting designer, dramaturgs, costume designer, assistant costume designers, and many more. The production of the show was highly interdependent—it required not only that each student fulfill their own function, but also that these pieces come together in an integrated way. This was not always so easy, as we will see.

One significant advantage of these roles is that they created many opportunities for leadership. Unlike during classes, students were given opportunities to direct their peers. Emily, the stage manager, compares her roles in class and school:

> Class to me is something you've done your whole life. It is kind of childish. Rehearsals are "Okay, this is a job." As you're getting older, this is what life is going to be like. I know a lot of friends and acquaintances that . . . [are] struggling with the whole "Oh gosh, I'm going to be an adult. I'm going to be in charge of myself." And I've been in charge of twenty people for the past couple of months. So, I'm not really too nervous about taking care of myself.

Talia, the student assistant director, describes how she had to gradually become more comfortable assuming responsibility, "And for me, when I was directing, I was not only learning the actual content of this is what it is to be a director; I was also learning leadership. I felt kind of weird directing, because I was [thinking], 'Wow, I think this person has more experience than me,' and it kind of psyched me out at first, but then I realized, 'No, I'm the director, I'm in this leadership position, I need to step up,' and I learned how to kind of get over myself, and be a leader."

For all the advantages of these roles, they posed the same challenge that exists in any midsized organization: if roles enable the differentiation needed for specialization, how can these roles be integrated into a coherent whole? As in many organizations, each of these departments came to see themselves as separate units; students spent the vast majority of their time with others in similar roles—the actors with other actors; the crew with the crew; the costumes people with the costumes people. These groups were often physically siloed so that each group could do their work: the costumes people had a room in which the costumes were made; a woodshop-type space was where the crew conducted much of its work; and the actors got the stage, except for days when light or set needed it and they were moved to the band room. While there was some movement across roles over time (that is, someone might be an actor in one show and do costumes for the next), there also were many people who stayed in their roles over years, which further intensified the departmental structure. Consequently when all the groups were together—such as in the tech run, students mostly hung out with people in their departments during breaks.

Given these dynamics, a key challenge for the show was to build integration across the teams, so that along the way they could learn lessons about teamwork, perspective-taking, and mutual respect. There were some formal integrating mechanisms. One was a series of meetings between Ben and Talia and costumes, set, and lighting at the beginning of the process to develop an overall vision for the show. Another was the Friday afternoon production meeting, run by Emily, in which each of the departments would have roughly five minutes to report on their progress and ask questions that required input from other departments. As I described one production meeting in my fieldnotes,

> About twelve students are sitting around two rectangular tables that have been pushed together. Naomi, Ross, Ben, and other adults are standing around the outside. Emily is leading the meeting and moving us down an agenda. Cody is typing, presumably about something else. Everyone else is paying attention with their eyes. One other girl is taking notes on a Mac. There are four water bottles. Max has a can of Pringles in front of him. Virtually everyone is wearing jeans— people look like they are at a meeting, waiting for their turns. Not enthralled, but also not misbehaving—just looks like adult life.

One way to understand what was happening here is to compare the hidden curriculum of classrooms to the hidden curriculum of theater. As Talia described the hidden curriculum of her classes, "I think when you're learning, there's two things you're really learning. So, one would be the content. So, if I was in English class, or learning about *Hamlet*, I'm learning about *Hamlet*, that's the content that I'm learning. And the other is the actual situation you're in. So, while I'm learning *Hamlet*, I'm also learning how to be in a class. And really, I'm not learning anything new, because I've been in classes before, and I'm learning how to sit down, and listen to this teacher, and take notes, and all that stuff." As hidden curriculum theorists like Philip Jackson have observed, the hidden curriculum of most classrooms is compliance; classes socialize students how to follow directions, work individually, and satisfy the demands of authority figures (teachers).[32]

In contrast, the hidden curriculum of theater is about learning how to function in a modern organization, in which expertise is distributed horizontally, and what participants need to learn is to respect the work of others, as well as how to negotiate problems that fall across different areas. For example, one issue that required considerable coordination in this show was the asides, moments when actors turned to speak directly to the audience. The idea was that the actor would turn, a spotlight would shine on him or her, the actor would speak his or her lines, then the actor would turn back, and the light would go off. But in practice this was challenging, because both the timing of this maneuver (turning on the lights exactly when the actor turned) and the positioning of it (having the actor stand exactly where the light was to shine) were hard to nail. It was so difficult that during a dress rehearsal two days before the show they considered scrapping the idea entirely. But ultimately they decided to keep the asides, and decided it was easier to move the actors than to move the lights. This decision then led the crew to strategically redo the marks on the stage that the actors used to position themselves—for example, giving one actor who was particularly struggling his own color of marks to make it easier to find his spot during the action. During one of the dress rehearsals, one of the actors was so far out of the light that he had to jump into the light, which brought a big laugh from the assembled group, and since the show was a comedy, they decided to keep that in. Thus, through a process of discussion, mutual adaptation, and a bit of improvisation, the group learned how to solve a problem that fell across departmental lines.

In teaching these skills of teamwork and mutual respect, the show had a considerable advantage: the adults involved themselves had long histories of working with one another with significant trust and mutual respect. As Naomi, the adult costume designer, said of Larry, the adult lighting designer, "He will just stop by and ask if I need something, and then he'll offer to do it, even if that is taking time away from what he is working on." The adults then extended this kind of mutual respect to the students, treating their roles and expertise as if it were on par with the adults. For example, at one production meeting, Naomi said that because of a family issue, she wouldn't be able to make it to the designer run, an important rehearsal in which the actors go through the show so that the various design teams can see it and adjust their work as necessary. She then, very tentatively, asked if the designer run could be moved from the following Friday to early the week after. Here are my notes:

> A lot of back and forth ensues. Ross, the crew director, says that it would work for him; they could use the extra time to make more progress on the set. Emily checks the schedule for Monday and Tuesday and discovers that two of the actors, including Pantalone, one of the leads, are going to be out that day. Ross asks whether they could check with the particular actors to switch. Ben says that he doesn't feel comfortable asking that. Ross says it is more than a week's notice, which is apparently the norm. Ben still demurs. Naomi concludes, "I only wanted to switch if it was easy." They agree to record the run and she will watch that and use it to give the costume department notes.

What is notable about this interchange is how respectful the adults are of one another and also of the students; Ross is trying to make it work for Naomi, but Naomi is unwilling to ask for the switch if it is inconvenient for the actors.

Students frequently described theater using the metaphor of work—not in the sense that it couldn't be fun and playful, but in the sense that it was a professional environment where the personal should take a back seat to the requirements of the work. As one actor said, in reaction to a question about what it was like to be part of a show where their fellow actors were chosen for them, "The bright side of that is that in theater we're thrown into a room with a bunch of people that we don't really know, and we don't really have a say. I had to work with them regardless. And getting that experience of having to deal with someone that you don't like and having to work together is definitely something that I'm glad that I had the opportunity to do." Students referred to one another as "professionals," as when Lisa, one of the actors, came over to the costumes people during a break in a rehearsal and they asked her opinion of her dress. "Oh, I don't know," she replied, "you guys are the professionals." Cody wryly quoted Patriots coach Bill Belichick in saying that the mantra of the program was "do your job," meaning that "whatever you choose to do, care about it. You may not like every little thing about it. You may not like—I got to sew that, I got to paint this. But, they really care about it . . . and that brings them back."

On the whole, both the students and adults characterized *Servant* as fairly successful in generating mutually respectful relationships while trying to build a very complex thing in a short amount of time. Sage, the assistant stage manager, said that it sometimes got "pretty fucking tense," but that on the whole, "it was just like everyone kind of had good relationships." As Naomi more eloquently described the show, "This was an incredibly respectful group of actors, and—as complicated as it was—I just felt like there was so much respect for each other's work product, sometimes that's the particular mix of personalities, or phase of the moon, this one was really remarkable."

Apprenticeship

Another critical aspect of theater, and one that made it distinctive from school, was the strong element of apprenticeship in students' learning. Students learned by doing, but they did so under the watchful eye of people who had more experience. This was particularly true in the production departments—lights, costumes, set, stage management— where students described a process of rising through the ranks and gradually gaining more responsibility. For example, Rosalind, the costume designer for the show, remembers initially shadowing in her first production as a freshman, then moving to becoming a "changer," someone who literally changes an actor's costume during the show, and then doing some design on some smaller shows before becoming the lead student designer for *Servant*. Older students would, when they had time, show younger ones exactly how things were done, as Sage describes how she learned stage managing in an earlier show from a girl named Amanda:

She showed me how to do everything, and she taught me how to set up the binder, and what line notes were, and how she took blocking notes for those shows, and how to do set lists, and ship lists, and all of that. I mean she taught me a lot of stuff, I didn't really do most of it, I guess for the most part. But, I was pretty okay with that. I was just kind of like, "Oh man, I get to sit next to a senior." So, yeah, I mean I think that was basically prelude for me.

As Sage describes, the older students are not simply imparting technical knowledge; they are also role models, and even being included among them can initially feel like an honor. This process is a more specific instantiation of what Lave and Wenger call legitimate peripheral participation, a theory of apprenticeship learning that suggests people learn by starting as "peripheral participants" in a domain and gradually gain expertise as they take on more central roles.[33]

This particular theater program had the benefit of having adults leading each of these departments, which gave students direct access to people who had significantly more expertise than even the most experienced students. These adults had similarly been through their own process of being mentored by more experienced people in their fields, and were paying it forward. For example, Larry, the adult lighting designer, had majored in light design as an undergraduate, and had worked with a number of professional theaters doing part-time work with lights. His position was originally part-time, and as the number of shows grew and the program expanded, it gradually became a full-time job. But he continues to work in summers and on weekends with professional and community theaters, and, on occasion, when a job came up where he was not available, had passed that opportunity to seniors or recent graduates whom he had trained. Thus the adults involved in the show had real, and in some cases recent or ongoing, experience in what they were training the students, and students sometimes had opportunities via these adults to participate in these domains beyond high school. This was in sharp contrast to most regular classroom teachers in our study, who had little ongoing connection to the professional work in the disciplines that they taught.

Apprenticeship learning also differs from classroom learning in what Roland Tharp has called the "jointness" of the endeavor between the adults and the students.[34] If in a regular class the student is trying to please the teacher, and the teacher is playing the role of judge or umpire in evaluating students' work, in a theater production, everyone is working together to make something for the audience. While the adults were careful to give students the final say, they also had considerable professional pride in what was being produced, and thus they worked together to make sure that the work achieved their standards. For example, Naomi, the beloved costumes designer, had decided to co-design the show with Rosalind, a junior. This decision had come about as a result of student demand, because students exiting the program had said that there was sometimes *too much* student leadership and that the students were losing out by not having the adults work directly with them.

Rosalind, in turn, described what it was like to work with Naomi, whom she described as "one of the kindest people I know." "I thought it was really special, because I'm not sure when the last time Naomi designed a show was. . . . It was really different than designing with a student, and really special. Because she is so knowledgeable, and she is so good at what she does, that I thought it gave me extra confidence in what I was doing. Because I knew—Naomi had my back throughout the whole thing really closely." Naomi and Rosalind went through the whole process together—researching the period, developing a design and a color scheme, creating an image board and a Pinterest, sewing the costumes, and then making adjustments as needed. In all of this, Rosalind found that Naomi was "very calm, and she's so, so knowledgeable. I don't know how she knows so much that she does, but she always has knowledge about these teeny-tiny little intricacies of time periods or even specific years, about different things. So, she can pinpoint really early on, 'Oh, no, that's not going to work, [it's not the right] time period' or . . . 'that's two years early, but no one will know.' Those sorts of little things. And I think that's really nice, to have that sort of backup." By working together to create something, Rosalind benefited from Naomi's considerable expertise, but she still had the experience of designing a show.

As students' roles increased as they got older, the tasks they were asked to do also increased in complexity, which, in turn, helped build more sophisticated understandings. Talia, for example, describes her shift from an acting to a directing role as a move from part to whole, from understanding the world only from the perspective of what she needed to do to seeing how the entire production fits together.[35] Larry, the adult lighting designer, similarly said that his work with Liam, the senior student lighting director, resembled more of a partnership than a teacher-student relationship, because Liam now had enough experience to see the same complexities that Larry did. For example, he said, students who were just starting out in lighting didn't have a picture in their head of what the whole show would look like, and thus while he could explain what they were doing and why, they didn't yet have a full mental model of what it is they were trying to create. But with Liam, who had designed a number of shows over the years, they could talk both broad vision and implementation of particular scenes from the start, because they could similarly envision what the final product might look like. Throughout the process, both students and adults deferred to Liam's decisions about lighting design, giving him respect that was commensurate with the expertise he had developed.

The Arc of a Powerful Learning Experience

The familiarity of theater masks the complexity of the learning that underpins it. For a show to succeed, actors need to understand something about the history of the show, its period, and the author's intent; develop a collective interpretation of how they are going to play the show; understand each and every one of their lines—who they are in that scene, what the purpose is of their words; develop actions and voice inflections that communicate those purposes; internalize their lines so that they can speak them without thinking about them; play off of the other characters in their scene; and integrate all of this with costumes, sets, and lighting. All of this is fraught with risk and vulnerability: the students need to develop interpretations of characters that may fall flat; they need to tap into parts of themselves and put those parts on display live in front of hundreds of people. To achieve all of that requires integrating spheres that are usually kept distinct: passion with precision, head with heart and hands, conscious memory and unconscious fluency, the individual parts and the collective whole. Part of why we see theater, and other extracurriculars, as such promising platforms for learning is that they have ways of enriching and integrating these many spheres of learning.

Setting a Foundation

The Servant of Two Masters was, everyone involved agreed, one of the most complicated shows that the school had ever put on. The show is an eighteenth-century comedy written by Carlo Goldoni in which the title character has not one but two masters, resulting in a number of comic mishaps such as being paid a debt "for your master" and not knowing to whom the money should go. But it is not only comedy; it is commedia dell'arte, an Italian style in which a troupe of actors are each given a stock character to play (the old hag, the young buck) and an outline for a show, which they then are supposed to improvise by drawing on the expected roles of those stock characters. In their version of *Servant*, they would follow the lines (and not improvise them), but they were also seeking to play the stock characters whom their roles represented. On top of that, they decided to follow an interpretation first put on by the Milwaukee Repertory Theater in 2004, in which rather than always being the characters, the actors were sometimes a theater troupe that was putting on the show. The audience would know whether they were seeing the "play" (actors as stock characters) or the "play prime" (the acting troupe scenario) because different parts of the stage (and different lighting schemes) were used for each. The action culminated with the servant lead Truffaldino getting married in the play, but falling sick and dying as an actor playing the role, a duality that the students had to communicate to the audience. As the actors themselves attested, when they began they knew little about *Servant*, commedia as a style, or the specific stock characters who they were playing. How, in eight short weeks, did they learn all of it?

The earliest part of the process was spent with everyone doing some research on the show, the time period, and the commedia style. Ben offered some overall framing thoughts that laid out how commedia was different from comedy, explained why they wanted to do the play prime version of the play, and introduced some historical context. The actors also watched clips from the United Kingdom's National Theatre of the different stock characters they would be playing. On their own, some of the actors watched YouTube videos of actors who had played their role in this play or the stock character their character was associated with. The show also benefited from two student dramaturgs, a new role that the students themselves had initiated and was being piloted with this show. The dramaturgs did their own research into the playwright's intent and the history of the show and presented it to the cast. Hence, in this early period, a variety of different forms of learning were being used to triangulate *Servant*—direct adult instruction, collective student analysis of videos of previous productions and interpretations of stock characters, individual research by actors (both text and video), and particular student roles (the dramaturgs) in which selected students developed a specialized expertise that was then shared with the group.

An adult troupe that specialized in commedia was also a critical resource. Found through social networks, this troupe came to a rehearsal, explained and demonstrated what many of the stock characters did, and played some games with students in which they tried out some of the stock characters and the physical motions that accompanied them. Many of the actors credited the time with the adult troupe as particularly important for helping them develop their "physicality," the movements that came with each of their characters. While most of the actors in the show had acted before, none had experience with the over-the-top motions that commedia requires, and several of them described that challenge as the most significant stretch that the show required. Working with the professional troupe had the benefits of injecting expertise, providing feedback, and showing that there was a real-world context for the students' work, all staple elements of theater that are absent from most classes.

Learning by Doing

Then it was on to rehearsals. At the beginning the students engaged in "table work," or reading through the play, line by line, trying to get familiar with the characters, the lines, and the rhythms between the actors. Some of this took place sitting cross-legged on the floor of the stage. Gradually the work progressed into more physical enactments of scenes, still with scripts in hand.

The major task in these early rehearsals was for the actors to venture an initial version of their characters. Ben's view, which is shared by many directors, is that taking this initial risk of putting something out there is critical to everything that follows. He says he learned this from his mentor, "Brother Ron," who was the director of his own high school shows: "What I get from Brother Ron is, he would always say,

'Don't talk, do.' And I am really all about doing something, and then analyzing the results, and not let's plan for two hours about what this kind of second scene is going to be." Following from this philosophy, Ben's most frequent piece of feedback was "make a choice," meaning that an actor needed to make a strong decision about what they were trying to do with each line and action. Particularly for the younger and less experienced actors, this was not always so easy: they would appeal to Ben for more direction, but his response was always the same: "you need to make a choice, you need to make a decision and try it." From Ben's point of view, it was always easier to give people feedback on whatever they tried, but you couldn't even begin until someone had ventured something. "Make a choice" was also a pragmatic reaction to the sheer volume of the task of putting on a play—there were, as Ben emphasized frequently in rehearsals, many too many lines and actions for Ben and Talia to try to direct each of them. Student initiative is thus not optional but rather a necessity if the play is going to come off at all.

A related point is that Ben was trying to encourage the actors to take risks in what they put forward. As he said on a number of occasions, "the greater danger is in *not* taking risks." Like a sculptor, once a lump of clay assumes an initial form, it can be molded into different shapes, but until it is created, there is nothing to mold it into. As Ben describes it, "It's way easier for me to pull back than to try to pull something out." More experienced actors understood this. Alex, the lead of the show who was also an experienced improv actor, described rehearsal as a process of trying out different possibilities, "If you think something is funny, you should try it and you should do it. If you think it's a good idea, definitely go for it, and it's not a big deal if you mess up. People aren't really going to think about it that much. It's just not a big deal." Alex lived up to this mantra during rehearsals; he tried a variety of different ways of prancing across the stage to emphasize his characters' attention-getting nature; he tried bawdy ways of delivering lines in seduction scenes. As he said, some of these worked and others did not, but he definitely got further faster by making these choices. In contrast, some of the younger and less experienced actors on occasion responded to Ben's "what choice were you making there?" with "I'm not sure" and the lack of these choices meant that it took a lot longer for them to develop their characters. Much as design thinking has a mantra of "fail faster" and advice columns say "nothing ventured, nothing gained," the same was true for actors developing their roles.

Part of why this was hard was that it required shedding deeply held inhibitions. When we interviewed the actors after the show, about half described themselves as extroverts who were "heightened versions of themselves" on stage, whereas the other half described themselves as introverts, for whom the stage enabled them to do things they would never do in real life. Renee, a very shy girl who played one of the female leads, Smeraldina, said that the character initially "terrified" her, because "she was bawdy, loud, overtly sexual—all the things that I'm not." And she was not the only one—a number of the actors said that they found the early rehearsals very challenging because they were essentially out there naked—just them, trying to find their character. Ironically, they said, performing in front of the audience on show night was comparatively easier, because by that point it was the character, not their real self, that was on display.

Another complicating dynamic in the early rehearsals was that the actors did not yet know each other that well, and some were trying to demonstrate that they belonged in the show. Raven, a sophomore, explains, "So, at the beginning of the process, I think it is really hard, because you haven't gotten a chance to know most of the kids in this cast. I mean I was familiar with all of them, but I mean I really did not know these kids, I didn't trust them. So, it seems like everybody is trying to impress one another. Like, 'Oh, I'm the best actor, I'm the best actor, you know. This is why I got this part.'" She was "definitely trying to impress everybody else as Raven, and—as Raven, I wasn't even focusing on Beatrice [her character]. I was trying to show everybody that I deserve this role, you know." Ben tried to counter these dynamics, said Liza, a freshman, but not always successfully: "I mean I noticed [Ben], he was always like 'You don't have anything to prove. You're already in.' But I felt I had to show that I was worth being in the show, and that yes, I could do it." Much as university freshmen spend the first month of the year trying to show that they are not an admissions mistake, actors' individual desires to show that they belonged got in the way of actually working together on the content of the play.

Tone and Culture

Given these challenges, establishing the right tone for the rehearsal process—one that was free of judgment, engendered trust, and encouraged people to take risks—was absolutely critical for the show's success. On the first day the group co-constructed norms that would reflect many of the major challenges of the process to come, including "try new things; make informed choices; focus on supporting others; have fun; create a warm, judgment-free environment; and expect to make mistakes." Both Ben and Talia had also thought a lot about the nature of their feedback and the notes they gave to actors; as Talia said, "the wrong note can break an actor." They tried to calibrate the amount of feedback they gave; Ben said one of the things he learned over his years directing was too give many fewer notes, because actors couldn't take in all of the feedback at once. Ben also explicitly tried to focus on praising them for making a choice: "whether or not the choice worked," he gave "positive feedback on them making a choice."

If part of the key to giving good feedback was its tone, the content of the feedback also mattered. Most of Ben's feedback was less about issuing a directive and more about offering an option. The actors really appreciated this style, because it put them in charge of developing their own characters but also provided ideas for what they might try. Says Matt, "Most of the feedback that he gave was not super like, 'This is the way that it's going to be, and there's no like argument about it.' Usually it was more like, 'What if you tried it this way, or think about this?' . . . And so, I do think that we definitely had our opportunities to think about our roles like ourselves, and not, you know, have him dictate everything." Ben also tried to situate the feedback as coming less from him and more from what the show needed: "If they think that I'm talking about my personal preference, then they have to buy into my personality, they have to buy into my set of values. . . . It's not about me, it's about what I am seeing as an audience member, and my interpretation of that. It's not like you need to do this for me, you need to do it for you, you need to do it for the audience." And because theater is a performance medium, it was frequently true that Ben's comments mirrored what we, as outsider observers, were seeing as prospective audience members. Some things the actors tried "worked" and others did not—hugs appeared natural or forced, jokes landed or fell flat—and thus much of what Ben did was simply gently anticipating the audience's reactions to what the actors were trying. This feedback was critical to creating the standards that would make the play worthy of a real audience.

These processes added up, and over time the actors became increasingly comfortable with each other and taking risks. Here Raven describes how things evolved from the initial days: "Once you have that foundation of trust in your cast, it's not about, 'Oh, who is watching me' anymore, it's about 'How do we create a space of taking risks together, and giving each other those notes.'" Over time, she says, it gets easier and more fluid, because "you're on stage with people you've grown to trust, grown to have very close friendships with, grown to love." Raven's description brings to mind research on how teams develop—moving through stages that scholar Bruce Tuckman memorably described as "forming, storming, norming, and performing"—with trust and time as the key elements that enables coordinated action.[36] Daisy, a freshman, adds that the way in which the directing team treated the actors mirrored what they were hoping the actors would do in the show, a parallelism that we earlier called symmetry:

> Ben and Talia were very good directors. They were directorial—they had enough of an influence to keep a bunch of rowdy high schoolers under control. But they also had enough leniency to let us have a little fun, have a little joke . . . make fun of the fact that somebody has a mask that has a footlong nose on it. And at no point was he like, "This is a theater show. You shouldn't be having fun. You should just be putting a comedy on for people." Because in order to put on a comedy, you're supposed to have fun yourself. And I think a big part of it was that a lot of us had a lot of fun.

Engaging Heads, Hands, and Heart

Even with the help of a supportive environment, the actors still had to figure out how to play their characters. "Making a choice" was harder than it looked. And Ben's other most quoted piece of advice—"play an action, not an emotion"—was intended to help them think about why their character was feeling a particular way in order to convey it to the audience. For instance, here Liza describes the problem with "playing sad." She says, "I mean if you play sad, there's no real motivation. You're just sad, but you don't know why, you don't know how you got sad. And it's just kind of shallow, and it's not really like real people. They have depth, they have—they have lives and they have experiences, and all that affects the emotion." So, how would you do that? "I think you have to do your research and really think about it. We had this script divided in beats, so each beat had a specific goal and action." We also see in

Liza's account an iteration between whole and part—she is both trying to think about her character's overall motivations and working on the purpose of specific lines and actions.

Many of the actors said that the key to finding their characters was finding the right "physicality" for the role. This suggests an intersection in their learning between the cognitive and the physical, the head and the body. For example, Raven was playing Beatrice, a woman who disguises herself as a man for most of the play, before reemerging as a woman at the end. She describes how she found her way into Beatrice, suggesting that through the reading of the script and the table work, she didn't really have it. The turning point, she said, was "getting the physicality of being a man, because that was my mentality. Once I got into the physicality, becoming that character would not be as hard. When really people say it's the other way around." She says that she consulted a transgendered friend. "I talked to my friend who's trans about what his transition was between womanly physicality to manly physicality. How to drop your voice, how to walk, and how to talk. So, once I got that down, I delved deep into her emotional state. . . . It went along in steps. I got my physicality down, then I got the mentality and my character down." Nico, who played Florindo, a blithely arrogant prince, said that watching a video of professional commedia actors playing his role was helpful, because the haughty physicality of a previous Florindo helped him understand his character. But translating this observation into action still didn't happen until he physically began to try the movements: "I think the first day that I didn't have my script in my hand was the first day I really discovered my character. Before that, I was very not sure of what my character was—I knew what my character was trying to accomplish, and what his goals were, because that's a lot of the stuff that we worked on, characterization, at rehearsals. But, I didn't really know what kind of physicality he had, or how to achieve his goals."

If part of finding the character was integrating mind and body, another part was summoning the emotions that animated their role. All of the actors said that even though they were playing eighteenth-century Italian characters, they needed to connect themselves to their roles, which is what gave the characters depth. Raven, for example, said that "I would take monologues from Beatrice, and I would translate it into my own words, and I would use my own emotion. I did it as Raven. And then, once I did it as Raven, I took from my emotion, and I took from what action I was supposed to put into these lines" and infused that into Beatrice. As Nico eloquently described the importance of emotion to powerful acting, "Teaching can be conveying information, but I think the essence of theater, like other art, is conveying emotion. So, you're trying to bring the emotion from your body to another actor's body, and then together to the audience, so that the audience can feel empathy, and then kind of have catharsis about what just happened in the show, feel those emotions in a way that would reflect on the show." Powerful learning often requires integrating the cognitive and the affective, the mind and the heart, and theater as a form consistently pushed actors to develop and use together these modes of understanding.

Layers of Learning

As the show moved into its middle and later stages, each week brought an additional layer of complexity to the actors' task. In short order, over the course of October, they went "off book," meaning that they needed to remember their lines rather than look at scripts; they blocked the show, meaning they had to remember movements as well as lines; they integrated costumes, lights, and props, meaning they had to learn to move in new garb and use new objects; and then finally they were doing three dress rehearsals and then three shows, meaning they had to run the whole show through without breaks. Each of these new layers had a "one step forward, two steps back," quality to it, with much of what had been developed in the previous stage temporarily lost as students tried to focus on the new dimension to be incorporated. For example, in one of the first rehearsals off book, Ben offered some stern feedback to the actors who were still a little shaky on their lines: "Hold. I want all actors on stage please. This is a reality check. Right now what we are watching is a line through. I'd rather have you calling for more lines. . . . There is no energy being passed back and forth. You need to stop thinking about next and think about now. This is a very safe run."

Scholars of expertise have described four stages of learning: unconscious incompetence (you don't know what you don't know), conscious incompetence (you know what you don't know), conscious competence (you can do something but only by thinking about it), and, finally, unconscious competence (you can do it automatically).[37] In the show, as new layers were introduced, things that had reached the stage of un-conscious competence (for instance, how the actors played the charac-ters) were temporarily lost as the actors tried to remember their lines (conscious competence). Thus, each new layer entailed loss as well as gain, until a new equilibrium was reached in which the actors had un-conscious competence over both their lines and their characters. The key to progress in each of these new phases was time to get acclimated. For instance, while the first dress rehearsal was by shared consensus a terrible run, by the third and final dress rehearsal the show was in good shape, not only because of corrections from the previous nights, but also because much of what had previously been established reemerged once actors became comfortable with the costumes, lights, and process of doing a full show.

Refining and Performing

If the beginning of the rehearsal process was about creation, and the middle was about consolidation and integration, the final step was about two things: increasingly detailed fine-tuning and performing. In terms of fine-tuning, the arc of the show resembled the arc of almost any act of production; anyone who has written an essay, developed a presenta-tion, or created a project knows that the end of the process requires careful attention to very small things to make the product shine. (One aphorism for this is the "ninety-ninety rule"—the last 10 percent takes 90 percent of the time, a mantra that acknowledges how time-consuming and important this last period is.) In the case of the show, the fine-tuning came in the form of increasingly lengthy rehearsals in the final two weeks, and feedback on increasingly small details. For example, in the notes after the second-to-last dress rehearsal, Ben tells Matt, "Open that downstage foot up a little more. We are seeing a lot of pro-file of that mask." He tells Jon, "Make sure when you are talking to June in the trunk scene, she was upstage of you, and thus you were speaking away from the audience." They also used some of their time to zero in on particular scenes or moments within scenes that were challenging, with a few scenes slated for an extra run-through before the final full dress rehearsal.[38] And, as described earlier, there was a lot of work on the asides, trying to get the timing exactly right between the turns of the actors and the appearance of the lights.

The other major task for this final period was preparing for the act of performance. Performing requires a combination of releasing energy and controlling anxiety. Particularly because it was a comedy, everyone was highly attentive to the pace of the show; for it to work, the lines should move quickly from one to another, heightening audience anticipation and building toward the verbal and physical punchlines. To build this energy, here was the scene at intermission back stage:

ANDRE: "Eight minutes to places."
TALIA: "When you're ready come into the little theater. Guys can you get into a circle."
Raven arrives. "The atmosphere is moving quickly."
ANDRE: "Five minutes to places."
TALIA: "What do we need? What do we need? What do we need?"
ACTORS: "Energy, energy, energy, energy."
They form a circle and begin bouncing off of each other. They are being thrown from one to another. It sounds like a fight scene. I can feel the energy, they are in a circle.
TALIA: "Okay, we are going to do two rounds of 'Ride that Pony.' And then energy, energy focus."
They form one inner circle, and a second outer circle: the inner circle moves one way and the outer circle moves the other, and they shake their rumps at each other as they go by. They start to chant, led by Talia but with everyone joining in: "Ride, ride ride that pony, back to back, side to side, this is what we do. Get up, get up, and ride that big fat pony. Ride, ride ride that pony; get up, get up, and ride that big fat pony. Energy, energy, energy, and then shake."
TALIA: "Andre, how many minutes?"
ANDRE: "Three minutes to places."
TALIA: "Take care of what you need to do in those three minutes."
ACTOR, ON THE WAY OUT: "Fan-fucking tastic—let's go to Act II!"

While building this energy, the actors were also trying to manage anxiety and channel their nervous energy toward the performance. Renee, for example, said that her strategy was to tell herself "obnoxiously positive mantras" backstage: "You can, you know you can, you can and you must, it's too late to back out now." Talia, who as a senior and assistant director was one of the leaders of the show, remembers her own moment of freaking out as a sophomore before a performance: "I remember one night, the first night of opening, I was just so over-whelmed by the pressure. . . . I couldn't handle it, and I just started bawling ten minutes before we were set to go on stage. And I remember I had to get it all out, and Mr. Black was comforting me outside, and I had to quickly finish up crying, get my make-up on, be fixed, and head out, and start right away." Cody says that managing this pressure to perform live is difficult, but a critical part of what makes it such a powerful learning experience. "You learn about yourself, and how to deal with those things. On stage, it's the live moment, there's no stop-ping. You can't stop, you have to keep going. You have to. You know, film, you can just cut, go back. [In theater], it's beginning to end."

All too quickly, performance night came. To someone who had seen the show at all stages of its construction—rehearsal in the band room with scripts in hand, the set halfway constructed, the lights hung but not fully programmed—it was remarkable to see the whole thing come together as one performance. The presence of the audience added the finishing layer to the show—after weeks of doing comedy with no one there to laugh, the presence of live laughter from people who hadn't heard the jokes a thousand times injected new energy into the performance and confidence into the actors. Renee, whose struggles with the flirtatious nature of her character were so noticeable at the first rehearsal we witnessed, brought the house down as a coquettish Smer-aldina: at one point she was unable to finish her lines because the audi-ence reaction to her previous line was so enthusiastic. The asides were not quite perfect, but close, and Nico's leap into the light brought a huge laugh from the crowd. As the show concluded, the actors filed past Ben backstage, which Ben remembers as his best moment of the show: "I mean the Friday night was their best performance, and the joyous moment backstage when I ran out after the curtain call, and just gave them all high-five on the way back. Their joy was a huge high." After eight weeks of hard work, the show night brought the kind of exhilaration that comes from a job well done.

Overall, the show, from its first rehearsal to its final performance, created space for different stages of learning—at the beginning, low-risk opportunities to develop creativity; at the middle, opportunities for consolidation and integration; and at the end, chances for detailed re-finement. It enabled students to gradually develop real expertise, moving incrementally from unconscious incompetence (never having heard of commedia dell'arte) to eventually a modest degree of unconscious competence (having the physicality of commedia be a part of their acting repertoire). It provided opportunities to integrate mind and body into one unified interpretation of the play. And it coupled the participants' passion for theater, which provided the spark and sustained the momentum, with high levels of precision, as they worked to perfect the production.

The Whole Game at a Junior Level

High school theater is an example of what learning scientist David Perkins calls the "whole game at the junior level."[39] Perkins's point is that in variants of games like little league baseball, players do not spend a year learning to catch and another to pitch and another to bat. Rather, they play the whole game from the start, just at the level at which they can play it. The idea is that playing the whole game at the junior level helps the players see how baseball as a whole works, as well why they would want to put practice time into learning the specific skills. The production we saw was a junior form of what college or professional actors do—although a professional theater would have more resources, more expertise, and potentially more time, much of what happened was the same. The student actors in the theater group were doing what professional actors do, just at the level they could do it—developing an interpretation of a role; preparing their minds, bodies, and voices; rehearsing and refining their characterizations within the larger context of the play; and ultimately, seeking to move an audience.

In so doing, they also could draw on many of the resources, or affordances, provided by theater as a field. Theater as a field provides a thick infrastructure for doing this work. It employs a series of familiar roles (set and lighting crew, costume designers, dramaturgs, stage manager, director) and expectations for what people in those roles will do. It offers a technical language, developed over many generations, that enables precise feedback in ways that are understood by everyone involved. It creates a rhythm or temporal arc to the work—table work, blocking, scene work, run throughs, tech week, dress rehearsals, show. It creates role models, in theater or movie stars, who are well-known and provide templates for what student-actors might someday become. And it builds in an external audience for the work; people who know what a production is and why one would want to attend a show. That it is a recognizable and valued form also helps secure the lengthy after-school time it demands of students each day as well as the public budget for the space and for the work of the adults involved in the program.

This was different from what we observed in many academic classes. In science, for example, students, even when they were doing labs, were mostly going through a series of steps to demonstrate a principle that had already been discovered by previous scientists. In a sense, this is the opposite of real science—actual scientists explore what is not known as opposed to trying to verify what is already known.

Or compare theater to project-based learning. A project-based teacher has many of the same goals as a theater director: she wants students to create an authentic product that will matter to the student, demonstrate some understanding of the content, and be valued by an external audience. But she has so much less to work with: she needs to explain to her students what the final product will be, even though they have never seen what it is they are trying to produce; if she wants students to take roles in their groups she needs to explain what those roles are and why they matter; if she wants to give feedback she has no specific shared technical language to rely on; if she wants to create an arc to the learning she needs to explain what the stages are in the development of a project and why they are important; if she wants peer mentoring and apprenticeship she likely will need to make special arrangements because more experienced students are likely in other grades and thus not in her class; she will likely need long blocks, especially toward the end of a project, but will be on a fixed schedule of short blocks; if she wants an audience for the work, she will have to make special arrangements to recruit one and she will have to explain to them what the students are doing and why; and finally, if she is going to develop resources for this project, she will need to convince the principal, the parents, and the school board of the value of a product and a mode of learning that they likely don't understand and may not value.

Scholar Barbara Rogoff has suggested that apprenticeships work on three planes: the individual, the interpersonal, and the community.[40] All of those dimensions are present in theater: individuals develop identities that link them to theater; the interpersonal plane is the level through which the participants develop the show together; and the community level provides the audience, the space, and the financial support for the performance. But our research suggests that there is another level that infuses the work, which is the way in which the field structures and enables much of what happens for the students in their own theater work. If we want to make the kind of powerful learning experiences that happen in theater more the norm in regular school, we likely will have to develop similar fields in more classically academic arenas.

Limits and Tensions

While there is much to admire about this theater production, some cautions are in order. The first is external generalizability. Theater at Attainment High is special—even compared to other similar large comprehensive high schools nearby, it has one of the most developed high school theater programs in the area. Its spirit and ethos reflect the influence of its director, Cody Black, whose particular mixture of community building, ability to help students find their authentic selves, humor, and political savvy was critical for setting the tone and building the program. Obviously there are theater programs where directors are tyrannical, students are cliquish and catty, and many other undesirable things happen. Thus theater is a *container*, within which both good and bad things can happen. The success of this particular theater program is due in part to the opportunities created by the traditions around theater, but those opportunities in turn depend on the judgment, wisdom, and humanity of the adults who develop what students experience. We see theater as a more promising container than the containers for many academic classes, but it is a container nonetheless.

More specifically, there were also some tradeoffs within this production that likely point to some broader tensions. One was the sheer number of hours needed to produce such a complicated show, which worked against the kind of experimentation that might have led to a deeper grappling with its subtleties and meanings. Specifically, the show needed to be blocked in order for the lighting team to do its work, which meant that much of the time in the middle weeks was spent trying to figure out exactly who was going to go where when, as opposed to developing characterization, which is what both the actors and the directors would have preferred to do. This allocation of time was intimately related to the length and size of the show—*Servant* is a full two act, two-hour (or more) play, with eleven actors, which meant that there were many, many lines to be learned and scenes to be blocked, important but prosaic tasks that took up much of the rehearsal time. If deeper learning frequently results from a "less is more" approach, that injunction was not heeded in this case. But at the same time, what might have been good for the depth of the actors' learning might not have met other important demands: in particular, cultural expectations that high school theater groups produce large full-length shows, which is something the actors look forward to and the audience expects. The theater program puts on some shorter plays each spring, but it is unwilling to buck the traditions of having several large dramas and a musical each year.

The short timeframe allocated for the play's production also limited students' understanding of some of its historical or cultural context. In our conversations with students as well as our observations of the rehearsal process, we did not see much evidence of a depth of understanding about Goldoni, his contemporaries, or the history, culture, art, politics, or music of Venice at the time. This would have required substantially more than the initial research of the students and the dramaturgs. Linking courses in English and history to productions in yearlong sequences would provide opportunities for deeper learning about the context out of which a play had emerged.

There is also a related tension between process and product. Ben's seminal theater experience was as a high school student in a small Catholic prep school, where a man named "Brother Ron" organized theater shows by putting the actors largely in charge. Brother Ron would sit in the back, or would leave the theater entirely, and, having given the actors a task or a scene, would let them develop it together. Says Ben, "And so, from a very early age, I learned the value of getting peer-to-peer feedback, and how to give peer-to-peer feedback, and just the idea like we were the creators in a lot of ways. He would come up with the design, but he gave us a lot of freedom which I really, really valued." When Ben first came to Attainment High, he tried to introduce this approach with his first show. As he describes it, it really didn't take: "It was a rough transition, it really was. I tried to hit it with the same kind of magic touch that Brother Ron had about like 'We're all working together, we're a troupe,' kind of arm them with knowledge, and let them go off, but it was just not jiving with the culture." Specifically, Ben says, people at Attainment High were used to a more "traditional" approach to theater, with the director organizing the action, leading warmups, and giving notes. The size and expected production values also inhibited more actor-led theater, because with a large cast and a number of departments that needed to be integrated, more pre-planning was needed to develop a coordinated show.

The version Ben eventually landed on was a bit of a hybrid—he gave actors as much freedom as he could to develop their interpretations, while retaining overall control and direction. This "happy medium," as he called it, enabled him to meet the various expectations of a show at Attainment High while also seeding some student initiative. But he still talked wistfully about the initiative and creativity that had been sparked by Brother Ron's methods. "The creativity was at an all-time high; we could do anything. We did a production of *Midsummer Night's Dream* that ended up with five different concepts, which is why it didn't do very well. There was a lot of room for creativity, growth was as much as you opened yourself up to the opportunity, and also that the older kids were really allowed . . . to do something, because it was a lot in their hands." By comparison, theater at Attainment High was a little safer, a little more adult-directed, which led to productions that were more consistently high-quality, but at the cost of more student initiative and raw creativity.

How Deep Learning Develops: A Theory

In the Introduction, we argued that those interested in "deeper learning" should be particularly attentive to three qualities: mastery, identity, and creativity. Mastery because you cannot learn something deeply without building up considerable skill and knowledge in that domain; identity because it is hard to become deeply learned at anything without becoming identified with the domain; and creativity because moving from taking in someone else's ideas to developing your own is a big part of what makes learning "deep." A fourth important quality is community, for it is in communities that this learning frequently takes place.

A THEORY OF DEEPER LEARNING OVER TIME

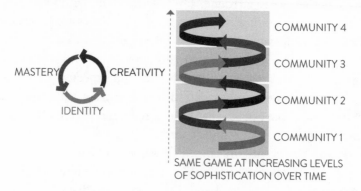

Part of what the example of theater enables us to do is to put these qualities into dynamic motion and see how they reinforce each other and create ever-deepening cycles of learning over time. We could imagine mastery-identity-creativity as a self-reinforcing upward spiral, where identity is the fuel and motivation, creativity offers the goal that stretches students' powers, mastery is the base that needs to be developed for the creative product to achieve quality, and community is the environment within which the learning takes place. This theory builds on previous work and integrates a variety of perspectives on learning into one vision of how significant learning accumulates over time.[41] This figure provides a visual depiction of this model.

We think this model can describe how deep learning develops in any domain, but we will stay with our example of theater to explain how it works. With respect to mastery, there are no value-added scores in theater, but there are a number of processes that produce increasing expertise over time. Within a given production, participants have an opportunity to play the "whole game" of theater: they learn how a show is put together from start to finish, they learn much of the technical language of theater, and they have opportunities to develop ideas and interpretations and to receive many rounds of detailed feedback on their work from more knowledgeable others. There are also opportunities to practice the particularly troublesome spots—while there is a lot of whole-game perspective, this is complemented by particular emphasis on the things that need work, which is a critical part of developing mastery. Over the course of a high school career, there will be many repetitions of this process, and, for many, increasingly larger roles as they demonstrate more expertise. There is also differentiation built into the process: relative novices have only a few lines to deliver, whereas more experienced actors have many more lines and may be assuming new characters that stretch their repertoire. In this way, everyone is pushed at their zone of proximal development.

All of this work is fueled by the motivation that is critical to any sustained learning. This motivation comes from students' identification with theater as a domain, as well as their desire to become better at their craft and to produce high-quality productions. Students described the theater program as a home within a large high school, one that provided both an individual identity for each participant and a collective identity as members of a shared artistic endeavor. Within theater, the opportunity to be an actor, or to work on lighting, costumes, or crew, provided a further chance to find a subgroup of people with whom one shared a set of interests and a community. Being part of theater and its community was what sustained students' participation, which they needed to stay in the learning "spiral" and build mastery over time.

What made this sustained work "deeper" was the element of creativity. Students not only needed to learn about the play, the roles, and the time period; they also had to develop their own interpretation of how the play would be performed. Participants described the difference between reading a play in class and putting one on as the difference between working in two dimensions and three. As Emily explained, "It's that distinction between analyzing and making something. I think analyzing can only go so far. . . . Whereas creation, you can make whatever you want." She contrasted reading *Romeo and Juliet* with staging it: "I stage-managed *Romeo and Juliet* last year, and so that was the first time I had, you know, stage-managed something that I'd read before. And that was a different experience, like you can see it come to life. Like when you're involved in a production, you watch it from nothing, go to, you know, set, lights, and everything."

Nico went one step further in contrasting the passivity of school to the activity of the stage:

Because classroom learning is not about expression, it's about absorbing. . . . As a student, you have to be the audience, you have to like absorb that information, and maybe use your personality to interpret it, which is I guess like completely opposite from theater I think.

How is theater the opposite?

Because theater as an actor, it's more like being a teacher, like you're taking this script, this like knowledge that other people have given you, like all this compiled information, all this storyline, and you're putting it in yourself, and then you're sending it out to many audience members, and many students. And then, being a student is more like being an audience member, because you're taking what the teacher is expressing and absorb it, and remember it.

If Bloom's taxonomy places remembering at the bottom and creating at the top, putting on a production pushes students to move through the levels of the taxonomy—remembering, understanding, and analyzing—but doing so in the service of an act of synthesis and creation.

If we imagined this self-reinforcing cycle of mastery, identity, and creativity as a spiral that leads upward over time, with participants circling back to the same tasks again and again at increasing levels of sophistication, another key idea is that each community in which the learner participates adds something important and distinct. A key part of the learning process is the nature of these communities, which have to be simultaneously safe enough that people feel open to taking risks and expressing vulnerability, but exacting enough to create real standards and give, when necessary, critical feedback. Each production creates such a community, and thus each one creates an opportunity to learn something a little different—with a different play, potentially a different director, and a different group of cast members. Alex, the lead in the show, describes what it was like to move from community theater to theater at Attainment High:

So, I first started in a very non-theater town. Like there was tons of opportunity, because there's tons of community theater, tons of community theater shows going on. But they weren't like high-quality production. But it gave me like the basics, and got me comfortable on stage. And then, I got to a point where like I wasn't learning anything from there anymore. Like the last role I did there, I was the main character, it was *Tom Sawyer*, and I was Tom

Sawyer. And I did fine in that, and that was good. And then I just felt like there wasn't anything that I was learning from each show. And then we moved here, and I started learning a bunch from being in the shows here. And I learned a ton from the comedy troupes for sure. And it encouraged me to do my own research, and I'm doing this independent study. . . . And I know, I'm definitely still learning things, because it's given me opportunity to do things on my own, but I don't feel like I'm being taught things.

Thus through repeated cycles, in different and increasingly sophisticated communities, Alex gradually grew as an actor.

This theory of how people become deep learners integrates quite different theories of learning, which is part of why we are attracted to it as a model. There is, in one sense, a very constructivist, learning-by-doing emphasis, which connects to the way that theater is a space of active learning where one learns in part through trial and error—and where if nothing is ventured, nothing is gained. It also is consistent with progressive visions of schooling in its emphasis on developing an authentic product, and tapping the intrinsic motivation, creativity, and passion of the learner. But at the same time, it is also a view in which the domain structures the learning, creates roles and an expected temporal arc, and leaves a large place for informed external feedback from more knowledgeable others. It also emphasizes heavily the role of disciplined practice, which we generally think of as hallmarks of more conservative or traditional visions of learning. There is also a balance between individual and community—it is the individual who has to develop new skills, who helps direct their learning, and who becomes more skilled over time, but it is the community that structures the learning and creates the context in which it happens. We see these many integrations as critical for a realistic theory of how people come to know, be, and do something deeply.

Beyond Theater

The following elements make theater a powerful learning environment:

- Purpose and performance
- Choice

- Community
- Interdependent roles
- Use of heads, hands, and heart
- An arc of learning
- Apprenticeship
- Offering the whole game at a junior level

There are good reasons to think that these same elements are critical in other extracurricular contexts.[42] Consider the making of a newspaper. Like theater, there is a purpose that is shaped by a public product. Like theater, people have chosen to be there, and, more specifically, they have chosen to work on different sections (arts, sports, news, design) because those sections are consistent with their interests and identities. These roles are interdependent, both in that all of them are required for the successful production of the paper, and, sometimes in the sense that they literally need to be aligned, such as when an illustration or a photo accompanies a story. Meetings are held that parallel the production meetings in theater, where different departments report in on their developing work and collective decisions are made. There is a temporal arc to the work, beginning with a brainstorming round (what should we cover? what special issues might we explore?), a middle stage where the different pieces are edited and integrated into one layout, and then a final stage of proofing, which focuses on very detailed refining of the work. Older students have more significant roles and younger ones have smaller roles, a situation that creates significant opportunities for apprenticeship and hands-on learning. Finally, while it is undoubtedly a junior version, the core tasks are the same as what happens for college or professional newspapers, and students have many opportunities over the course of their high school career to play the "whole game" of creating a newspaper.

High school debate is another promising arena. In a separate paper with Pooja Bakhai, we report on the results of a study that we conducted of high school debate that was similar in methods and scale to this study of theater.[43] The study was conducted in a pair of schools where more than 75 percent of students received free or reduced-price lunch and all of the participants in debate were students of color. Here we observed a number of similar themes: the authentic public purpose created by public debate motivated considerable study and practice;

students had chosen to be there (and, for more experienced students, chosen to stay); and there were interdependent roles, because students debated in teams and needed to find complementary ways to build off of their partners' strengths. Students remarked on the integration of head, hands, and heart, explaining that a good debate lay at the intersection of logos (logic), pathos (passion), and ethos (empathy), and that they might be strong in one but need work on another. Themes of apprenticeship were highly present: there were four levels of debate, beginning with "novice" and moving up through "open," which enabled students both to form peer communities with students at their level and to apprentice students who were earlier in their trajectories. The most experienced debaters had formed communities not just at their school but also with other debaters in the city, whom they met with on their own time and used as feedback and research partners. Debate was also particularly good as a vehicle for learning academic content—the debate topic at the time of our study was U.S. foreign policy with regard to human rights in China as well as the South China Sea, and the students researched the ins and outs of this topic as if it were life or death. Debate, like theater, shaped students' identities: those who had been debating for longer saw it as a core part of their selves, and talked passionately about how it had changed them—in particular, how it had made them better able to advocate effectively in other arenas of their lives. While there were some differences with the theater program at Attainment High created by socioeconomic disparities—for example, the Attainment High students enjoyed full dinners during tech week, paid for by the parents, whereas the debaters had granola bars and fruit during practice that were paid for by the organization that sponsored their debate league—the core learning processes seemed remarkably similar. In some ways, debate was a potentially even more powerful vehicle than theater because in debate students could choose their own words, and because the agency that students experienced in debate was in sharp contrast to the very controlling atmosphere of their high-poverty schools.

Athletics similarly possesses many of these same elements. There is a clear purpose, an external audience, students choose to be there, they build community, there are interdependent roles, they use minds and bodies, there is a mixture of creative expression and disciplined practice, there is playing the whole game, it helps define individual and collective identity, and there are apprenticeship and mixed-aged group-ings. A study that compared students' experiences in basketball practices with the same students' experiences in math class found that "the prac-tice of basketball supported deep engagement as players had greater ac-cess to an understanding of the domain, were assigned and took up a unique role that was integral to the practice, and had opportunities to express themselves and feel competent," whereas math classes afforded similar opportunities only for the most successful math learners.[44] The learning is less academic—in theater, newspaper, or debate there is a more immediate connection to the kind of questions might one pursue in school—but within what the domains offer, there is a thick and multi-dimensional approach to learning it.[45]

This research suggests that theater, debate, and by implication other extracurriculars, bring together a powerful combination of purpose, passion, and precision. They constitute their own, second, "grammar of schooling," one that sits in plain sight right alongside the grammar that governs most of the nation's core academic classes. This second grammar embodies a very different set of principles than the first, by emphasizing

- students as active producers rather than passive recipients
- learning by doing rather than by transmission
- clear purposes and external audiences rather than simply working to please the teacher
- multi-age groupings rather than age-graded classrooms
- integration of students with different skill levels rather than tracking, and
- learning through apprenticeship rather than didactic instruction

Extracurriculars, in other words, are not just fun and engaging, but also highly aligned with a powerful mode of learning.

To be sure, extracurriculars benefit to some degree from their spe-cial circumstances. The fact that they are chosen is critical to their suc-cess, because such choice is important for building communities of mutual interest. Extracurriculars also benefit from being shielded from some of the constraints of the core curriculum; there are no expectations for what should be taught, the students are not tested on what they learned (or didn't learn), and they have traditionally been free of at least some of the pressure to attain a score or "win" that will help a student get into college. These characteristics enable the learning to follow the natural rhythms of their subjects, and they free students from the instrumental mindset—is this going to be on the test?—that is so common in the more conventional part of school.[46]

At the same time, there are ways to inject more of these qualities into the traditionally academic part of the curriculum. Elective classes, as we have seen, also enable student choice and the formation of communities of interest in a particular subject, but within the academic curriculum. Electives in certain domains, like English, can be normed, so that while students have choice about which content they read, the core skills are common across the domains. Courses can also be pitched in ways that are much clearer about their purposes, and students can produce final products that are connected to real-world domains. Thus, rather than focusing on the ways in which extracurriculars are structurally special, perhaps we should think more about whether there are ways to engender some of the same qualities of learning in core classes. There is much that the periphery can teach the core, if only we open ourselves to the possibilities created by this second grammar of schooling.

7

Deeper Teaching:
Rigor, Joy, and Apprenticeship

We have seen how extracurricular and elective activities can provide platforms for powerful learning experiences. How can similar qualities be created in core academic classes? While we struggled to find whole schools where consistent excellence in core classes was the norm, we did find individual teachers who had achieved it in their classrooms. They worked in all kinds of schools (traditional public, charter, and private); they handled a variety of subjects; and they taught students in lower tracks as well as higher ones. What were these teachers doing differently? How did their backgrounds and life experiences differ from those of their colleagues? How did they achieve deeper learning with students who were struggling to build basic skills? And how can the work of these teachers inform a broader effort toward deeper learning?

We identified these teachers by focusing on three primary criteria: cognitive challenge, engagement, and participation. With respect to cognitive challenge, we sought out classrooms where the task that students were confronted with was in the top half of Bloom's taxonomy—with students asked to analyze, synthesize, or create—or were in levels three or four of Webb's depth of knowledge scale, which similarly focuses on complex thinking as opposed to recall or application.[1] With respect to engagement, we were interested in the ethos of the classroom: was it a place where there was energy in the room, where students spoke with both knowledge and enthusiasm about the work they were doing? Did their body language and vocal or written contributions suggest that they were "in task" as well as "on task," rather than counting the

minutes until the bell rang? Our third criterion was participation. We
picked classes where at least three-quarters of the students were actively
engaged with the task; running a great class for a few students isn't
enough. In addition to these observational criteria, we triangulated with
other information: these were also classes that were highly recommended by faculty and students, classes that people in the schools we
visited said we had to see if we wanted to see the "deepest" teaching at
their school. They were the classes where discussions spilled out into
the hallway and cafeteria. Predictably, they were also the classes that
older students reported remembering years later.

To write about these teachers, we drew on class observations, lengthy
interviews, artifacts including planning documents and students' work,
and conversations with students. We used Mill's methods of agreement
to identify what was in common among these "deeper teachers" and
Mill's methods of difference to verify that these characteristics were different from those of the many other teachers in our study.[2] Our coding
process began inductively, although having attended the classes, we
could see some clear differences in the choices that teachers were
making. Those observations informed our subsequent analytic journey.
As we read through our data, we began to see strong links between how
they saw their purpose (the why), the nature of their classrooms (the
what), and their own identities as teachers and as people (the who). Thus,
we organized our second round of coding around these three dimensions of the teachers and their practice.

In an era when test scores reign supreme, some readers might find
this way of choosing teachers to be anachronistic. We understand this
critique but think it is misguided. First, the majority of state tests used
during the time of our study have been shown to measure mostly low-
level cognitive processes; hence we could not use them as indicators of
"deeper" learning.[3] Second, studies that have tried to identify teachers
using value-added methodology have found, not surprisingly, that many
of the teachers who are "most effective" using these methods are those
who teach directly to the state tests.[4] Third, some subjects we were
interested in lack standardized testing. Fourth, given our view that significant learning accumulates over the long run, we were particularly
interested in teachers who inspired their charges, who were successful in
planting seeds that might grow into longstanding interest in a subject.
Focusing on teachers who inspired this passion in the moment or who

were identified by older students as particularly good teachers seemed like good proxies for identifying teachers with lasting influence. And fifth, these were teachers who students and colleagues alike testified were exceptional, which afforded us a rare opportunity to learn from the practice of such skilled teachers.

To other readers, looking across disciplines will obscure important differences in deeper disciplinary teaching. From one perspective, we think this is a fair point; it would certainly be possible to delve "deeper" into pedagogical and content techniques within particular disciplinary arenas, and we build on discipline-specific work at certain points in the chapter. But, at the same time, we found striking similarities among these teachers, even across disciplines, in how they thought about their fields, how they related to their students, how they saw the purpose of their work, and how all of this was shaped by who they were. By telling their stories, we hope to reignite an integrative conversation about teaching that builds on the best of the discipline-specific work but re-engages the shared question of what makes for powerful teaching.

We draw on the work of seven teachers in this chapter (all names are pseudonyms):

- Jeff Fields, an English and philosophy teacher at Attainment High;
- Nick Collins and Nathaniel Clarke, math teachers at a high-poverty traditional public school in the Northeast;
- Kyle Hogan, an English teacher at a high-poverty traditional public school in the Northeast;
- Joel Wolf and William Duchin, science teachers at Midwestern Math and Science Academy;
- Megan Marino, a chemistry teacher at a high-poverty traditional public school in the Northeast.

All but one of these individuals have been teaching at least ten years; their ages range from early thirties to near seventy, with the median age early forties. Although they teach in a range of contexts, it is worth noting that all of them teach in traditional public schools, and that four of the seven teach in unselective schools in high-poverty urban districts. All of these teachers identified as white; this fact reflects the disheartening reality that very few of the teachers we observed in our research were people of color—which is itself a reflection of the fact that more than 80 percent of the U.S. teaching workforce remains white. There were also five other teachers we found who had similar practices and perspectives; in the interest of space we do not present their stories, but our analysis of them is consistent with the argument we advance here, as is much of our analysis of electives teachers in Chapter 6.[5]

The story that we tell about these teachers is a holistic one, in every sense. We are interested not only in their practices, but also in their identities, their journeys, and their accounts of what they are trying to do with their students. In so doing, we seek to broaden the conversation around teaching, moving away from questions such as "What are best practices for increasing value-added test scores?" and toward questions such as "What dispositions, skills, orientations, and identities do we want to cultivate in teachers if the goal is to inspire and motivate the next generation of students?" Because we see a tight link between who these people are and how they teach, our story perhaps will be frustrating to those who seek best practices or simple technical solutions. Yet we hope that our rich account of some of the most compelling educators we encountered will help future teachers as they embark on their own journeys toward deeper teaching, as well as illustrate what policies and practices are needed to support the development of such consequential work.

We also hope that this approach will contribute to the scholarly literature on the subject. There is writing about good teaching, there is writing about teachers' identities and beliefs, there is writing about the life cycle of teaching, but there is very little writing that links teachers' own learning experiences, identities, and stance toward their subjects and their students to observations of how they actually teach.[6] Since we believe that it takes significant time to become a "deeper teacher," it is critical to understand the nature of these trajectories and the evolving relationship between teachers' identities and their practices. To the degree that previous scholars have made these links, they have focused on teacher preparation and the first several years of teaching; this research allows us to examine exemplary experienced teachers and how their trajectories unfolded over longer spans of time.[7]

There are some limits to our approach. We are deeply exploring only seven teachers, so the generalizability of our findings awaits future research. The ways that they teach in their disciplines are not the only ways to do so; there are many ways to skin each disciplinary cat. Their accounts of their journeys are offered retrospectively, and thus are subject to the usual presentist biases that can be present in such reconstructions. Despite these limitations, it is rare to have a chance to explore the practice, journey, and identities of such compelling teachers; we hope that doing so will stimulate more research of this type.

Jeff Fields: Existential Explorations

The classroom has a wall of windows that looks out on wooded lands, a picturesque backdrop for a philosophical discussion. Mr. Fields is an athletic-looking guy in his early forties with a laid-back energy and a deep voice. He has a buzz cut and wears a linen shirt with rolled-up shirtsleeves and khakis; when class begins, Mr. Fields sits at a desk facing the horseshoe of other desks and puts on a pair of glasses. About twenty students are sitting in the horseshoe, expectantly facing forward. They are dressed casually. This is a philosophical literature honors class at Attainment High.

The students come in and two boys talk with me briefly. When I say what I'm here for, one of them says, "You can't get deeper than this." I ask what that means and he says, "It's a philosophy class so we just talk about everything . . ." His peer interrupts, "Everyone comes in pretending they understand the reading—but I really only ever understand one part of it, but what ends up happening is that we all understand different parts, so then by the end of class we all understand all of it."

Class begins. The topic of today's class is Descartes's famous postulate: "I think, therefore I am." Written on the board are four questions: "1. Basis of D's argument that all he can know is that he exists? 2. What is he? 3. From there, how prove God, and thus reality, exists? 4. Responses?" There are no SWBATs, no agenda, just the questions.[8] The room is humming with energy, as students begin talking with one another in small groups about these four questions. Mr. Fields prompts them to rejoin the large group: "Thoughts on the first question? Ideas from the text?"

One student begins: "If he is thinking a thing, then he must exist." Mr. Fields interjects: "Do you have language that supports?" The student looks through the text. "Perhaps it should also come to pass that if I were to cease thinking, then I would cease to exist," he reads from Descartes's Meditation Two. Another student, Anna, jumps in: "If he didn't exist, he wouldn't be able to think." Mr. Fields offers, "What I'm hearing you saying is a little different than what he writes. What I heard him say in the text is that if I'm not thinking, I don't exist." A third student asks, "Do you ever stop thinking?" A fourth responds, "How would we know?"

They continue to deconstruct the text in this manner for about fifteen minutes. Students are doing most of the talking, and they are sometimes challenging each other, asking for textual support for their arguments. Students draw on heavily marked-up texts. Eyes are attentively tracking the speaker. Then Mr. Fields shifts the discussion from "what" to "why." "Why is Descartes bothering with this? What's the point?"

A student answers: "The only thing I can count on is that I exist. Even if these perceptions are wrong, I exist." (Here they are taking up Descartes's idea of "the deceiver"—what if there were someone, Matrix-style, who was trying to convince you of a reality that wasn't actually real.) Another student adds, "There has to be something which is being deceived. Since everything he is sensing doesn't have to be real, but the thing that is thinking has to exist." "But," adds another, "the question I have about [another student's] argument is what does it mean to exist? God sets out your plan before you—you still exist as a person but you don't have free will. Does the argument fall apart if something is making your decisions? Is that a different level of existence?"

Toward the end of the period, Mr. Fields invites them to shift from unpacking Descartes's thesis to evaluating his argument. "What about computers?" says one student. "They seem to think, but they don't exist," he argues. "Or what if you are in a vegetable state," says another, "then you can't think, but you still exist." Other students take up these hypotheticals, offering their views on what is necessary and sufficient to demonstrate existence.

The clock reaches 8:50, the end of the period. Time has flown by. Mr. Fields attempts to wrap up the discussion: "Tomorrow, we are going to see how Descartes shows that if we exist, God must exist." A chorus of cries break out across the room—how does the fact that we exist show that God exists? Skepticism, once let out of the bottle, can't easily be contained. As the students pack up, they continue the discussion; as one tells us later, "After every class pretty much, we like argue about it or discuss it for fifteen minutes after class. We walk down the halls talking about whatever we had just talked about. People probably think we're nuts, arguing about the nature of existence in the hallways."

What makes this class tick? If you listen to the students, it begins with Mr. Fields's enthusiasm for the subject and the intensity of his respect for students' ideas about it: "In other classes, teachers are a little bit condescending," said one. "Mr. Fields genuinely wants to know what we have to say. He feels very genuine when he speaks to us." To support this claim, the students pointed to the fact that when they were citing a passage, "Mr. Fields will flip to it with us," and when they said something interesting, he would pause, and take some time to think about what they were saying. Added another, "You can tell that he is so passionate about the material, he really wants to know what everyone thinks about it. . . . All the really good teachers I've had really know their material well and are really invested—not even just in teaching, but in the material. . . . It's contagious."

Students took particular note that Mr. Fields recently had been ordained as a Zen priest, which meant that in the readings on Buddhism, he was as interested in them as they were. "When we learned that he had become a Zen priest," one student said, "we saw him as a person, and in some ways, as another student. He was learning the material as well with us, although he knew it already." Author Parker Palmer argues that the best classes are dominated not by student or teacher but by subject, which he calls "The Great Thing" that orients the inquiry. This class had that feeling: while Mr. Fields was clearly the more knowledgeable reader, the tone of the class was one in which students and teacher were co-exploring philosophical texts.

Part of what enabled this exploration was the way in which the students had come to understand the discipline in which they were participating. Rather than seeing philosophy as a fixed body of eternal truths established by great minds throughout history, they saw it more as a field in which they could and should seek to divine truth for themselves, with texts serving as contributors to their journey. "I think the reason that people think philosophy is interesting is because there is no right answer, the way there is in biology and math," one student said. (This was not necessarily true in the most powerful science and math classes, as we will explore later.) In turn, this made students' critical task not to remember but rather to interpret the texts. In the students' telling, this created an unusual and exciting atmosphere in the class—one that was less focused on whether they were right or wrong and more on whether, as a class, they had worked together to deepen their understanding. They also noted that they had become more confident in their abilities to offer these interpretations over time, and that this growing confidence was one of the most important things they had gained from the class.

Much as in the theater production, the ethos of Mr. Fields's class was one that blended passion and precision, and that was grounded in a clear sense of purpose. Class often began with simply, "Who wants to start?"—an invitation for students to lead off with their thoughts on the previous night's text. There were some rules for conversation, particularly that students build on one another's points and stay close to the text. Sometimes the atmosphere was fun and light—such as when a student exclaimed "Star Wars is such a Buddhist series of films!" to roaring laughter from his classmates—and other times it was deadly serious, as when students were pondering a deep philosophical conundrum. Not once did we hear anyone ask whether something was on the test or whether one could get points for this or that; such questions would have been highly discordant with the norms of the class. While there was a lot of energy created by the existential questions at hand, there also was considerable precision in how students talked—making a claim, referring back to the text, and being challenged by Mr. Fields and one another on whether one could really make that claim based on that piece of text. In so doing, they were being inducted into some of the key norms of philosophy as a field, in which learning how to defend and support one's claims is critical.

Supporting this learning was a highly evolved, if almost invisible, pedagogical approach. Mr. Fields had been teaching for twenty years; he had learned through long practice how to set up a supportive and collaborative classroom culture that, once established, could almost run itself. Much as in Socratic seminars at universities or Harkness tables at Exeter, there was not much variance in the day-to-day approach; the task was to talk about great texts, sometimes briefly scaffolded with some pre-writing or small-group discussion, but mainly students were asked to read and share their understandings.[9] Mr. Fields had, through much trial and error, come to four questions that guided the exploration of each text: (1) What? (What did the author say?); (2) Why? (Why was the author making that argument?); (3) Connect? (How does this connect to other passages in the text or to other texts?); and (4) Significance? (Why does it matter and what do we think of it?). These questions moved the discussion gradually outward in concentric circles, with students first deciphering the text, then connecting the text to other works, and only at that point, once they were sure they understood it, evaluating what they were reading. These questions also touched on a number of the qualities associated with deeper learning: the first two focused on mastery, asking students to accurately unearth what a particular author was saying and why he was saying it; the third asked for transfer, pushing students to connect what they were learning in a particular text with other readings; and the fourth invoked values and identity, asking students their views of the significance of what they were reading. All of the questions were open-ended and asked for analysis as well as recall.

Like other teachers in this chapter, Mr. Fields often privileged depth over breadth. Sometimes, particularly with dense philosophy, the readings were only a few pages a night. He often had students read particular passages out loud, a practice that focused the discussion and centralized the text for shared interrogation. He had found that focusing on one passage could solve a number of related pedagogical dilemmas: it could equalize access to understanding, engender widespread engagement, and build deeper understanding of the text. As he described it:

> First somebody reads the passage and they hear it, but to them it feels just like dead language. It doesn't pique their interest or curiosity in any way. Then you ask the question, "So what's actually being said in this?" Half of them are disengaged because they don't actually understand what's even being said in the passage. Somebody in the class will say, "Well, here's how I'm reading this." Then another student says, "Oh, that's not how I thought of it." Then they start to discuss it. By doing that, the people who didn't understand the passage gain access to it. There you've got interest because more have access to the actual passage. And by layering one interpretation over another, students gradually deepen their understanding of the text.

Mr. Fields also had a different approach to relevance than many other teachers. Earlier in his career, he said, he had been more tempted to start with a personal connection. But, he said, he had found that "as soon as you switch to talking about the text from the personal, it's like all the air gets let out of the balloon. They've been really excited to talk about themselves and their personal connections to a topic. They think it has nothing to do with the book. Then you bring the book in and they go, 'Oh shit. He tricked us. This is actually about the book.'" As he became more experienced, he reversed the equation, beginning with the text, asking less about the personal connection and more about "why does this matter to us as people." The ideal, Mr. Fields said, is that there is a recursive loop between what was learned in the text and something one cares about in life: "Because the text is primary. 'What's this text saying?' Rather than them being primary. It's more like their interest is all personal but it fuels their interest in the text itself. What does the text have to teach me about how I see my family? Does this change the way that I look at reality, or meaning in my life, or things like that? Then they make the connection, whoa, this is true in my life, too. That's where there's often a kind of light bulb like wow, this actually means something. And then that realization becomes the energy that feeds the inquiry back into [the] text."

A critical part of Mr. Fields's growth as a teacher was learning how both to share his passion for the subject and to acknowledge that students might find different things in the text than he would. Mr. Fields had majored in literature, was married to a philosophy professor, and continued to study philosophy as part of his Buddhist training. After one unfulfilling year after college as a consultant, he felt that he had found his life's calling in teaching literature and philosophy to high school students, which he now had been doing for close to twenty years. So it was not hard for him to express his passion for the subject: "If you personify your subject as dead and kind of boring," he chuckled, "kids are not gonna invest. If you personify it as meaningful and really important somehow, and transformative, 'This changed my life,' kids feel that. They feel it and they wanna know how. How did it change your life? Why is it so important to you?" In addition, he said, a critical turning point was when he stopped trying to lead students through the text using a series of questions that he had preselected. Students can read that attitude in a teacher, he says, because when you pose questions that you know the answers to, then "it's not really an open discussion; it's more like an oral quiz."

In more recent years, Mr. Fields had shifted his approach to letting students pick the passages to discuss: "Actually learning to withdraw from the conversation I think is really essential. Learning to ask the question with passion because you do care about it, but to say, 'The reason it matters to me doesn't have to be the same reason that it matters to you. This is really important material. It has changed my life. It's transformed the way that I see relationships. It's transformed the way that I think of love.' Then you say, 'What's it do for you?'" He found that decentering his role had both increased students' engagement—they were talking about the passages that mattered to them—and signaled his respect for his charges as people whose interests were as important as his own.

This shift, while now foundational to his approach, had not come easily because it meant reconceiving his role as a teacher: "When I first started doing this, it felt revolutionary because I decided to go into the room and abandon what I knew about the text. I was no longer the authority on the text. I'm the teacher. Your identity as a teacher is wrapped up in being the one who knows. I think that there's something terrifying about that because, for a teacher, you're walking in, saying to students, 'Well, I have my own thoughts about it but they're not actually what matter,' or, 'I don't claim to know the bottom line about this book. I can tell you my own personal feelings about it but I don't have the answer.' I think that's really scary for a lot of teachers 'cause basically what you're doing then is you're walking into a big question mark. In fact, you are the question mark."

But if making this change was initially scary for Mr. Fields, it did have the empowering effect that he sought in his students. They described it as refreshing not to be rehashing the "not like the nine thousandth billionth, trillionth essay on *The Great Gatsby* about the motif of death." And they respected that Mr. Fields didn't always have the answers: "His attitude is not like, 'I know everything.' He's really open to the fact that he probably doesn't know everything and no one really does." Other teachers might get "defensive" when they didn't know the answer, but students thought that it actually "builds respect for the teacher when they are willing to admit that they don't know everything."

A further benefit of this approach was that it gave everyone the responsibility for "deepening" the learning. The goal of the class was to wring everything there was out of a given piece of text, and this was something that the group could do better than any individual, including the teacher. Mr. Fields saw this as part of his own growth as a person— realizing that his perspective was as colored by his background and experiences as anyone else's—and thus that trusting the wisdom of the crowd would lead to richer understandings of the text than what he alone could provide. Students saw it as about equality; that this wasn't a class where one person knew all the answers but rather where a diversity of opinions was critical for deeper understanding.

At a school where there was a lot of niggling for grades, this class stood out as one in which there was unadulterated joy in pursuit of existential questions. As one student summed up: "I think what I love about this is that we have thought about these questions our entire lives. We just didn't know how to put a name to these questions. I feel like I'm getting a glimpse of what people thought, not how individual people think, but how humans think. I think that's really cool."

Nick Collins and Nathaniel Martin: Math as an Activity

It's one thing to develop an appreciation for open-ended inquiry in philosophy, but what about mathematics? In our travels, most of the math instruction we saw was consistent with researchers' descriptions of American mathematics teaching: teacher-led lessons in which an instructor explained a rule or algorithm, went over it on the board, and then had students apply it to "practice problems" that varied only slightly in their particulars.[10] The reactions to this approach from students, depending on their interest and skill in math, ranged from workmanlike compliance to outright boredom and disengagement. We did see a small number of classes, however, where students were engaged in mathematical reasoning, and, relatedly, were much more engaged and interested in their work. Most of these were in elite or advantaged settings—at an elite private school known for its distinctive pedagogy, at a statewide math and science magnet school, and in a few of the revamped math classes at Attainment High. But we were particularly interested in whether a similar approach could be implemented with more disadvantaged students, which brought us to Bryant High School.

Bryant is a school that serves exclusively high-poverty students, all of whom are students of color, in a major Northeastern city. The classroom we describe here was run by Nick Collins, a "master teacher" who was recruited by the city's teacher residency program both to teach in this school and to mentor a new teacher, Nathaniel Martin, who was in his first year of teaching mathematics.

I arrive at Bryant at about 8:15. The building is an old public school building—very tall ceilings give off the feel of a large comprehensive high school constructed in another era. It is early June, but fortunately not too hot. The lights are off in the main hallway, presumably to save money. We enter the room of Mr. Collins and his student teacher, Mr. Martin. Only Mr. Martin is present. The room has a worn linoleum floor, which has X and Y axes taped onto it with masking tape. Students are sitting at tables of two to four, facing front. All are students of color. They are wearing dark blue shirts with the name of the school on them. A sign on the wall reads, "Math is an activity: questioning, noticing, calculating, exploring, organizing, persevering, making sense, understanding, applying connections."

The younger teacher begins the lesson by projecting a picture of the front of a package of balloons on the overhead. He asks the students to call out and write down, "What do you notice?" "What can you count or measure?" "What do you wonder?" [This is an adaptation of a well-known protocol used in constructivist teaching: "see, think, wonder."] The students respond, "The Balloon is red." "There is a six on the package." As they talk, he is blowing up a balloon. "Don't pass out, man," a student calls, and there is shared laughter; the tone of the class is light. A student points out, "The picture of the balloon on the package is round, but the one you are blowing up is not quite round." The teacher encourages them to think about why and a short discussion ensues. "What other questions could you ask?" he asks. And, "What does this balloon stuff have to do with math class?" A student asks, "How can you measure a balloon?" and the teacher asks this back to the class—"How can you measure the balloon?" The students call out that there is the diameter, the radius, and the circumference. The teacher asks them to define these terms, and they establish that you could measure the circumference but would have to compute the radius or the diameter. Then, the teacher asks, "How many breaths will it take to fill this balloon?" "Is it fully inflated? How would we know?" The students ponder this, intrigued but unsure. And, he says, with a dramatic pause, how many breaths would it take to fill a bigger balloon? At this point the other teacher, Mr. Collins, walks in the door with a HUGE purple balloon, almost as big as he is. "How many breaths would it take to fill this balloon?" he asks.

The teachers hand out balloons of varying sizes. The students set to work in small groups. Each group has a white board next to its table where students can capture their work. The process is to blow a breath, watch the balloon inflate, measure the circumference, and chart it on a two-column chart. The goal is to figure out what kind of function relates the numbers of breaths (the Xs) and the circumference (the Ys). All of the groups are working assiduously; only one student asks to go to the bathroom. I ask one group how they are going to solve the problem. "We have to start with the input," says one. "The only way really to figure it out is to try it," says another. Over time, students begin to fill out their tables. The teachers are circulating, offering help and asking for questions. The period ends before students can graph their results or turn them into a function. We talk some with the students; they say that this is a very different approach to math than anything they have previously experienced: "more fun" and "more thinking like a mathematician."

A new group of students files in. This class is an elective, "discrete mathematics." Because this is a STEM-themed school (though not a magnet or otherwise selective school), the students take additional math classes; this class, the teachers explain, was an elective for the teachers, if not for the students (who had to take it to fill their slate of math classes). The teachers chose it because they liked the subject and because they wanted the students to see something very different from what they were learning in algebra. (Discrete math is about understanding arithmetic in different bases, modular arithmetic, and graph theory.) The main task for this class is a math game. The game features "trees" comprised of a series of connected lines and dots. Each player makes a move by putting a slash line through one of the lines, and then everything above that line is eliminated from the game. The players take turns, and whoever has to make the last cut loses. At each configuration, the teachers prod them: "Do you want to go first, do you want to go second, or does it matter?" The students try out different possibilities, often playing through the same tree more than once, to see whether various opening moves lead to different results. There is fairly rapt attention—everyone is playing a version of this game, and the students want to win. Energy is high at the beginning and gradually flags as the period moves toward its conclusion, but this is the kind of draining of energy that comes from thinking hard— it's what you might see at a chess club. The teachers are circulating, trying to get students to think more generally. "Why," they ask, "do in some of these cases you want to go first and others not? What's the more general rule here?"

These two classes differ considerably from most math classes we saw in our research. They were both organized around a single essential question—in the first case, what sort of function will explain how many breaths it takes to blow up a balloon; in the second, what rule will explain the winning strategy in a particular mathematical game. Both approaches treated students as meaning-makers—while there were some processes to be followed, students were being asked to develop their own theories and ideas about what could explain the outcome. The questions were also intrinsically interesting—in the first, engagement was motivated by a demonstration, and in the second, the task took the form of a game, which was itself fun, challenging, and purposeful. In all of these respects these math classes differed from most others we saw, where the common approach was for the teacher to provide an algorithm and for the students to apply the rule to a series of practice problems. The atmosphere was also different from that in most math classes we observed: the students were at ease with the teachers, with a relaxed, light tone in the balloon class and a highly focused spirit in the math games class.

How did these teachers learn to teach this way? For Mr. Collins, it was a gradual process. He grew up in an affluent district nearby where he had been a math whiz. From early on, he had been good at math and he initially embraced the competitive timed tests, the "can I do my multiplication tables faster than you" approach to math. As he got older, he became more interested in the way in which math posed puzzles—and the challenge to figure out these puzzles was what kept him interested in the field. Interestingly, he was less taken by the applications of math—for example, physics or economics—because while these made the math more "real world," from his perspective they often made the math itself less interesting. He found himself more drawn to fields like computer science, where there was a big task to do, and lots of freedom and flexibility to figure out how to do it.

Over the years, Mr. Collins had gradually figured out how to translate this commitment to "puzzling through" into a set of workable pedagogical principles for high school students. Part of his approach came through his university teacher-prep program, which had taken a strong stance about the constructed nature of mathematical knowledge. Part came from his own reading—a book that argued that "math was an activity" rather than a "body of knowledge" was particularly influential.

And then he described the most important influence (what he called "the biggest revolution" in his teaching)—his finding of "math Twitter," an online community with influential figures like Berkeley professor Jo Boaler and practicing math teacher Dan Meyer. This group had a similar stance toward math, and across Twitter they shared ideas, teaching strategies, and, most of all, sample problems that were "low floor, high ceiling"—meaning that they were simple enough to offer an easy on-ramp for all learners, but had enough room to play to be challenging for the most mathematically inclined. In our conversation, Mr. Collins identified particular posts from Dan Meyer and others as significantly shaping his practice, particularly the idea that "real world did not necessarily mean real math," which was consistent with his overall mathematical philosophy and interests.

For Mr. Martin, it had been a godsend to find Mr. Collins as his mentor. Mr. Martin had been homeschooled for the first eight years of his life, and thus had become used to working independently and finding answers to his own questions. He later attended what he described as a typical high school and, afterward, spent the first two years of college doing work that was "fairly traditional—sit there and take notes as the teacher talks." He continued, "I didn't start getting into actual math— proofs and algebraic thinking—until junior and senior years," and what he describes in retrospect as a "very procedural education." But once he recovered from that initial setback, he found this latter part of college very stimulating, and the kind of math he did then helped him to think about what he was trying to do with his students. "I often think: what would an actual mathematician do?" To answer that, "I think I'm drawing on having studied math in college—not just when I was taking the derivative but when I was doing proofs. . . . I was inducted into the community of mathematicians by my college professors, and I can share that with my students." Just as the director of the theater production had been apprenticed into theater and then, in turn, apprenticed his students, Mr. Martin saw himself as bringing his experiences in college mathematics to his high school students.

The result of his training was that Mr. Martin, like Mr. Collins, had come to see math less as a field of right answers than it is usually perceived to be. "Does math have right answers?" we asked. "Well," the twenty-three-year-old responded, "as a community of humans, we've decided that numbers are a good way to think about things," and, given that, he said, "certain things are true." But real math, he continued, was less about knowing the right answers, and more about "I'm going to try this out, conjecture, and revise," and that was what he was trying to share with his students. Working with Mr. Collins had been a godsend, he said, because Mr. Collins "set the tone for collaboration—math is about you seeing random things and trying to make sense of them; he very much set the expectation that math is something students do rather than something they receive."

Mr. Collins's and Mr. Martin's students appreciated this attitude. They told us that "just so you know, this school sucks—they care more about the rules than the education," but added "[the two math teachers] are awesome." Why is that, we asked? One Latina girl explained, "When we get frustrated, he knows we are thinking hard. I know that he cares about us. He uses a different form of grading—a rubric—[that emphasizes] effort and reasoning. It is different from doing problems and seeing whether we get the right answer. He cares about us and our learning. When we get too frustrated, he tells us to take a drink and take a walk." An African American student added, "This class is different because we are thinking more like mathematicians. . . . Math is about finding different ways of understanding something, and looking for patterns." Adds a third, "This class is great, A+++. They really care about whether we learn, this class involves a lot of playing with numbers, when we get something they move on, but if we are struggling they don't tell us, they ask us again and again, give us different problems, they are always asking us to think. They show that they care by always being available at lunch, after school, helping us to think. It's fun."

Both Mr. Collins and Mr. Martin saw their work in math as not only about building mathematical interest but also about empowering their students. As Mr. Martin said, "Our purpose is not to get them into college; our purpose is to give students power. The idea is to help students become mathematicians, which means they have to do what real mathematicians do—discover, innovate, and meet a real intellectual need." Thus there is congruence between their approach to math—which is more about building mathematical identities than about covering content—and their ultimate goals for their students.

In fact, the only other places where we saw students asked to develop their own interpretations in math were highly elite settings. At one

highly regarded private school, the Harkness method had been adapted
to math, and every class began with each student writing an answer to
a problem on the board, which other students then built upon and critiqued. (The school's faculty had also replaced the textbook with materials they themselves had written, a spiraling curriculum of problems
that they hoped would introduce students to math as an integrated
field—instead of as different, siloed branches, which is how students
often experienced it.) At the Midwestern Math and Science Academy,
an exam school for the strongest math and science students in the state,
students worked in a similar inquiry-oriented way: they were exposed
to the mathematical mysteries in calculus and linear algebra by working
collectively on one hard problem at a time. What Mr. Collins and
Mr. Martin's class demonstrated was that an equivalent approach was
possible with students who were less privileged and entered with less
knowledge of math; it simply required a willingness to recast math in
a way that made it more inviting for these students.

Pedagogically, this meant puzzles, games, and low-floor, high-ceiling
problems, through which the duo sought to advance understanding of
core mathematical content. As Mr. Collins says, "My underlying philosophy is that math and mathematical thinking and solving puzzles is
something which is innately enjoyable. It's not so much that I have to
convince them; it's more that I have to remove the reasons that it's not
coming to life for them." Mr. Collins himself also continued to enjoy
what he called recreational math—games and puzzles that he himself
liked to do—and he brought these in and shared them with the students.
Particularly at the beginning of the year, they made a considerable
effort to reframe the ways in which students experienced math,
which for many had been a painful subject. By reintroducing math as a
field rife with puzzles that could gradually be unraveled, they hoped to
awaken students' mathematical interests. When we asked Mr. Martin
whether, as a first-year teacher, he had had problems with classroom
management, he responded that Mr. Collins had developed a very
strong collaborative culture by creating a "task environment" in which
math is "seen very much as something you do rather than receive"; from
there, his job had simply been to sustain it.

Overall, their teaching illustrates a parallel to what we saw in electives at Attainment High: if you want to change students' experiences
in core disciplines, you need to change the "what" of what students are

being asked to do. Mr. Collins and Mr. Martin had not found some magical way to make traditional mathematics more engaging. Rather they had simply, and significantly, changed the tasks asked of students— play mathematical games, reason collectively about puzzling mathematical conundrums—and, through those processes, they were gradually teaching topics like discrete mathematics and statistical analysis. Like other "deeper teachers" in our sample, they led with authentic complex tasks, and embedded within those tasks the basic skill-building needed to take on those tasks. They also drew on Mr. Collins's knowledge of the field to make these selections. Mirroring Jerome Bruner's contention that real mastery is the ability to see the structure of how knowledge is organized in a field, Mr. Collins chose problems or exercises based on his sense of the arc of mathematical learning in different topical areas.

Mr. Collins had also made changes to his ways of assessing students' progress and success in his class. Like the organic chemistry teacher at Attainment High, he had been frustrated by the process of grading quizzes; giving students a "70" just seemed to tell them that they weren't good at math rather than that they were struggling with particular concepts or subtopics. Instead, like Adam, he had moved toward a mastery-based system: students were assessed on particular elements of math, and, if they did not pass, were given opportunities to do the material again, with different questions, until they showed mastery of a particular skill or idea. He also had tried some collective performance assessments: students worked together to solve problems in a group, thus modeling on the assessments the same kind of collaborative culture they were creating in class.

The duo's class also shows what is possible through an apprenticeship model of teacher training. While Mr. Martin was part of a teaching residency program that itself provided significant training, he named Mr. Collins as by far the most significant influence on his teaching. They planned together; they debriefed lessons together; and sometimes, within lessons, they moved from one teaching to the other teaching. This total immersion helped Mr. Martin see, concretely, what it would mean to actualize this approach to mathematics, to practice it extensively, and to refine and revise it with actual students. The balance of the teaching also shifted over time, with Mr. Collins doing most of the teaching at the beginning of the year and Mr. Martin doing the majority by the end. This was by design, as part of the "residency" program; much as in medical residencies, the younger professional gradually assumes more responsibility as she or he demonstrates competence. While such an approach is only as good as the "master" teacher—we saw some pairs where the apprentice had taken on much of the formulaic approach to teaching of the lead teacher—it does show the power of co-teaching as a mechanism for learning the craft. Everything about Mr. Martin—how he talked about the nature of his field, how he thought about pedagogy, and what he actually did with students—were qualities that we otherwise observed only in veteran teachers, who had been through many rounds (and often years) of trial and error before they unlearned their initial methodology and reset-tled into a more collaborative, open-ended approach. His is only one example, but it does show that such a learning curve can be greatly ac-celerated in the hands of the right mentor.[11]

Kyle Hogan: Building Skills, Empowering Learners

In our travels, we saw a stark discrepancy between English classes serving affluent and higher-track students on the one hand, and classes serving higher-poverty and lower-track students on the other. In affluent settings, English was frequently the discipline where we saw the most opportunities for meaning-making, analysis, and interpreta-tion, perhaps because discussion is the coin of the realm. But in less ad-vantaged settings, we saw significantly less of this. For example, at one highly tracked comprehensive high school that included both a magnet program serving predominantly affluent white and Asian students and a "regular track" serving predominantly black students, we saw the higher-track students being asked questions like "What choices did the author make in organizing the narrative?" while the lower-track stu-dents were simply reading the story aloud and answering comprehen-sion questions, with no opportunities for interpretation or meaning-making. These observations are consistent with a large body of litera-ture that indicates that opportunities for extended thinking are more present in higher tracks and more affluent settings.[12]

Enter Kyle Hogan. Mr. Hogan teaches almost exclusively high-poverty black and Latinx students in a traditional public school in a major Northeastern city. His mission in life is not only to educate but also to empower those students: to build their skills and knowledge, but also to teach them how to read critically canonical texts as well as analyze words in all of their forms in the world around them. Mr. Hogan—who is in his mid-thirties, has a joint master's degree in philosophy and education, is working on an education doctorate, and teaches novice English teachers at a well-regarded university—describes his own practice as only a work in progress. How to integrate skill-building with critical reading is both the topic of his doctoral thesis and a lifelong dilemma.

To describe aspects of Mr. Hogan's approach, we focus on a set of classes about a Ta-Nehisi Coates article, "In Defense of a Loaded Word."[13] The article, published in the *New York Times* in November 2013, is a defense of sometimes using the word "nigger," suggesting that rules regarding usage should not be absolute but rather should take into account the nature of the context, the race of the speaker, and the relationships among the parties. The classes described here took place less than two weeks after the article was published. We describe a three-class arc: the first one devoted to deciphering the text, the second to a discussion of it, and the third to an analysis of the form of the writing.

Mr. Hogan is a thirty-something guy, slim, dressed in a sports jacket and tie. He has short buzzed hair and the overall impression I get is a bit preppy. There are twenty students in all. Two are chattering away in what I discover is Haitian Creole, while others speak in Spanish. There are thirteen boys and seven girls.

They are sitting around a horseshoe arrangement of tables. Mr. Hogan jumps right in, reminding the group about the analytic essay due on Monday. He asks me to introduce myself. When I say that I'm looking for classrooms where students are learning deeply, a few students clap and another says, "This is your man."

Mr. Hogan introduces the Coates piece. "We're going to talk about his central argument—which he doesn't state directly! I don't really know what he's saying—so you're going to help figure it out, and to figure out why he doesn't just say it flat out," he says. A student responds, "You *really* don't know what he's saying? Because then I ain't gonna be able to figure it out either." The students laugh.

Mr. Hogan smiles but moves forward with the task, and the group quickly quiets down. He directs the group to look at the writing assignment due next Monday, which is a choice between two prompts. The choice involving the Coates article is as follows:

In his essay, Coates never states his thesis directly; instead, he implies his central argument by building ideas from paragraph to paragraph. Your task is to state Coates' central argument in your own words and then defend, challenge, or qualify it. Support your argument with evidence from your reading, observation, and experience.

Mr. Hogan says that the *New York Times* is "the most challenging daily paper," and holds up a copy. "Some people make fun of me because I have this delivered to my house every day," he says. He then explains what op-eds are: "Most of the newspaper is factual stories, but at the back there are arguments and opinions."

The class starts to look at the essay. "We're going to use a reading strategy where in a few words you summarize what he's saying in each paragraph. . . . We've done this before. We'll do the first paragraph together and then I'm going to let you work in groups or on your own with the rest." Mr. Hogan pauses after a few sentences and asks what one of the sentences mean, and several students help to clarify. Mr. Hogan follows up: "Does anyone else have this experience that they're called something in your family that would be uncomfortable if someone from outside the family called you?" There are loud assents.

Mr. Hogan asks students to turn and talk with their partner about what the first paragraph is about. There is one minute of conversation; Mr. Hogan then asks what students came up with. A boy raises his hand: "That relationships with different people affect your language in terms of what you call them?" Another student adds: "The fact that other people that might not be as close to him call him dad is a problem."

Mr. Hogan asks if they want to do another paragraph together and there are some murmurs of assent. He leads them through the next section, feeding them questions: "What is he implying here? . . . If I were to call my wife 'baby' is that okay? What about if you called her baby?" One student says that he thinks this article is about the n-word and Mr. Hogan directs them to look back at the title. Mr. Hogan ask students to put the key sentence of the second paragraph in their own words: "Right names depend on right relationships," one student offers. Mr. Hogan prompts the students to annotate all of their thoughts and responses in the margins of the text. With the first two paragraphs done, Mr. Hogan releases his students to spend ten to fifteen minutes working through the rest of the article.

I sit down with two boys, who tell me that they find this strategy to be very useful—"because later I can look back on it and see what I was thinking, since we're going to write an essay on it and stuff." I come back to the pair where I have stationed my computer. They have finished the next two paragraphs and tell me what they think: "He hints at how race might have to do with how we use the n-word," one of them tells me. They have underlined lots of words and drawn arrows to their annotations in the margins. I turn to the other side and talk to a student who is working on his own. He says that he thinks Coates is in between thinking that the word is and isn't acceptable, referring to a paragraph that describes how frequently the n-word recurs in black music and culture. I move to a pair of girls who affirm that they find the strategy useful—"I do it on my own," she says.

In this first class, we see a highly scaffolded effort to help students make sense of the text. Recognizing that his students lack dominant cultural capital, Mr. Hogan explains what the *New York Times* is and what an op-ed is. He models by sharing his own enthusiasm for the *Times*. And he helps them work through the eleven-paragraph op-ed, annotating paragraph by paragraph, until they each have developed their own summary of the piece. In so doing, he is responding to where the students are—supporting them by breaking a full-length op-ed into paragraph-long chunks—but not lessening his expectations that they can read a significant contemporary author and engage with his ideas. He also models that this is a topic on which there can be different viewpoints, starting with his opening comment that it is the students' job to help him make sense of the essay.

A day later, we return for the discussion of the Coates text:

Mr. Hogan begins: "What I'd like to do is have a discussion about whether you agree, disagree, or want to qualify his claim, but before we do that you need to know what his claim was. Try to write it down in a sentence or two." I walk around—it seems that roughly half of the students have grasped at least the idea that Coates is defending the n-word as a choice that black people can make in certain contexts. Mr. Hogan has put a continuum on the board, running from "defend" to "qualify" to "challenge" and says that students who think they have a sense of the central argument should put their initials in the appropriate column. A number of students get up and do so. A bunch of them fall between "defend" and "qualify," with only two toward "challenge."

"Let's start talking about this," Mr. Hogan says.

STUDENT 1: "I believe that he's arguing that in certain situations you have to use certain words. . . . There are certain graces that we are allowed to say to each other. If you say the n-word to Jamal, he might get offensive about it . . . the coach was using the word in an aggressive way."

MR. HOGAN: "Do you think that [student 1] is correct in his assessment? Raise your hand if so."

STUDENT 2: "I think he says that certain words are for certain people."

MR. HOGAN: "Does anyone think they understand what [student 2] is saying and can paraphrase it?"

STUDENT 3: "It's like the example of calling your spouse, 'baby' . . ."

STUDENT 2: "No. I think he's saying that certain words are meant for certain people."

MR. HOGAN: "What's been said so far and what do you want to add to it?

STUDENT 4: "[Student 1] was saying that it's mostly race . . . and [student 2] was saying that depending on race you can't say certain things like the n-word or spic, but [student 3] says it depends on the relationship, and I agree with that. There are certain words that hold a negative connotation no matter what. With the n-word there is a difference between the -er and the -a. I think that Coates thinks that language does have to do with certain words and certain situations that you're put in."

MR. HOGAN: "Can we agree that Coates is saying the words we use depend on the situation?" Students say yes. "So to what extent does Coates think that race is part of the situation?"

STUDENT 5: "I think it's just about the relationship. . . . I mean, if I have a white friend who calls me that, I'm not gonna care, but if it's a random stranger I would."

MR. HOGAN: "Do you think that Coates would think it's okay for black people to use the n-word in some situations and context?"

STUDENT 6: "I thought he was saying that that word holds a negative connotation, so I think he would say it's never okay even for people of color because it brings back the history."

MR. HOGAN: "So we need to go back to the text because we have some disagreement here about what Coates is saying. We need to figure this out."

STUDENT 7: "Generally, I think he thinks that in some situations he thinks it's okay." [He reads a quote from the text.]

STUDENT 8: "I feel like he's trying to say that it's okay when there's an "a" but it can go back to something negative otherwise. . . . I think it's not negative when you use it among your type of race."

MR. HOGAN: "Does Coates think that?"

STUDENT 9: "I think so, because right here it says"—and he offers a quote from the text—"When Matt Barnes used the word 'niggas' he was being inappropriate. When Richie Incognito and Riley Cooper used 'nigger,' they were being violent and offensive."

STUDENT 10: "I agree because he's saying that the n-word for when some races use it is like a symbol of saying that they've overcome something . . . like in the last line, 'It tells white people that, for all their guns and all their gold, there will always be places they can never go.' So no matter what the white people do they will never be able to use that word in the same way."

In this discussion, we see the students grappling with the complexities of Coates's argument. The students' comments build on one another; there is some "barn-raising" in the way that the students' cumulative responses create an increasingly complex argument. They consider the questions of whether different races can and should use the word, whether "nigger" is different from "nigga," and how, if at all, context and relationships shape when the word should be used. The exclusively black and Latinx students are also unself-conscious about saying the word, even in front of a white teacher, and have no trouble developing an analytic discussion on a potentially very sensitive topic. Finally, unlike the *Waiting for Godot* pattern that we described in Chapter 1— where teachers promised that the "deeper" day was coming on some unspecified future date—here the unpacking work of the previous class becomes a platform for a deeper discussion of ideas.

In a third class, Mr. Hogan prompts the students to think more about the *structure* of the argument than its content, which leads into their writing assignment:

"We're going to start by talking about whether Coates's implied thesis was effective, and then we're going to focus on your introduction and thesis paragraphs," he says. He says that the homework is to write a draft of the introduction to their argument essay.

"When I say implied thesis, what do I mean?" Mr. Hogan asks. "What his intention is—what he's implying to other people," a student says. "If you imply something you don't say it—like you don't actually say it." Adds another. "You're hinting at it; it's subliminal," says another. "Subliminal is going too far," Mr. Hogan says.

"If we take a look at his first paragraph," Mr. Hogan says, and gestures for them to look at the text, "Do we see a thesis statement there? No. So what I want you to do is to write—on a scale of zero to five—write whether you like his implied thesis." A student asks, "What is his implied thesis?"

Student: "I think what he's saying is that saying niggers depends who you are ... it depends who you are and who you have a relationship with— if I'm a Negro and I say nigger then it's one thing, but if I'm white, it's like not okay."

Mr. Hogan asks the students to turn and talk about where they sit on the one-to-five scale in terms of how effective they found Coates's implied thesis. Mr. Hogan asks students to share out loud what their partners were saying, and asks one student to summarize what his partner said.

STUDENT 1: "What she said is because his writing have [sic] too much information—it started far away and it's not connected and it confuse people a lot. The point he makes is there but because of the connections it's not as clear."

MR. HOGAN: "So tell me if this is right: you've got a bunch of different stories and they are too far from the central point?"

STUDENT 2: "I'm in the middle because it's like it's good what he says but he taking too long to get to the point."

MR. HOGAN: What would you have preferred that he did?

STUDENT 2: "In the end he shoulda just stated his fact and went to the point."

STUDENT 3: "I think the stories and all the stuff does match—you just have to put thought into what he's saying. All the stories he gave about Matt Barnes and stuff are all prime examples of relationships and where it's coming from and how it works. I'm still not exactly sure what he's getting at so that's why I'm at a 2.5. It's basically like a riddle to me."

MR. HOGAN: "When you think about the effect, do you think he intentionally put his thesis under the surface to make you think?"

STUDENT 4: "I feel like in order to prove his point he had to give different examples of different situations—I think he's trying to get the reader to see it from a different point of view rather than just one so they could choose which one they agree with the most."

The discussion continues and then Mr. Hogan prompts them to begin work on their own essays. The prompt is to "state Coates' central argument and then to defend, qualify, or challenge what Coates is saying." In preparation for this task, they look at an AP English test essay from a student from the year before. Mr. Hogan asks them to analyze it, not for the specifics but for the structure of how the author has organized the text. One student says that "you should have a thesis—explain your opinion on the subject." "Does Coates do that?" Mr. Hogan asks. "No," says the student. "So we want to keep that in mind—putting your argument first is more of a guideline, since writing is an art, not like in math where two plus two is four no matter where in the world you go."

I talk with two students who are still confused about the argument— they are looking back at the passage to figure it out. Mr. Hogan projects one student's intro on the document camera for the class to read—by a Latino student who was working on his intro yesterday during a study hall:

> In the passage, "In defense of a loaded word," the writer, Ta-Nahesi Coates, argues that when it comes to a solid relationship between two people, they have certain rights to call one another any name they feel comfortable with. More specifically, name calling can impact the relationship with one another negatively or positively, depending on how the other person reacts to the name calling. Others might say using expletives has no place in civilized relationships. Ultimately I think this language can be offensive but it is up to the individual to decide with consideration to whether this language is appropriate or not.

Mr. Hogan prompts students to use this as an inspiration and to keep going. "The best way to write a good paper is to write a bad first draft—you just have to go for it," he says.

In this third lesson, Mr. Hogan shifts the focus from the content of Coates's argument to the nature of persuasive writing. One reason he had chosen the Coates text was that it differed from what students were frequently taught in school about essay writing: it did not lead with a thesis, and, in fact, the thesis was never directly stated. As a teaching tool, Mr. Hogan saw the implied thesis as having double benefits—it pushed his students to decipher the argument, and it showed them that real writing does not always conform to the hamburger-essay template that is so familiar in school. In so doing, he was inducting them into the world of real writers, where there is no fixed template, but rather only an intentionality about the effects of different authorial choices. In our interview with him, Mr. Hogan, unprompted, cited David Perkins's "whole game at the junior level" as key to his thinking: he wanted to show students the "whole game" of professional persuasive writing and within that have them practice the parts that were particularly difficult.

Mr. Hogan also was seeking to support the transfer of skills that cognitive scientists have identified as a critical component of mastery. Thus he had students read both the Coates and the former AP English example for their structures, then he asked them to think about what they implied for their own writing. In a meta-move, the students were writing an essay about the nature of another essay, and thus they were having to make the same choices that they were asking of the author they were reading. Mr. Hogan ends by encouraging students to see their work as just the first draft of their thinking, consistent with the idea that production of worthy products comes through multiple drafts and revisions, another meta-lesson about the writing process.

How did Mr. Hogan come to teach this way? Like many of the other teachers in our sample, he had taken a significant journey to reach this point. He was, he told us, initially shaped by what Dan Lortie called "the apprenticeship of observation," because his own experiences as a student had "a huge effect" on his initial practice as a teacher.[14] The thinking was that "we would look at literature and discuss it and ultimately come to what seemed like reasonable, supported interpretations, and when we weren't coming to what struck me as these reasonable, supported interpretations, I didn't know what else to do but say, 'Well, here it is.'" That led to "student assessments that looked more like, unsurprisingly, regurgitation." He also remembers that he just taught the books that were assigned from the curriculum, and that, at the beginning, it felt like the question was how was he going to fill up all the classes in the school year.

Over time, he had reflected more on what his actual, as opposed to inherited, goals were for students. As part of this reflection, he went on a college tour, where he followed up with his former students as well as a number of their professors and asked them what they were struggling with in college. He found that "students weren't struggling at the next level because they couldn't read and understand *Hamlet*." The problem, he discovered, was not so much whether they could remember this text or that one, but rather "what was holding them back was their ability to critically read, analyze what they were reading, make arguments, and synthesize a variety of [ideas] into their viewpoints." Thus, he realized, if he had limited time with students, while exposing them to a variety of texts was still important, the most important thing he could do was to take enough time with each text to make sure that students built up their abilities to analyze, interrogate, and write, which were portable skills that they would need in college.

At the same time, Mr. Hogan coupled this hard-headed analysis with a desire to induct students into his own love of all things text. Mr. Hogan described himself as "having an obsession with the written word . . . I just love reading and writing in essentially every genre." Shakespeare, Proust, Dickinson, Baldwin, Coates, fiction and nonfiction, historical and contemporary, were all of interest to Mr. Hogan. He continued to read voraciously, bringing new texts to class as he got interested in them and thought they would spark something for the students. He described himself as having a "pedagogical lens" on everything he sees: "When I read the newspaper, when I watch a movie, when I see an ad, I'm almost always thinking, at least in the back of my mind, 'How might this fit into my teaching?'" Mr. Hogan's students described gradually adopting this attitude themselves; as one reported, "I used to just like see ads and not think about it and now I think about how they're targeting certain audiences."

As someone with a master's degree from a divinity school, Mr. Hogan saw teaching as an almost spiritual endeavor, a "calling" of sorts. In an interview with Sarah, he flatly disputed Jal's account from a previous book that teaching should professionalize along the lines of medicine or law, because those dry fields, in his view, did not compare to teaching:

I think there's really something missing there. I think it's more like teachers as architects where there's a more artistic component, teachers as ministers where you have this more spiritual component, almost a more theological component. . . . It's a way of living in the world in the same way that I think some religious folks would argue that they wake up every morning and look at the world through a lens of what would the Honorable Prophet Muhammad do or what would the Buddha do or what would Jesus do. Teaching is an identity, a way of being in the world, a way of seeing the world that means that my teaching is going to inform the way that I'm looking at almost everything outside of school. Similarly, the things that I encounter outside of school are really going to be informing the choices that I make as a teacher.

Thus, he concluded, "Dewey was right" when he said that school was not preparation for the real world. But rather, "for students who are here hours and hours and hours every day, this is the real world. Then that's when I want to make this world—which is part of the real world; it's the real world for me and them for much of our lives—I want to make it vital to their experience as human beings."

These convictions organized many of Mr. Hogan's choices. The essential question for the year was, "How do you use literacy skills to influence change in your life and the lives of others?" a question he picked because he wanted to show students the way in which literature could be a force for social mobility. Within that overarching purpose, he looked for texts that would likely both be of interest to the students and embody issues of "perennial" or vital interest. He then gave himself some flexibility to pick texts as the interests of the class developed:

Okay now might be an excellent time to bring in Judith Ortiz Cofer, "The Myth of the Latin Woman." This might be a good time to bring in—we've already done some stuff with Richard Rodriguez. This might be a good time to bring in Randall Kennedy out of Harvard who writes about our use of the N-word. It might be a time to bring in Anzaldúa. At that point, I can say, "Okay. Now I can connect some of these classic pieces to the Coates piece and do a sort of thematic unit on language."

Far from his initial practice of moving lockstep through a set of pre-assigned texts, he now felt the rhythm of the class and thought about which texts would best expand its web of knowledge. If the job of the Deweyan teacher is to connect the web of knowledge in learners' heads to the tree of knowledge in the world, he used his wide-ranging knowledge of literature to pick texts that would likely extend their growing understanding.

Mr. Hogan also had grappled with how exactly to make the skill-building piece come alive. Many classes began with some vocabulary words—for example, juxtaposition, antithesis, delectable—which he challenged students to use and combine. Examples offered were: "the antithesis of dapper is frumpy"; "the antithesis of brief is long-winded"; "two antithesis foods such as broccoli and fried chicken in juxtaposition to each other make the broccoli seem less delectable" (students cheer because the sentence contains all three words). By making vocabulary playful, inviting students to consider different ways of using the words, Mr. Hogan was trying to show them that these weren't just words to be memorized but rather they could use them in different ways as writers. One powerful "aha" for Mr. Hogan was his discovery that re-framing grammar as an instrument of power enabled him to see how to integrate it with his other goals. "When I stopped seeing grammar as rightness and more as making choices to express ideas, that really helped—at first I just couldn't see how to integrate it at all. So a lot of the beginning of the year is setting up what the classroom means for us as people who want to be successful in an unjust world—we need to be able to make a choice about the kind of language we use to make sure that we're able to use it to further our purposes."

Finally, Mr. Hogan's experiences had led him to take a different stance than many of the other teachers we interviewed. While many other teachers in our sample, encouraged by today's data-saturated climate, tended to reflect on what their students did not know how to do, Mr. Hogan started with a conviction that students' thinking was often ahead of their writing: "Students are ready to think deeply about issues of public discourse—they're ready for that intellectually but they're not at a place where they know that you're supposed to put a comma before the coordinating conjunction when you have two independent clauses." Thus while for many teachers the common pattern we saw was "Bloom as ladder"—do the lower-order tasks now on the assumption that higher-order tasks will follow at some future date—Mr. Hogan's approach was "Bloom as web," moving back and forth between complex texts and the skill-building needed to decipher and write about them.

Joel Wolf, William Duchin, and Megan Marino: Scientific Inquiry

On a visit to an urban charter school early in our travels, the science department chair, a woman in her mid-twenties, pulled us aside and said, "If you really want to see deep learning, you should visit the school where I went to high school—the Midwestern Math and Science Academy [a pseudonym]." MMSA, as we will call it, is an exam school created by a governor and a Nobel Prize winner with a twofold mission—to educate some of the strongest math and science students in the state, and to develop new approaches to schooling that could serve as models for the state and the nation. We visited MMSA in 2013 for seven research days, with a particular interest in how they approached science instruction. While we realize that there are some who are skeptical of what can be learned from a selective magnet school (and the school certainly benefits from the strong skills and motivation of its students), we felt that this school had found particularly thoughtful things to do with its students, perhaps generating ideas that could be useful across the spectrum.

Part of what made MMSA distinctive was its strong constructivist stance that students should be treated as inquirers who need to figure things out for themselves. This was a consistent theme in our interviews with both students and faculty. As one student said,

> They don't just give you information and expect you to regurgitate it—you have to develop things on your own. They encourage discovering things. Like with math classes, at my previous school they would give us the information and then have us give it back to them on a test. Here they will give us [the material] and then will ask you to draw your own conclusions based on the evidence that you've gained—it gives you deeper understandings because you understand the math behind it.

Another student said that many of the questions on tests in science were "transfer questions, where they change the scenario; you can't just memorize it the day of; you need to know it and have a good understanding of it." In language, "Before you had to memorize vocab and grammar; here it's all discussion and immersion based." From the teachers' perspective, this was a huge shift from what the students were used to in their previous schools. As one teacher told us, "The shift is so hard to do—the first semester of sophomore year is like hell because they come in, and they're like this is how I was successful for so many years." The result is that "students can be uncomfortable early on because their idea of what teachers are supposed to do is different from what happens here. 'My teacher doesn't teach; they always answer questions with questions.'" Over time, both students and teachers said that students adjusted, gradually becoming more comfortable with uncertainty and the notion that knowledge is not given but constructed.

A significant part of helping students make this shift is a required sophomore course called Methods of Scientific Inquiry (MSI), which is designed and taught by a team of teachers. The purpose of the course is to teach students what it means to do scientific inquiry, and the goal is for students to write a scientific paper that could be submitted to a journal. Students begin by learning some basic statistics—how to run a t-test, and how to test the relationship between x and y variables by doing a correlation analysis or running a regression. Students then are exposed to some of the scientific literature, because, as Joel Wolf, one of the teachers of the course, says, "many of the students have not seen or read the peer-reviewed professional literature," only textbooks. Mr. Wolf and his colleagues then walk students through how to use databases to find things in the scientific literature. They do a simple lab on buoyancy, the purpose of which is to show how to label axes of a graph and put the dependent variable on the y axis and the independent variable on the x axis. Thus in the first several months of school, students learn the things they need to know, big and small, to at least begin to write a scientific paper.

Then there is a scaffolded process of developing the research for the paper. The first step is brainstorming—what are they interested in, what data do they have access to or might they be able to collect? Mr. Wolf helps to fine-tune the brainstorming process, helping students to figure out what is "feasible or reasonable and what might not work." Then they develop a project proposal, which Mr. Wolf describes as a critical step in the process. Here they have to define the question, the methods they will use, how they plan to analyze the data, as well as how they will address "safety concerns and privacy issues." They also make a list of the materials they will need for their project, and develop a timeline for what they plan to do on specific days. Students submit a draft of this proposal, which gets marked up by Mr. Wolf, then submit a revision that responds to his questions.

The rest of the semester follows a similar pattern. Each step in the project is closely structured, but students have full control over the substance of the experiment and the content of the paper. The elements of a scientific paper are isolated—introduction, literature review, data and methods, findings, and discussion—and each piece has to be separately turned in for feedback from Mr. Wolf. Some of the components are extensively scaffolded; for example, for the literature review, students have to write an annotated bibliography of at least ten sources before they actually try to integrate that research into their literature review. The last steps are writing an abstract and a title. As Mr. Wolf describes the goal, "We talk about—like in an art class. Products of art would be the painting, the sculpture, but what's that product of science? It's that publication, and we want them to generate that paper at the end that looks like a peer-review journal article." The project concludes with students developing a poster for the project, and sharing their results and conclusions with their classmates.

Over the years, students have chosen a wide range of topics. Mr. Wolf remembers projects seeking to understand plant growth, comparing organic and nonorganic apples, and a product-testing project where students measured the absorption levels of different kinds of paper towels. There also have been projects in the social sciences; for example, he remembers one where a teacher delivered the same short lecture in a monotone and then in a livelier way: the experimenters then gave students a content assessment and asked them to rate the quality of the teaching across the two versions. One group we observed was testing whether students were more likely to remember lyrics of a song if they listened to the song or were shown the lyrics visually. (They found no statistically significant difference.) In a given year, some students would likely be in the chemistry lab, some in the greenhouse, and some out in the field, which avoided the problem of competing for scarce resources.

The class generally has about twenty-four students, working in pairs, meaning that Mr. Wolf is supporting twelve projects at once, which he finds to be a significant but manageable workload, especially because at any given stage of the process some students will need more help than others.

These semester-long mini-projects sophomore year feed into the Student Inquiry and Research program in junior and senior years. MMSA gives over much of Wednesdays to these projects, which are larger scientific investigations, either designed by the students on campus or in college labs. The school has established partnerships with two well-regarded universities for students to work in labs, and buses take students back and forth to these labs on Wednesdays. The school has a full-time coordinator for this program, who works to find mentors, checks in with matches as they develop, and conducts site visits at the labs and other off-campus sites where students are placed. Students choose their projects; about 75 percent of these projects are in STEM, but some students do work in other disciplines, including literature (writing novels) and music (composition). As in the MSI course, the process is scaffolded: students have to submit a proposal, keep notebooks that document what they are learning, and present to the community at the end of the year. Substantively, the projects here are more ambitious. The year we visited, one student was running regressions on the effects of homelessness; another was exploring whether the universal declaration of human rights was truly universal; and a third, in a university lab, was evaluating the effects of different drugs on heart disease. Roughly 5 to 10 percent of these projects are presented at research conferences or are published. Students described the MSI course as critical preparation for these larger projects: "Sophomore year was big . . . in teaching us how to learn on our own; how to bring all different types of data together and synthesize and boil it down to prove something."

Interestingly, the way that MSI was working during our visit wasn't the way in which it had initially been envisioned. In its earlier iteration, said Mr. Wolf, the skill-building part took most of the semester, and the project happened only in the final three weeks. But when a team conducted a review of the course, they found that students did not find the skill-building part particularly engaging or relevant, because it was divorced from the context in which it would be used:

The students were not seeing the relevance to all of the skill-building activities. They didn't understand why they were expected to do all that stuff that didn't seem to have a context. . . . The project is what gives it context. When they're reading literature they're reading literature because it's relevant to the research that they're doing, and they're writing about it so that their conclusions can be understood in a broader context and not in isolation, for example. Background can be given so that the reader of their paper has some knowledge about their topic before they get into the specifics of what they've learned. Now it has a context and a meaning, and it's relevant to them, and they understand how it fits in.

As a result, they had shortened the skill-building portion to just the first few weeks of the course, then integrated additional tools through the development of the scientific research. From Mr. Wolf's perspective, this shift not only had the benefit of making the work more engaging; it also helped students to think more like scientists, for whom integrating hypotheses, literature, data, and findings are the core tasks.

Thus the MSI example parallels the apprenticeship and induction approach that made the extracurriculars described earlier so powerful. It draws on the motivation of students' intrinsic interest in their topics, develops learning in a contextualized rather than a decontextualized way, has a clear purpose, and is incentivized by a public presentation of work at the end. At the same time, it also features ample feedback from an experienced teacher and a carefully scaffolded process that helps students gradually gain the tools they need to conduct real scientific research. There is "playing the whole game at the junior level" in the MSI project, followed by the gradual move toward becoming part of the larger community of scientists, as students become more experienced and many join college labs. Much as Mr. Hogan did with English language arts, the building of basic skills is subsumed within a larger arc that has meaning and purpose.

What was it about Mr. Wolf and his fellow science teacher Duchin (known on campus as Dr. Duchin) that enabled them to construct this arc for their students? Mr. Wolf said that the model for his teaching stemmed from the part of his own educational career that looked most like real science: "Another interesting thing is—I think back at my own education. It wasn't until I did an independent study in my senior year that I really got involved in doing some of the kinds of things that we ask the students to do in the MSI class, my senior year in college. I really didn't get good exposure to a lot of stuff until I became a grad student and started doing research of my own. That was a whole different experience than all the coursework that I had taken prior to that." Dr. Duchin, who also taught MSI and had been a fixture at MMSA for several decades, described the way his own doctoral training shaped his teaching: "I suppose, if I didn't go to graduate school, I wouldn't be the same person I am. I'm a constructivist, because that's the training that I have. I practiced constructing models that reflect the data that I collected. I can't separate that experience from who I am now, as a teacher of these kids."[15] Many of the teachers at MMSA have Ph.D.'s in their subjects, and it was this exposure to building and creating knowledge themselves that had enabled them to apprentice students into a similar mode.

MMSA's schoolwide commitment to inquiry-oriented teaching dramatically shortened the period of trial and error that characterized the first years of many of our other teachers. Dr. Duchin describes initially coming to MMSA after working for a few years as an adjunct lecturer on the college circuit, and finding a fit between his beliefs about the subject and his beliefs about teaching. "In college, I'm a lecturer. I'm supposed to communicate the theory, the concept, the thought pattern of the discipline, and then test students on it. Here, I came to discover very early that it was a constructivist atmosphere, not an instructivist one. It appealed to me tremendously, particularly in my career, coming out of science, which is constructivist. It just seemed to make sense that we should educate our science students in a constructivist manner. It was a good fit for me." In an environment filled with students and colleagues who had similar beliefs, Dr. Duchin had many opportunities to grow and reshape his teaching in a supportive environment.

Megan Marino was trying to do something similar but in a much less privileged environment. After earning a Ph.D. in chemistry with a focus on science education, Ms. Marino had been teaching in a large, comprehensive, traditional public high school in a Northeastern city. Most of her students were African American or Latinx, and they were almost uniformly recipients of free or reduced-price lunch. One of the classes that we observed her teaching was a Methods of Scientific Inquiry class:

Ms. Marino has told me that this class is an eleventh- and twelfth-grade elective, which functionally means that it's a "dumping ground" for students whose schedules put them in the time slot. She says that there is a huge range of skills and interests but "that's the point—I don't care if students start by thinking of themselves as science students or not."

The sun streams through the tall windows on one side of the room. Even with the blinds partially closed I can see the city skyline to the west of the school. The students have been working on corrosion; yesterday they did an experiment and have brought in their results. Class begins immediately with the bell. There are about twenty students in the room. Most appear to be black or Latinx with three who appear to be white and one boy in ROTC uniform who appears to be Middle Eastern. Ms. Marino says that the students will be continuing their steel wool experiments from the day before—they will be designing a second experiment based on the results of the first. "You're going to come up with a new question based on what you see, based on what is interesting to you," she continues, and asks students to take out their notebooks and their handouts from yesterday. She prompts students to look at the post-lab questions, briefly explains the plan for the class, and says that she will be checking homework. The students get going within five minutes of the bell. "You are going to do the same things that you did for the first experiment . . . create a question, identify your variables." They have done a little background work about rusting before the lab (they read an article), but Ms. Marino tells me that "I'm more of an explore-first kind of teacher, so the pre-work was pretty sparse." She gives me the article, which provides some basic information about corrosion in the context of discussing vintage cars and how they rust differently in different parts of the country.

There is a one-page outline of instructions for the lab. In Phase 1, students could choose one of three questions to explore—the first question, for example, is "How does water temperature affect the rate of corrosion of steel wool?" Then they had to identify the variables (and check with Ms. C before moving on), state a hypothesis, create a materials list, write a detailed procedure (check with Ms. C), carry it out, and record results. Today, in Phase 2, they are to design a follow-up experiment based on what was most interesting in their first results. The follow-up questions are as follows:

1) What does your original experiment show about the relationship between your dependent and independent variables? Answer this question for both experiments.
2) Comment on your hypothesis in light of your results.
3) Explain your thinking around your follow-up experiment. What about your original results led you to choose the particular follow-up experiment?
4) Explain why corrosion happens more quickly under some conditions than others, according to your experiment. This should include a discussion of the chemical reactions involved in corrosion and how the conditions affect this reaction.

The students immediately move from their desks to spaces around the room, checking on their results. I talk to a pair of girls, one with long black hair and a slight lisp who tells me that she is part of the science mentors program, the other with a messy bun. They tell me that they picked the question about which liquid or solution resulted in the fastest corrosion. They tested water, vinegar, and lemon juice, and show me the test tubes where they have put the samples of steel wool with these solutions. They have hypothesized that water will corrode the wool the most "because water is polar and steel isn't . . . that's just what we thought." I ask how they will know about the levels of corrosion and they say just by looking— but when I come back later they have decided to measure the mass of the steel wool.

Ms. Marino is talking to a pair who is having a hard time deciding on a second experiment—a Latina girl and a black girl. They chose to look at how salt water, regular water, and vinegar corroded the steel wool by measuring the mass of the wool before and after it soaked in the solutions. The salt water didn't change the mass of the wool, as they had thought it might. Ms. Marino says, "It's up to you—you could even decide to duplicate the same experiment with different solutions," she adds. "Because, would we ever decide we know for sure with just one experiment?" They shake their heads. When I follow up a few minutes later, they tell me that they've decided to design a new experiment to see if higher concentrations of salt will result in greater corrosion. I ask why, and they say, "Water is everywhere, so it's related to real life—so we'd know what would happen if metal was in the ocean." When I ask why they think in this pair of labs students are designing different experiments rather than all following the same procedure, one of them says, "Well this is an elective class so we get to choose what we want to do."

The feeling in the room is busy but focused. Many students wear safety goggles without seeming self-conscious about it; at some point Ms. Marino says to a student, "Dear, I need you to wear your goggles," and he puts them on without fuss. All students are engaged in measuring, weighing, taking notes, talking about the experiments, or conversing with Ms. Marino or Tiffany, a former student who works as an assistant. Throughout, when I ask students questions about the experiments—like which solution they originally thought would be the most corrosive—I'm struck by the fact that many of them look uncertain and check their notebooks rather than responding extemporaneously. My impression is that this is the effect of their general lack of confidence in this kind of work. They don't seem to have the big picture, that this is about learning to think like a scientist, but they are doing so nevertheless—my guess is for one of the first times. It is also October, still relatively early in the year.

At the end of the period Ms. Marino prompts clean-up, and all the students put their labeled experiments-in-progress on the windowsill. Ms. Marino gives a few reminders: she checked notebooks today so anyone who didn't get checked needs to show her theirs. "By tomorrow we need to have our follow-up experiments completely set up and we'll be working on the analysis questions. Later in the week we'll have time in the computer lab to work on processing some of this and formatting it as a lab report."

This class reveals what an inquiry-oriented stance looks like in a less advantaged setting. As at MMSA, students are employing the scientific method, have some control over the nature of their investigations, and are evaluating their hypotheses through evidence. While they are somewhat unsure of their footing, given that this is their first exposure to doing real science, they are able to work through the steps of the scientific process. The room also shares the affective qualities we have seen in other powerful classrooms—a hum of busy focus that is driven by the students. It is also notable that it is an elective—students, freed of some of the coverage constraints of other science classrooms, can make some choices about what they investigate, which helps to pique their interest. Finally, unlike many of the scientific labs we saw—where the purpose was to replicate existing experiments—there was in this room a genuine sense of the unpredictability that characterizes real science, as students tried different materials to arrive at their results. The experimental work was also linked to underlying content in chemistry, creating the basis for the conclusions of the experiments.

Like the other teachers profiled, Ms. Marino had made a series of decisions that produced the classroom we saw. Because the class is an elective for juniors and seniors, it is not subject to state tests. As a teacher with a strong reputation within a school with loose administrative oversight, Ms. Marino also had significant autonomy in designing the course. She had, over time, decided that certain ideas and associated procedures within chemistry that she initially had held dear could be sacrificed in favor of greater conceptual understanding of core ideas, while inducting students into the use of the scientific method. As a result, she had made participating in the science fair a required component of the course, and threaded development of the science fair project through the learning across the year.

Pedagogically, she had taken the task of scientific inquiry and broken it into many components. One strategy she used, especially early in the year, was that on the first day she would design an experiment, which students would carry out; then they would design the follow-up experiment. In so doing, she both actively demonstrated the steps of the scientific method and gave students some freedom to develop their own ideas. The science fair project was the culmination of this evolution, as she gradually gave over responsibility to the students to take charge of their own scientific explorations. Much as Mr. Fields hoped that each discussion of a text would produce something new, Ms. Marino similarly thought that the key was for students not to feel as if they were the thousandth student to perform an experiment but rather that they were investigating something original. Creating choice over the science fair project was one part of this—"if you hate cooking but love sports, don't pick a project on sugar crystallization," she said—but even in day-to-day instruction, she thought that students making choices gave the work life. "That whole idea of really asking students to kind of come at it from who they are. I think every student is more engaged in a lesson if they think it's different because they're there. Because they're taking part in it; that [their presence] has somehow changed what has happened," she told us.

At the same time, while Ms. Marino placed a heavy emphasis on inducting students into the methods and epistemology of real science, she also made sure to integrate a core knowledge of chemistry: "I always tell kids and I mean it. I see the world in chemistry. It organizes my perspective, my vision on the world," she said. One of Ms. Marino's goals is for students to become scientifically literate, and to achieve that, she seeds an accumulating series of chemistry lessons within her largely active approach to teaching. Much as the National Research Council has argued that deeper understanding requires fusing content with skills, Ms. Marino believed that scientific inquiry is necessarily built on a growing base of scientific knowledge.[16] At the same time, as Magdalene Lampert does in math, she would often foreground an investigation, then gradually bring in the scientific content, rather than the reverse.

As with many of our other teachers, coming to teach this way had been an evolution. Ms. Marino described herself as someone who learned well from the book, the traditional way, and she had begun her teaching in a rather conventional manner. When she began teaching high school, however, she quickly discovered that this did not work for many of her students. While completing a master's degree in education, she struck up a relationship with her science methods professor, who was beginning a large NSF-funded grant on inquiry-based science teaching. Ms. Marino became a doctoral student on this project, and did her own research comparing more and less inquiry-based ways of running labs. At the same time, she got her Ph.D. in chemistry, not science education, and thus had to complete some bench chemistry research as well. This combination had both grounded her in doing research in the discipline and given her an opportunity to do dissertation-level research about different teaching practices. These experiences informed the work she was doing with her own students.[17]

Ms. Marino now teaches others who are trying to learn inquiry-based methods of teaching science. Her key piece of advice? "One of the first things is be not afraid. It is a little messier. . . . Push yourself to let go of the idea of a very tight kind of classroom control and have faith that if you kind of give students the reins that it will be okay." Much like other teachers in our sample, she embraces the value of growth over correctness: "One of my other refrains to kids is, 'It is hard. It is difficult. You shouldn't feel bad. It takes time and repeated effort and that's okay. Everything we do, every effort you provide is advancing you towards the ultimate goal even if you're not there yet. Even if you get the wrong answer, it doesn't mean that it was a waste.'" As was true at Attainment High, she noted that this message is counter-cultural to what students normally receive, and that it requires some unlearning on their part to get used to it.

Like a coach, Ms. Marino employs a variety of methods to acclimatize students to this new way of being. For example, she refuses to grade the multiple-choice sections of tests if students have not taken a real shot at doing the open-response sections. Because she has found that some students freeze up at the writing stage of developing lab reports, she urges them to first talk out their ideas, then write down their thoughts. A central goal of her teaching is to build a culture in which students try out scientific ideas with one another, ultimately making them responsible for creating and regulating a space infused with scientific norms.

In line with Dewey, who urged that the teacher should be an active researcher of her own practice, and a reformist superintendent who in 1893 advocated teacher learning so that students could "drink from a running stream rather than from a stagnant pool," Ms. Marino frequently adjusted and experimented with her own practice.[18] Unlike the teachers at MMSA, she was not part of a school committed to the kind of teaching she was employing, so she did not have the benefit of the kind of community that they had on-site. As a result she eschewed most schoolwide discussions and focused on her classroom. In her city, however, she had found a community of people who shared similar missions and goals: through this community she both shared what she learned, and learned from others' shared experiences. In particular, through videotaping herself teaching and asking a group of friends from across her networks to provide feedback, she continued to strengthen her own teaching.

What Do These Teachers Do Differently?

These teachers differed from their more traditional colleagues in a variety of interlinked ways. They had a different conception of their purpose (the why), which in turn was linked to a different teacher identity (the who), which in turn was linked to a different set of pedagogical choices (the what and how).

Table 7.1 A Different Stance: Traditional versus "Deeper" Teachers

	Traditional teachers	"Deeper" teachers
Educational goal	Cover the material	Do the work of the field; inspire students to become members of the field
Pedagogical priorities	Breadth	Depth
View of knowledge	Certain	Uncertain
View of students	Extrinsically motivated	Creative, curious, and capable
Role of student	Receiver of knowledge	Creator of knowledge
Role of teacher	Dispenser of knowledge	Facilitator of learning
View of failure	Something to be avoided	Critical for learning
Ethos	Compliance	Rigor and joy

Tying these together was a different *stance*, a different way of viewing what they were trying to do, which came out of their experiences and informed their work. While leading work by Lee Shulman emphasizes the different sorts of knowledge that teachers possess—substantive knowledge, pedagogical knowledge, pedagogical content knowledge— our work suggests that it is the perspective or stance that teachers take toward their work that is critical.[19] (Knowledge certainly contributes to the formulation of such a stance, but it is not sufficient.[20]) A number of the key dimensions of this stance and how they fit together are en- capsulated in Table 7.1.

The Why: How Deeper Teachers See Their Purpose

The starting point for understanding these teachers is that they had a different view from most teachers of what they were trying to do with their students. At essence, they began with a set of goals about what they wanted for the young people in their charge—not just knowledge, but a set of capacities and dispositions that they thought were impor- tant for facing the world. They sought to empower their students; they wanted them to be able to approach both their fields and other life sit- uations as people who could act on the world and not simply have the world act on them.

While their hopes for the students as people came first, they cared about their students *through* their disciplines or subjects. In other words, in contrast to the role of parents, as teachers they expressed love for their students by showing them the corner of the world that inspired them. In so doing, they hoped to modestly but fundamentally change their charges, helping them to develop new interests, new understandings, and, potentially, new identities that would integrate what they were learning into revised notions of their core selves.[21] Their goals were at once both less and more ambitious than those of other teachers we encountered: less ambitious in that they were less concerned with whether students remembered particular pieces of content; and more ambitious in that they hoped to create seminal learning experiences that would affect their students beyond the specific content of the course: they tried to plant seeds that might inspire many years of inquiry into their subject.

This approach reflected the different way in which these teachers understood their disciplines. To a person, they saw their disciplines as open-ended rather than close-ended fields, meaning that they saw their fields as places where people had constructed provisional knowledge, rather than as places where there was a finished set of answers that needed to be passed on or "professed" to others.

While teachers' epistemological understandings of their disciplines might seem like an arcane point, we found that it was critical for everything that followed. If teachers saw their fields as fixed or inherited bodies of knowledge, teaching as transmission seemed like a logical and efficient approach. Students might be given opportunities to process more interactively, but the fundamental goal was to push students to absorb established knowledge. Conversely, if the fields were understood as places where different people would develop different interpretations, experiments, and approaches to problems, it seemed natural to invite students into this process of inquiry, connecting them to the generations of scholars and seekers of knowledge who had come before.

At the same time, even while teachers were giving their students room to develop their own approaches and interpretations, they were pushing them to think hard about how they would defend the arguments that they were making. The teachers loved their fields and disciplines, and with that love came a belief in the way those disciplines embodied standards about which arguments passed muster and which did not. They indicated this through their feedback, both verbal and written, and by the standards that governed what happened in their classes. When possible, they tried to teach students to enforce these standards, making the task of rigor something that was collectively owned. In English classes, for example, students would often be vigorously prompted to support interpretations with particular pieces of text, with other students asked to evaluate whether they thought those inferences were warranted. In math, it could come through assigning some students to present problems that they had solved on the board, and asking others to verify their chains of logic. If the conventional approach to instruction is "I do / we do / you do" with respect to a particular piece of content or skill, the approach of these teachers was "I do / we do / you do" with respect to the *standards of the field;* with the goal of gradually shifting responsibility for the learning itself to the students as a collective.[22]

In many ways, these teachers were paralleling the induction processes that we saw in theater and other extracurriculars in the previous chapter. Much of what they were trying to do was to close the gap between the "game of school" way of approaching the field or discipline and the way in which professional participants in those fields do those same activities. Mr. Hogan, for example, used the Ta-Nehisi Coates article to show his students that good, real-world writers did not always conform to the five-paragraph essay form that they had been taught, then invited them to make similar authorial choices in their own work. The instructors at MMSA walked students through the scientific process on a small scale, then connected them to college labs where they could participate in the creation of real science. Even when students were not yet in a position to contribute to the field—for example, in math and philosophy—their teachers tried to induct them into the kind of thinking and methodology that disciplinary experts employ. They did this not because they thought that all of their students would become professionals in these disciplines, but rather because it was a way of empowering their students; showing them that they, too, could develop and create knowledge and ideas.

These commitments were particularly apparent in teachers who were teaching high-poverty students and students of color. These teachers were well aware that these were the students who historically had not received an empowering education, and they saw their missions as heavily shaped by a commitment to social justice. But they did not frame their students in deficit terms; nor did they, like many of the teachers in our sample, see the urgency of "catching students up on the basics" as precluding the kind of thinking that they wanted for their students. Instead, they made sensible adjustments—shortening the pieces of text they asked students to read; scaffolding unfamiliar terms or concepts; embedding skill-building within larger investigations—but kept their fundamental stance toward students as highly capable meaning-makers.

These teachers also had a different view of expertise than is sometimes found in the literature. Much of the literature, especially in cognitive science, emphasizes the importance of the differences between experts and novices: experts can see patterns that novices cannot, and thus the role of teaching is to use this expertise to help bring novices along a trajectory toward expertise.[23] These teachers did not deny that they had greater expertise in their subjects than their students, but their stance was rather one of co-investigators. As Dr. Duchin describes it, "What developed for me was a subject-centered learning community. I have to be part of the learning community, not that intercessor between the content and the students. I think that's where the truth comes out, and students know it." These teachers were hoping that as a text was analyzed, an experiment conducted, a proof worked out, their students would come up with something they hadn't seen, that new ideas would be unearthed. Having sought to inspire their charges to love their subjects, they welcomed having others with whom they could explore their fields.

The Who: Teachers' Journeys and Identities

This stance, in turn, was heavily shaped by the life trajectories and identities of those teachers. As we noted at the outset, all but one of the teachers in our sample had been teaching at least ten years; the median level of experience was twenty years. They had reached their stance only after a considerable journey, with their sense of what matters most for teaching as well as their hopes for young people crystallizing over a long period.

Many of the teachers in our sample had started teaching in the traditional way—cover content, assess results, batch-process students, rinse and repeat—and had gradually come to see the limits of that method, which had motivated a search for a new approach. Ms. Walsh, the IB teacher at IB High, recalled that her very first experience was teaching on a Fulbright in Malaysia. Around October of her first year, she said, one of her students came up to her and said, "Miss, you seem like a very nice lady, but you have to stop talking!" She described this somewhat sobering encounter as the beginning of her journey into how students were experiencing her teaching, which had so evolved that, by the time we saw her twenty years later, she was hardly talking at all. Many of the teachers had made similar journeys. This was not an easy shift—it required destabilizing their initial conception of what they were supposed to do as professionals—so the evolution toward this approach could take a long period of reflection, as they gradually came to hold a different view of their role.[24]

While it may have taken time for them to find a teaching equilibrium, they generally credited a *seminal learning experience* for shaping how they viewed their field or purpose. For some, this had come in the last two years of college or in graduate school, which was the time in their own schooling when they had finally shifted from being told information acquired by others to participating in the development of knowledge.[25] For the humanities teachers, it came from participating in Socratic seminars or other joint meaning-making activities in their own schooling, which they sought to pass on to their students. If Dan Lortie emphasized the ways in which the apprenticeship of observation was normally a conservative force that replicated transmission-style teaching, our teachers suggested that the opposite is also possible: drawing on the best experiences of schooling could provide models for a different kind of teaching.

One particularly striking instance of this relationship between how teachers learned their fields and how they taught them came in a discussion we had with a teacher in an advantaged school who was teaching both history and AP psychology. We had visited her history class, which, while not perfect, had given students opportunities to interact with documents and try to develop historical interpretations. We had also visited her AP psychology class, which had none of the life of the history class, because students were being asked to memorize definitions of different kinds of conditioning. As we interviewed her to probe the reasons for the differences between these classes, we asked how she saw the two disciplines. To paraphrase, she said that history is very much an open discipline. People think it's all names and facts, but it's not.

Why do you say that? we asked. In college, she said, we had this two-year required course in Western Civilization, co-taught by four professors, in history, English, theology, and philosophy, and we got to see how the same events could be understood through different lenses. What about psychology, we asked? Oh, she said, unlike history, psychology is all about right answers, it is a very closed discipline. From these starkly different answers we can see that even in the same person, very different teaching can result from very different understandings of various fields or disciplines.[26] Perhaps not surprisingly, given our apprenticeship view of powerful teaching and learning, it was only when teachers had themselves experienced the nature of their disciplines as open or constructed that they could create the same experience for their students.

Depth of knowledge about their fields was also important for other reasons. All of our most compelling teachers had at least an undergraduate degree in their subject, with some who had masters' or even doctoral degrees. This depth of knowledge helped them think about how to structure the work in their fields; in particular, it helped them to decide which readings, questions, or problems would be likely to open up the widest range of possibilities for their students. It also was critically important for giving them confidence in their ability to teach in more open-ended ways; for other teachers in our study, moving off-script or asking open-ended questions felt perilous because it could expose the limitations in their knowledge of their fields. These teachers, by contrast, were hoping that students' questions and ideas would take them to unfamiliar territories, confident in their ability to handle such terrain because they were secure in their underlying knowledge of the field. Ironically, as students in Mr. Fields's philosophy class told us, when teachers admitted that they didn't know everything, students thought more, not less, of them.

If the roots of these teachers' approach to teaching were deeply grounded in their initial learning in their fields, they were sustained by an ongoing passion for their subjects and for finding ways to teach them. The humanities teachers were voracious readers, continuing to explore different tributaries of their subjects. Mr. Fields had recently been ordained as a Buddhist priest, which was the culmination of a sustained multiyear interest in Buddhism. Mr. Hogan said that he saw everything in his life—movies, television shows, books, magazines,

even advertisements—as texts carrying messages that could be decon-
structed; he was always on alert for materials that he could bring into
the classroom. Mr. Collins continued to love to do what he called "recreational math," which he then shared with his students. Students, not
surprisingly, could sense the ways in which these fields were alive in
their teachers, describing this passion and interest as "contagious."

If part of their identity was continued immersion in doing the work
of their fields or disciplines, these teachers were also equally alive in
thinking through the work of teaching, constantly tinkering with and
revising aspects of their practice as they tried to figure out what would
land well with their students. Much as Dewey described teaching as a
form of action research, these teachers were continually experimenting
in ways small and large. In so doing, they stayed plugged into new cur-
rents developing in their fields and disciplines, considering whether
these approaches would work for them and their students. For some,
this was facilitated by technology and the growth of online teacher
communities; for others, by colleagues or critical friends in their geographic areas. Much as we have described deep learning for students as
occurring over long periods of time in spirals of mastery, identity, and
creativity, these teachers were part of similar cycles as they enriched
their teaching. Such cycles also sustained these teachers, preventing
the kind of burnout that is so common in more structured teaching
situations.

Finally, there was an interaction between these teachers' growing
sense of what mattered for their students, their understanding of their
fields, and their pedagogical approaches. Initially, for many of these
teachers, these elements had been misaligned: the ways they were
teaching felt incongruent with their own views of their fields, and
while they were meeting external expectations for their students (for
instance, by keeping up with pacing guides), their own assessment of
what their students were learning fell short of their expectations. Over
time, as they gained experience or tracked student outcomes over
time (including the years after students left their classrooms), they
had come to realize that less really was more—that more important
than what was covered was developing students' abilities to think and
to take ownership of the tools of their field or discipline. This realization enabled them to shift their goals and to some degree their curriculum, which in turn enabled them to develop pedagogical practices

consistent with both their hopes for students and their views of their fields or disciplines. While they continued to iterate and revise, part of what was striking about these teachers was the way in which they had found an equilibrium that integrated their knowledge, their teaching, and their selves.

The What and How: Inducting Students into the Disciplines

The ways in which these teachers taught were highly varied. Consistent with the aphorism from the National Research Council report—"asking which teaching technique is best is analogous to asking which tool is best—a hammer, a screwdriver, a knife, or pliers"—the pedagogical approaches that these teachers employed differed depending on their disciplines, goals, and teaching philosophies.[27] Some, like Mr. Fields, used essentially only one modality, which had the advantage that students knew how they were going to be working and could both focus on the content and gradually assume ownership of the process. Others, like Mr. Hogan and Mr. Collins, varied the pedagogical modalities depending on what they were teaching and what method would best suit that task.

If the pedagogical modes varied, what was common in their approaches was that they aimed to be simultaneously inspiring and exacting. All of them saw their fields as something worthy of considerable devotion, something that could be this way for everyone, if, as Mr. Collins said, the obstacles to such devotion were removed. But at the same time, they also all had high standards for what good work in their fields looked like, and they instantiated those standards by asking hard questions and by requiring students continually to revise and revise both their thinking and their written work.

In many ways, their classes exemplified many of the same qualities that were present in the extracurriculars: purpose, choice, community, apprenticeship, and the sense of "playing the whole game at the junior level." As in theater, classes were grounded in an attention-grabbing purpose or question: How do we know if we exist? How many breaths would it take to blow up a huge balloon? Under what circumstances is it appropriate to say "nigger"? What do we want to investigate scientifically? Within this overarching purpose, there was often choice: Mr. Fields let students start with the passages that meant something to them; the Methods of Scientific Inquiry classes let students choose what they wanted to explore and how they would design an experiment to explore it. The work happened within a community that the teachers had expertly created, one that was playful and productive, warm in affect but focused in energy. Students knew the rules and norms of how the space worked, so they could push one another on things large and small, such as reminding classmates to put on their goggles or pressing them to refer to texts.

All of this happened within the context of apprenticeship and playing the whole game at the junior level: the teachers, as the expert guides to the field, were gradually showing students how their domains worked, with students learning by doing the work of the domain. In taking this stance, teachers emphasized learning over performance; failure was not something to be avoided but rather an expected part of striving toward the difficult tasks of thinking and creation. Finally, all of these classes shared a culture of respect for students as capable and intelligent young people, whose opinions and ideas had real value, and where challenging those ideas was a sign of intellectual seriousness.

These teachers also had a distinctive approach to choices about time and coverage. Most teachers we saw were highly concerned with what was covered, and would rush or lecture if they worried that they were "falling behind" their expected goals. The teachers featured in this chapter, by contrast, were more concerned with whether students were adopting the habits and dispositions of inquirers in their disciplines. Thus when students became particularly interested in an idea or question, the teachers saw that as a critical opportunity to ignite learning rather than as a threat to subject-coverage goals. For example, a teacher who teaches American history to predominantly poor black and Latinx students in a prominent urban center remembers that he had been taught to teach in what he calls "developmental" lessons, where you ask students a series of questions that leads to a preset destination—whatever points you, the teacher, want to get across about the topic. He remembers clearly that one day a mentor asked him to try something different—it was an elective on popular culture, and the item in question was the Michael Jackson video *Thriller*—by soliciting students' ideas rather than leading them to his planned conclusions about the video. The ensuing discussion had a kind of life and energy that was absent from classes with his previous approach. This discovery became the beginning of a long teaching journey, in which he gradually learned the techniques of how to run a classroom discussion, how to honor students' interests while also integrating core content, and how to balance breadth and depth. As part of this shift, he had found that when students got particularly interested in a subject—such as, for example, the founding fathers and slavery—it served him well to go into those topics in depth, creating opportunities for students to take more ownership over their reading, writing, and analyses.

Ted Sizer once said that "to change anything, you need to change everything."[28] These teachers had taken that point to heart. In particular, they had not created greater purpose or engagement through some magical teaching technique; rather they had changed the pacing and the goals of their courses in ways that were more congenial to their induct-into-the-disciplines approach. Specifically, they had prioritized depth over breadth, they had given students some choice, and they had picked topics that they thought would appeal, in different ways, to the adolescent mind. To create these departures, they had to find ways to buffer themselves from external expectations. Some did this by teaching in the elective curriculum, some did it by moving to schools like MMSA that were supportive of these approaches, while some were simply so beloved by students and parents that they had enough political clout to do things differently. All sought out situations that were not monitored by external tests. Thus while a big part of becoming a compelling teacher was building empowering classrooms with students, an equally important part was creating the political space to redesign their courses.

∽

These teachers show what is possible in high school education. Working in settings ranging from the country's most elite state academies to its highest-poverty urban public schools, they demonstrate how teachers can create spaces that enable students to become knowledgeable, skillful, and deeply invested in the core academic disciplines.

The cases in this chapter also show how difficult it will be to achieve such outcomes. These teachers had each undertaken significant personal journeys to reach their present teaching approaches, involving not only thousands of hours of practice, but also ongoing cycles of reflection and experimentation. Their teaching was not something that could come off the shelf; they hadn't adopted the latest in "best practices." Rather, they had forged consequential identities around the type of teachers they wanted to be, which was connected to their personal evolution and their understanding of their fields. As they had become surer of their footing over the course of their careers, they had become more confident in their visions of what they wanted for students, and had developed wider repertoires of techniques to accomplish those ends. Ultimately, they had discovered ways to create coherent teaching identities that integrated their goals, their pedagogy, and their broader selves.

But if it is true that the teaching identities and skills of these teachers developed only over years, it is also true that they were working within a system that was not supporting, and, in many cases was actively subverting, their growth and development. The paucity of such teachers discovered by our research is itself an indictment of the absence of such systems to generate and nurture this kind of teaching practice. With the exception of the teachers at MMSA, these teachers largely had to figure this out through a long process of trial and error, aided by occasional fortunate infusions of knowledge from friends or experts. In many cases, not only were they not supported by their environments; they also had to actively contravene or buffer the expectations of administrators, district officials, or state tests.

What would it look like to create a different kind of ecosystem of schools? One that was organized in such a way that such teaching could be rule rather than exception? We turn to these questions next.

8 ~

Mastery, Identity, Creativity, and the Future of Schooling

Sᴄʜᴏᴏʟɪɴɢ ᴛᴏᴅᴀʏ seeks a different future, but is heavily constrained by its past. Efforts to create twenty-first-century skills sit uncomfortably on top of a U.S. educational system that, at its foundation, is still employing a late-nineteenth-century grammar of schooling. While the research for this book was conducted in the United States, the dilemma is global—educators and officials in many countries are trying to rethink inherited practices in order to create learners ready to meet the challenges of the modern world. When we offered an executive education program on deeper learning at Harvard in the summer of 2017, the majority of our enrollees were international; they too were searching for ways to integrate rigor with joy, precision with passion, mastery with identity and creativity.

What should we tell them? The lessons from this book are necessarily partial; no one has it all figured out. But what we found, perhaps, was a path forward: we found a series of forays, at the level of classrooms, extracurriculars, clubs, and sometimes whole schools, that, in one way or another, were trying to move away from old realities and toward new and powerful learning environments. American public schools are in the early days of their journey toward deeper learning; old practices are still entrenched in many ways.[1] We have a public system that was founded on the idea of teaching as transmission, and on an industrial model devoted to sorting and batch-processing students. What we witnessed were a series of efforts to break away from those realities and establish something new. But such efforts are themselves embryonic. Different individuals and institutions are beginning to put in place different pieces of the puzzle, but the creation of an integrated whole is still very much a work in progress.[2]

At the same time, a few things became clear to us: across our different powerful learning environments there were important commonalities; among our deeper teachers there was a shared stance and often a remarkably similar journey; and across our successful schools there was a common set of elements that allowed them to translate espoused visions into enacted practices. There was also agreement on the ways in which the broader system was inhibiting efforts to enact deeper learning. To this end, many of our most successful examples (electives, clubs, extracurriculars, charter schools) were in some ways buffered from the external system and its current demands. Thus the critical questions became: *What would it take to make the exception the rule? How might we create a system where it wouldn't be necessary to work against the grain to be successful?*

In the pages that follow, we take up these questions. Our thesis can be captured in one sentence: *We need to change student learning, so we need to change schools, so we need to change systems.* We advance this argument by working outward in concentric circles. We begin by exploring what we learned about the nature of powerful learning experiences. Then we turn to teachers and teaching, asking what kinds of preparation and career trajectories they would need to lead such experiences. Then we move to schools, considering what kinds of leadership, culture, norms, processes, and organizational designs they would need to support such learning for both students and teachers. Finally, we move outward to the system level, considering how we might remake policies and structures to support such work closer to the ground. We include a discussion of politics and values because the question of whether or how to transform our country's schools is not in the end a technical one, but one related at its core to how we see the purpose of education.

What follows is not intended as an all-or-nothing proposition. While we lay out the changes that would need to happen at each level to create a system oriented toward deep learning, individual teachers, administrators, schools, teacher-preparation institutions, and others can take some concrete steps in this direction without waiting for wholesale system change. The United States has more than 13,000 districts and almost 100,000 public schools within a fairly decentralized system of governance. This frustrates those who desire rapid and centralized change, but it also creates opportunities for a deeper-learning agenda to flourish in different corners as it acquires local political support.[3] We can well imagine the change looking more like a social movement or an Othello board, where, as some places flip toward deeper learning, momentum builds for similar change in surrounding classrooms, schools, or districts.

The Nature of Powerful Learning Environments

Across the variety of settings that we studied, some clear commonalities emerged among those learning environments that students and teachers described as the most powerful. In all of these environments, learning started with a purpose—something that was not preparation for life later but could grab the interest of a young person in the present. Students were treated as producers, that is, as people who could offer interpretations, solve problems, develop products of value, and otherwise create in ways consistent with the norms of the field or discipline. Subjects were treated as open-ended rather than closed; there was a belief that what students were discovering or creating had significant value, not that knowledge had been previously discovered and needed only to be transmitted. Students were invited to "play the whole game at a junior level"—that is, while there were opportunities to work in depth on particular subsections, students were immersed in whole projects, such as putting on a production, designing experiments, or engaging in mathematical problem-solving. While traditional classes used an "I do / we do / you do" formula, powerful learning environments gradually transferred ownership of the process of learning itself. Such a shift could empower students either individually or in small groups—as in the projects at Dewey High, or the self-paced organic chemistry modules or design projects at Attainment High—or it could empower the group collectively, as in Mr. Fields's philosophy classes, Harkness tables at Exeter, or the student production team in *Servant of Two Masters*. While traditional classes often had only two roles— teacher and student—powerful learning environments built communities of learners in which students could teach as well as learn, capitalizing on both the distributed expertise that exists in any group of learners and the motivational benefits of peer-to-peer learning. These powerful learning environments were also cognitively challenging. "This is the class that makes my brain hurt" was a refrain we heard more than once. At the same time, they were also passionate places where the passion sustained students' motivation when the learning was hard. To enable these experiences, the teachers had carefully built communities that were challenging yet vulnerable, where students sought to give their best but were willing to be wrong.

Such environments also tended to mobilize two very different sets of virtues. In their emphasis on intrinsic motivation, creativity, and student empowerment, these environments evoked liberal or romantic virtues—and, in so doing, stayed consistent with the Rousseauian metaphor of learning as more "igniting a fire" than "filling a container." At the same time, these were places that emphasized classical virtues. They had real standards for learning and emphasized the importance of practice, revision, and repetition to get work exactly right. Whether it was Mr. Simmons having students move forward in organic chemistry only after they had shown complete command of the previous unit, students developing draft after draft of their projects at Dewey High in preparation for public exhibitions, or the *Servant* production team patiently refining the angle of an actor's foot, there was a fierce attention to detail and an insistence on mastery.

In other words, the most powerful learning experiences we observed were neither at the progressive pole of self-guided learning nor at the conservative extreme of direct instruction. Rather, they assumed the model of apprenticeship or induction, in which students became motivated by a domain and worked to develop or make something within that domain, but did so under the watchful eye of expert mentors.[4] Our findings are consistent with two recent syntheses of decades of work on project-based learning and problem-based or inquiry-oriented learning, both of which find that such modes can have strongly positive results if (and only if) they are organized with appropriate scaffolding and necessary direction from more knowledgeable others.[5] John Hattie's meta-analysis of practices aligned with effective teaching similarly emphasizes a number of the elements that we identify here, including the importance of feedback, deliberate practice, and scaffolding.[6]

In emphasizing this duality, we seek to integrate two very different traditions of school commentary. On the one hand, this study builds on a long lineage of progressive figures—from J. M. Rice in the 1890s to John Goodlad in the 1980s—who at different points over the past 120 years have similarly argued that schools are unnecessarily stultifying places where textbooks, bell schedules, and the view of teaching as transmission cut students off from the enlivening possibilities of learning. On the other hand, this study also draws from work on expertise (which emphasizes practice and feedback from knowledgeable others); the notion that fields possess standards that guide the creation of good work (we can see this in IB, among other places); and the old-fashioned idea that things of quality can be produced only through significant amounts of hard work, practice, and revision. In so doing, we offer a bridge across ideological divides, and suggest that powerful learning environments integrate elements from what are frequently seen as opposed positions.[7]

We also suggest that deep learning accrues over time through an upward spiral of mastery, identity, and creativity. Our argument is that there is a cycle that integrates developing one's knowledge and skill in a domain (mastery), becoming deeply and personally invested in that domain (identity), and trying to make or do something fresh in that domain rather than simply receiving knowledge passively (creativity). Over time, students play the "whole game" at more and more complex levels, participating in the same activities but at increasing levels of sophistication. We saw this clearly in our observations of extracurricular activities; a similar theory of learning was at work in project-based schools that emphasized multiple cycles of revision as students worked toward a culminating project.

It is also important to name what we are *not* arguing. As should be apparent, deep learning is not synonymous with student-centered learning, project-based learning, blended learning, or competency-based learning. These are modalities of learning that can be either deep or shallow in practice. We think of mastery, identity, and creativity as rather stringent criteria against which particular learning experiences can be evaluated. In advancing this argument, we are seeking to give some teeth to what it means to learn "deeply," creating a demanding standard to which students, teachers, and other stakeholders can aspire.

Expanding a Parallel "Grammar" of Schooling

Our adoption of an apprenticeship perspective also sheds light on why we found electives and extracurriculars to be such promising platforms for learning. David Tyack and Larry Cuban have powerfully argued that the core "grammar" of schooling—featuring teaching as transmission, age-graded classrooms, short blocks—is not hospitable to powerful modes of learning.[8] But what Tyack and Cuban missed is that in high schools there is a second, parallel grammar that many students are experiencing every day, one with many characteristics that make it promising for learning: purpose, choice, community, interdependent roles, learning with heart and hands as well as head, apprenticeship, and the "whole game at the junior level." While books like *The Adolescent Society* and *The Shopping Mall High School* have faulted the periphery for distracting students from the academic core, our account suggests that the core might have much to learn from the periphery when it comes to organizing learning experiences.

Part of what makes this parallel "grammar" so promising is that it connects to longer and older traditions of learning, particularly traditions of apprenticeship. Efforts to transform learning in core disciplines to make students more active learners date only to Dewey and his disciples beginning a century ago, and, as we have seen, these efforts have proceeded in fits and starts, never having been really tried on any scale in public schools. By contrast, learning in theater and debate goes back at least to the Greeks, and thus we have millennia of aggregated knowledge about how best to prepare aspiring actors or debaters to enact their craft. These traditions are unambiguous that learning must happen through doing, that trying and failing is a necessary part of improvement, and that coaching and feedback from more skilled others is critical for learning. These fields have also developed structures that create rhythm to the learning, a set of roles that are endemic to the field, and a technical language that allows people to communicate with precision, all of which are linked to the adult work that it emulates. These characteristics either do not exist or are less developed when it comes to the teaching of core disciplinary subjects; that area has much catching up to do if it is to provide the same kind of infrastructure that supports peripheral modes of learning.

Recognizing the importance of extracurriculars also has important equity implications. Opportunities to participate in these arenas are unequally distributed; low-income students are three times as likely as their non-poor counterparts "to participate in neither sports nor clubs" (30 percent versus 10 percent); some research suggests that this gap is widening over time in concert with growing income inequality.[9] In the high-poverty school where we studied debate, it was the only non-sports extracurricular offered, in contrast to the vast array of options at Attainment High. Our research suggests that equalizing opportunities to powerful learning experiences across race and class lines requires paying significant attention to inequities in these peripheral spaces as well as to inequities in core academic classes.

Unlearning and Double Loop Learning

Our study also suggests that achieving these challenging integrations will require as much *unlearning* as learning. For traditional comprehensive high schools, it will be impossible to realize powerful learning environments without giving something up. For example, the rush of teaching and testing for enormous amounts of content in various subjects, with all that entails, would need be to be rethought if the goal were to give students a deeper learning experience in those subjects. Such a goal would also require teachers to rethink what are, for some, fundamental aspects of their identities, moving from deliverers of content and repositories of knowledge to skillful facilitators of deep explorations into particular domains.

Schools that are committed to particular thematic approaches—exemplified by Dewey High's commitment to projects and No Excuses High's emphasis on traditional modes of achievement—gain part of their collective identity not only by what they are but also by what they are not. This can make it difficult to incorporate part of the other into their approach. These schools tend to be good at what Chris Argyris called "single loop learning," which he defines as getting better *within* one's existing paradigms and goals.[10] So, for example, we once visited a no-excuses school and asked the leader what the school was working on, and he said, "Our scholars are using forty-four of the forty-nine minutes of a period productively; we'd like to get that up to forty-seven minutes." This is textbook single loop learning. But what our schools were gradually realizing was that they needed to engage in what Argyris calls "double loop learning," which requires questioning fundamental goals and paradigms. At No Excuses High, school leaders realized that their overwhelming emphasis on control strategies was inhibiting their students' ability to function in the more open-ended environments of college, so they were trying to incorporate more self-directed and project-based learning. Conversely, at Dewey High, teachers and administrators were realizing that sometimes they were struggling to ensure that foundational skills were being built through students' projects, and that conventional data should not be considered a four-letter word. Noticing and naming these absences was one thing, but really taking them on was quite another because much of the worldview of these schools—their existing systems, culture, and organizational DNA—was bound to a seemingly ironclad set of commitments. Change thus requires significant undoing and unlearning.

At the same time, while such changes will undoubtedly be difficult, achieving these integrations is arguably the central challenge for schools and even entire educational systems moving forward. As we progressed through our travels, we found that people were increasingly aware of the limitations of approaches that emphasized only one side of the coin: no-excuses networks are now building schools that they hope will result in more empowered and self-directed learners; East Asian nations that have been leading the PISA rankings are now interested in whether they are taking care of their students' mental health and whether they are sufficiently fostering creativity; and conversely, project-based and competency-based networks beyond Dewey High are beginning to recognize the importance of continuous improvement and careful skill-building, especially if such schools are to realize their aspirations with respect to equity. We are also encouraged that there seems to be more dialogue across different models. When we began the study in 2010, most schools were talking to counterparts similar to themselves; by 2018, many were involved in networks that crossed pedagogical divides. If we are not simply to continue the pendulum-swinging nature of reform, bringing together these opposing qualities will be critical to achieving lasting success.

Deeper Teaching

While the schools and networks in our study generally struggled to integrate these qualities, we did find a number of skillful teachers who were able to create powerful learning experiences for their students, and who share some common characteristics:

- Significant and substantive knowledge of their disciplines or fields;
- A view of these disciplines or fields as open-ended rather than closed;
- High levels of pedagogical knowledge in their preferred approach to teaching;
- A stance toward teaching as an act of igniting interest rather than as an act of transmission;
- One or more "seminal learning experiences" in their pasts that caused them to view their domains, their students, and their purpose, in this fashion.

Truly knowing their subjects was critical to these teachers. It gave them the deep understanding that they were trying to give to their students; it made them comfortable with ambiguity and not having all the answers because they were fundamentally secure in their control of their field; and their passion for their subject engendered student passion for those same fields. Further, the seminal learning experiences often came in their junior or senior years of college or in graduate school. Moving beyond survey courses and actually doing their discipline were key in helping them to understand how knowledge is created. That, in turn, helped them to induct students into a fellowship of people who are part of a given discipline.

Thus while Dan Lortie was right that the lengthy apprenticeship of observation that future teachers undergo as students is perhaps the most important impediment to significant change in teaching, he missed that the opposite can also be true; future teachers' best experiences (in school, college, or even graduate school) can be the launching point for a different kind of teaching.[11] Prospective teachers experience dozens of teachers over the course of their lives, but they are not all equally influential; even one really good experience can provide the spark for what teachers are trying to accomplish. Again, an apprenticeship perspective is helpful here; all of our most compelling group had been apprenticed by their own most valued teachers into a way of being that they then sought to pass on to their students.

A related point is that what characterized these teachers was a specific and particular *stance*, which was connected to their own disciplinary or field-specific identities. Their stance encompassed a number of related ideas—that inspiring charges to become members of the field was more important than "covering the material" and so depth was more important than breadth; that students could construct as well as receive knowledge; that historically marginalized students could achieve in powerful ways if given the chance; that failure was a critical part of learning; and that discovering how to engage in the overarching processes of a field was more important than the acquisition of any particular piece of knowledge. These stances were born both out of their own experiences in doing the work of their fields and out of their experiences with students, which reconfirmed for them that orienting their teaching in this direction would serve their charges well in the long run. Given that the systems that they were in did not prioritize these ends, these teachers had to make what Robert Kegan calls a "subject to object" shift—in other words, they had to move from being subject to the expectations of the current system to a stance in which they took the existing system as "object" and made their own decisions about whether expected practices and goals would truly support their students' learning. In the case of AP teachers, for example, the shift highlighted the difference between teachers who "taught to the test," and teachers who had their own goals for the subject matter, saw the test as one constraint in their designs, and then developed units that both met their goals and enabled their students to pass the tests.

The importance of stance and teachers' disciplinary identities complicates Lee Shulman's famous formulation that good teaching involves substantive knowledge, pedagogical knowledge, and pedagogical content knowledge.[12] These realms of knowledge are critically important, but our research suggests that good teaching also needs to be anchored in a clear vision of what the work of the relevant discipline or field actually looks like, as well as in the conviction that students (including disadvantaged students) are capable sense-makers who can engage in such work. There is again a parallel here to student learning: much as was true for students' powerful learning, forging this kind of teaching identity brings together the cognitive and affective in a powerful way that can fundamentally orient and shape teachers' trajectories.

How might we more consistently engender these qualities in our teachers? As we have seen, content knowledge is crucial, thus a critical starting point is to reduce "out-of-field" teaching by making every effort to ensure that teachers teach the subjects they actually studied in college. Our research expands on this point: it shows that teachers need not only to know the subjects they teach, but also to have had some experience actually doing the work of their fields or disciplines (much as teachers in the periphery had experiences in their domains). The implication is that teacher preparation programs should work with disciplinary departments to help their students have real experiences doing science in labs, writing history based on primary research and original documents, and in other ways immersing themselves in doing the work of the fields that they aspire to teach. Much as Finnish teachers have to complete a research thesis as part of their training, it would be good if prospective American high school teachers similarly had to produce research—one project focused on an educational problem, overseen by education school faculty, and one piece of disciplinary research in their fields, overseen by faculty in the disciplines. For those aiming to teach less classically academic subjects, such as modern instantiations of vocational education, we would expect that they would spend time similarly apprenticing in real-world equivalents. The core principle here is not that teachers need to become more academic, but rather that they need to immerse themselves in the real-world versions of the subjects they aspire to teach, which, depending on the domain, may or may not sit within the university.

With this substantive knowledge in place, the next question concerns how teachers learn how to teach. The most compelling teachers in our sample had a median experience level of fifteen years. In part this is unavoidable, because it takes time to accrue skill.[13] But these teachers also described very long periods of trial and error, in which their transmission mode of teaching had to be gradually undone and replaced by a different mode of pedagogy. The example of Mr. Martin, the first-year math teacher who had spent a year co-teaching with one of the strongest teachers in our sample, suggests that this learning trajectory might be greatly accelerated if new teachers were apprenticed to master teachers. This relationship was successful in part because it was true co-teaching—the two teachers planned together, taught together, and debriefed together, with the ratio of teaching gradually shifting more to the newer teacher over time. Consistent with our emphasis on apprenticeship as a powerful mechanism for learning, this example suggests that teachers will best learn to teach from other teachers.

Formalizing this idea, in the past decade we have seen the creation of a number of teacher residency programs in cities around the country. Modeled on medical residencies, the idea is that all new teachers should spend one year being carefully trained by master teachers. As in the math case described earlier (which was part of a teacher residency), there is a gradual transfer of responsibility from the veteran to the new teacher as the new teacher shows that she can handle different aspects of teaching. Studies have shown that residency programs can have positive effects on teacher retention and teacher quality, and help fill shortages in hard-to-staff subjects.[14] A recent report from the National Commission on Teaching and America's Future (of which Mehta is a member) called for every new teacher to complete one year in a residency program.[15]

If such residency programs provide promising *containers* for teacher training, our research suggests that it is what happens inside these containers that shapes whether or not teachers learn to teach in ways that challenge, engage, and empower students. In particular, it is important that these residencies take a specific stand on the nature of good instruction, emphasizing the qualities of the powerful learning environments that we have described here. The recent movement toward developing high-leverage practices for teacher education that support "ambitious" instruction in a variety of disciplines is a step in this direction, because it is granular, concrete, and inquiry-based in its vision of good instruction.[16] At the same time, these practices need to become not ends in themselves, but ways of actualizing broader stances toward teaching. Our research suggests that helping teachers reflect on and understand the reasons for these stances (particularly the shift away from teaching as transmission and toward students as junior-level participants in their fields) is critical if teachers are going to stand for deeper learning and teaching.[17]

This vision, in turn, needs to guide the selection of master teachers and, when possible, the schools into which new teachers are placed. Part of the challenge for an apprenticeship vision of deeper instruction is that most teachers don't teach this way, so having existing teachers apprentice new teachers into inherited ways of doing things will produce only more of the same. Thus residency programs need to be selective in their choice of master teachers; this generation's exceptional teachers need to train what we hope will become the new normal of the next.[18]

Deeper Schools

While there is currently much interest in the preparation of teachers, learning how to teach "deeply" will not happen in a year. It is also not reasonable to assume that new teachers, no matter how well prepared, can change the institutions they enter. Thus a commitment to training teachers in new ways, if it is to succeed, needs to be coupled with the building of different types of schools. Deeper schools may also need to rethink the grammar of schooling to give students more purpose, more choice, more community, and other qualities that have proven intrinsic to deeper learning experiences.

What would such schools look like, and how might they be organized? Part of what motivated this project was that there was writing about effective schools, writing about "ambitious" teaching, but little to nothing on "ambitious schools." We set out to fill this gap, but answers were elusive. We found that most schools were not consistently able to enact a vision, any vision, because they lacked the organizational mechanisms that would enable such change. In addition, the schools we found that did have some consistency in their practices often were better at realizing some goals of learning than others.

As far as we can tell, then, there appear to be a series of mechanisms that are critical for mounting an ambitious program of instruction (the how), but those elements need to be tied to a thick vision of powerful learning that integrates rigor and joy (the what). Thus, if we were to advise a future school leader who wanted to build a deeper learning school, we would suggest that he or she define a vision of learning in ways that are consistent with our earlier description of the "nature of powerful learning environments," then enact that vision using the mechanisms described below.

With respect to the "how," there were some shared characteristics of those schools that, regardless of their vision, had discovered how to turn their espoused values into enacted practices. They were:

1. *A specific and granular vision of good instruction*, which was the north star to which everything was oriented;
2. *Thick mechanisms for adult learning*, which enabled all adults in the building to learn together how to achieve this vision;
3. *Symmetry*, that is, the ways in which adults worked with and learned from one another paralleled the ways in which they hoped students would learn;
4. *Visibility*, which means that student work (and by implication, teachers' teaching) was public and shared, which both de-privatized teaching and created some collective accountability around the enactment of the instructional vision;
5. *A collective identity* that connected to the instructional vision and anchored student and faculty commitment to this way of working; and
6. *An organizational design* that aligned all structures in support of the instructional vision.[19]

In comparison to the "effective schools" correlates, these elements are much more instructionally tied, and together form an intricate web that can support the enactment of an instructional vision.

Having these elements helped schools move away from the classroom-to-classroom variation we saw in the vast majority of schools we visited. By defining a granular instructional vision, the schools featured in earlier chapters were able to have highly specific conversations about the nature of good instruction and about what more and less rigorous versions of this instruction would look like. By creating thick mechanisms for adult learning, they helped to de-privatize teaching, countering the phenomenon we saw in other schools whereby teachers knew that other teachers were doing great work but had no access to understanding how and why they were doing what they did. Symmetry, that is, the mirroring of the school's values in the design of leadership and adult learning, was a particularly key ingredient. In one sense, all schools we visited were symmetrical: in schools where administrators controlled and distrusted teachers, teachers controlled and distrusted students; in schools where administrators empowered teachers and treated them as designers (as at Dewey High), teachers more often treated students as capable and thoughtful human beings. While we came to think that symmetry was simply a natural property of schools as social institutions, skillful leaders regarded their work with faculty as opportunities to model the kinds of interactions they hoped the teachers would have with their students. Symmetry was also important in a more specific sense: teachers can't teach in ways that they themselves have not experienced, and thus the most skilled school leaders used professional learning time to give teachers the kinds of learning experiences that they hoped teachers would recreate in their classrooms.

The fourth element—visibility of student work—was another mechanism to de-privatize the classroom and to act as a check on the rigor of what was being produced. At Dewey High, this came in the form of public exhibition of projects. Seeing the work of one's students and one's colleagues' students not only exerted some modest pressure for performance but also promoted collective dialogue among faculty about the nature of high-quality student work. International Baccalaureate exams played a similar role at IB High, creating a common scaffold and anchor that situated the collective work of the faculty. Building a collective identity—at Dewey High around projects, at IB High around making IB possible for non-elite students, and at No Excuses High around closing the achievement gap—was critical to sustaining motivation, purpose, and energy at these schools. Finally, these schools were meticulously designed to bring all elements of their structure into alignment; everything from hiring to teacher development to assessment flowed from these schools' instructional vision and overall purpose. In contrast, at most schools we visited, some elements (such as the teacher evaluation system) were grossly misaligned with other elements (for example, the professional learning strategy).

In the case of large comprehensive schools, it may be unrealistic to expect the kind of thoroughgoing alignment around a single instructional vision that we saw at small charter schools. In these larger schools, the department can be the right vehicle for deepening instruction.[20] But what such disciplinary groupings need to do at a departmental level is largely the same as what certain smaller schools were doing schoolwide.

The math department at Attainment High, for example, set a specific and granular vision of instruction, particular to itself, focusing on mathematical practices it wanted students to develop, drawing in large part on Common Core expectations. Because a state assessment based on the Common Core had not yet been developed, the department couldn't teach to a test. Instead, they had to work together to define how the broader Common Core standards would translate to curriculum and teaching, a need that provided a rich opportunity for dialogue and learning. Over time, many in the department became enthusiastic about this work and began to draw boundaries between the new ways of doing math and their older approaches. In so doing, they developed a collective identity that built motivation and also tied the department to the larger community of math educators and researchers moving toward reform. There also was a strong and aligned organizational design to this work, because the department introduced the new approach in ninth grade and gradually carried it through the later years.

Cross-cutting these mechanisms was the *culture* of the schools. Powerful learning environments that we observed in electives, extracurriculars, and core classes had an ethos in which student risk-taking was the norm, productive struggle was expected, and failure was embraced as a critical part of learning. Schools that prioritized these qualities in a symmetrical way in classrooms created a similar culture for teachers, in which they could make decisions and take risks. Failure was seen not as a dereliction of duty but as a critical part of learning and growth. Especially if the goal is for teachers to work in a mode different from the one in which they have been working, creating a culture that supports such unlearning and learning is critical.[21] With that culture often comes a flat organizational structure in which decision-making is shared among faculty; there is a recognition that the wisdom of the group creates a much stronger platform for learning than knowledge flowing top-down from the center. Such a culture also brings with it a changed attitude toward students, whose ideas, interests, and capabilities are to be respected, and who should participate in making some decisions about their education and their schools. Schools like No Excuses High, which began, in their history and organizational imprint, with a very different set of assumptions—emphasizing hierarchy, control, and fear of failure—would need to undergo a significant process of unlearning if they are going to shift from one cultural and structural mode to another.

Finally, there is no substitute for a mature set of humanistic values that adults model and that guide key decisions at the school.[22] IB High, for example, sought a tricky balance that would enable it to be a school that was highly committed to equity and yet not all-consumed by scores on IB exams. Holding this balance was what made the school what it was. On the one hand, had its leaders fallen into the trap of many other schools, by trying simply to maximize scores, they would have increased the test-prep focus and drained much of the intellectual vitality from the school. On the other hand, had they not been so committed to equity, reducing the focus on outcomes could have significantly lowered standards and increased inequality. More generally, having adults who really cared about their students, who knew when to push and when to support, was critical to the success of all the good schools that we encountered.

Reimagining the Grammar of Schooling

These organizational elements, when cross-cut by a strong and clear vision of what deeper learning means, can enable the creation of a deeper school that works *within* the current grammar of schooling. IB High is the best example in our sample. There, a pedagogical vision organized around inquiry-based instruction, an external measurement system oriented toward deeper competencies, a strong learning culture for adults, and a commitment to equity enabled the school to create a culture of thinking and respect for student ideas that was truly impressive. For many schools, then, this could be a model for how to create deeper learning schoolwide without making fundamental changes to subject areas, age-graded classrooms, boundaries between schools and their external communities, and other taken-for-granted aspects of schooling.

At the same time, peeking through in examples from Dewey High at its best, in some of the electives at Attainment High, in clubs and extracurriculars, and in certain other schools that have been profiled in the literature, is a different way of organizing learning experiences. In the interests of pushing the envelope, we will present such a vision in its full-blown form. But one can also regard what follows as options on a continuum. School leaders might keep much of what they have in place but try some of these ideas with one grade level, or they might preserve a disciplinary approach to math while adopting an interdisciplinary approach in the humanities. Thus, while we will present a different grammar of schooling as a full-blown alternative, it could be adopted in pieces and married to a more conventional structure.

Central to this vision are a set of presumptions about students, development, and learning that were shared across these environments but are often not present in traditional schooling. The first presumption understands students as purposeful, curious, capable beings who have interests that can be developed and who value being treated as responsible people. Consequently, for education in this mode to work, students need some choice and agency over their learning, coupled with guidance from more experienced students and adults. While agency and choice are important, we cannot lose sight of the fact that adolescents fundamentally are seeking *community*, people with whom they can both learn and relate. This priority leads to the further presumption: that powerful learning is fundamentally about *connections*—between students and teachers, between students and other students, between students' selves and the subjects they are studying, between subjects and other subjects, between students and out-of-school mentors, between subjects and their applications in the world beyond school. Such learning is also dynamic and responsive to the surrounding world—each year, the world is a little different, and thus slightly different things will seem important to students and teachers. Clubs respond to such shifts by growing and changing, but subjects often seem frozen in place. Finally, all of these presumptions need to be made about adults as well as students—adults need purpose in their work, they need both choice and community, they need time to work with one another and to connect with knowledgeable others beyond school walls, and they need an opportunity to revise as fields evolve, as the world changes, and as new ideas become salient.

While some teachers can realize these ends within regular classes, for an institution to achieve them schoolwide and on a consistent basis would require significant changes to the grammar of schooling. Such a re-envisioning would begin with defining a clearer sense of the purpose of a powerful education, and move from there to making changes in roles, time, space, assessment, and a variety of other dimensions of schooling (see Table 8.1).

Table 8.1 Reimagining the Grammar of Schooling

	Existing grammar of schooling	New grammar of schooling
Purpose	Assimilate preexisting content	Engage student as producer in variety of fields and worthy human pursuits
View of knowledge	Siloed and fixed	Constructed, interconnected, and dynamic
Learning modality	Teaching as transmission	Learning through doing; apprenticeship; whole game at junior level
Roles	One teacher, many students	Vertically integrated communities: teachers, students as teachers, and field members providing expertise
Boundaries between disciplines	Strong	Permeable
Boundaries between school and world	Strong	Permeable
Places where students learn	Schools	Various, including schools, community centers, field sites, online
Choice	Limited	Open, multiple
Time	Short blocks of fixed length	Longer, variable blocks, time for immersive experiences
Space	Individual classrooms	Linked spaces, variable spaces
Assessment	Seat time, standardized tests	Creation of worthy products in the domain: projects, portfolios, performances, research
Organizational model	Linear, top-down planning	Distributed leadership; spirals of inquiry
Stance toward community	Defensive; keeping out	Welcoming; inviting in

Central to this rethinking would be a determination to break down the barriers we put around learning. A conventional classroom in a disciplinary subject (say, biology) is cut off from people who do that discipline in the world (biologists), from students in older grades who might know more about the subject, from adults other than the teacher who are knowledgeable about that field, from the knowledge about the subject that isn't prescribed by the teacher, and from work in related disciplines that would inform the subject.

In a revamped vision of schooling, students would be connected to various sources of learning. The central image we have in mind, borrowed from the arts, athletics, graduate school, and the world of work, is what we think of as a *vertically integrated community*, in which the purpose is clear, the need for the learner to produce is a driving force, learners master more and more complex skills by being in a community of people who have those skills, and apprenticeship is a primary mode of learning.[23] Such communities have the advantage of engendering the different virtues needed for serious learning: opportunities for practice and oversight from more knowledgeable others build mastery; engagement in the domain and gradually becoming an effective producer in the domain build identity, and the need to make real products for real audiences unleashes creativity. Over time, as students engage with increasingly sophisticated communities of people who are doing what they want to learn, they deepen their understanding and ability to act in those domains. Animating this approach are two core ideas: first, that knowledge exists in an interconnected web to which students should have access; and second, that gradually inducting students into apprenticeship-based communities is a powerful way to encourage the creation of passionate and skilled learners. It is our view that, together, these ideas could be the foundation of a revamped grammar of schooling.

How might we organize schools with these ideas in mind? Imagine a statistics strand curated by an adult at the school in which students analyzed statistical claims in the news, sampled from college lectures or essays on the manipulative use of numbers to further political agendas, did mini-lessons on key statistical topics (either taught by the teacher or organized into self-paced modules), then developed a project that used statistical analysis to explore a topic of interest. Some students within this statistics strand might dual-enroll in a college statistics course, others might intern with a local pro team to see how analytics are being used in sports, and still others might intern at a government agency to see how statistics are employed there. A humanities teacher might help them think about who gets to construct statistics, how they have been used, and to what end, with a particular focus on the relationship between numbers and power. There could be a presentation day when students and their mentors would come together to discuss the uses of statistics in these various arenas. Such an approach would show students the many tributaries into which statistics runs, meet the students' differing interests and abilities where they are, encourage students to reflect critically on the role of numbers in society, ask them to use this learning to produce something that matters to them, and connect students to academic or real-world uses of numbers to deepen their mathematical and/or practical understanding of statistics.

While bringing together all of these elements is beyond what most schools have thus far tried, we did come across models that have implemented some of these ideas. For example, to the degree that schools want to retain disciplines as their primary units of study, some have connected to colleges to show students what happens when people produce knowledge in those subjects. For example, at the Midwestern Math and Science Academy, students spend half of every Wednesday working in college laboratories. While arranging this is not easy—buses have to be chartered, professors and doctoral students have to be vetted to ensure they give the high school students real work and follow through on their commitments—it does show students what actual science is. No Excuses High does something similar by placing students in nearby labs, showing that such an approach need not be limited to highly selective schools. Early College High Schools offer a systematic way of pursuing such a vision, enabling high school students to enroll in college courses while still in high school; evaluations of this program suggest that it has had a large impact in increasing college enrollment.[24]

Rethinking the grammar of schooling also creates opportunities for interdisciplinary or even transdisciplinary study. Most high school students are not enthralled with the disciplines per se; rather, they are more interested in questions in the world that draw on disciplines to answer them. Project-based schools already have a good model for this—schools like Dewey High help students find consequential questions, have them leave the school to investigate them, and then produce artifacts that they hope will matter to real audiences.[25] One central challenge here, as we stressed in our chapter on Dewey High, is to develop and sustain serious standards of quality to guide the work. The best projects often involve considerable feedback from experts in the relevant fields—as was true of some of the most successful design projects at Attainment High—which can help to integrate the standards of the broader field into the work of the school and the minds of students.

Such a recharged educational vision would also create opportunities for many more types of institutions and adults to offer learning experiences to students. Architectural firms, hospitals, community centers, design studios, artists' collaboratives, museums, theaters, and many more institutions might be potential sites for student learning. For example, the Philadelphia Science and Leadership Academy, a school in which 70 percent of students are of color and 50 percent are eligible for free or reduced-price lunch, partners with the Franklin Institute, a world-renowned science museum named after Benjamin Franklin, to have students take "mini-courses" taught by Franklin Institute scholars on a range of scientific topics, including astronomy, computer programming, and project design. The students use the museum's enormous resources to do hands-on work and further their studies in different domains.[26] At the MC² STEM school in Cleveland, a partnership with General Electric enables students to work alongside scientists, engineers, and managers to build robots, solar-powered phone chargers, and other products that connect theory and practice in physics.[27] Exactly what partnerships are possible depends on the specific location and context of the school, but the core principles are the same.

Such an approach should also give students more choice about what it is they want to learn and where they want to learn it. If becoming interested in a domain is a necessary ingredient for sustained study and learning, giving students some choice over what and where they study is a critical first step. At Avalon Charter School, a teacher-run school in Minnesota, the school year starts by asking ninth graders "What do you want to learn?" and "What would you like to do better?"; the year's curricula are then developed from those questions.[28] At the I School in New York, students nominate and rank elective topics; then faculty rank which of those they would be interested in teaching. Electives for the following year sit at the intersection of student and faculty interests. In addition to such on-site opportunities, as MOOCs and other online courses continue to expand, there will be opportunities for interested students to study a much more varied set of subjects than traditionally has been offered in school. Teachers' responsibilities in these instances would be to use their adult judgment to assist students in choosing among potential options, to help them process what they are taking in through such courses, and, as needed, to scaffold the learning in ways that connect where students are to what is being offered online.

Reorganizing the role of time is another important part of this equation.[29] Many private high schools and some public high schools have moved to a schedule where students study three to four subjects for ninety minutes at a time, rather than retaining the seven forty-five-minute blocks per day that were the norm. Other schools have moved to create periods of time during the year (two- to three-week blocks) during which students work intensively on only one topic, enabling concentrated effort and creating opportunities to go off campus for field-embedded or project-based learning.[30] A more ambitious version of this idea is to send students to other parts of the country or, ideally, to other countries to get to know different cultures and to complete a service project with members of the receiving community. Doing so would encourage students to build both civic and global skills, improve their second-language abilities, and see beyond the borders of their local communities and their nation.

Assessment would also shift. Rather than evaluating students on seat time in conventional classes or on the results of standardized tests, the goal would be to evaluate students on the basis of their performance in domain-specific arenas. The "assessment" of the students in *The Servant of Two Masters* was their show night; the assessment of students who produce the student newspaper is the quality of that newspaper; the assessment of project-based learning is the quality of the final artifact that is presented or performed. In the more conventional academic disciplines, we might require that for high school graduation a student needs to produce one substantial piece of work in the natural sciences, the humanities, and the social sciences. A social science "thesis," for example, would require students to review the literature, develop hypotheses, create a strategy for data gathering, collect and analyze the data, write up an argument, and reflect on limitations. If a student could successfully achieve a product of that magnitude in the social sciences, and equivalent ones in the natural sciences and the humanities, he or she would have demonstrated significant familiarity with the tools and methods of three broad modes of inquiry that shape how we understand the world.

A renewed vision of schooling would also include a different approach to how space is used within a school.[31] The way space is currently organized reifies many of the most regressive tendencies of industrial schooling: each teacher is alone in a classroom of twenty to thirty-five students, with limited opportunities for collaboration or flexible group-ings. A whole field of twenty-first-century school design is emerging that seeks to organize space in ways that would parallel the future of learning.[32] Proposed innovations include creating rooms of varying sizes to accommodate different learning modalities, using glass walls to preserve some privacy while also integrating classrooms into the broader environment, and building "hubs" that link different classrooms and promote exchanges of both student and teacher learning. Movable partitions can also enable two classes to come together (say for project-based or interdisciplinary blocks) but be separated for other learning modalities. Some of the best learning spaces we visited intentionally sought to soften the institutional feel of schooling by using rugs, lamps, beanbag chairs, and other warm touches to make classrooms feel personal and welcoming. While there are certainly examples of unin-spired, stultifying learning experiences set in beautiful physical spaces, the development of a new space can spark a discussion about what kind of teaching and learning a school is seeking, and how a new space can support new collaborations and learning goals.

All of these changes in what students experience would need to be paralleled in changes to the work of teachers. For example, schools would need to give teachers some choice over their teaching and learning, opportunities to collaborate both with one another and with outside sources of knowledge, methods of assessment of their work consistent with the highest standards of their domain, and so forth. Perhaps the most critical ingredients here are time and symmetry. American teachers teach more and have much less time to plan with their colleagues than do their counterparts in other nations.[33] If we are asking teachers to change their routines and develop quite dif-ferent new practices, we need to give them substantial time to work together to develop such practices, or any initial momentum will be quickly lost. Teachers, especially newer teachers, also need fewer "preps" (classes to prepare each day) which would enable them to work in more depth on each class. On symmetry, if teachers are going to create an environment in which students are treated as capable agents whose views should be respected and whose interests should be devel-oped, they need to experience an equivalent level of consideration and a similarly welcoming and respectful environment in the schools that employ them.

As schools move in this direction, they will need to be attentive to maintaining the critical qualities of mastery, identity, and creativity. It is quite possible to place students in real-world settings where they are not doing interesting work, to create interdisciplinary learning that is shallow rather than deep, to create projects where students learn much about the part and nothing about the whole. Relaxing the grammar of schooling creates a more varied set of containers, a potentially more transformative set of educational possibilities, but whether that potential is realized still depends heavily on what happens inside those containers. Teachers and school leaders need to be vigilant about the quality of the reimagined experiences they put forward if a changed grammar is actually going to translate into improvements in students' quality of learning.

The Politics

A major part of the challenge of building deeper learning schools is to create the political space they need. Schools have two potential strategies, which are not mutually exclusive. The first, which we might call advocating, is to try directly to cultivate support for their work among parents, school boards, and district administrators. The second, which we might call buffering, is to find a way to meet the expectations of those external audiences by acquiescing to conventional benchmarks, while also creating enough space to do the work that the school actually cares about. The strategies are not mutually exclusive. In either case, the internal work of organizing teaching and learning has to be linked to an effort to manage the external environment.

To take the first strategy first, advocating, clearly the preferable approach is to talk directly with stakeholders about the value of deeper learning. School leaders can articulate the importance of "twenty-first-century skills" in the contemporary economy and can emphasize that the kind of learning being attempted will build the skills students will need for college and careers.[34] Creating powerful learning experiences that involve connections with partners or applications that connect theory and practice will also help to enlist the advocacy of students, who can in turn convey to their parents what is special about the school. Dewey High has found that highly public exhibitions of learning are an effective way of showing what students have learned to parents and community members, and thereby to build momentum and support. Stressing that this kind of work does not mean sacrificing core academic skills, and, in fact, that such skills can be better developed through these methods, is also a necessary and important part of the message. For high schools in particular, college acceptance rates and placements can become the key metric (as opposed to test scores); parents are willing to grant flexibility if they are confident that the end result will still be a strong college option.[35]

The schools featured in this book faced the usual pressures associated with test scores, Carnegie Units, and other external constraints that could not be directly altered. But they employed a form of double bookkeeping—they satisfied the external metrics, but they were also clear internally about what they thought was actually important—thus buffering the school from outside expectations. For example, until recently Dewey High downplayed the importance of test scores, stressing to its teachers that students needed to pass state tests (thereby satisfying the external authorities) but not to score particularly highly on them, while teachers would be evaluated on the quality of their students' products. Downplaying the test scores created an internal alignment of expectations. At the New York City I School, all students are asked to take and pass the Regents Examinations by the end of tenth grade (with test prep provided, if necessary); they then take an all-elective curriculum for eleventh and twelfth grades. The same school also has found a way around Carnegie Units—the high school graduation requirement that students accumulate a certain number of credits in each disciplinary subject—by creating interdisciplinary classes and allocating half of the credits to each of the disciplines involved, so that a history of science class, for example, is counted as half history and half science.

Other school leaders are banding together and working with researchers to find ways to measure other competencies—social-emotional learning, strong academic writing, powerful project-based learning—initiatives that will, in the long run, enable them to measure what they actually value.[36] New assessments are critical because otherwise students will continue to be measured on tests that may or may not align with the school's core missions. Once a school passes a basic minimum of mandated external markers, school leaders of deeper learning schools can use the fact that they are distinctive to create a self-reinforcing virtuous cycle that both strengthens the school and protects it from external skeptics. In the case of both Dewey High and IB High, their initial wins and innovative approaches made it easier to attract ambitious teachers, as well as like-minded parents and students. It also bought them some protection from their respective districts, which did not want to disturb politically popular school options.

Creating Deeper Systems

At the same time, a school that is succeeding in producing powerful learning should not find it necessary to "buffer" itself from its own district or school board. In the long run, if deeper learning is to go to scale, these systems and their expectations will themselves need to change.

Balancing Breadth and Depth

The first specific issue on which district leadership could be helpful is by developing a new balance between breadth and depth. Teachers consistently told us that their biggest obstacles to "deeper" learning were the pacing guides developed by districts that dictated the rate at which students were supposed to learn. These guides, and the subjects they referred to, were developed out of a healthy appreciation of what it means to be an educated citizen. Who could argue that a high school graduate should not know something of Shakespeare, Newton, Darwin, Baldwin, Langston Hughes, American and world history, and other elements of a liberal arts education?

The problem arose in translating theory into practice. The crush of information that students were asked to know, and all that that entails, precluded deep exploration of any subject and meant that students had considerable trouble remembering what they had, in theory, learned. Conversely, almost all of the best learning experiences we saw involved students immersing themselves in a discipline and learning how it actually worked rather than confronting a canned version of it. When, judging with adult eyes, we saw significant comprehension of a subject—an ability not only to *know* but to *do* the things in the domain—it was almost always when students had gone "deep" into a field. At the same time, rather ironically, developing "deep" knowledge in a domain also requires breadth—understanding how a particular topic, fact, or event fits into the bigger picture is critical to developing real expertise in an area.

There are ways to marry breadth and depth. Consider ninth-grade world history, a subject we saw again and again in our research. The class usually raced from ancient history to the French revolution in a single year, through a blur of dynasties and an endless stream of dates and names that went in one ear and out the other. Imagine if that same course was reorganized around the following essential question: "Why do civilizations rise and fall?" This question forces coverage, as students examine the Greeks, Romans, Mayans, and others, but it also casts students into the role of a historical social scientist as they seek to develop theories, weigh evidence, and consider context. Such a course also would inevitably bring to the fore, in vital and relevant ways, questions of economics, government, culture, and many other forces and their interactions—presumably a central reason that we are interested in these different civilizations in the first place. Such an examination could connect to the contemporary debate about whether America is or is not a civilization in decline, a question recently raised by some noted commentators.[37] It might also help students to remember longer at least some of what they have learned, because historical events would no longer resemble a string of facts but rather become part of a pattern of meaning that the students themselves had developed.

In this vein, newer approaches have urged the development of standards that emphasize a small number of core ideas or essential questions rather than a laundry list of discrete pieces of content or skills. American districts that have made a shift toward twenty-first-century competencies as well as leading provinces abroad, such as British Columbia, have moved in this direction.[38] Critical to the success of this approach is building opportunities for teachers to adapt mandated core courses that have preestablished goals and objectives. Let's say a school or district decides that all ninth graders should learn something about different civilizations in world history, something about why they rise and fall, as well as something about how historians and social scientists would adjudicate the questions of why they rise and fall. Within that shell, it would be wise to create some flexibility, letting teachers spend more time on eras or periods that they or their students are particularly interested in. If, for example, students became curious about whether there are parallels between the fall of Rome and America today, they could research the topic, looking at differences as well as similarities; critically examine the work of commentators who have made this comparison; and perhaps conclude with a public debate or set of essays or blogposts on the subject. Creating the space and flexibility for this kind of exploration is what brings learning alive—no longer are students among a sea of teenagers to learn about Rome; now they are the first students to enter into an ongoing debate about what Rome's example means for leading powers in the contemporary world. If the goal were to explore five civilizations over nine months, such an in-depth exploration would not sacrifice the goal of helping students see the range of ways in which people have chosen to live.

Schools and districts could also hold firm on certain skills they want students to develop—to be able to analyze texts, to write with skill and authority, to develop and carry out a scientific investigation, to do effective research, and to reason quantitatively—even as they gave schools and teachers more flexibility in the amount of time devoted to particular subjects. Ms. Morgan, the English chair at Attainment High, held this position: she gave teachers some flexibility in choosing the texts they taught, receiving in return the promise that they would agree to common goals focused on building students' reading and writing skills.

Assessments and Curricula That Support Deeper Learning

When we first started our study of deeper learning in high schools, David Cohen, a wise University of Michigan professor, said to us, "Well, have you found any yet? There are no incentives for it." His words proved to be prophetic: everywhere we went, teachers and students told us that the external assessments were pushing against deep learning. In the early years of our study, these were state tests under No Child Left Behind; they also could be state tests that were required for student graduation. Even Advanced Placement tests were often described by teachers, in spite of the College Board's claims, as emphasizing breadth over depth and superficial content knowledge over deeper understanding of core processes and concepts in the disciplines. As we described earlier, many of the most powerful examples of deep learning that we found were in electives and extracurriculars, precisely because these are domains where students' skills are not tested.

Thus, if American society is to get serious about deeper learning, we will need to change how schools and students are externally assessed. There is no shortage of potential models that could be adopted or adapted. The United States could follow the International Baccalaureate model, or examination systems in other countries such as England, Singapore, and Australia, and develop district or state-level assessments that measure deeper learning competencies.[39] In these models, assessments usually feature a culminating "sit down" exam that entails a series of essays or other open-ended problems, as well as a series of specified tasks within the classroom that require learners to demonstrate the variety of skills and knowledge important in a domain. This classroom portion could mean the development of a portfolio of work, as in the English examination system, or it could be a longer investigation of a single problem, such as in the Singaporean science exams, which require students to develop a hypothesis, plan an investigation, record reliable data, interpret experimental results, and reflect on the methods used. This classroom portion is most often scored internally with a rubric, but it is also possible to have panels of experts evaluate the work, or, as IB does, to audit a sample of the classroom-level scoring to ensure that external standards are being upheld. It is also possible to organize systems for external scoring of portfolios; for example, the New York Performance Standards Consortium, a group of more than forty public secondary schools, allows students to submit graduation portfolios rather than take parts of the Regents exams. The key to any of these systems is that they do not incentivize the narrowing of curricula or reward the ability to succeed on low-level multiple choice tests; instead, they position the accountability system to reward deeper learning.

A powerful, if under-recognized, player in potentially bringing about these desired shifts is college. Specifically, in our travels we saw a mismatch between what high schools thought that colleges wanted and what college faculty actually wanted. High school teachers thought that college faculty wanted content knowledge—students who had learned certain themes in Shakespeare or who could recite the key components of a molecule. But unless students have AP credit, a freshman college instructor can't assume that a freshman has any particular piece of content knowledge, so freshman courses usually require very little specific knowledge. What does help students in college are skills: the ability to write well, to think analytically, to persevere in solving hard problems and deciphering difficult texts. Not surprisingly, then, those are the skills that college faculty value. They know they can teach the content, but they want students who have developed the disposition to learn and who have had practice with writing and analysis.[40] Standing between the college and high school faculties are the tests given by the College Board (particularly the SAT IIs and the APs) and the college admissions offices, which need an efficient way to process tens of thousands of applications. But while the current modes are efficient, they are not capturing the qualities that college faculty actually value. If colleges were to recast their admission procedures and start valuing other markers of achievement—including IB, portfolio assessments, or other yet-to-be-developed assessments—high schools would follow suit, and the new system would better reflect the values of both high schools and colleges.[41]

Deeper learning also demands a different approach to curriculum design. While teachers, especially experienced teachers, may develop or adapt their own curricula, it is unrealistic to expect wholesale changes in teaching without materials that would support such a shift.[42] In different disciplines, efforts have cropped up that begin to do this work. For instance, Sam Wineburg, a Stanford professor and former history teacher, has developed an American history curriculum and set of lessons that can be taught in forty-five-minute periods. They feature opportunities for student meaning-making, along with analysis of primary sources and debate, and they cover much of the same ground as would be found in most American history courses.[43] The George Lucas Educational Foundation has developed curriculum modules for AP Environmental Science and AP Government; these modules are organized into five project-based units that still prepare students for the exams.[44] Early research has found that students going through these curricula do as well as control groups on the AP tests, but are much stronger with respect to deeper learning competencies such as working in teams and designing social inquiry approaches.[45] The reform math community, which is comprised of thousands of teachers and researchers around the country, shares over Twitter "high ceiling, low floor" math problems, which provide materials to both engage and challenge students in math.[46] There can and should be more efforts of this type. As Expeditionary Learning's Ron Berger has pointed out, even within the existing standards, there are often more and less interesting ways to teach the same standard. Well-designed curriculum materials can help teachers find the more powerful approaches.[47]

Districts: Inverting the Pyramid

While the focus of our study is schools, it is clear that districts are a big part of the problem and thus could become a big part of the solution when it comes to deeper learning. Outside of college pressures, the three biggest barriers to deeper learning that teachers cited were district pacing guidelines, teacher evaluation systems, and pressure from state tests. All of these are manifestations of a systemic problem: districts were created a century ago in a command and control, compliance-oriented model that is antithetical to modern learning. In the spirit of symmetry, the qualities associated with student deeper learning—having opportunities to take risks, acknowledging that failure is part of learning, having some control and choice over one's learning—should instead characterize the adult culture in our schools and districts.

While there are some specific strategies that districts could undertake to support deeper learning, the biggest and most fundamental shift needed is cultural. Like most public bureaucracies, districts tend to avoid risk, seek control, and have "the many" implement the ideas of "the few."[48] More developed professions, as well as modern learning organizations of all types, work in a different way. Instead of placing their faith in a small administrative class to supervise a weak practitioner class, they realize that the work is too complex and variable to be easily standardized from above, and thus that they should invest more in the selection and training of the practitioners. With this as a foundation, there becomes less need for administrative oversight. Making this shift from a bureaucratic approach to a more professional one is imperative if the goal is to support teachers in teaching for deeper learning.[49]

As with schools that have been organized hierarchically, this change will require significant unlearning. District personnel, who have been socialized to believe that "fidelity of implementation" is king and that their job is to direct outcomes, will need to re-culture themselves to see that students and teachers are paramount and that the district's fundamental role is to support and catalyze these learning communities. As with teachers who initially feel that if they are not directly instructing they are not really teaching, district officials will need time and space to transition from "command and control" to "empower, fertilize, and catalyze."[50]

If district leaders and personnel were to adopt this different orientation, then a host of more specific strategies that districts could undertake to deepen learning for both teachers and students become viable. Districts that have adopted this orientation have frequently begun by using an EdLeader21 tool called "portrait of a graduate," through which a variety of community stakeholders come together to define the skills and competencies that they want students to acquire.[51] While the specifics vary, when asked to reflect seriously about their values, most communities choose a version of the following: they want their students to think critically, collaborate with others, build character, and otherwise develop into thoughtful and ethical human beings. With this goal established, a district could revisit the decisions it makes. With respect to curriculum, for instance, it could do a "deeper learning audit": working with teachers, it could name the core skills and knowledge that are sought for a particular subject and grade, then revamp the curriculum to develop a few extended investigations to explore that topic (for example, turning a world history survey course into a comparative investigation of five civilizations). If such an audit were consistently carried out over grades and disciplines, district expectations for teaching would line up with teachers' efforts to go deep rather than broad. If the district were then to make different decisions about assessment—moving toward the more performance-based, integrationist approach described earlier—then the whole system would become more aligned with twenty-first-century standards.

The next step would be to revamp the approach to teacher learning. Professional growth is especially important given the magnitude of the shift that we need in what teachers know and can do. Unfortunately, current approaches to professional development violate the tenets of deeper learning as well as what is known about powerful adult learning. Teachers frequently sit through presentations on topics they haven't chosen. As one report quoted a frustrated teacher, "We walk into a room and get the handouts. We sit and listen to a PowerPoint, usually without paying attention. Then an hour goes by and we go to the next session."[52] Another teacher in the same report said, "PD is something we go and do. We line up to get vaccinated." A better approach would significantly change this paradigm in a number of respects: teachers would have a major role in shaping school and district priorities for professional learning; there would be substantial opportunities for teachers to learn from one another rather than solely from external experts; and teachers would have some choice over the trajectories of their professional learning.[53] Much as significant learning for students comes through long trajectories in which students spiral through cycles of mastery, identity, and creativity, we need to create opportunities for teacher learning to do the same. In addition to whatever collective professional learning is organized by schools and districts, teachers also should be able to propose topics that they want, or even need, to learn more about and there should be sustained time for them to acquire this learning. There is no shortage of potential models for how to achieve these changes—the problem is not a technical one. The challenge is rather that districts would have to change their mindset—seeing teachers less as widgets to be slotted into their preexisting plans and more as talented people who need opportunities to grow in directions that they themselves control and direct.[54]

If deeper learning were the goal, the approach to evaluation would also need to change radically. Teachers in our study spoke bitterly about how district administrators, who knew little about the content or context of their lessons, would ding them because they didn't have the right things on their bulletin boards or because what they taught in a given fifteen-minute observation did not meet a pre-established rubric. The issue here, again, is one of professional respect—there is no world where a supervisor would watch fifteen minutes of a surgery or a trial and make consequential decisions about a doctor's or lawyer's professional performance. The current systems also focus more on individual performance than on improving collective capacity.[55] A more humane system would remember that evaluation is just one small part of a much larger project of developing people, and that a critical objective of evaluation is to not alienate high-quality people whom the field needs to recruit and develop. Again, there are professional systems of evaluation, such as, for example, the ones used in many consulting firms— in which the individual and the supervisor collectively define a set of goals for the year, and a 360-degree evaluation system (relying on a wide variety of different kinds of evidence) is used to pinpoint where there is growth and where someone needs a leg up. None of this precludes dropping bad performers, but retaining employees and helping them grow professionally are key to any school's long-term success, and systems of evaluation should be developed accordingly.

Districts also have the power to open up opportunities and time for deeper learning. If the goal were to provide students with more powerful learning experiences more of the time, then students would likely need to have more choice, more opportunities to work across disciplines, and more chances to connect their learning to the world. Districts have the power to make all of this possible. They could enable block scheduling, give students more choice, expand electives, break down the silos between disciplines, and broker connections between schools and a variety of external learning opportunities.

Finally, districts cannot expect deeper learning to flourish without exercising considerable skillful leadership. Most teachers teach as they were taught, and most of our educational structures still bear the imprint of their industrial-era origins. Thus creating change will require significant leadership. While most teachers are not opposed to having students think more or become more engaged, they need to see what it would look like—so they need to be asked to change in manageably sized chunks; and even so, many will need some outside support to make even modest changes. Change is possible, and once teachers and students begin to experience what it looks and feels like to do captivating work, energy can snowball in a positive direction. But these changes go against the grain, and will require vision and active leadership to get started.

On Equity and Deeper Learning

One criticism leveled against progressive or constructivist approaches to education is "that's fine for kids who come to school with significant amounts of social and cultural capital, but for kids who don't have that background, they need to learn it in school." While there is truth in part of this observation—students do learn different amounts of dominant cultural knowledge at home—much of what has followed from this assumption in terms of educational practice has been harmful. This line of thinking tends to foreground students' deficits over their assets; it serves to justify teaching as transmission and what Paulo Freire called the "banking model" of education. Writ large, this line of thinking is a powerful force for social reproduction—that is, no matter how well-intentioned it is, the result in practice is that, yet again, the most privileged students are being taught how to think whereas less advantaged students, who are often students of color, are being taught how to follow the directions of authorities.

Our time in schools persuaded us of the truth of something close to the opposite proposition. For students who came with high levels of dominant cultural capital, who were willing to follow rules, who were either intrinsically interested in academic subjects or willing to play the game of school to get to college, school as it currently stands is functional. As we've suggested, we think more could happen for these students if school were remade, but the status quo works well enough to get them to college. For the rest of students, however, the changes we suggest are necessary to get them engaged in their education. For example, we once witnessed a biology teacher teaching a fairly traditional class about DNA to two different sections of kids. The lesson included some mini-lecture, some work with manipulables (strands that the students could use to assemble DNA), and some worksheet questions. This was an experienced teacher—he was energetic, he was very good at classroom management, and his lesson was clear and biologically accurate. And he was committed to equality: he taught exactly the same lesson to his middle-track and lower-track students. The way this lesson was received, however, varied greatly. The middle-track students did what he asked—they dutifully listened to him lecture, manipulated the strands when he told them to, and filled out the worksheet. The lower-track students did not—despite a lot of skillful cajoling, they looked out the window, and, in some cases, refused to do what he asked. After both classes were over, he asked us for feedback. We don't have any feedback on what you did, we said. Within the constraints of what you were trying to do—a teacher-led lesson on DNA—you did it about as well as it can be done. But, we asked, have you ever done anything that has had more success, particularly with the lower-track group of students? As it happens, he said, yes. To paraphrase, he said: I teach this senior elective, where students get to pick the biological topic they want to investigate, and they have to do research and create some sort of product that reflects what they learned. Some of my students who had their heads on their desks today were great in that setting.

Our chapter on the most compelling teachers in our sample reached similar conclusions. In math, science, English, and social studies or history, we found fundamentally similar approaches among our high-challenge/high-engagement/high-participation teachers in their elite and their highly disadvantaged settings. All of these teachers constructed powerful learning environments with clear purpose, and supported students as producers, depth over breadth, disciplines as open-ended rather than closed, and students playing the whole game at a junior level. In settings where students had weaker reading or math skills, teachers slowed down, focused on shorter pieces of text, and included more scaffolds, but the fundamental approach was the same. Some social studies teachers also drew upon the critical tradition—critical approaches to race, gender, class and other subjects—and found that this tradition contained within it a "deeper" approach to understanding social processes as well as a stance that was particularly resonant for marginalized student populations.[56] Thus while Lisa Delpit's well-known work has been seen as arguing that different and more-structured learning environments are appropriate for disadvantaged students and students of color, our research suggests that it is precisely these students who would benefit most from an approach that integrates mastery, identity, and creativity.[57]

To put it another way, these are often the students for whom traditional school has worked least well, who are most disengaged from school, and whose interests and racial identities have been largely denied by traditional school priorities.[58] Thus, perhaps not surprisingly, it is they who are most in need of a new approach. As Milbrey McLaughlin and Joan Talbert describe it, "Nontraditional students appear to be more at home and successful as learners in classrooms where teachers connect them to subjects in new ways. The students we interviewed recognized and appreciated teachers' efforts to get to know them and to create classroom settings that encouraged academic engagement and expression of ideas. Yet nontraditional students describe most of their classes as highly structured, teacher-controlled and regimented."[59]

Taking the perspective one step further, farsighted provinces like British Columbia have begun actively to integrate the funds of knowledge that exist in indigenous communities, which traditionally have been marginalized by mainstream schooling. Through cultural exchange programs and by welcoming community elders as additional adult mentors to students, British Columbia is actively trying to show all students the varied traditions of powerful learning that exist in different communities. First People principles, for example, emphasize learning by doing, apprenticeship learning, cross-generational learning, and learning that is deeply informed by history.[60] Deep learning exists in many different registers. Schools of the future might incorporate these varied registers, and, in so doing, both help to educate privileged students about other cultures and create a sense of belonging and identity for students who historically have been marginalized.

There Is a Way, but Is There the Will?

As we put this book to bed in June of 2018, we are struck by the incongruence between our interest in "deep learning" and the values of a large segment of the American polity. The 2016 presidential election of Donald Trump was not simply a routine swing of the ideological pendulum; it represented the apotheosis of a certain brand of populist politics that distrusts any form of expertise, is skeptical of science, and is overtly hostile to people of color. Enlightenment values themselves are under attack and anti-Enlightenment values—nativism, xenophobia, distrust of reason and evidence—have come to the forefront. Nor did the election of Trump come out of nowhere. Rather, it is the culmination of trends that since the 1960s have been growing on the Right—leading to a racially coded politics that is highly antagonistic toward non-whites, skeptical about knowledge, dismissive of expertise, distrustful of educated people, and enamored of authoritarian values as the way to restore order and national greatness. Every element on this list runs counter to the values that support "deeper learning."

For our purposes, these trends are particularly important because public schools are public institutions. Education also has an underdeveloped technical core—by which we mean a weak foundation of professionally accepted definitions of the nature of the work and the ways it should be carried out—which has made it particularly vulnerable to changing public priorities. Thus, reforms that have succeeded—the creation of the public school system in the first place, standardized tests, age-graded schooling, extracurricular activities, tracking—all have met the needs of teachers or parents or both. Reforms that have struggled—particularly reforms, like those discussed in this book, that would make education more intellectually lively and demanding—have failed nationwide not only because they have not solved problems that teachers think they have, but also because they have never built a public constituency powerful enough to establish them. At the same time, they have succeeded in niches—either individual schools, or subsystems like Montessori, IB, or some progressive charter management organizations—that have managed to build the needed political support among voluntary groups of parents and students. This perspective explains why such education can thrive in specific communities, even when the national political picture is unfavorable to deeper learning.

If the changes that we have described here are to transpire, we see no alternative but for public school leaders—governors, mayors, superintendents, principals, teachers, and even students—to make a loud, sustained, and convincing case for deeper learning. Making schools places where our children learn to think, where they create, where they pursue things that matter to them, where they seize the skills that will help them master their lives, should be an easy sell. But we recognize that it is not. It can be seen as threatening for students not to learn in the ways their parents were taught. Much as parents can fear sending their children to college because they may end up rejecting the ways of the parents, schools that aspire to deeper learning can similarly arouse fear and skepticism in parents educated in a different way.[61]

An enormous amount depends on whether or not we can summon the courage and the will to make this shift. Schools lay the foundation of our economy and our path to equity—they train future workers and (we hope) mitigate some of the inequalities of this generation by empowering the next. These are important purposes. But perhaps the most important role they play is training our future citizens. These are people who will need to be able to tell truth from fantasy, real news from fake news; they will need to understand that climate change is real; and they will need to be able to work with people from other countries to solve the next generation of problems. If we cannot shift from a world where learning deeply is the exception rather than the rule, more is in jeopardy than our schools. Nothing less than our society is at stake.

Appendix

Notes

Acknowledgments

Index

Methodology

IN 2010, we set out on what became a six-year study of American high schools. At the time, our study went by the banner "Good Schools Beyond Test Scores." Still in the throes of the No Child Left Behind era, we envisioned a project that would look at a variety of different types of high schools and offer a holistic appraisal of the nature of "goodness" in the best of those. Then two things happened that altered the trajectory of our work. First, as we began to visit schools, we became particularly focused on what was happening in classrooms; students spent at least 80 percent of their time in classes, and thus it was hard for a school to claim to be "good" if it hadn't found interesting, engaging, and challenging ways to use that time. Second, the world began to shift a bit under our feet. No Child Left Behind and its unrelenting emphasis on basic skills began to wind down, and in its place came the Common Core. The Hewlett Foundation crystallized the term "deeper learning" as an umbrella for the range of skills students would need in order to participate in modern life: critical thinking, problem solving, collaboration, and the ability to direct one's own learning. Hewlett also began to devote its entire educational portfolio to deeper learning, funding districts, schools, charter networks, researchers, assessment designers, policymakers, and many others who were seeking to move in this direction. With funding from Apple, XQ launched a ten-million-dollar competition for new school designs. While at the beginning we felt on the periphery of the school reform conversation and could find only drips of funding, as the project matured we found more and more people interested in our research, as they, too, were trying to develop "deeper learning" schools.

Early in our project, we focused on public schools—some charters, some traditional—with high reputations and with declared progressive or "deeper learning" orientations. As we visited these schools, we often found that there was much less there than met the eye—either the classrooms were virtually indistinguishable from traditional classrooms, or their espoused missions far outran their actual practice. In total, we visited nine such progressive schools, the strongest of which we describe in Chapter 2. In the spirit of developing a diverse sample of schools, we also visited four "no excuses" schools—very strict schools, serving almost exclusively high-poverty students of color, with a college prep mission and curriculum. While some see such schools as the antithesis of "deeper learning," in our initial visits we saw one in which students were engaging in sophisticated discussions of academic subjects. This school became the focus of Chapter 3. We also became interested in International Baccalaureate as an approach to instantiating deeper learning systematically, and thus chose five schools that had made IB a significant part of their approach. We chose the strongest of those schools for Chapter 4. We were interested in how regular comprehensive high schools were navigating toward deeper learning, and thus we visited three of them, including one, a highly regarded suburban school, that became the subject of Chapter 5. Finally, as we moved toward the end of our study, we picked out a few schools from which we wanted to learn particular things. These included an elite private school using the Harkness method as a platform for "deeper" mathematics; one private and one charter school whose missions were to send low-income students to college; a statewide exam school for math and science that was highly recommended as a place to observe inquiry-based teaching; a well-regarded alternative school that built apprenticeships into its work; and a "next generation" blended learning school that had greatly expanded the role of electives and of student choice. We drew on these schools as we made recommendations for what might be possible in Chapter 8.

In total, we visited thirty schools, representing a wide but still limited sample of American high schools. They were drawn from a range
of American cities—Boston, New York, Providence, Cincinnati, Chicago, Denver, Oakland, San Diego, and San Francisco—and thus are
mostly urban (with a couple of suburban) schools in politically blue
states or blue cities. We do not have schools from the South or rural
areas in our sample. Thus the question of how to instantiate "deeper
learning" in highly politically conservative areas is not part of our study.

The timing of our study is also important. Over the past few years,
there has been an explosion of new school models that are more personalized, or competency-based, or that seek to reinvent schooling in
other ways. These schools were too new to be in our sample. Our sample
draws heavily from schools that were either longstanding comprehensive schools or schools that were created in the 1990s or 2000s. In some
ways, this study captures the matured version of the most recent generation of school reform, including some of the early charter models
and some of the New York City small schools of choice. The timing
also matters with respect to the external policy environment: the early
years of our study capture the end of the No Child Left Behind era,
and the later years the beginnings of Common Core era.

We sought to use a mix of schools to balance breadth and depth. Four
of the schools—one no excuses, one progressive, one IB, and one
comprehensive—became sites of deep dives. At each of these schools,
we spent twenty to thirty days, trying to understand in detail what made
these schools tick, how they realized their visions, and what the tradeoffs were in their models. Each of these schools became an anchor case
for one of the chapters of the book. Another six became sites for medium dives—here we spent five to ten days at each, examining particularly distinctive elements of their models, or, in some cases, why they
were struggling to achieve what they aspired to. The remaining twenty
we visited for one to four days. In total, we spent more than 750 hours
in schools and interviewed more than three hundred teachers, administrators, and students.

As the focus of our work shifted toward "deeper learning," there was
the question of what we could write about learning on the basis of an
observational study like this one. As one friend said to us early in the
process, "Wouldn't you just like to line up all of the schools in your
study and give them a test and see who did the best?" Entertaining this

as a thought experiment shows its limits as an idea: (1) It would not have been practical; we visited many schools and had to negotiate access to each one. If we had insisted that each school have its students take a test, we would have had to greatly limit our sample; (2) It would not have been fair; students at different schools studied different things and different schools were trying to realize different values; and (3) We would have had no way of controlling for selection or drawing a comparison group, thus there would have been no way of assessing the contribution of the school to the test results. Consequently we do not make any causal claims about the schools' independent contribution to learning, as measured by a common standard.[1]

As has been the case with previous qualitative research on schools, we focused on what we could observe in classrooms. In particular, we zeroed in on three dimensions: (1) the cognitive rigor of the task, (2) the observed engagement level of the students, and (3) how many of the students in the class were doing the task and were engaged by the work. For the cognitive rigor of the task, we used Bloom's revised taxonomy, with its six categories: recall, comprehend, apply, analyze, synthesize, create. While there are other more recent ways of capturing classroom activity that we like, such as Karin Hess's adaptation of Norman Webb's depth-of-knowledge scale, as well as more specific tools for different disciplines, Bloom's taxonomy had the advantage of being clear and widely applicable to very different kinds of classrooms and contexts.[2] In general, if the task asked students to analyze, synthesize, or create, we counted it as a higher-order task; if it asked students to recall, comprehend, or apply, we counted it as a lower-order task. Of course, there is no school where at every moment of the day students are analyzing, synthesizing, or creating; there are times when new information needs to be introduced or routine tasks performed. Nevertheless, in our observations of a great many classrooms, schools, and school days, it was possible to see general patterns of the task distribution. Following Fred Newmann's argument about engagement as a precondition for significant and sustained learning, we also looked for signs of engagement or disengagement in the classroom. For engagement, we looked at students' demeanor, we listened to their conversations with one another, and we talked with them about their classes. While such observations cannot yield fine distinctions, they do allow one to capture the differences between classes where students are actively disengaged (heads down, staring out the window, watching the clock, gossiping with one another, not doing the stated task of the class) and ones where students are actively engaged (eyes following the speaker, doing the task, displaying enthusiasm in their conversations or actions). To measure participation, we counted the ratio of students doing the task and engaged in the work.

While in the book we used the term "deeper learning" in order to join the conversation on the topic, if we were going to be precise we would say that what we were witnessing in classrooms were "deeper learning opportunities." While engaging in higher-order tasks is no guarantee of deeper learning, it is fairly safe to assume that *if there are no opportunities to engage in higher-order thinking tasks, or if students do not engage with these tasks, then students will not be able to think deeply in that domain*, unless similar opportunities are offered and embraced outside of school. Thus in this study we are building on the "opportunities to learn" literature, which shows fairly conclusively that what students can do is related to what they are consistently asked to do.[3] Some of the most well-known qualitative work on tracking also takes this approach. Jeannie Oakes's famous study *Keeping Track*, based on classroom observations and student interviews, focuses on how differences in what students are asked to do vary across tracks.[4]

While we consistently monitored the three learning dimensions in our notes on classrooms, we embedded them in narrative field notes. These narrative field notes, featured throughout the book, sought to capture in a holistic way what was happening in classrooms. They included the three corners of the instructional triangle—teachers' actions, students' responses, and the nature of the task. This narrative approach has been used by a number of prominent authors in the past, including in such well-known studies as *The Shopping Mall High School, The Good High School*, and *A Place Called School*, and was particularly useful for our study for several reasons. First, when we tried another approach, such as using rubrics to classify different aspects of classroom activity, we found it difficult to really "see" what had happened in the class. We think this is because the narrative form puts the elements of a class into conversation with each other, and the contextual information those elements provide (it was the beginning of a unit; it was after lunch and there was little energy in the room) contributes to a holistic picture that helps us make sense of a given class. Second, as we discuss in more detail in Chapter 8, we came to think that good classrooms need to be understood *ecologically*, meaning that it is not any one factor that makes them successful, but rather the interaction of a number of elements. Whether asking a "higher-order question" did or did not lead to a good class depended on whether students were given opportunities to really answer that question, whether the question was embedded within the narrative arc of the class, and whether there was a productive level of trust among students, and between students and the teacher, among other factors. Third, given that we were interested in the plurality of approaches that teachers and schools brought to their work, narrative field notes enabled us to avoid fitting classrooms and schools into pre-conceived categories, and instead to capture on their own terms what they were trying to do.

We drew on these data in different ways in different chapters. In Chapter 1, we looked at some of the overall patterns that we observed in the data as a whole. While the sample was not a representative pic-ture of American schools, it did offer a current look into a diverse array of American schools. Because the schools were recommended, we could also think of our sample as an "upper bound" estimate of what is hap-pening in American classrooms. Since key findings from the data as a whole were not encouraging, we think it likely that a representative sample of American schools would yield even more sobering findings. We corroborated our findings by consulting national quantitative evi-dence, which has reached similar conclusions.

In the spirit of seeking to understand different approaches to real-izing deeper learning, we organized the next four chapters around different school models. Chapter 2 explores a progressive, project-based school; Chapter 3 describes a no-excuses school; Chapter 4 examines an International Baccalaureate school; and Chapter 5 looks at "shopping mall," or comprehensive, high schools. In examining these schools' dif-fering approaches, we concluded that none could claim a monopoly on "deeper learning," but rather they each tended to bring out different qualities important to learning, and those same design choices often precluded other important virtues.

If one question was about the strengths and weaknesses of different models, another was about what it took to successfully realize a given vision, no matter the stripe. One of the early findings of the study was that there was often a considerable gap between a school's *espoused values*

and its *enacted practices*. In other words, what the school said about itself on its website, in its mission statement, or in our interviews with its
administrators was not consistently supported by what we saw in classrooms. There were a few exceptions to this pattern, schools that were
able to realize their intended visions. The anchor cases that we chose
for Chapters 2, 3, and 4 were these schools. They were schools—one
progressive, one no excuses, and one International Baccalaureate—
that had found ways to successfully instantiate their visions across
many, if not all, of their classrooms. So while they were quite pedagogically varied, they also had commonalities—in their structure,
processes, culture, and way of managing their external environment—
that enabled them to realize their visions. We attempted to describe
these elements and how they interacted, and we hope our analysis will
be useful to future school leaders, regardless of the vision that they are
trying to achieve.

We constructed these four deep-dive chapters as classic organizational case studies in the sociological sense. At each of these
schools, we spent twenty to thirty days; we interviewed at least fifty students, teachers, and administrators; we observed at least twenty classes;
and we collected artifacts and documents along the way. Our general
procedure was to spend our first few days observing a wide cross-section
of classes, often by shadowing students through the course of their days.
Once we had an overall picture of the patterns of instruction, we moved
to interviews, talking to faculty and administrators about the forces and
mechanisms that shaped instruction in the school. Since we were interested in how they had broken the usual pattern of high variance from
class to class, we focused some of our questions on understanding the
mechanisms that had produced this consistency, giving greater credence
to those mechanisms that were identified by multiple different groups
of respondents and by our own observations. We also talked to faculty,
administrators, and students about what they saw as the strengths and
weaknesses of the school, and asked them to describe the broader forces
that had produced these outcomes. We stayed at the schools until we
had reached saturation, meaning that additional observations and interviews were consistent with our developing theories for what explained
the patterns of instruction and engagement at those schools.

In doing this work, we also drew on the well-developed sociological
logic that determines when to use case as opposed to variable-oriented

research.[5] Variable-oriented research is useful when the goal is to use large-n samples to explore the relationship between a given x and a given y, especially when there is a fairly well-developed theory to be tested. Case-oriented research is particularly useful for generating hypotheses, for understanding mechanisms, and for considering how different dimensions of a situation interrelate.[6] In this case, we were more interested in the latter—in trying to understand how schools as organizations develop mechanisms to support deeper learning and how they manage internal processes as well as external stakeholders in doing so. Given that aspirations for deeper learning are fairly new, a hypothesis-generating, case-oriented approach is appropriate. We also were particularly interested in the diversity of approaches to realizing these goals. Comparing a no-excuses school seeking to maximize test scores with a project-based school seeking to maximize twenty-first-century skills is not meaningful. Instead, by giving each kind of school its own chapter, we were able to explore the strengths and weaknesses of each approach on its own terms.

We also took advantage of the "negative" cases that our data supplied, which were schools with similar aspirations that had made less progress in closing the gap between their espoused values and enacted practices. For the project-based, no-excuses, and IB schools, we had other schools in our sample that had similar philosophies but wider gaps between what they were trying to do and what they were actually accomplishing. In the case of the no-excuses and project-based schools, we had very similar comps—other schools that were also charters and were serving similar demographics of students. For the IB school, our successful IB school served more middle-class students than our struggling IB schools, and thus in the chapter we indicate that they had made much progress in bringing IB to non-elite middle-class students, but we do not yet know what it would entail to successfully bring IB to highly disadvantaged students.

While we had initially focused our study on core disciplinary classes, as we spent more time in schools we found that some of the most engaged, vital places in these high schools were on the "periphery"—in arts, music, electives, and extracurriculars. In Chapter 6, we explored this idea by taking a deep dive into the creation of a high school theater production. We attended ten rehearsals; spent time with actors, faculty, staff, and crew; watched the production; and interviewed everyone involved. Here we drew on another strength of the case study method—its ability to capture the contribution of parts to a whole.[7] Through observations and interviews, we developed a theory of the different elements that were important in putting together a theater production—purpose, choice, community, apprenticeship, "playing the whole game at a junior level," and more—and suggested the ways in which these factors interacted to produce what students and faculty described as a highly powerful learning environment. Creating this theory was an iterative process: we developed an initial list of what we saw as the important elements, shared that list with some of our respondents, revised it based on their feedback, then added questions about additional elements in subsequent interviews. We again stopped at the point of saturation, when interviews and observations were no longer yielding new information and were confirming our theoretical frame.

We built on these ideas in Chapter 7, where we returned to the data as a whole to characterize the most powerful classrooms that we saw. Here we focused on those classrooms that featured cognitive challenge, engagement, and widespread participation, and sought to understand what made those classrooms tick. More formally, we were using Mill's method of agreement, by which scholars take a set of phenomena that produce a similar outcome (in this case, classes that were cognitively challenging and characterized by high engagement and widespread participation) and identify the common factors that produced that outcome. In this case, some of these factors related to the teachers—how they themselves had been taught, and the stance they took toward students and knowledge—while other factors related to the way in which they had organized their classrooms and the arc of the learning. We also used Mill's method of difference to see whether these same factors were absent in other classrooms that were not as powerful. The many classrooms we saw that were not cognitively challenging and engaging, and the interviews we did with those teachers, were "negative" data that we could use to contrast with the compelling teachers we hone in on in Chapter 7. Modern applications of Mill's methods in qualitative research frequently not only use absence or presence to identify the factors but also examine the mechanisms by which those factors affect the outcome, and we did so here.[8] For example, if Mill's methods suggest that powerful teachers took a different stance toward learning—privileging more *how* to think than *what* to think—and then students said, "Mr. X's class is really powerful, and I think that is because he cares less about what we learn than that we think it through"—then we would take that as confirmation of the importance of taking a different stance toward learning.

Further complicating this point is that when we analyzed the data, we found that what mattered was less the presence of particular individual factors and more the coming together of a constellation of factors to produce a powerful classroom. Classrooms, as well as schools, we argue, should be understood as ecologies or environments where a number of elements need to coalesce to produce an outcome. Case methods were again well-suited to understanding these ecologies, because they enabled us to let each class stand on its own, while also looking for features that were common across powerful learning environments.

These choices of sample and method have both strengths and limitations. In terms of limits, we will mention four. First, as mentioned earlier, this is not a study of the "effect" of schools on measured outcomes; such a study would require a very different methodology. Second, as with any case study research, there is the question of the external generalizability of our conclusions. We have talked about our findings many times with teachers, principals, superintendents, and the general public, and have found that much of what we say resonates with these audiences, including international audiences, who report seeing similar things in different guises. Thus while hard evidence of external generalizability awaits future research, we have substantial reason to think that the ideas developed here have a broad reach. Third, we were particularly interested in these schools from the perspective of teachers and administrators seeking to create deeper learning. Given this perspective, we spent much of our interview time with teachers and administrators, and the questions that we asked students focused heavily on how they were experiencing their learning environments. This means that we did not investigate much about the peer culture of schools, social media, or students' lives outside of school, all of which would be important topics if we were seeking to explore student learning more from the perspective of the students. Fourth, as a study that took schools as the units of analysis, there were some limits to the depth with which we could explore reform in particular disciplines. We drew on such disciplinary work as we evaluated particular classes, but a study with a disciplinary orientation could go deeper on these topics.[9]

At the same time, we think that there are some distinctive strengths that come with this methodology and approach. We hope that it balances breadth and depth, drawing together a wide sample of American high schools with some deep dives on particular models. It is, as far as we are aware, the only contemporary study that considers different kinds of schools—project-based, IB, no excuses, comprehensive schools—together, and tries to assess the strengths and weaknesses of different models. Our argument about the periphery and the core—that peripheral environments like extracurriculars and electives are often more promising platforms for learning than core subjects—is another argument that we think is largely original to this book.[10] And while there were some tradeoffs concerning the depth with which we could study particular disciplines, foregrounding schools as units of analysis had some significant advantages, particularly given the importance of asking how the grammar of schooling might be reinvented in more innovative directions. Finally, for the reasons sketched earlier, we think that the case study method that we have employed is particularly well-suited to address this range of questions.

Notes

Introduction

1. Throughout this book, we have followed the academic convention of giving pseudonyms to all of the schools, as well as all of the individuals, in our study. This reflects part of the agreement we made with our institutional review board, and it allows us to be candid in discussing the limitations as well as the strengths of what we witnessed. Ethically, it also seems like the right thing to do because the places we visited were generous with their time, and thus when we do call out shortcomings, it seemed better not to name places publicly. We did wish that we could identify schools about which we had largely positive things to say, but even in these cases, there were often also tradeoffs that we did not necessarily wish to discuss publicly. Also, the promise that the schools would not be identified allowed our respondents to speak more candidly then they otherwise might have been willing to do.

2. See Theodore Sizer's *Horace's Compromise: The Dilemma of the American High School* (New York: Houghton Mifflin, 1984), Sara Lawrence-Lightfoot's *The Good High School: Portraits of Character and Culture* (New York: Basic Books, 1983), Arthur G. Powell, Eleanor Farrar, and David K. Cohen, *The Shopping Mall High School: Winners and Losers in the Educational Marketplace* (New York: Houghton Mifflin Harcourt, 1985), and John Goodlad's *A Place Called School* (New York: McGraw-Hill, 1984).

3. National Center for Education Statistics, *The Nation's Report Card: Trends in Academic Progress 2012* (Washington, D.C.: National Center for Education Statistics, Institute of Education Sciences, U.S. Department of Education, 2013).

4. Organisation for Economic Co-operation and Development and Programme for International Student Assessment, *PISA 2015 Results*, vol. 1: *Excellence and Equity in Education* (Paris: OECD, 2016). In the 2015 PISA, the United States ranked nineteenth in science, twentieth in reading, and thirty-first in math among 35 OECD countries: see https://www.oecd.org/pisa/PISA-2015-United-States.pdf, 18 (accessed August 21, 2018).

5. Ross Brenneman, "Gallup Student Poll Finds Engagement in School Dropping by Grade Level," *Education Week*, March 22, 2016.

6. Hewlett Foundation, "Deeper Learning Competencies" (2013), https://www.hewlett.org/wp-content/uploads/2016/08/Deeper_Learning_Defined__April_2013.pdf (accessed August 21, 2018); National Research Council, Committee on Defining Deeper Learning and 21st Century Skills, *Education for Life and Work: Developing Transferable Knowledge and Skills in the 21st Century* (Washington, D.C.: National Academies Press, 2012).

1 ∿ The State of Deeper Learning in American High Schools

1. Hewlett Foundation, "Deeper Learning Competencies" (2013), https://www.hewlett.org/wp-content/uploads/2016/08/Deeper_Learning_Defined__April_2013.pdf.

2. National Research Council (U.S.), Committee on Defining Deeper Learning and 21st Century Skills, *Education for Life and Work: Developing Transferable Knowledge and Skills in the 21st Century* (Washington, D.C.: National Academies Press, 2012).

3. Paulo Freire, *Pedagogy of the Oppressed* (New York: Seabury Press, 1970).

4. Alfred North Whitehead, *The Aims of Education and Other Essays* (New York: Macmillan, 1929).

5. Joseph Mayer Rice, *The Public-School System of the United States* (New York: Century, 1893).

6. Magdalene Lampert et al., "Keeping It Complex: Using Rehearsals to Support Novice Teacher Learning of Ambitious Teaching," *Journal of Teacher Education* 64, no. 3 (2014): 226–243.

7. In linking to these antecedents, we connect the current interest in "deeper learning" to older ideas about serious or powerful education, and, conversely, differentiate ourselves from those who associate "deeper learning" with technology, blended schools, or competency-based or personalized education. Our perspective is that these are modalities of learning, which can be either deep or shallow, depending on how they are carried out.

8. For 1970, see Linda Darling-Hammond et al., *Criteria for High Quality Assessment* (Stanford, Calif.: Stanford Center for Opportunity Policy in Education, 2013), 11. For 2015, see World Economic Forum, https://www.inc.com/melanie-curtin/the-10-top-skills-that-will-land-you-high-paying-jobs-by-2020-according-to-world-economic-forum.html (accessed September 10, 2018).

9. John Bransford, A. L Brown, and R. R. Cocking, eds., *How People Learn: Brain, Mind, Experience and School* (Washington, D.C.: National Academy Press, 1999).

10. Ibid.

11. Ibid., particularly chapters 1, 2, and 7. Jon Star makes a similar argument about the need for the integration of procedural and conceptual knowledge in mathematics: see Jon R. Star, "Reconceptualizing Procedural Knowledge," *Journal for Research in Mathematics Education* 36, no. 5 (2005): 404–411.

12. Hilda Borko and Carol Livingston, "Cognition and Improvisation: Differences in Mathematics Instruction by Expert and Novice Teachers," *American Educational Research Journal* 26, no. 4 (1989): 473–498.

13. Jerome Bruner, *The Process of Education* (Cambridge, Mass.: Harvard University Press, 1960).

14. Milbrey W. McLaughlin and Joan E. Talbert, "Introduction: New Visions of Teaching," in David Cohen, Milbrey McLaughlin, and Joan Talbert, eds., *Teaching for Understanding: Challenges for Policy and Practice* (San Francisco: Jossey Bass, 1993), 1.

15. Ibid, 2. See also Deborah Walker and Linda Lampert, "Learning and Leading Theory: A Century in the Making," in *The Constructivist Leader*, ed. Linda Lampert et al. (New York: Teachers College Press, 1995), 1–27.

16. Magdalene Lampert, "Deeper Teaching," in *Students at the Center*, Deeper Learning Research Series (Boston: Jobs for the Future, 2015), available at https://www.researchgate.net/publication/319230890_Deeper_Teaching (accessed September 10, 2018).

17. Fred Newmann, "Introduction," in Fred Newmann, ed., *Student Engagement and Achievement in American Secondary Schools* (New York: Teachers College Press, 1992), 2.

18. Ibid., 3.

19. Benjamin Bloom, *Developing Talent in Young People* (New York: Ballantine Books, 1985); Daniel Coyle, *The Talent Code* (New York: Bantam Books, 2009).

20. This idea of a spiral came from a group of students in our deeper learning class, as part of a class assignment to analyze data we had collected through interviews with deep learners. The students in that group were Meredith Innis, Ben Johnson, Jessica Lander, David Sabey, Jesse Tang, Julia Tomasko, Tat Chuen Wee, and Olivia Werby. The idea was also influenced by reading Bloom, *Developing Talent in Young People*. While this group came up with the idea of seeing deeper learning as a spiral, the identification of the key components of that spiral as mastery, identity, and creativity is original to this work.

21. Jean Lave and Etienne Wenger, *Situated Learning: Legitimate Peripheral Participation* (New York: Cambridge University Press, 1991).

22. A Collins, J. S. Brown, and S. E. Newman, "Cognitive Apprenticeship: Teaching the Craft of Reading, Writing and Mathematics," in L. B. Resnick, ed., *Knowing, Learning, and Instruction: Essays in Honor of Robert Glaser* (Hillsdale, N.J.: Erlbaum, 1989).

23. Carl Bereiter and Marlene Scardamalia, *Surpassing Ourselves: An Inquiry into the Nature and Implications of Expertise* (Chicago: Open Court, 1993).

24. Ronald Edmonds, "Effective Schools for the Urban Poor," *Educational Leadership* 37, no. 1 (1980): 15–18, 20–24.

25. Elizabeth A. City et al., *Instructional Rounds in Education: A Network Approach to Improving Teaching and Learning* (Cambridge, Mass.: Harvard Education Press, 2009).

26. Anthony S. Bryk, *Organizing Schools for Improvement: Lessons from Chicago* (Chicago: University of Chicago Press, 2010).

27. Paul Cobb and Kara Jackson, "Towards an Empirically Grounded Theory of Action for Improving the Quality of Mathematics Teaching at Scale," *Mathematics Teacher Education and Development* 13, no. 1 (2012): 6–33. The quotation is from pp. 7–8.

28. Lampert et al., "Keeping It Complex"; Pamela L. Grossman, *Teaching Core Practices in Teacher Education* (Cambridge, Mass.: Harvard Education Press, 2018).

29. Tom Vander Ark and Carri Schneider, "Deeper Learning for Every Student Every Day," https://www.hewlett.org/wp-content/uploads/2016/08/Deeper%20 Learning%20for%20Every%20Student%20EVery%20Day_GETTING%20 SMART_1.2014.pdf (accessed September 10, 2018), 78.

30. There is no precise definition of a "no excuses" school; some schools use this term in describing themselves and others do not. Our list of ten no-excuses networks includes schools that either self-name themselves as "no excuses" schools or have been repeatedly described as such by those writing about the schools: Achievement First, Aspire, Democracy Prep, Green Dot, IDEA, KIPP, Noble, Success Academies, Uncommon Schools, and Yes Prep. It is also the case that, in recent years, some of these schools have begun to distance themselves from the "no excuses" label; we discuss these issues in Chapter 3.

31. Michael McShane and Jenn Hatfield, "Measuring Diversity in Charter School Offerings," (Washington, D.C.: American Enterprise Institute, 2015), https://www.aei.org/wp-content/uploads/2015/07/Measuring-Diversity-in -Charter-School-Offerings.pdf (accessed September 10, 2018).

32. For 1999, see The Hechinger Report, "Will Common Core Undermine a Massachusetts College-Prep Program's Diversity Goal?," *U.S. News and World Report*, March 14, 2016, available at https://www.usnews.com/news/articles/2016-03 -14/will-common-core-undermine-an-elite-college-prep-programs-goal-of -diversity; for more current data, see the International Baccalaureate Organization's data on the United States, available at https://www.ibo.org/about-the-ib /the-ib-by-country/u/united-states/(both accessed September 10, 2018).

33. Sarah Sparks, "International Baccalaureate Saw Rapid Growth in High-Poverty Schools," *Education Week* (July 31, 2015), available at http://blogs.edweek .org/edweek/inside-school-research/2015/07/international_baccalaureate_poor _students.html (accessed September 10, 2018).

34. Tom Kane and Douglas Staiger, *Gathering Feedback for Teaching: Combining High-Quality Observations with Student Surveys and Achievement Gains* (Seattle: Bill & Melinda Gates Foundation, 2012), 24. We are not aware of a similar representative study of high schools.

35. Sonja Santelises and Joan Dabrowski, *Checking In: Do Classroom Assignments Reflect Today's Higher Standards?* (Washington, D.C.: Education Trust, 2015), 4.

36. Martin Nystrand and Adam Gamoran, "The Big Picture: Language and Learning in Hundreds of English Lessons," in Martin Nystrand, *Opening Dialogue: Understanding the Dynamics of Language and Learning in the English Classroom* (New York: Teachers College Press, 1997), 33.

37. Ross Brenneman, "Gallup Student Poll Finds Engagement in School Dropping by Grade Level," *Education Week*, March 22, 2016. The study does not explore the reasons for this drop, which could be attributable, at least in part, to extra-school factors or to student peer dynamics, as opposed to schools' practices per se.

38. Helen Marks, "Student Engagement in Instructional Activity: Patterns in the Elementary, Middle, and High School Years," *American Educational Research Journal* 37, no. 1 (2000): 153–184.

39. Ethan Yazzie-Mintz, *Charting the Path from Engagement to Achievement: A Report on the 2009 High School Survey of Student Engagement* (Bloomington, Ind.: Center for Evaluation & Education Policy, 2010), 6. Earlier editions of the HSSSE survey reported almost identical results.

40. Ibid, 7.

41. Ibid, 11.

42. Marks, "Student Engagement."

43. Yazzie-Mintz, *Charting the Path*, 17.

44. Ibid., 16.

45. Kane and Staiger, *Gathering Feedback for Teaching*, 24.

46. Yazzie-Mintz, *Charting the Path*, 10.

47. In a study of middle schools, Hilary Conklin similarly found elements of humor, play, and joy, even in the absence of accompanying intellectual rigor. See Hilary Conklin, "Toward More Joyful Learning: Integrating Play into Frameworks of Middle Grades Teaching," *American Educational Research Journal* 51, no. 6 (2014): 1227–1255.

48. Tony Wagner, *The Global Achievement Gap: Why Even Our Best Schools Don't Teach the New Survival Skills Our Children Need—and What We Can Do about It* (New York: Basic Books, 2010).

49. David Perkins, *Making Learning Whole: How Seven Principles of Teaching Can Transform Education* (San Francisco, CA: Jossey-Bass, 2010).

50. In some subjects and in some teachers' hands, AP can result in rapid coverage of content at the expense of deeper or more developed explorations of fewer topics, and for that reason, some of the most elite schools, public and private, have moved away from AP. At the same time, Advanced Placement courses are intended to mirror college courses in similar subjects, and so often require a greater command of the content as well as significantly higher reasoning about the content than most high school courses demand. There also has been some revision of Advanced Placement exams in recent years, particularly in the sciences, as the College Board, responding to criticisms that the tests its wider than they are deep, has tried to ask for more reasoning focused on fewer topics. Thus, we argue that Advanced Placement can be either an asset for or a constraint on deeper learning, depending on the subject and on the way in which the teacher prepares students for the exam.

51. David Cohen, "Teaching Practice: Plus ça change . . . ," in *Contributing to Educational Change: Perspectives on Research and Practice*, ed. P. W. Jackson (Berkeley, Calif.: McCutchan, 1989): 27–84.

52. David B. Tyack and Larry Cuban, *Tinkering toward Utopia: A Century of Public School Reform* (Cambridge, Mass.: Harvard University Press, 1995).

53. David Tyack, *The One Best System: A History of American Urban Education* (Cambridge, Mass.: Harvard University Press, 1974); Patricia Graham, *Schooling America: How the Public Schools Meet the Nation's Changing Needs* (New York: Oxford University Press, 2007).

54. Jal Mehta, *The Allure of Order: High Hopes, Dashed Expectations, and the Troubled Quest to Remake American Schooling* (New York: Oxford University Press, 2013).

55. Rice, *Public School System*.

56. Larry Cuban, *How Teachers Taught: Constancy and Change in American Classrooms, 1890–1980*, Research on Teaching Monograph Series (New York: Longman, 1984).

57. John Goodlad, *A Place Called School* (New York: McGraw Hill, 1984), 229.

58. Dan C. Lortie, *Schoolteacher: A Sociological Study* (Chicago: University of Chicago Press, 1975).

59. On niches, see David K. Cohen and Jal D. Mehta, "Why Reform Sometimes Succeeds: Understanding the Conditions That Produce Reforms That Last," *American Educational Research Journal* 54, no. 4 (2017): 644–690.

60. Susan F. Semel and Alan R. Sadovnik, *"Schools of Tomorrow," Schools of Today: What Happened to Progressive Education* (New York: P. Lang, 1999).

61. Diane Ravitch, *Left Back: A Century of Battles over School Reforms* (New York: Simon & Schuster, 2000).

62. William Julius Wilson, *The Truly Disadvantaged: The Inner City, the Underclass, and Public Policy* (Chicago: University of Chicago Press, 1987); Doug Massey and Nancy Denton, *American Apartheid: Segregation and the Making of the Underclass* (Cambridge, Mass.: Harvard University Press, 1993).

63. Jean Anyon, "Social Class and School Knowledge," *Curriculum Inquiry* 11, no. 1 (1981): 3–42; Jeannie Oakes, *Keeping Track: How Schools Structure Inequality* (New Haven, Conn.: Yale University Press, 1985).

64. Samuel Bowles and Herbert Gintis, *Schooling in Capitalist America* (New York: Basic Books, 1976); Melvin Kohn, *Class and Conformity* (Chicago: University of Chicago Press, 1977).

65. Linda Perlstein, *Tested: One American School Struggles to Make the Grade* (New York: Holt, 2007).

66. Richard Hofstadter, *Anti-Intellectualism in American Life* (New York: Knopf, 1963).

67. Peter Dow, *Schoolhouse Politics: Lessons from the Sputnik Era* (Cambridge, Mass.: Harvard University Press, 1991).

68. Theodore Sizer, *Horace's Compromise: The Dilemma of the American High School* (Boston: Houghton Mifflin, 1984).

69. Sarah Fine, "A Slow Revolution: Toward a Theory of Intellectual Playfulness in High School Classrooms," *Harvard Educational Review*, 84, no. 1 (2014): 1–23; Anyon, "Social Class and School Knowledge."

70. Cohen and Mehta, "Why Reform Sometimes Succeeds."

71. Robert Stake, Jack Easley, et al., *Case Studies in Science Education* (Urbana, Ill.: Center for Instructional Research and Curriculum Evaluation, 1978).

72. Lortie, *Schoolteacher*; Arthur Levine, *Educating School Teachers* (Washington, D.C.: Education Schools Project, 2006).

73. Milbrey W. McLaughlin and Joan Talbert, *Professional Communities and the Work of High School Teaching* (Chicago: University of Chicago Press, 2001).

2 ∿ The Progressive Frontier: Project-Based Learning

1. Robert Halpern, *The Means to Grow Up: Reinventing Apprenticeship as a Developmental Support in Adolescence* (New York: Routledge, 2009).

2. David Cohen, "Dewey's Problem," *Elementary School Journal* 98, no. 5 (1998): 427–446.

3. Ibid.

4. David B. Tyack, *The One Best System: A History of American Urban Education* (Cambridge, Mass.: Harvard University Press, 1974).

5. Ibid.; Jal Mehta, *The Allure of Order: High Hopes, Dashed Expectations, and the Troubled Quest to Remake American Schooling*, (New York: Oxford University Press, 2013).

6. John Dewey, *The Child and the Curriculum, Including the School and Society* (New York: Cosimo Classics, 2008).

7. David Cohen, "Teaching Practice: Plus ça change . . . ," issue paper, Michigan State University, National Center for Research on Teacher Education, 1988, available at https://www.educ.msu.edu/NCRTL/PDFs/NCRTL/IssuePapers /ip883.pdf (accessed September 10, 2018).

8. Dewey, *The Child and the Curriculum*.

9. John Dewey, *My Pedagogic Creed* (New York: E.L. Kellogg, 1897), 81.

10. Halpern, *Means to Grow Up*.

11. Michael Fullan, Joanne Quinn, and Joanne McEachen, *Deep Learning: Engage the World, Change the World* (Newbury Park, Calif.: Corwin Press, 2017).

12. Richard Elmore, personal communication, September 22, 2011.

13. Cohen, "Teaching Practice."

14. Lee S. Shulman, "Knowledge and Teaching: Foundations of the New Reform," *Harvard Educational Review* 57, no. 1 (1987): 1–23.

15. Dewey, *The Child and the Curriculum*.

16. Ibid.

17. Dewey, *My Pedagogic Creed*.

18. Patricia Graham, personal communication, September 19, 2012.

19. Graham, *Schooling America: How the Public School Meet the Nation's Changing Needs* (New York: Oxford University Press, 2005), 56.

20. Andrea Di Sessa, "A History of Conceptual Change Research: Threads and Fault Lines," in R. K. Sawyer, ed., *The Cambridge Handbook of the Learning Sciences* (New York: Cambridge University Press, 2006), 265–282; Kenneth Strike and George J. Posner, "A Conceptual Change View of Learning and Understanding." In L. H. T. West and A. L. Pines, eds., *Cognitive Structure and Conceptual Change* (New York: Academic Press, 1985), 211–231.

21. Cynthia E. Coburn and Sarah L. Woulfin, "Reading Coaches and the Relationship between Policy and Practice," *Reading Research Quarterly* 47, no. 1 (2012): 5–30.

22. Author Sarah Fine's experience is echoed by data presented in Richard Elmore, *School Reform from the Inside Out* (Cambridge, Mass.: Harvard Education Press, 2004).

23. Mordechai Gordon, "The Misuses and Effective Uses of Constructivist Teaching," *Teachers and Teaching: Theory and Practice* 15, no. 6 (2009): 737–746; Tina A. Grotzer, "Understanding Counts! Teaching for Depth in Math and Science," in *Cognitive Issues That Affect Math and Science Learning: Math / Science Matters* (Cambridge, Mass.: Harvard Project on Schooling and Children, 1996).

24. E. D. Hirsch, *Why Knowledge Matters: Rescuing Our Children from Failed Educational Theories* (Cambridge, Mass.: Harvard Education Press, 2016).

3 ⚬ No Excuses Schools: Benefits and Tradeoffs

1. Deborah Walker and Linda Lampert, "Learning and Leading Theory: A Century in the Making," in Linda Lampert et al., eds., *The Constructivist Leader* (New York: Teachers College Press, 1995), 1–27.

2. David Whitman, *Sweating the Small Stuff: Inner-City Schools and the New Paternalism* (Washington, D.C.: Thomas B. Fordham Institute, 2008).

3. Ibid. In George Lakoff's terms, no-excuses schools embrace the "strict father" morality, which is the idea that young people need to be disciplined if they are going to resist their natural urges and become productive and self-disciplined citizens. Lakoff contrasts this to the "nurturant parent" worldview, in which people are considered inherently good and the role of the parent is to teach children to care for other people. While many in the no-excuses world think of themselves as liberals because they are concerned with equity and social mobility, their view of how to achieve those ends is conservative in the Lakoff sense. See George Lakoff, *Moral Politics: How Liberals and Conservatives Think* (Chicago: University of Chicago Press, 2002).

4. Quantitative research has generally found that no-excuses schools, unlike charter schools as a whole, have positive effects on math and reading scores on state tests and on college enrollment: see Atila Abdulkadiroğlu, Joshua D. Angrist, Susan M. Dynarski, Thomas J. Kane, and Parag A. Pathak, "Accountability in Public Schools: Evidence from Boston's Charters and Pilots," *Quarterly Journal of Economics* 126, no. 2 (2011): 699–748; Joshua Angrist, Parag A. Pathak, and Christopher R. Walters, "Explaining Charter School Effectiveness," *American Economic Journal: Applied Economics* 5, no. 4 (2013): 1–27; Joshua D Angrist, Sarah Cohodes, Susan Dynarski, Parag A. Pathak, and Christopher Walters, "Stand and Deliver: Effects of Boston's Charter High Schools on College Preparation, Entry, and Choice," *Journal of Labor Economics* 34, no. 2 (2016): 275–318; Will Dobbie and Roland G. Fryer, "The Medium-Term Impacts of High-Achieving Charter Schools," *Journal of Political Economy* 123, no. 5 (2015): 985–1037. One recent study by Dobbie and Fryer finds little impact of attending no-excuses schools on labor market outcomes, suggesting that perhaps the short-term human capital effects are not translating to students' acquiring the underlying skills that are valued in the labor market: Will Dobbie and Roland G. Fryer, "Charter Schools and Labor Market Outcomes," NBER working paper no. 22502 (2016), available at http://www.nber.org/papers/w22502 (accessed September 10, 2018).

5. Katrina Bulkley, *Between Public and Private: Politics, Governance and the New Portfolio Models for Urban School Reform* (Cambridge, Mass.: Harvard Education Press, 2010).

6. Joanne Golann, "The Paradox of Success at a No Excuses School," *Sociology of Education* 88, no. 2 (2015): 103–119.

7. KIPP Foundation, *The Promise of College Completion: KIPP's Early Successes and Challenges*, 2011, available at http://www.kipp.org/about-kipp/results/college-completion-report (accessed September 10, 2018).

8. Joan F. Goodman, "Charter Management Organizations and the Regulated Environment: Is It Worth the Price?" *Educational Researcher* 42, no. 2 (2013): 89–96.

9. Katherine Merseth et al., *Inside Urban Charter Schools: Promising Practices and Strategies in Five Urban Charter Schools* (Cambridge, Mass.: Harvard Education Press, 2008); Joanne Golann, "Scripting the Moves: Class, Control and Urban School Reform," Ph.D. diss., Princeton University, 2016; Seneca Rosenberg, "Organizing for Quality in Education: Individualistic and Systemic Approaches to Teacher Quality," Ph.D. diss., University of Michigan, 2012.

10. The data about the school's performance come from the school's published fact sheet.

11. Data on attrition at no-excuses charters are surprisingly difficult to come by. A study by Mathematica of KIPP middle schools found attrition of 34 percent between grades five and seven, which was not statistically different from attrition in district middle schools: see Ira Nichols-Barrer et al., "Student Selection, Attrition, and Replacement in KIPP Middle Schools," *Education Evaluation and Policy Analysis* 9 (2016): 36–58. There do not appear to be attrition studies on other no-excuses charter networks. Despite the absence of more systematic evidence, many charter researchers and observers have significant concern about high attrition rates at no-excuses CMOs; from this perspective, what we witnessed at No Excuses High seems fairly similar to what other knowledgeable observers have witnessed at other similar schools.

12. Ron W. Zimmer and Cassandra M. Guarino, "Is There Empirical Evidence That Charter Schools "Push Out" Low-Performing Students?" *Educational Evaluation and Policy Analysis* 35, no. 4 (2013): 461–480.

13. Arthur Powell, Eleanor Farrar, and David Cohen, *The Shopping Mall High School: Winners and Losers in the Education Marketplace* (Boston: Houghton Mifflin, 1985).

14. Jerome Bruner, *The Process of Education* (Cambridge, Mass.: Harvard University Press, 1960).

15. Magdalene Lampert, *Teaching Problems and the Problems of Teaching* (New Haven, Conn.: Yale University Press, 2001).

16. James Hiebert et al., "Mathematics Teaching in the United States Today (and Tomorrow): Results from the TIMSS 1999 Video Study," *Educational Evaluation and Policy Analysis* 27, no. 2 (2005): 111–132.

17. Rosenberg, "Organizing for Quality in Education."

18. Terrenda White, "Charter Schools: Demystifying Whiteness in a Market of "No Excuses" Corporate-Styled Charter Schools," in Bree Picower and Edwin Mayorga, eds., *What's Race Got to Do with It?* (New York: Peter Lang, 2015), 121–145.

19. Chris Argyris, "Double Loop Learning in Organizations," *Harvard Business Review* (September 1977).

20. Because no-excuses schools began as middle schools in the mid- to late 1990s, it was only by about 2010 that it was possible to begin gathering data on college completion rates for students from these networks. The first internal study of Bay Area KIPP schools found that 36 percent of students who had graduated from their high schools had completed college in six years: see KIPP Foundation, *Promise of College Completion*. These findings crystallized the concerns of many in no-excuses networks that despite the extensive effort put in by the schools and the students, there was still more work to be done to get the students to college graduation.

21. Jal Mehta, "Unlearning Is Critical for Deeper Learning," Learning Deeply Blog, *Education Week*, January 6, 2015, available at http://blogs.edweek.org/edweek/learning_deeply/2015/01/unlearning_is_critical_for_deep_learning.html (accessed September 10, 2018); Jal Mehta and Sarah Fine, "The Elusive Quest for Deeper Learning," *Harvard Education Letter* 30, no. 4 (2013).

22. See Project Lead the Way at https://www.pltw.org (accessed September 10, 2018).

23. Justin Jansen et al., "Structural Differentiation and Ambidexterity: The Mediating Role of Integration Mechanisms." *Organization Science* 20, no. 4 (2009): 797–811.

24. This is a more specific manifestation of the more general notion of contingency in organizational design. The idea is that different organizational structures are appropriate for personnel with different levels of skill, and for tasks that vary in their level of complexity. See P. R. Lawrence and Jay Lorsch, *Organization and Environment: Managing Differentiation and Integration* (Brighton, Mass.: Harvard Business Press, 1967).

4 ∿ International Baccalaureate: A System for Deeper Learning?

This chapter draws in part on research and field notes drafted by Maren Oberman.

1. Jay Mathews and Ian Hill, *Supertest: How the International Baccalaureate Can Strengthen Our Schools*, 1st trade paper ed. (Chicago: Open Court, 2006); Jerusha Conner, "From International Schools to Inner-City Schools: The First Principles of the International Baccalaureate Diploma Program," *Teachers College Record* 110, no. 2 (2008): 322–351.

2. In IB global history, for example, teachers choose three topics to cover from a list provided yearly by the International Baccalaureate Organization; the exams require students to use what they have studied to explore a series of open-ended analytic questions such as "How far would you agree that single party states have been more interested in controlling the minds of young people than in providing genuine education?" By comparison, most American standardized world history exams rely heavily on multiple-choice questions and require students to have working knowledge of the history of seven continents over three millennia.

3. David Williamson Shaffer and Mitchel Resnick, "'Thick' Authenticity: New Media and Authentic Learning," *Journal of Interactive Learning Research* 10, no. 2 (1999): 195–215.

4. Conner, "From International Schools to Inner-City Schools," 334.

5. Gail Gerry, Tom Corcoran, and Consortium for Policy Research in Education, "Expanding Access, Participation, and Success in International Baccalaureate Programmes (IB Access Project): Evaluation Report Year Two," Consortium for Policy Research in Education, September 1, 2011; Laura W. Perna et al., "Unequal Access to Rigorous High School Curricula: An Exploration of the Opportunity to Benefit from the International Baccalaureate Diploma Programme (IBDP)," *Educational Policy* 29, no. 2 (March 2015): 402–425.

6. Vanessa Coca et al., "Working to My Potential: The Postsecondary Experiences of CPS Students in the International Baccalaureate Diploma Programme" (Chicago: Consortium on Chicago School Research, 2012).

7. Tristan Bunnell, "The International Baccalaureate in the USA and the Emerging 'Culture War,'" *Discourse: Studies in the Cultural Politics of Education* 30, no. 1 (2009): 61–72.

8. Mathews and Hill, *Supertest*.

9. Bunnell, "International Baccalaureate in the USA," 62.

10. David K. Cohen et al., *Improvement by Design: The Promise of Better Schools* (Chicago: University of Chicago Press, 2014); Jal Mehta and Sarah Fine, "The Why, What, Where, and How of Deeper Learning in American Secondary Schools," Deeper Learning Research Series (Boston: Jobs for the Future, 2015).

11. These are raw scores; they do not control for the socioeconomic status or motivation of the students.

12. These statistics come from IB High's school-specific version of the report "How Your School Compares Internationally: OECD Test for Schools (Based on PISA)." A sample version of this report is available at http://www.oecd.org/pisa /aboutpisa/Golden_e-book_1_example.pdf (accessed October 10, 2018).

13. Magdalene Lampert, "Deeper Teaching," Deeper Learning Research Series (Boston: Jobs for the Future, 2015).

14. As of June 2016, after the period during which we collected data at IB High, Mr. Stone replaced Mr. Weber as IB High's executive director.

15. Cohen et al., *Improvement by Design*; David K. Cohen and Susan L. Moffitt, *The Ordeal of Equality: Did Federal Regulation Fix the Schools?* (Cambridge, Mass.: Harvard University Press, 2009).

16. Elizabeth Green, *Building a Better Teacher: How Teaching Works* (New York: W.W. Norton, 2015).

17. In 2015, the IBO released an "Approaches to Teaching and Learning" resource guide that describes the constructivist and student-centered pedagogical practices that the organization believes can best support students in developing the dispositions specified in the Learner Profile. Although this document is narratively rich and grounded in a range of high-quality research on learning and teaching, in our view it does not drill deeply enough into the particulars of pedagogy to provide more than a loose framework for instructional practice. Furthermore, school leaders noted the lack of program-imposed accountability for adhering to the guide's framework, especially when compared to the high level of accountability of the IB assessments.

18. Carol Dweck, *Self-Theories: Their Role in Motivation, Personality, and Development*, 1st ed. (Philadelphia: Psychology Press, 2000).

19. A few students talked about having considered transferring to the nearby regional high school to play sports at a competitive level, but most describe the scrappy nature of IB High's teams with affection.

20. As of 2016, the city had promised to build a new facility for the school, but construction had not yet begun.

21. Recent research reveals that while the IBDP increasingly has been made available in schools that are racially and socioeconomically diverse, actual participation in the program still tends to occur disproportionately among the most advantaged students (see Perna et al., "Unequal Access"). This research further contends that one of the mechanisms fueling this pattern is that many schools uphold strict grade-point-average cutoff policies to determine eligibility for entry and ongoing participation. The case of IB High suggests that if such schools were to embrace more inclusive policies, build an inclusive culture, and develop robust supports for those with a lower baseline of academic independence, they would be able to engage a much broader range of learners in the program. This would constitute a significant improvement over the current state of affairs.

5 ～ The Comprehensive High School: Performance versus Learning

1. Michael Sedlak, *Selling Students Short: Classroom Bargains and Academic Reform in the American High School* (New York: Teachers College Press, 1986); Arthur Powell, Eleanor Farrar, and David Cohen, *The Shopping Mall High School: Winners and Losers in the Educational Marketplace* (Boston: Houghton Mifflin, 1985).

2. Carol Dweck, "Motivational Processes Affecting Learning," *American Psychologist* 41 (1986): 1040–1048.

3. Richard Elmore, personal communication, September 2016.

4. Robert Kegan, *In over Our Heads: The Mental Demands of Modern Life* (Cambridge, Mass.: Harvard University Press, 1994).

5. David Labaree, "Public Goods, Private Goods: The American Struggle over Educational Goals," *American Educational Research Journal* 34, no. 1 (1997): 39–81, quotation on p. 56.

6. What we see in the top track at Attainment High is not sui generis. A 2009 book by Peter Demerath, *Producing Success*, found similar patterns in another affluent school—high levels of student stress, overscheduled students, cheating, parents pressing for every advantage for their children, extensive tutoring—which suggests that what we observed at Attainment High is fairly representative of the challenges of engaging students in deep learning in the top tracks of affluent public schools today. See Peter Demerath, *Producing Success: The Culture of Personal Advancement in an American High School* (Chicago: University of Chicago Press, 2009). It is worth noting that these challenges are not insurmountable. As we show in Chapter 7, there are teachers who are able to pull students into the inner worlds of their fields and leave behind questions of "performance" and "how many points did I get."

7. Reba Page, *Lower Track Classroooms: Curricular and Cultural Perspective* (New York: Teachers College Press, 1991).

8. These numbers are calculated by slots and not by students; thus if one student takes three upper-level courses, she or he is counted three times. This way of counting can both overvalue and undervalue the percentage of minorities taking higher-level courses. It can overvalue, because one Black or Latinx student taking three courses would count three times in the data, even if two other minority students weren't taking any upper-level courses. It can also undervalue the minority share in these courses, because if a white or Asian student is taking five honors courses, then that one student would count five times in the data.

9. Kun Yuan and Vi-Nhuan Le, *Estimating the Percentage of Students Who Were Tested on Cognitively Demanding Items through the State Achievement Tests* (Santa Monica, Calif.: Rand Corporation, 2012).

10. Some of the facts in this paragraph, as well as the quotation from the student, came from the school newspaper. We do not provide links to the articles in order to keep the school anonymous.

11. Leslie Siskin, *Realms of Knowledge: Academic Departments in Secondary Schools* (Philadelphia: Taylor and Francis, 1994); Pamela Grossman and Susan Stodolsky, "Content as Context: The Role of Schools Subjects in Secondary School Teaching," *Educational Researcher* 24, no. 8 (1995): 5–23.

12. Powell, Farrar, and Cohen, *Shopping Mall High School*.

13. William Deresiewicz, *Excellent Sheep: The Miseducation of the American Elite and the Way to a Meaningful Life* (New York: Free Press, 2014); David Brooks, "The Organization Kid," *Atlantic* 287, no. 4 (2001): 40–54.

14. Dorothy Holland, *Identity and Agency in Cultural Worlds* (Cambridge, Mass.: Harvard University Press, 1998). We also see this argument as consistent with the research of Daphna Oyserman and Mesmin Destin, who argue that different roles can bring forth different identities, which is precisely what we witnessed in these

students. See Daphna Oyserman and Mesmin Destin, "Identity-Based Motivation: Implications for Intervention," *Counseling Psychologist* 38, no. 7 (2010): 1001–1043.

6 ∾ Deeper Learning at the Margins: Why the Periphery Is More Vital Than the Core

1. David Perkins, *Making Learning Whole: How Seven Principles of Teaching Can Transform Education* (San Francisco: Jossey Bass, 2009).

2. Arthur Powell, Eleanor Farrar, and David Cohen, *The Shopping Mall High School: Winners and Losers in the Education Marketplace* (Boston: Houghton Mifflin, 1985); James Coleman, *The Adolescent Society* (New York: Free Press, 1961).

3. This was not true of all classrooms; in Chapter 7 we discuss some of the most compelling ones we saw.

4. Powell, Farrar, and Cohen, *Shopping Mall High School*; Herbert Kliebard, *The Struggle for the American Curriculum, 1893–1958* (New York: Routledge, 2004); David Angus and Jeffrey Mirel, *The Failed Promise of the American High School* (New York: Teachers College Press, 1999).

5. Powell, Farrar, and Cohen, *Shopping Mall High School*, 257.

6. Robert Lynd and Helen M. Lynd, *Middletown* (New York: Harcourt Brace, 1929): 211–222.

7. Ibid., 218.

8. Ibid., 215.

9. Ibid.

10. Coleman, *Adolescent Society*.

11. Diane Ravitch, *Left Back: A Century of Failed School Reforms* (New York: Simon and Schuster, 2000); Angus and Mirel, *Failed Promise*.

12. The debate around Hall and the Cardinal Principles is expertly and fairly described by Kliebard, *Struggle for the American Curriculum*.

13. Ravitch, *Left Back*; Angus and Mirel, *Failed Promise*.

14. Joseph Mayer Rice, *The Public-School System of the United States* (New York: Century, 1893).

15. As Powell, Farrar, and Cohen describe it in *Shopping Mall High School*, "It seems, then, that the reforms discussed here produced the worst of both worlds; new courses, content, and academic standards were less intellectual and more practical, and a style of teaching that was as dull as reformers had once complained of in Latin and medieval history courses" (267).

16. Lynd and Lynd, *Middletown*, 195.

17. Powell, Farrar, and Cohen, *Shopping Mall High School*, 257.

18. Coleman, *Adolescent Society*, 320–322.

19. David Cohen, "Teaching Practice: Plus ça change . . . ," in *Contributing to Educational Change: Perspectives on Research and Practice*, ed. P. W. Jackson (Berkeley, Calif.: McCutchan, 1989): 27–84.

20. Jennifer Fredericks and Jacquelynne Eccles, "Is Extracurricular Participation Associated with Beneficial Outcomes? Concurrent and Longitudinal Relations," *Developmental Psychology* 42, no. 4 (2006): 698–713; Joseph Mahoney, Reed Larson, and Jacquelynne Eccles, eds. *Organized Activities as Contexts for Development: Extracurricular Activities, After School, and Community Programs* (Mahwah, N.J.:

Lawrence Erlbaum, 2005); Poh-Sun Seow and Gary Pan, "A Literature Review of the Impact of Extracurricular Activities Participation on Students' Academic Performance," *Journal of Education for Business* 89, no. 7 (2014): 361–366.

21. Fredericks and Eccles, "Is Extracurricular Participation Associated with Beneficial Outcomes?"; Jennifer Fredericks and Sandra Simpkins, "Promoting Positive Youth Development through Organized After-School Activities: Taking a Closer Look at Participation of Ethnic Minority Youth," *Child Development Perspectives* 6, no 3 (September 2012): 280–287.

22. Alyce Holland and Thomas Andre, "Participation in Extracurricular Activities in Secondary School: What Is Known, What Needs to Be Known?" *Review of Educational Research* 57, no. 4 (Winter 1987): 437–466; Herbert Marsh and Sabina Kleitman, "Extracurricular School Activities: The Good, the Bad, and the Nonlinear," *Harvard Educational Review* 72, no. 4 (December 2002): 464–515.

23. Helen Marks, "Student Engagement in Instructional Activity: Patterns in the Elementary, Middle, and High School Years," *American Educational Research Journal* 37, no 1 (Spring 2000): 153–184.

24. The original study was Mihaly Csikszentmihalyi and Reed Larson, *Being Adolescent: Conflict and Growth in the Teenage Years* (New York: Basic Books, 1984). A more recent piece reviews the research on flow in schools: see David Shernoff and Mihaly Csikszentmihalyi, "Flow in Schools: Cultivating Engaged Learners and Optimal Environments" in Michael Furlong et al., eds., *Handbook of Positive Psychology in Schools* (New York: Routledge, 2014). A study that directly explores out of school learning is D. L. Vandell et al., "Activities, Engagement, and Emotion in After-School Programs (and Elsewhere)," *New Directions for Youth Development* 105 (2005): 121–129.

25. Joseph L. Mahoney et al., "Adolescent Out-of-School Activities," in *Handbook of Adolescent Psychology* (New York: John Wiley & Sons, 2009). The authors note that this is the first time that out-of-school issues have warranted a chapter in this prominent handbook, arguing that it is a relatively young field worthy of significantly more research. Similarly Shirley Bryth Heath in a 2001 *Educational Researcher* article argued that little was known about the kind of "third spaces" represented by extracurriculars. See Shirley Brice Heath, "Three's Not a Crowd: Plans, Roles, and Focus in the Arts," *Educational Researcher* 30, no. 7 (2001): 10–17.

26. Milbrey McLaughlin, *Community Counts: How Youth Organizations Matter for Youth Development* (Washington, D.C.: Public Education Network, 2000).

27. In fact, this work by Sam Intrator and Don Siegel, takes the argument one step further and argues that these out-of-school environments are actively structured in ways that are more conducive to learning than formal schooling. They point out the following contrasts: schools are compulsory, but programs are voluntary; schools feel like they belong to the adults, while programs feel like they belong to the youth; schools emphasize individual work, but programs operate through meaningful collaboration; schools emphasize pure thought, whereas programs emphasize doing; schoolwork happens in the classroom, but learning happens everywhere in out-of-school programs; schools have many formal structures, but out-of-school programs are informal spaces; school curricula strive for scope and sequence, whereas out-of-school programs emphasize authentic

problems; high-stakes tasks in schools happen at desks, while in out-of-school programs they happen in the public spotlight; and schools emphasize hard work, whereas programs merge play with work. While these are ideal types—we encountered classrooms that had some of the qualities associated here with out-of-school programs—they do reveal the range of ways in which organized youth activities can avoid some of the stultifying nature of school, and instead infuse learning with vitality, purpose, collaboration, and authenticity. See Sam Intrator and Don Siegel, *The Quest for Mastery: Positive Youth Development through After School Programs* (Cambridge, Mass.: Harvard Education Press, 2014).

28. Robert Halpern, *The Means to Grow Up: Reinventing Apprenticeship as a Developmental Support in Adolescence* (New York: Routledge, 2009).

29. Jean Lave, "A Comparative Approach to Educational Forms and Learning Processes," *Anthropology & Education Quarterly* 13, no. 2 (1982): 181–187.

30. We depart from the convention that we have used elsewhere in the book in calling teachers "Mr." and "Ms." and instead refer to them by first names in keeping with the greater informality and equality between students and adults in the theater program.

31. Parker Palmer, *The Courage to Teach: Exploring the Inner Landscape of a Teacher's Life* (San Francisco: Jossey Bass, 1998).

32. Philip W. Jackson, *Life in Classrooms* (New York: Holt, Rinehart, and Winston, 1968).

33. Jean Lave and Etienne Wenger, *Situated Learning: Legitimate Peripheral Participation* (New York: Cambridge University Press, 1991).

34. Roland Tharp, "Institutional and Social Context of Educational Practice and Reform," in Ellice A. Forman et al., *Contexts for Learning: Sociocultural Dynamics in Children's Development* (New York: Oxford University Press, 1993), 269–282. See also Vivian Chavez and Elisabeth Soep, "Youth Radio and the Pedagogy of Collegiality," *Harvard Educational Review* 75, no. 4 (2006): 409–434.

35. In Talia's words, "I think one thing that's really special about designing is the way that you get to really individually interact with the script, and interact with the story. Because when you work as just a crewmember on a show, you're helping create someone else's vision. And you never get a script, unless you're crew managing, or designing the show, otherwise you just go see runs, and you develop an understanding for the show, but you never really get to read it and figure out for yourself what you want."

36. According to Tuckman, new groups go through four stages: *forming*, a period where new members are polite but have not yet coalesced as a group; *storming*, a period of friction created by conflict in personalities and work styles as people try to figure out how to work together; *norming*, a period where a group develops its own culture and norms for how it will do the work; and *performing*, the final period where the group builds on its common culture and trust to produce something. See Bruce Tuckman, "Developmental Sequence in Small Groups," *Psychological Bulletin* 63, no. 6 (June 1965): 384–399.

37. This model was developed by Gordon Training International employee Noel Burch in the 1970s. The model is summarized in Linda Adams, "Learning a New Skill Is Easier Said Than Done," n.d., available on the Gordon Training International website at http://www.gordontraining.com/free-workplace-articles /learning-a-new-skill-is-easier-said-than-done (accessed September 10, 2018).

38. This is what David Perkins calls "working on the hard parts" within a learning experience intended to take on the whole game; see Perkins, *Making Learning Whole*.

39. Ibid.

40. Barbara Rogoff, "Observing Sociocultural Activity on Three Planes: Participatory Appropriation, Guided Participation, and Apprenticeship," in J. V. Wertsch et al., eds., *Sociocultural Studies of Mind* (Cambridge, Eng.: Cambridge University Press), 139–164.

41. This theory is consistent with the more general ideas offered by Jean Lave and Etienne Wenger on legitimate peripheral participation and is aligned with the broader socio-cultural perspective on learning; see Lave and Wenger, *Situated Learning*.

42. This is hypothesis-generating research; further research is needed to determine whether the elements identified here appear in other extracurricular activities.

43. Jal Mehta and Pooja Bakhai, "When the Periphery Is More Vital Than the Core: Theater and Debate as Platforms for Powerful Learning," working paper, forthcoming, Harvard Graduate School of Education.

44. Na'ilah Suad Nasir and Victoria Hand, "From the Court to the Classroom: Opportunities for Engagement, Learning, and Identity in Basketball and Classroom Mathematics," *Journal of the Learning Sciences* 17, no. 2 (April 2008): 143–179.

45. We are aware of the critiques of high school athletics: that they pull students away from academics; that they are breeding grounds for anti-intellectualism; that, in some communities, high school football and basketball can greatly overshadow and take resources away from academic programs; and that, for some disadvantaged youth, sports can falsely seem like an easier way to achieve social mobility than does school success. Proponents conversely claim that sports are promising places to help mold character, that they provide constructive outlets for youth (particularly boys) to use their physical energy, and that they are a better place for young people to spend time after school than unsupervised settings. This debate is beyond the scope of our chapter. Our point is simply that they provide an effective learning environment for building skill in their domains, comparable to other extracurriculars. One significant source of the power of this learning draws in part from the high esteem in which sports are held: many young people see professional athletes as role models, and they receive praise from the school and the community for their athletic accomplishments. As Coleman has argued in *Adolescent Society*, part of the challenge of getting students similarly energized about academic subjects is to build similar communities, and societal esteem, for the more traditional academic domains.

46. To the degree that in recent years extracurriculars have become increasingly critical for college admissions, these domains have lost some of this special intrinsic quality: students at competitive high schools now compete to head these extracurricular domains not only because they are interested, but also because leadership in these domains will improve their college résumés.

7 ∾ Deeper Teaching: Rigor, Joy, and Apprenticeship

1. For Karin Hess's adaptation of Webb's depth of knowledge scale, see http://static.pdesas.org/content/documents/M1-Slide_22_DOK_Hess_Cognitive_Rigor.pdf.

2. John Stuart Mill, *A System of Logic: Ratiocinative and Inductive* (1843; New York: Harper and Brothers, 1846).

3. Kun Yuan and Vi-Nhuan Le, *Estimating the Percentage of Students Who Were Tested on Cognitively Demanding Items through the State Achievement Tests* (Santa Monica, Calif.: Rand Corporation, 2012).

4. Jennifer Booher-Jennings, "Below the Bubble: 'Educational Triage' and the Texas Accountability System," *American Educational Research Journal* 42, no. 2 (2005): 231–268; Julie Cohen, "Challenges in Identifying High Leverage Practices," *Teachers College Record* 117, no. 7 (2015): 1–41.

5. In focusing on this small group of particularly compelling teachers, we do not mean to cast aspersions on all of the other teachers we saw. Teaching skill is on a continuum, and there were many teachers in our sample who were competent, if not inspiring, teachers.

6. As one review of the research on teacher beliefs described it, "The majority of the studies in this review have examined identity in isolation of classroom practice. Little attention has been afforded to . . . teachers' identities in reference to their classroom roles and pedagogic practice as teachers." See Lucy Avraamidou, "Studying Science Teacher Identity: Current Insights and Future Research Directions," *Studies in Science Education* 50, no. 2 (2014): 145–179. The quotation is from p. 168.

7. One of the few articles that does seek to link identities and practices is Charles J. Eick and Cynthia J. Reed, "What Makes an Inquiry-Oriented Science Teacher? The Influence of Learning Histories on Student Teacher Role Identity and Practice," *Science Education* 86, no. 3 (2002): 401–416. But this study focuses on teachers in the first year of practice.

8. SWBAT is short for "students will be able to"; many classes we saw used this educational jargon to organize their agendas.

9. Harkness tables are an approach to student seminars that have been developed at Exeter and have since spread to other schools. They involve students leading discussions, and the heavy use of supporting texts. See Katherine Cadwell, "What Is the Harkness Method?," available at https://katherinecadwell.wordpress.com/what-is-the-harkness-method (accessed September 10, 2018).

10. James W. Stigler and National Center for Education Statistics, *The TIMSS Videotape Classroom Study: Methods and Findings from an Exploratory Research Project on Eighth-Grade Mathematics Instruction in Germany, Japan, and the United States* (Washington, D.C.: U.S. Department of Education, 1999).

11. The movement toward developing practice-based teacher education reflects many of these beliefs. See Pam Grossman, Karen Hammerness, and Morva Mc-donald, "Redefining Teaching, Re-Imagining Teacher Education," *Teachers and Teaching: Theory and Practice* 15, no. 2 (2010): 273–289; and Magdalene Lampert et al., "Keeping It Complex: Using Rehearsals to Support Novice Teacher Learning of Ambitious Teaching," *Journal of Teacher Education* 64, no. 3 (2014): 226–243. Of course, the shift to practice-based teacher education does not obviate the need for broader reflection on the overall aims involved in this approach to teaching. As Sharon Feiman-Nemser writes in her essay about practice-based approaches across the years, while the development of core practices is important, "still, it leaves open the question of what the core skills consist of and how to help beginning teachers transfer those skills to the classroom, integrate them into a coherent performance, and develop the professional judgment to decide what to do when." See Sharon

Feiman-Nemser, *Teachers as Learners* (Cambridge, Mass.: Harvard Education Press, 2012), 22.

12. We discuss the literature on this point in Chapter 1.

13. Ta-Nehisi Coates, "In Defense of a Loaded Word," *New York Times*, November 24, 2013.

14. Dan Lortie, *Schoolteacher* (Chicago: University of Chicago Press, 1975).

15. Previous work in math also suggests the importance of how teachers view the discipline. Tasos Barkastas and John Malone write that, "Our interpretation of Ernest's (1989) statements . . . is that it is not possible to separate mathematics teachers' views about mathematics from their views about mathematics teaching and learning." Anastasios (Tasos) Barkastas and John Malone, "A Typology of Mathematics Teachers' Beliefs about Teaching and Learning Mathematics and Instructional Practices," *Mathematics Education Research Journal* 17, no. 2 (2005): 69–90, quotation on p. 80. Also see Paul Ernest, "The Knowledge, Beliefs and Attitudes of the Mathematics Teacher: A Model," *Journal of Education for Teaching* 15, no. 1 (1989): 13–33.

16. John Bransford et al., *How People Learn: Brain, Mind, Experience, and School* (Washington, D.C.: National Academy Press, 1999), 22.

17. There is literature that corroborates the links between teachers' beliefs about the nature of the field and their practices. In math, see Dionne I. Cross, "Alignment, Cohesion, and Change: Examining Mathematics Teachers' Belief Structures and Their Influence on Instructional Practices," *Journal of Mathematics Teacher Education* 12, no. 5 (2009): 325–346; in science, see Randy Yerrick, Helen Parke, and Jeff Nugent, "Struggling to Promote Deeply Rooted Change: The 'Filtering Effect' of Teachers' Beliefs on Understanding Transformational Views of Teaching Science," *Science Education* 81, no. 2 (1997): 137–159, and David Stroupe, "Ambitious Teachers' Design and Use of Classrooms as a Place of Science," *Science Education* 101, no. 3 (2017): 458–485. Research does suggest that classroom practice is also shaped by contextual factors in the local environment, which can lead teachers' beliefs to be inconsistent with their practices. See Anne M. Raymond, "Inconsistency between a Beginning Elementary School Teacher's Mathematics Beliefs and Teaching Practice," *Journal for Research in Mathematics Education* 28, no. 5 (1999): 550–576. Even this study, however, suggests that teachers' underlying beliefs about mathematics (as opposed to their beliefs about teaching mathematics) shape their practice in deep ways.

18. J. M. Rice, *The Public-School System of the United States* (New York: Century, 1893), 112.

19. Lee Shulman, "Knowledge and Teaching: Foundations of the New Reform," *Harvard Educational Review* 57, no. 1 (1987): 1–23.

20. On the importance of mathematical knowledge for math teaching, see Heather C. Hill, Brian Rowan, and Deborah Loewenberg Ball, "Effects of Teachers' Mathematical Knowledge for Teaching on Student Achievement," *American Educational Research Journal* 42, no. 2 (2005): 371–406.

21. Other scholars who have similarly taken a sociocultural perspective have emphasized that good teachers seek to develop not only students' knowledge but also their identities, helping them to think of themselves as "math people" or otherwise members of the field. Magdalene Lampert calls these academic identities "intellectual virtues" and James Greeno calls them "intellective identities." See

Magdalene Lampert, *Teaching Problems and the Problems of Teaching* (New Haven, Conn.: Yale University Press, 2001); James Greeno, *Students with Competence, Authority, and Accountability* (New York: College Board, 2002); Leslie Rupert Herrenkohl, *How Students Come to Be, Know, and Do: A Case for a Broad View of Learning* (New York: Cambridge University Press, 2010).

22. Elisabeth Soep offers a similar argument about students gradually taking ownership over the standards of the field through the process of critique, particularly in the arts. Elisabeth Soep, "Critique: Assessment and the Production of Learning," *Teachers College Record* 108, no. 4 (2006): 748–777.

23. Tina A. Grotzer, "How Conceptual Leaps in Understanding the Nature of Causality Can Limit Learning: An Example from Electrical Circuits," American Educational Research Association (AERA) paper, 2000, available at http://citeseerx .ist.psu.edu/viewdoc/download?doi=10.1.1.36.774&rep=rep1&type=pdf (accessed September 10, 2018).

24. Sharon Feiman-Nemser suggests a similar trajectory in her book *Teachers as Learners*. Drawing on her four decades of research, she argues that initial teacher preparation can help to create professional identities that orient teachers toward the complexities of teaching, but that it takes many cycles of teaching and experimentation to translate that preparation into high-quality teaching (143).

25. In the teachers' own narratives of how they had come to their current mode of teaching, they emphasized these seminal learning experiences, so we highlight them as well. One study exploring the origins of inquiry-oriented science teachers found that they described themselves as children who liked to explore and experiment, thus putting the weight more on early individual predispositions than the nature of their influential learning experiences. The reality is that some combination of personal preferences and earlier teaching experiences probably helps shape one's teaching stance, which in turn shapes practices. See Judith A. Morrison, "Exploring Exemplary Elementary Teachers' Conceptions and Implementation of Inquiry Science," *Journal of Science Teacher Education* 24, no. 3 (2013): 573–588.

26. That subject-matter orientation can lead to very different modes of teaching in the same teacher is not a point that is well represented in the literature. One study that offers a similar analysis, at the elementary level, is James P. Spillane, "A Fifth-Grade Teacher's Reconstruction of Mathematics and Literacy Teaching: Exploring Interactions among Identity, Learning, and Subject Matter," *Elementary School Journal* 100, no. 4 (March 1, 2000): 307–330.

27. Bransford et al., *How People Learn*, 22.

28. Sizer was discussing the organization of schools, but the same point applies to classrooms. Quoted in Francis M. Duffy, *Designing High-Performance Schools: A Practical Guide to Organizational Reengineering* (Delray Beach, Fl.: St. Lucie Press, 1996), 23.

8 ✑ Mastery, Identity, Creativity, and the Future of Schooling

1. David Cohen, "Teaching Practice: Plus ça change . . . ," in *Contributing to Educational Change: Perspectives on Research and Practice*, ed. P. W. Jackson (Berkeley, Calif.: McCutchan, 1989): 27–84. It is particularly early for public schools, as well as schools that are seeking to enact deeper learning for a wide range of students. As described in Chapter 1, there is an older tradition of such work in private

progressive schools in the United States. See Susan F. Semel and Alan R. Sadovnik, eds., *"Schools of Tomorrow," Schools of Today: What Happened to Progressive
Education* (New York: P. Lang, 1999).

2. Other studies of new models are also starting to show that these changes
make for difficult sledding; a national RAND study on personalized or competency-
based schooling similarly found that these models were early in their development.
Benjamin Herold, "6 Key Insights: RAND Corp. Researchers Talk Personalized
Learning," *Education Week*, November 8, 2017, available at https://www.edweek
.org/ew/articles/2017/11/08/6-key-insights-rand-corp-researchers-talk.html (accessed September 10, 2018).

3. In an article on why reform "sometimes succeeds," David Cohen and Jal
Mehta argue, drawing on a review of a century's worth of school reforms, that reforms can succeed in what they call "niches"—protected subspaces that have
political support—even if they cannot succeed across the whole system. See
David K. Cohen and Jal D. Mehta, "Why Reform Sometimes Succeeds: Understanding the Conditions That Produce Reforms That Last," *American Educational Research Journal* 54, no. 4 (August 1, 2017): 644–690.

4. Allan Collins, John Seely Brown, and Susan E. Newman argued for the
value of what they called "cognitive apprenticeship" in approaching school subjects in a widely cited chapter published in 1989. See Allan Collins, John Seely
Brown, and Susan E. Newman, "Cognitive Apprenticeship: Teaching the Crafts
of Reading, Writing, and Mathematics," in Lauren B. Resnick, ed., *Knowing,
Learning, and Instruction: Essays in Honor of Robert Glaser* (Hillsdale, N.J.: Lawrence
Erlbaum, 1989), 32–42. We share similar presumptions when it comes to the value
of apprenticeship learning, although the authors' article was particularly interested
in how notions of apprenticeship would need to change to support in-school
learning. For example, they emphasized that elementary school teachers might employ "read-a-louds" to model the process of reading. Perhaps because our focus
was on high schools and we included extracurricular domains, we argue that
teaching is often most effective when it simply models and links to adult work in
the domain, with as few modifications for its high school context as possible.

5. Cindy E. Hmelo-Silver, Ravit Golan Duncan, and Clark A. Chinn, "Scaffolding and Achievement in Problem-Based and Inquiry Learning: A Response to
Kirschner, Sweller, and Clark (2006)," *Educational Psychologist* 42, no. 2 (April 26,
2007): 99–107; Barbara Condliffe, "Project-Based Learning: A Literature Review,"
MDRC working paper, 2017, available at https://eric.ed.gov/?id=ED578933 (accessed September 10, 2018).

6. John Hattie, *Visible Learning: A Synthesis of over 800 Meta-Analyses Relating
to Achievement* (London: Routledge, 2009).

7. Some of the scholars and writers we most admire, like John Dewey, Jerome
Bruner, and Ted Sizer, have offered similarly integrative accounts of powerful or
deep learning.

8. David B. Tyack and Larry Cuban, *Tinkering toward Utopia* (Cambridge,
Mass.: Harvard University Press, 1995).

9. Robert Putnam, *Our Kids: The American Dream in Crisis* (New York: Simon
and Schuster, 2015), 176–177.

10. Chris Argyris, "Double Loop Learning in Organizations," *Harvard Business Review* 55, no. 5 (September 1, 1977): 115–125.

11. Dan Lortie, *Schoolteacher* (Chicago: University of Chicago Press, 1975).

12. Lee Shulman, "Knowledge and Teaching: Foundations of the New Reform," *Harvard Educational Review* 57, no. 1 (1987): 1–23.

13. John Papay and Matthew Kraft, "Can Professional Environments in Schools Promote Teacher Development? Explaining Heterogeneity in Returns to Teaching Experience," *Educational Effectiveness and Policy Analysis* 36, no. 4 (2014): 476–500.

14. Urban Teacher Residency United, "Building Effective Teacher Residencies: A Research Report," 2014, available at https://nctresidencies.org/wp-content/uploads/2015/09/Research-Report.pdf (accessed September 10, 2018).

15. National Commission on Teaching and America's Future (NCTAF), *What Matters Now: A New Compact for Teaching and Learning* (Arlington, Va.: NCTAF, 2016).

16. Pam Grossman, Karen Hammerness, and Morva Mcdonald, "Redefining Teaching, Re-Imagining Teacher Education," *Teachers and Teaching: Theory and Practice* 15, no. 2 (2010): 273–289; Magdalene Lampert et al., "Keeping It Complex: Using Rehearsals to Support Novice Teacher Learning of Ambitious Teaching," *Journal of Teacher Education* 64, no. 3 (2014): 226–243.

17. Sharon Feiman-Nemser, *Teachers as Learners* (Cambridge, Mass.: Harvard Education Press, 2012).

18. An ongoing study of programs that seek to enact deeper learning competencies in teacher education reaches similar conclusions. See Learning Policy Institute, "Teacher Preparation and Deeper Learning," proposal submitted for 2018 American Educational Research Association (AERA) meetings, available on request from the authors.

19. We describe these six factors in more depth in Jal Mehta and Sarah Fine, "Bringing Values Back In: How Purposes Shape Practices in Coherent School Designs," *Journal of Educational Change* 16, no. 4 (2015): 483–510.

20. Leslie Siskin, *Realms of Knowledge: Academic Departments in Secondary Schools* (Philadelphia: Taylor and Francis, 1994).

21. David Cohen and Carol Barnes, "Conclusion: A New Pedagogy for Policy?" in David K. Cohen, Milbrey McLaughlin, and Joan Talbert, eds., *Teaching for Understanding: Challenges for Policy and Practice* (San Francisco: Jossey Bass, 1993), 240–275, esp. p. 247.

22. Deborah Meier, *In Schools We Trust: Creating Communities of Learning in an Era of Testing and Standardization* (Boston: Beacon Press, 2002).

23. Carl Bereiter and Marlene Scardamalia describe something similar, which they call "knowledge-building communities," in their book on what education can learn from studies of expertise. See Carl Bereiter and Marlene Scardamalia, *Surpassing Ourselves: An Inquiry into the Nature and Implications of Expertise* (Chicago: Open Court, 1993).

24. Andrea Berger et al., *Early College, Early Success: Early College High School Initiative Impact Study* (Washington, D.C.: American Institutes for Research, 2013).

25. Monica Martinez and Charles McGrath, *Deeper Learning: How Eight Innovative Schools Are Transforming Education in the Twenty-First Century* (New York: New Press, 2014), 123–126; and Grant Lichtman, *#EdJourney: A Roadmap to the Future of Education* (San Francisco: Jossey Bass, 2014).

26. Martinez and McGrath, *Deeper Learning*, 108–109.

27. Ibid., 118–119.

28. Ibid., 23. Similar approaches are discussed in Lichtman, *#EdJourney*, 126–129.

29. Mary Moss Brown and Alisa Berger, *How to Innovate: The Essential Guide for Fearless School Leaders* (New York: Teachers College Press, 2014).

30. Lichtman, *#EdJourney*, 12.

31. Space mattered in the schools that we studied, for both good and ill: Dewey High used its hallways and walls to display spectacular student work that set the tone for the entire building; Attainment High's teacher lounges were organized by disciplines, which promoted disciplinary collaboration but inhibited cross-disciplinary work; No Excuses High assigned new and experienced teachers to the same classrooms, so that new teachers would be watching more experienced ones teach as they graded papers in their off periods, and the younger teachers would always be in the rooms of the more experienced teachers.

32. Prakash Nair, *Blueprint for Tomorrow: Redesigning Schools for Student-Centered Learning* (Cambridge, Mass.: Harvard Education Press, 2014). For examples, see http://www.bobpearlman.org/Learning21/new%20learning%20environments .htm#videos (accessed September 10, 2018).

33. Linda Darling-Hammond, *The Flat World and Education: How America's Commitment to Equity Will Determine Our Future* (New York: Teachers College Press, 2010).

34. A related strategy is to co-design with parents and other key stakeholders. By working collectively to define a rich portrait of what the community hopes students will be able to know, do, and be, schools can build wide support for deeper learning.

35. Ron Berger has argued that one advantage available to deeper learning high schools that is not available to elementary and middle schools is that college acceptances provide a clear external signal of success other than test scores. In high schools, learning that is less focused on tests can still be validated by this high-status marker.

36. Lichtman, *#EdJourney*.

37. Fareed Zakaria, *The Post-American World* (New York: Norton, 2008).

38. On American districts, see Ken Kay and Valerie Greenhill, *The Leader's Guide to 21st Century Education: 7 Steps for Schools and Districts* (Boston: Pearson, 2013). On British Columbia, see https://www2.gov.bc.ca/gov/content/education -training/k-12/teach/curriculum (accessed September 10, 2018).

39. David Conley and Linda Darling-Hammond, *Creating Systems of Assessment for Deeper Learning* (Stanford, Calif.: Stanford Center for Opportunity Policy in Education, 2013), 10–13. Note that while the assessment instruments of the countries listed here are directed toward deeper learning competencies, the overall systems that they are housed in are subject to many of the critiques we raise in this book. The English system has long been critiqued as creating a highly tracked and stratified model of schooling, and the Singaporean model is increasingly being seen as creating highly anxious and stressed students. Thus while the particular assessment instruments themselves are models, the overall systems are still struggling to achieve the balances we outline as needed for a healthy school system.

40. More than 99 percent of university faculty respondents identified "develop[ing] the ability to think critically" as an "essential" or "very important" aim of education. See J. A. Lindholm et al., *The American College Teacher: National*

Norms for the 2004–2005 HERI Faculty Survey (Los Angeles: UCLA Higher Education Research Institute, 2005).

41. Richard Weissbourd, *Turning the Tide: Inspiring Good for Others and the Common Good through College Admissions* (Cambridge, Mass.: Making Caring Common Project, 2016); Grant Lichtman, *Moving the Rock: Seven Levers We Can Press to Transform Education* (San Francisco: Jossey Bass, 2017), chap. 5.

42. David Cohen and Monica Bhatta, "The Importance of Infrastructure Development to High-Quality Literacy Instruction," *Future of Children* 22, no. 2 (2012): 117–138.

43. These lessons can be found at the Stanford History Education Group website: https://sheg.stanford.edu (accessed September 10, 2018).

44. Anna Saavedra, *Knowledge in Action Pilot Study*, unpublished summary (n.d.), University of Southern California, Dornsife Center for Economic and Social Research.

45. For more on these results, see the Lucas Education Research website at https://www.lucasedresearch.org/projects.html (accessed September 10, 2018).

46. Jo Boaler (@joboaler), Dan Meyer (@ddmeyer) and the math Twitter blogosphere (@exploreMTBoS) are all good Twitter handles to learn about this work. Ilana Horn's *Motivated: Designing Math Classrooms Where Students Want to Join In* (Portsmouth, N.H.: Heinemann, 2017) summarizes some of this work and provides links to more resources.

47. Ron Berger, Libby Woodfin, and Anne Vilen, *Learning That Lasts: Challenging, Engaging and Empowering Students with Deeper Instruction* (San Francisco: Jossey Bass, 2016).

48. Jal Mehta, *The Allure of Order: High Hopes, Dashed Expectations, and the Troubled Quest to Remake American Schooling* (New York: Oxford University Press, 2013); James Q. Wilson, *Bureaucracy: What Government Agencies Do and Why They Do It* (New York: Basic Books, 1989).

49. Mehta, *The Allure of Order*; also Jal Mehta, "From Bureaucracy to Profession: Remaking the Educational Sector for the 21st Century," *Harvard Educational Review*, 83, no. 3 (2013): 463–488.

50. William Bridges, *Transitions: Making Sense of Life's Changes* (Boston: Da Capo Press, 2004).

51. For more on this tool, see https://portraitofagraduate.org (accessed September 10, 2018).

52. Laurie Calvert, *Moving from Compliance to Agency: What Teachers Need to Make Professional Learning Work* (Oxford, Ohio: Learning Forward and NCTAF, 2016), 7.

53. Ibid., 5.

54. Robert Kegan, *In over Our Heads: The Mental Demands of Modern Life* (Cambridge, Mass.: Harvard University Press, 1994).

55. Michael Fullan, "Choosing the Wrong Drivers for Whole System Reform," 2011, available at https://edsource.org/wp-content/uploads/old/Fullan-Wrong-Drivers11.pdf (accessed September 10, 2018).

56. Jeff Duncan-Andrade and Ernest Morrell, *The Art of Critical Pedagogy* (New York: P. Lang, 2008); Sarah Fine, "Why Dewey Needs Freire, and Vice Versa," 2016, available at http://blogs.edweek.org/edweek/learning_deeply/2016/11/why _dewey_needs_freire_and_vice_versa_a_call_for_critical_deeper_learning.html

(accessed September 10, 2018); Pooja Bakhai, "Why Dewey Needs Freire, But Not Vice Versa; Critical Consciousness-Raising as a Form of Deeper Learning," http://blogs.edweek.org/edweek/learning_deeply/2017/07/why_dewey_needs_freire_but_not_vice_versa_critical_consciousness-raising_as_a_form_of_deeper_learnin.html (accessed October 9, 2018).

57. Lisa Delpit, "The Silenced Dialogue: Power and Pedagogy in Educating Other People's Children," *Harvard Educational Review* 58, no. 3 (1989): 280–298.

58. For the ways in which traditional schooling mutes the identities of students of color, see Angela Valenzuela, *Subtractive Schooling: U.S.-Mexican Youth and the Politics of Caring* (Albany: State University of New York Press, 1999). For more on skilled teaching of students of color, see Gloria Ladson-Billings, *The Dreamkeepers: Successful Teachers of African American Children* (San Francisco: Jossey-Bass, 1994) and Jeannie Oakes, "Learning That Is Equitable and Oriented towards Social Justice," working paper, Learning Policy Institute (Washington, D.C., 2018).

59. Milbrey McLaughlin and Joan Talbert, *Professional Communities and the Work of High School Teaching* (Chicago: University of Chicago Press, 2001), 36.

60. For more on this effort to include the experiences of indigenous peoples, see First Nations Pedagogy Online, https://firstnationspedagogy.ca/storytelling.html (accessed September 10, 2018).

61. Richard Sennett and Jonathan Cobb, *The Hidden Injuries of Class* (New York: Vintage, 1972).

Appendix: Methodology

1. With these caveats in mind, we do use some information from state tests, APs, or IB tests as part of developing holistic case studies of our deep dive schools.

2. For Hess's adaptation of Webb's depth of knowledge scale, see http://static.pdesas.org/content/documents/M1-Slide_22_DOK_Hess_Cognitive_Rigor.pdf.

3. Lorraine McDonnell, "Opportunity to Learn as a Research Concept and a Policy Instrument," *Educational Evaluation and Policy Analysis* 17, no. 3 (1995): 305–322; Andrew Porter, "The Effects of Upgrading Policies on High School Mathematics and Science," in Diane Ravitch, ed., *Brookings Papers on Education Policy* (Washington, D.C.: Brookings Institution Press, 1998), 123–164.

4. Jeannie Oakes, *Keeping Track: How Schools Structure Inequality* (New Haven, Conn.: Yale University Press, 1985).

5. Charles C. Ragin and Howard S. Becker, eds., *What Is a Case? Exploring the Foundations of Social Inquiry* (New York: Cambridge University Press, 1992); Charles Ragin, "Turning the Tables: How Case-Oriented Research Challenges Variable-Oriented Research," *Comparative Social Research* 16 (1997): 27–42.

6. John Gerring, *Case Study Research: Principles and Practices* (New York: Cambridge University Press, 2006); Henry Brady and David Collier, *Rethinking Social Inquiry: Diverse Tools, Shared Standards*, 2nd ed. (Lanham, Md.: Rowman and Littlefield, 2010).

7. Gerring, *Case Study Research*.

8. James Mahoney, "Nominal, Ordinal, and Narrative Appraisal in Macro-causal Analysis," *American Journal of Sociology* 104, no. 4 (1999): 1154–1196.

9. John Bransford et al., *How People Learn: Brain, Mind, Experience, and School* (Washington, D.C.: National Academy Press, 1999), 155–189, reviews much of the literature on deep learning in math, science, and history.

10. There is some literature on the power of out-of-school learning spaces and youth development that is relevant to this argument. We reviewed that literature in Chapter 6.

Acknowledgments

Many people have helped us develop our thinking over the years we have been working on this book. As we have argued throughout, learning stems in large part from the communities of which one is part; with this in mind, we feel immensely grateful for the variety of communities that have shaped us and our work.

We owe thanks first to the many administrators and teachers who welcomed us into their schools and classrooms. Often with little more than an email by way of introduction to our project, these educators allowed us to observe them, shared their in-process work with us, and voluntarily gave up their lunches and planning time to tell us about their successes and struggles. We are extremely grateful for their openness and candor, and we hope that synthesizing some of what we learned will serve as a small token in return for all they have given us. We also would like to thank the students, who were penetrating ethnographers of their own settings, and who, contrary to stereotypes about today's teenagers, were unflaggingly polite and forthcoming.

We want to extend a particularly hearty thanks to the leaders, teachers, and students in the schools we described in Chapters 2 through 7. We learned an extraordinary amount from these folks about the nature of powerful education, and their work continues to inform our thinking, writing, and teaching. Although our decision to anonymize all of our participants means we cannot honor them by their real names, we hope they know we are immeasurably in their debt.

The field research that generated the data for this project—research that spanned six years and thirty different sites–was energizing but also grueling. We are deeply grateful for the contributions made by three talented doctoral students, Maren Oberman, Nicole Simon, and Elizabeth Stosich, each of whom spent considerable time in the field, building relationships and observing the rhythms of the schools where they were stationed. Their sharp observations and incisive analyses were critical to the project's evolution, and in several places in the book we draw on their beautifully crafted notes.

A large number of people from the world of educational scholarship helped to stimulate the thinking in this book. David Cohen, David Perkins, Richard Elmore, Robert Kegan, and Sara Lawrence Lightfoot are all, in their varying ways, scholars who attend to the needs of practice and who take a humanistic stance toward the nature of learning and teaching. These pages reflect their perspectives as well as their specific advice, critiques, and support. David Cohen has been a particularly generous thought partner, sharing his immense accumulated wisdom while at the same time expressing the utmost interest in our evolving work. We feel very lucky to count him as an intellectual companion and friend.

Many colleagues read drafts and offered thoughtful reactions, including Amelia Peterson, James Noonan, Jenna Gravel, Max Yurkofsky, Robert Halpern, Sarah Leibel, Scott Davies, Steve Brint, and Victoria Theisen-Homer. For being supportive colleagues and thought partners, we also want to thank Andres Alonso, Andrew Hargreaves, Bill Penuel, David Steiner, Don Peurach, Ebony Bridwell-Mitchell, Eric Shed, Fernando Reimers, Heather Hill, Helen Malone, Howard Gardner, Jeannie Oakes, Jim Spillane, Joe Blatt, Jon Star, Josh Glazer, Judy Halbert, Julie Reuben, Karen Mapp, Linda Darling-Hammond, Lee Teitel, Linda Kaser, Mary Grassa O'Neill, Michael Fullan, Monica Higgins, Natasha Warikoo, Rick Hess, and Steve Mahoney. Jal cotaught with Elizabeth City during much of the time the book was in development; he feels very lucky to count her as a friend and thought partner.

Jim Ryan, former dean of the Harvard Graduate School of Education, was the epitome of a dean: supportive, enthusiastic, and always ready to engage. Having Jim in our corner helped give us confidence in this somewhat unconventional project. Last but certainly not least, Meira Levinson has been a steadfast friend and intellectual companion to both of us over many years. She has tirelessly read drafts and talked through writing-related quandaries, offering a balance of encouragement and critique and helping us to keep sight of our broader purposes.

There are also folks from the world of educational practice who have had a profound influence on the project. In addition to the many unnamed colleagues at the schools we researched, we would like to thank a few whose work has been particularly influential in shaping our thinking. Foremost among them is Ron Berger, teacher and professional learning leader extraordinaire. Ron is a powerful living example of what it means to combine precision and play in service of the deepest learning. Alisa Berger has been another valuable partner in the journey; she puts into practice what we talk about in theory. Finally, Rob Riordan offered wisdom, encouragement, and gentle reminders that the most important thing of all, when it comes to organizing schools and classrooms, is the belief that all children are curious and capable when given the chance to be so.

For financial support, we thank the Spencer Foundation, including its president Na'ilah Nasir and program officer Michael Barber; the Carnegie Foundation, including then program officer Leah Hamilton; and the Hewlett Foundation, particularly former program director Barbara Chow and program officers Chris Shearer and Marc Chun. As we write in the Introduction, when we first undertook this project there was not much interest in "deep learning" or innovative learning environments; we are thankful that these three foundations were willing to join us on the front lines and support making deeper learning a more popular notion. Jal is also indebted to the Radcliffe Institute, particularly its incomparable fellowship director Judy Vichniac, for providing a year's sabbatical to finish the research and complete much of the writing of the book. Many thanks also to the Radcliffe fellows for our many conversations over the course of that year.

We would be remiss if we did not thank our own students, particularly those in our "Deeper Learning for All" course at the Harvard Graduate School of Education. Having the opportunity to try out some of the ideas in the book with an enthusiastic yet discerning group of students each year has helped us tremendously in refining our thinking. We've also learned much from the teaching fellows who have helped with the course over the years: Dan Wise, Jim Heal, Kelly Kovacic, Kim Frumin, Pooja Bakhai, Rebecca Grainger, and Tyler Thigpen. Jal also would like to thank the students in the Education Leadership program; teaching them has helped him to think through what it would take to bring deeper learning to scale, and he has felt inspired by their shared commitment to equity and social justice. Thanks also to seminar participants at Johns Hopkins, the Ontario Institute for the Study of Education, and the University of Buffalo for listening to earlier versions of these ideas and helping us to refine and deepen them.

We want to thank Michael Aronson for initially signing the book for Harvard University Press, and Andrew Kinney for taking on the book and making it his own. Andrew has been a first-rate editor—always mindful that we were writing a book for both an academic and a public audience, and helpful in our task of finding the balance between the two. Julie Carlson was a meticulous and enthusiastic copy-editor, showing that rigor and joy can and do coexist. We also want to thank two anonymous reviewers for Harvard University Press, whose comments greatly helped us to sharpen our focus concerning the main contributions of the book.

We could not have written the book without the love and support of our friends and families. Book writing—even book co-writing—is a long and sometimes lonely endeavor; having people in your life who support the process and give you a reason to do something else is critical. To this end, Jal would like to thank John MacLachlan, a kindred spirit who is equally comfortable talking sports, politics, or schooling, and is always up for a trip to Dairy Joy. Jal is also thankful for the rest of the Lincoln crew: Becky Bermont and Alex Benik, Craig and Katie Nicholson, Jon and Kristen Ferris, Lara MacLachlan, Rebecca and Paul Blanchfield, and Tera Kemp. He'd also like to thank Ami Regnier, Andrew and Zoe Clarkwest, Ethan Gray, Jeff Israel, Susannah Tobin, and Will Reckler for their longstanding friendship.

Jal wants to offer particular thanks to his parents, Louise and Xerxes. Mom and Dad, you have really been everything one could ask for as parents: loving, warm, supportive, and caring, in ways that range from large to small. As I parent my own children, you provide an inspiration for what parents should be. I also appreciate the many hours we spent talking through ideas and considering what it entails to be an educated person. Finally, you read every word of the manuscript and offered highly skilled and helpful responses. I also want to thank my Aunt Kathy, who recently passed away, who was the kindest and most loving aunt any nephew could ask for. Cheryl, it seems hard to believe that what started in an Adams House dorm room more than twenty years ago could have developed into the rich and full life we share together today. Thanks especially for your unshakable confidence that it would work out, if only I just put some words on the page! I love you! Alex and Nico, with the book done, I will finally jump in the lake, and I look forward to many more hours playing together. You guys are the best part of our lives, and there is no close second.

Although Sarah lives three thousand miles away from her parents, she is deeply indebted to them for their love and support—now and always. My mother, Deborah Hirschland, has worn an astonishing array of hats throughout this process: cheerleader, therapist, thought partner, doting grandmother, and occasional line editor. My father, Jeffrey Fine, contributed wisdom, humor, and curry, all of which always managed to hit the spot. Thank you also to my sister, Shoshanna Fine, for inspiring me to think and live more boldly than I might otherwise, and to her wonderful wife, Laurel Gabler.

As the parent of two young children, I needed as much help with childcare as I possibly could get in order to have time and space to complete this project. My two sets of parents-in-law, Robyn Perlin and Ed Duncan and Ruth and Joel Perlin, were extraordinarily generous in providing such help, allowing me to "lean in" while still trusting that my children were benefiting from the loving gaze and companionship of their family. Their unwavering love and support have meant the world to me.

Finally, I am deeply indebted to Micah, Avi, and Sasha—the partner and children who collectively serve as both my anchor and my compass. Avi, at five, is full of a sweetness and intensity that inspire me to be my best self. Sasha, at two and a half, has a delight in the world that fills me with gratitude and joy. Micah, my partner of more than a decade, sustains me through it all. I don't think that he had any idea what he was signing up for when I told him that I was going to co-author a book; for that matter, neither did I. Even so, he has been in it with me every step of the way, making me cups of tea while I labored over grant proposals, caring for our children while I spent time at research sites, taking in stride the absentmindedness that accompanied my work on the manuscript, and, throughout, insisting that I never put my work before my well-being. I am eternally grateful for his love and support.

As a final gesture of gratitude, we would like to thank each other. While co-authorship, especially among two perfectionistic writers, is not always easy, we have managed to come out the other side of the process with an enduring friendship, a profound respect for each other's ways of seeing the world, and—we hope—a book that reflects our complementary perspectives and skills. We have been forever changed by each other and by the process of working together, and for that we are deeply grateful.

Index

Note: Page numbers followed by the letter *t* refer to tables.